THE UPANISHADS

THE
UPANISHADS

*Katha, Iśa, Kena, Mundaka, Śvetāśvatara,
Praśna, Māndukya, Aitareya, Brihadāranyaka,
Taittiriya, and Chhāndogya*

BY

SWAMI NIKHILANANDA

ABRIDGED EDITION

HARPER TORCHBOOKS
THE CLOISTER LIBRARY

HARPER & ROW, PUBLISHERS
NEW YORK AND EVANSTON

PREFACE

This volume of the Upanishads, containing *Katha, Iśa, Kena, Mundaka, Śvetāśvatara, Praśna, Māndukya, Aitareya, Brihadāran-yaka, Taittiriya,* and *Chhāndogya,* is a presentation in abridged form of the four volumes of the Upanishads translated by myself and published by Harper & Brothers in New York and Phoenix House in London. These are the major Upanishads and they are regarded as the basis of the Vedānta philosophy, the outstanding contribution of the Hindu thinkers to the philosophical thought of the world.

In the arrangement of these Upanishads no chronology has been attempted. Modern scholars, from the standpoint of linguistics and of the evolution of religious and philosophical thought, have formulated several chronologies. But Hindu tradition regards the whole of the Vedas, with their rituals and philosophies, as a simultaneous revelation of certain truths which cannot be perceived by the sense-organs or arrived at through reasoning based upon sense data. These truths are conceived as being eternal, without beginning or end, and not creations of the human intellect.

In this volume I have omitted certain portions of the text of the four original volumes: those dealing mostly with upāsanā, or ritualistic meditation, as described especially in the Brāhmana part of the Vedas, which would appear recondite to modern readers. The place of upāsanā in Vedic thought and its usefulness in the practice of spiritual disciplines have been discussed in the introduction to the *Chhāndogya Upanishad* in the present volume. The bulk of the original volumes has been further reduced by condensing the notes and explanations, enough of which, however, have been kept to enable a perceptive reader to grasp the meaning of the text. For a deeper comprehension the regular edition will be useful. The number given in parentheses at the end of each verse is the number of the verse in the original Upanishad. The quotations in the two introductory chapters, if not specified otherwise, are from the Upanishads. The exact references are given in the regular four-volume edition of the Upanishads translated by the present author.

A comprehensive glossary deals with the Sanskrit terms to be found in the volume. I have prepared this glossary as a sort of Upanishadic dictionary and attempted to give various meanings of the words, often italicizing those meanings especially pertinent to the Upanishadic texts. In preparing it I have profitably consulted the Sanskrit-English dictionary of Monier Williams. Here I take the opportunity to express my profound gratitude to Dr Herbert W. Schneider, former Professor of Philosophy in Columbia University, who urged me to prepare this abridged edition and who has kindly suggested important changes in the two introductory chapters.

This abridged edition of the Upanishads is expected to be especially useful for students in colleges, universities, and theological seminaries where the Upanishads are studied in connexion with comparative religion or world literature. It is unfortunate that the importance of the Upanishads as world philosophy has not yet been recognized by philosophers in the West. For those already familiar with the Upanishads, who wish to have the best parts of the texts readily available, the book will be convenient to carry about.

The distinctive feature of my translation, apart from whatever literary merit it may possess, is that it explains the texts in the light of the commentary of Śri Śankarāchārya (AD 788–820), whose non-dualistic interpretation of the truths of the Upanishads is accepted by the majority of Indian students of the Upanishads as giving coherent and satisfactory meaning to many difficult passages.

As I stated in the preface to the first volume of *The Upanishads*, the vast Vedic literature of the early Indo-Āryans is like a trackless tropical forest, full of lush underbrush, weeds, thorns, and stately trees. Travellers in it often become dismayed, bewildered, and lost; yet if they courageously and patiently push on, they are rewarded by the discovery of blossoms of rare beauty and fragrance. The present volume contains these blossoms.

NIKHILANANDA

Thousand Island Park
New York
September 1962

CONTENTS

LIST OF ABBREVIATIONS

Ai. Br.	. .	Aitareya Brāhmana
Ai. Up.	. .	Aitareya Upanishad
Ath.	. .	Atharva-Veda
B. G.	. .	Bhagavad Gitā
Br. Su.	. .	Brahma Sutras
Br. Up.	. .	Brihadāranyaka Upanishad
Chh. Up.	. .	Chhāndogya Upanishad
Iś. Up.	. .	Iśa Upanishad
Ka. Up.	. .	Katha Upanishad
Kau. Up.	. .	Kaushitaki Upanishad
Ke. Up.	. .	Kena Upanishad
Mā. Up.	. .	Māndukya Upanishad
Mai. Up.	. .	Maitrāyani Upanishad
Mu. Up.	. .	Mundaka Upanishad
Pr. Up.	. .	Praśna Upanishad
Ri.	. .	Rig-Veda
Śa. Br.	. .	Śathapatha Brāhmana
Sām. Kā.	. .	Sāmkhya Kārikā
Sām. Su.	. .	Sāmkhya Sutras
Śvet. Up.	. .	Śvetāśvatara Upanishad
Tai. Up.	. .	Taittiriya Upanishad
Yog. Su.	. .	Yoga Sutras

Note: References to *The Upanishads*, Vols I–IV, are to the original four volumes published by Harper & Brothers in New York and Phoenix House in London, of which the present work is an abridgement.

NOTE ON THE PRONUNCIATION
OF SANSKRIT WORDS

The vowels are pronounced almost as in Italian, except that the sound of *a* approaches that of *o* in *bond* or *u* in *but*, and *ā* that of *a* in *army*; *ē* has the sound of *a* (prolonged) in *evade*. The consonants are generally as in English, except that *ḍ* is a cerebral; *t* and *d* are usually dentals, as in French; *bh*, *chh*, *dh*, *th*, etc., are the simple sounds plus an aspiration; *jn* is a nasalized *gn*; and *ś* is pronounced as *sh*.

GENERAL INTRODUCTION

THE VEDAS ARE the basic scriptures of the Hindus and their highest authority in all matters pertaining to religion and philosophy. They are, moreover, the earliest extant Indo-Āryan literary monuments. The Hindus regard them as eternal, without beginning, without human authorship. The primary meaning of the word *Veda* is uncreated Knowledge, super-sensuous wisdom. The secondary reference is to the *words* in which that Knowledge is embodied. And so the term *Veda* denotes not only the religious and philosophical wisdom of India, but also the books in which the earliest utterances of that wisdom are preserved. The Hindus look upon these books with the highest reverence. They are known as the Word-Brahman, the Śabda-Brahma.

Knowledge is of two kinds. The first is derived from the sense-organs and corroborated by varied evidence based upon the experiences of the sense-organs. This is the form of knowledge that falls within the scope of the physical sciences. The second, however, is transcendent and is realized through the mental and spiritual discipline of yoga. And this is the subject matter of the Vedas. According to Patanjali, the traditional master of the yoga doctrine, it is not the words of the Vedas that are eternal, but the Knowledge conveyed through them. This Knowledge, also called the Sphota, has existed always. At the conclusion of a cycle both the Sphota and the created universe merge in the undifferentiated causal state, and at the beginning of the new cycle the two together again become manifest. The Lord brings forth the universe with the help of the Knowledge of the Vedas. He is the first teacher of Vedic truth. Though the words may be different in different cycles, the ideas conveyed through them remain unalterable: no human intellect can interfere with them.

The Vedas are called Śruti (from *śru*, to hear), since they were handed down orally from teacher to disciple. The Hindus did not at first commit them to writing. Either writing was unknown to them at that early period of history or they considered the words of the Vedas too sacred to set down. Written words become the common property of all, whereas the Vedas were to be studied only by those who had been initiated by a qualified teacher. Such was the high esteem in which the Hindus held the words that, once the Vedas had been systematized, they did not make the slightest change even in the pronunciation while passing them on from generation to generation. Hence, though committed to writing only many centuries after their composition, the Vedas as we now possess them may well contain the exact words and ideas of the Indo-Āryan ancestors of the Hindus.

THE DIVISIONS OF THE VEDAS

The Vedas have been divided in various ways. The two most general divisions according to subject matter are known as the Karmakānda and Jnānakānda. The first deals with karma, ritualistic action, sacrifices, etc., the purpose of which is the attainment of material prosperity here on earth and felicity in heaven after death. The second is concerned with the Knowledge through which one is liberated from ignorance and enabled to realize the Highest Good.

In the Purānas it is stated that Vyāsa was commanded by Brahmā to make a compilation of the Vedas. Vyāsa is reputed to be the author of the *Mahābhārata*, of which the Bhagavad Gitā forms a part. He lived at the time of the battle of Kurukshetra. With the help of four disciples, so the tradition goes, this great saint and poet arranged the Vedas in four books, namely, the Rik, Yajur, Sāman, and Atharva. He was thus the classifier of the Vedas, though not their author. Vyāsa compiled the Rig-Veda by collecting the riks. Of the sāmans he composed the Sāma-Veda, while the Yajur-Veda he composed of the yajus. The Rig-Veda, which may be called a book of chants, is set to certain fixed melodies. The Sāma-Veda has no independent value; for it consists mostly of stanzas from the Rig-Veda. The arrangement of its verses is solely with reference to their place and use in the Soma-sacrifice. The Yajur-Veda contains, in addition to verses taken from the Rig-Veda, many original prose formulas which may be called sacrificial prayers. The Atharva-Veda consists of a special class of Vedic texts known as chhandas. These deal with spells, incantations, and kingly duties, as well as exalted spiritual truths. Western scholars sometimes exclude this compilation from their consideration of the Vedas; but according to the Hindu view it definitely belongs among them. The name Trayi, or Triad, often used to denote the Vedas, is collectively applied to the Rig-Veda, the Sāma-Veda, and the Yajur-Veda, the Atharva-Veda being excluded from the Triad because it has no application to sacrificial actions. Nevertheless, one of the four priests officiating in all Vedic sacrifices had to be thoroughly versed in the chhandas.

Each of the four Vedas falls into two sections: Mantra and Brāhmana. The Mantra is also called the Samhitā (from *sam*, together, and *hita*, put), which means, literally, a collection of hymns, or mantras, used in the sacrifices. The offering of oblations for the propitiation of the devatās, or deities, is termed the sacrifice, or yajna. This was a highly important ceremony through which the ancient Indo-Āryans communed with the gods, or higher powers. The Mantra comprises the prayers and hymns, while the Brāhmana contains the rules and regulations for the sacrifices, deals with their accessories, and also reveals the meaning of the Mantra, which otherwise would remain obscure. Therefore both the

Mantra and the Brāhmana were indispensable for orthodox worship and propitiation of the gods.

A further development of the Brāhmana, and included in it, was the Āranyaka, or 'forest treatise'. This was intended for those people who had retired into the forest in accordance with the ideal of the third stage of life, and were consequently unable to perform in the usual way the sacrifices obligatory for all twice-born householders, and especially brāhmins. The sacrifices required many articles and accessories impossible to procure in the forest. Hence the Āranyaka prescribes symbolic worship and describes various meditations that were to be used as substitutes for an actual sacrifice. To give an illustration from the first chapter of the *Brihadāranyaka Upanishad*: instead of actually performing the Vedic Horse-sacrifice (Aśvamedha), the forest-dweller was to meditate in a special way upon the dawn as the head of the horse, the sun as the eye, the air as the life, and so on. The worship was lifted from the physical to the mental level.

THE FOUR STAGES

The full life-period of an Indo-Āryan was divided into four stages, namely, brahmacharya, gārhasthya, vānaprastha, and sannyāsa. The first stage was devoted to study. The celibate student led a life of chastity and austerity and served his teacher with humility. He learnt the Mantra and the Brāhmana sections of the Vedas. And when he left the teacher's house, after completing his studies, he was commanded not to deviate from truth and not to forget to persevere in the study of the Vedas. The second stage was devoted to household duties. The young man took a wife. Both together performed the Vedic sacrifice with the hymns of the Mantra and in accordance with the rules laid down in the Brāhmana. The third stage commenced when the hair turned grey and the face began to wrinkle. The householder consigned the responsibility of the home to his children and retired with his wife into the forest. He was then known as a vānaprashthin or āranyaka, a forest-dweller. The Āranyaka portion of the Vedas prescribed for him sacrifice by meditation and symbolic worship.

The final stage, called sannyāsa, was the culmination of the strictly regulated life of an Indo-Āryan. During this period, having totally renounced the world, he became a sannyāsin, or wandering monk, free from worldly desires and attachments and absorbed in the uninterrupted contemplation of Brahman.[1] He no longer needed to worship God by means of material articles or even mental symbols. It was for him that

[1] According to a Vedic injunction, one can renounce the world whenever one feels distaste for it. Thus one can become a sannyāsin from any stage The normal course, however, is to proceed through the series of the four stages.

the Upanishads (which are mostly the concluding portions of the Āranyakas) were generally intended.

Thus the Indo-Āryan seers arranged the Vedas to conform to the four stages of life. The brahmachāri studied the Samhitā, the house-holder followed the injunctions of the Brāhmana, the forest-dweller practised contemplation according to the Āranyaka, and the sannyāsin was guided by the wisdom of the Upanishads. According to the Hindu view, all four portions of the four Vedas were revealed simultaneously and have existed from the very beginning of the cycle. They are not to be regarded as exhibiting a philosophical development or evolution in the processes of thought.

According to tradition, Vyāsa systematized the Vedas in four books. He taught the Rig-Veda to his disciple Paila, the Yajur-Veda to Vaiśampāyana, the Sāma-Veda to Jaimini, and the Atharva-Veda to Sumanta. The Yajur-Veda has two versions: the one is called the Krishna Yajur-Veda, or Black Yajur-Veda, containing the *Taittiriya Samhitā*, and the other, the Śukla Yajur-Veda, or White Yajur-Veda, containing the *Vājasaneyi Samhitā*. The latter version was taught by Yājnavalkya, one of the great teachers of the *Brihadāranyaka Upanishad*, to his disciples.

The four basic Vedas gradually branched off into many recensions, or śākhās, at the hands of various teachers, after whom they were named. Thus the *Śatapatha Brāhmana* of the Śukla Yajur-Veda survives in the Kānva and Mādhyandina recensions, according to the two disciples of Yājnavalkya. They differ from each other greatly in content as well as in the number and arrangement of the sections and chapters, the former having seventeen and the latter fourteen sections. The concluding portion of the last book of both recensions is the *Brihadāranyaka Upanishad*; but here again the two versions often differ. Śankarāchārya based his commentary on the Kānva recension.

Each of the Vedas contains its own Brāhmanas. In most cases the concluding portion of the Āranyaka is the Upanishad—also called the Vedānta because in it the Vedic wisdom reaches its culmination (*anta*). It shows the seeker the way to Liberation and the Highest Good. Usually there is a full series from the Samhitā, or Mantra, through the Brāhmana and Āranyaka to the culmination in the Upanishad. For example, the *Taittiriya Samhitā* is followed by the *Taittiriya Brāhmana*, at the end of which comes the *Taittiriya Āranyaka*; and this is concluded by the *Taittiriya Upanishad*. But in rare instances an Upanishad may come directly at the conclusion of the Samhitā, as is the case with the *Iśa Upanishad*.

Following are a few hymns from the Rig-Veda and the Atharva-Veda:

PURUSHASUKTA[2]

A thousand heads had Purusha, a thousand eyes, a thousand feet.
He covered earth on every side, and spread ten fingers' breadth beyond.

The Purusha is all that yet hath been and all that is to be;
The lord of immortality which waxes greater still by food.

So mighty is his greatness; yea, greater than this is Purusha.
All creatures are one-fourth of him, three-fourths eternal life in heaven.

With three-fourths Purusha went up: one-fourth of him again was here.
Thence he strode out on every side over what eats not and what eats.

From him Virāj was born; again Purusha from Virāj was born.
As soon as he was born he spread eastward and westward o'er the earth.

When gods prepared the sacrifice with Purusha as their offering,
Its oil was spring, the holy gift was autumn; summer was the wood.

They balmed as victim on the grass Purusha born in earliest time.
With him the deities and all Sādhyas and Rishis sacrificed.

From that great general sacrifice the dripping fat was gathered up.
He formed the creatures of the air, and animals both wild and tame.

From that great general sacrifice Richas and Sāma-hymns were born:
Therefrom the metres were produced, the Yajus had its birth from it.

From it were horses born, from it all creatures with two rows of teeth:
From it were generated kine, from it the goats and sheep were born.

When they divided Purusha, how many portions did they make?
What do they call his mouth, his arms? What do they call his thighs and
    feet?

The Brāhman was his mouth, of both his arms was the Rājanya made.
His thighs became the Vaiśya, from his feet the Śudra was produced.

The moon was gendered from his mind, and from his eye the Sun had birth.
Indra and Agni from his mouth were born, and Vāyu from his breath.

Forth from his navel came mid-air; the sky was fashioned from his head;
Earth from his feet, and from his ear the regions. Thus they formed the
    worlds.

Seven fencing-logs had he, thrice seven layers of fuel were prepared,
When the gods, offering sacrifice, bound, as their victim, Purusha.

[2] *Ri.* X.90 (*translated by R. T. H. Griffith*).

Gods, sacrificing, sacrificed the victim: these were the earliest holy ordinances.
The mighty ones attained the height of heaven, there where the Sādhyas, gods of old, are dwelling.

HYMN TO PRAJĀPATI[3]

In the beginning rose Hiranyagarbha, born only lord of all created beings.
He fixed and holdeth up this earth and heaven. What god shall we adore with our oblation?

Giver of vital breath, of power and vigour, he whose commandments all the gods acknowledge:
Whose shade is death, whose lustre makes immortal. What god shall we adore with our oblation?

Who by his grandeur hath become sole ruler of all the moving world that breathes and slumbers;
He who is lord of men and lord of cattle. What god shall we adore with our oblation?

His, through his might, are these snow-covered mountains, and men call sea and Rājā his possession:
His arms are these, his are these heavenly regions. What god shall we adore with our oblation?

By him the heavens are strong and earth is steadfast, by him light's realm and sky-vault are supported:
By him the regions in mid-air were measured. What god shall we adore with our oblation?

To him, supported by his help, two armies look while trembling in their spirit,
When over them the risen sun is shining. What god shall we adore with our oblation?

What time the mighty waters came, containing the universal germs, producing Agni,
Thence sprang the gods' one spirit into being. What god shall we adore with our oblation?

He in his might surveyed the floods containing productive force and generating worship.
He is the god of gods, and none beside him. What god shall we adore with our oblation?

[3] *Ri.* X.121 (*translated by R. T. H. Griffith*). The last line of each verse is rendered in English by Hindu translators as: 'He it is to whom we offer our oblation.'

Ne'er may he harm us who is earth's begetter, nor he whose laws are sure,
the heavens' creator,
He who brought forth the great and lucid waters. What god shall we adore
with our oblation?

Prajāpati! Thou only comprehendest all these created things, and none
beside thee.
Grant us our hearts' desire when we invoke thee: may we have store of
riches in possession.

HYMN OF CREATION[4]

Non-being then existed not nor being:
There was no air, nor sky that is beyond it.
What was concealed? Wherein? In whose protection?
And was there deep unfathomable water?

Death then existed not nor life immortal;
Of neither night nor day was any token.
By its inherent force the One breathed breathless:
No other thing than that beyond existed.

Darkness there was at first by darkness hidden;
Without distinctive marks, this all was water.
That which, becoming, by the void was covered,
That One by force of heat came into being.

Desire entered the One in the beginning:
It was the earliest seed, of thought the product.
The sages searching in their hearts with wisdom,
Found out the bond of being in non-being.

Their ray extended light across the darkness:
But was the One above or was it under?
Creative force was there, and fertile power:
Below was energy, above was impulse.

Who knows for certain? Who shall here declare it?
Whence was it born, and whence came this creation?
The gods were born after this world's creation:
Then who can know from whence it has arisen?

None knoweth whence creation has arisen;
And whether he has or has not produced it:
He who surveys it in the highest heaven,
He only knows, or haply he may know not.

[4] *Ri.* X.129 (*translated by A. A. Macdonell*).

PRAISE OF TIME[5]

Time drives as a horse with seven reins, thousand-eyed, unageing, possessing
much seed; him the inspired poets mount; his wheels are all beings.

Seven wheels doth this time drive; seven are his naves, immortality for-
sooth his axle; he, time, including all these beings, goes on as first god.

A full vessel is set upon time; we indeed see it, being now manifoldly; it is
in front of all these beings; it call they time in the highest firmament.

He indeed together brought beings; he indeed together went about beings;
being father he became son of them; than him verily there is no other
brilliance that is higher.

Time generated yonder sky, time also these earths; what is and what is to
be stands out sent forth by time.

Time created the earth; in time burns the sun; in time are all existences;
in time the eye looks abroad.

In time is mind, in time is breath, in time is name collected; by time, when
arrived, all these creatures are glad.

In time is fervour, in time is what is chief, in time is the brahman collected;
time is the lord of all, who was father of Prajāpati.

Sent by it, born by it, in it is this set firm; time, becoming the brahman,
bears the most exalted one.

Time generated progeny, time in the beginning Prajāpati; the self-existent
Kaśyapa from time, fervour from time was born.

THE UPANISHADS

Now about the number and divisions of the Upanishads. With the
disappearance of many of the recensions of the Vedas, many Brāhmanas,
Āranyakas, and Upanishads also disappeared.[6] The fact that the sacred
books were not committed to writing in ancient times is partly responsible for this loss. Furthermore, among the works surviving, it is difficult
to ascertain the exact number that should be regarded as authentic
Upanishads. A religious system is considered valid in India only when
it is supported by Śruti (the Vedas); hence the founders of religious

---

[5] *Ath.* XIX.53 (*translated by W. D. Whitney*).
[6] The Rig-Veda is said to have existed in twenty-one recensions, the Yajur-
Veda in a hundred, the Sāma-Veda in a thousand, and the Atharva-Veda in nine.
But there are differences of opinion among the authorities on this subject.

sects have sometimes written books and called them Upanishads in order to give their views scriptural authority. The *Allāh Upanishad*, for instance, was composed in the sixteenth century, at the time of the Mussalmān emperor Ākbar.

One hundred and eight Upanishads are enumerated in the *Muktika Upanishad*, which is a work belonging to the tradition of the Yajur-Veda. Among these, the *Aitareya Upanishad* and *Kaushitaki Upanishad* belong to the Rig-Veda; the *Chhāndogya* and *Kena*, to the Sāma-Veda; the *Taittiriya*, *Mahānārāyana*, *Katha*, *Śvetāśvatara*, and *Maitrāyani*, to the Krishna Yajur-Veda; the *Iśa* and *Brihadāranyaka*, to the Śukla Yajur-Veda; and the *Mundaka*, *Praśna*, and *Māndukya*, to the Atharva-Veda. It may be stated, also, that these Upanishads belong to differing recensions of their respective Vedas. Thus, for instance, the *Mundaka Upanishad* belongs to the Śaunaka recension of the Atharva-Veda, while the *Praśna Upanishad* belongs to the Pippalāda recension. The *Brahma Sutras*, which is the most authoritative work on the Vedānta philosophy, has been based upon the *Aitareya*, *Taittiriya*, *Chhāndogya*, *Brihadāranyaka*, *Kaushitaki*, *Katha*, *Śvetāśvatara*, *Mundaka*, *Praśna*, and possibly also the *Jābāla Upanishad*. Śankarāchārya wrote his celebrated commentaries on the *Iśa*, *Kena*, *Katha*, *Praśna*, *Mundaka*, *Māndukya*, *Aitareya*, *Taittiriya*, *Chhāndogya*, *Brihadāranyaka*, and possibly also the *Śvetāśvatara Upanishad*. These latter are regarded as the major works.

The teachings of the Upanishads, the *Brahma Sutras*, and the Bhagavad Gitā form the basis of the Vedānta philosophy. Three main schools of Vedānta exist: the Dualist, Qualified Non-dualist, and Non-dualist, their principal teachers being, respectively, Madhvāchārya (AD 1199–1276), Rāmānujāchārya (AD 1017–1137), and Śankarāchārya (AD 788–820). Madhvāchārya has written commentaries on some of the major Upanishads according to Dualistic doctrines. Some of the disciples and followers of Rāmānujāchārya have done likewise to prove that Qualified Non-dualism is the underlying philosophy of Vedānta. But neither of these systems has won such wide acceptance and prestige as that of Śankarāchārya.

Śankarāchārya's interpretation of the Upanishads, Bhagavad Gitā, and *Brahma Sutras* is the supreme Hindu contribution to the philosophical wisdom of the world. This remarkable genius appeared at a critical period of Indian history. The sun of Buddhism had already passed below the horizon. Various invading peoples, such as the Śaks, the Tartars, the Beluchis, and the Huns had entered India with their grotesque religious ideas and ceremonies and embraced Buddhism. At their hands the religion of Buddha had become greatly distorted. A Hindu revival was struggling into existence, and numerous Hindu sects, such as the old Vedic ritualists and the yogi ascetics, were asserting their contrary yet equally dogmatic views. A veritable babel was reigning in India when the youthful Śankarāchārya appeared on the scene.

According to his followers, this great pillar of Hinduism was the perfect embodiment of the Vedic wisdom. Endowed with a keen intellect and with rare forensic powers, he courageously challenged all opponents. He cut through the cobweb of conflicting views with a direct and consistently rational interpretation of the authoritative texts, supported by his own profound spiritual experiences. Within his short lifetime of only thirty-two years, he travelled the length and breadth of India, preaching his doctrines and reforming the sannyāsin organizations. He founded four monasteries at the cardinal points of the country. And meanwhile he produced a body of literary work that includes not only his great Vedāntic commentaries but also many hymns addressed to the Hindu deities, through worship of whom the aspirant's heart is purified and his spirit qualified for the Knowledge of Brahman. When one considers the lofty height reached by Śankarāchārya in his philosophy, and at the same time the soul-melting love permeating his hymns, one cannot but marvel at the mighty sweep of his mind, the catholicity of his heart, and the austere purity of his philosophical thinking. He was indeed a saviour of the Hindu world.

The subject matter of the Upanishads is abstruse. There are, besides, apparent contradictions, by which unwary students may easily become confused. Therefore, from ancient times, books have been composed to explain and harmonize their mysteries. Among these the *Brahma Sutras*, also called the *Vedānta Sutras* and the *Śāriraka Sutras*, is the best known. It formulates the teachings of the Upanishads in concise aphorisms which reconcile the many apparent contradictions. Vyāsa is its reputed author. The Bhagavad Gitā and the *Brahma Sutras*, together with the Upanishads, constitute what are called the three Prasthānas, the canonical books, which are the foundation of the religion and philosophy of Vedānta.

Side by side with Śruti, or the Vedas, there exists another body of scriptural treatises known as Smriti. These works are regarded as having come into existence through human authorship. They derive their authority from the Vedas and include such majestic books as the *Mahābhārata*, the various Purānas, and the *Manusamhitā*. In ancient India only those people who belonged to the three upper castes were permitted to read the Vedas. The teachings of Smriti, however, were accessible to all. And they too opened the door to Liberation.

In AD 1650, fifty Upanishads were translated into Persian under the patronage of Prince Dārā, the son of Sājāhān, Emperor of Delhi. From the Persian they were translated into Latin, in AD 1801–1802. Schopenhauer studied this Latin translation and in later years declared: 'In the whole world there is no study so beneficial and so elevating as that of the Upanishads. It has been the solace of my life; it will be the solace of my death.'

THE MEANING OF UPANISHAD

The word *Upanishad* has been derived from the root *sad*, to which are added two prefixes: *upa* and *ni*. The prefix *upa* denotes nearness, and *ni*, totality. The root *sad* means to loosen, to attain, and to annihilate. Thus the etymological meaning of the word is the Knowledge, or Vidyā, which, when received from a competent teacher, *loosens totally* the bondage of the world, or surely enables the pupil to *attain* (i.e. realize) the Ātman, or Self, or *completely destroys* ignorance, which is responsible for the deluding appearance of the Infinite Self as the finite embodied creature. Though the word primarily signifies knowledge, yet by implication it also refers to the books that contain that knowledge. The root *sad* with the prefix *upa* also connotes the humility with which the pupil should approach the teacher.

The Knowledge of Brahman was considered a profound secret and was itself sometimes given the name of Upanishad. It is to be noted that the instructions regarding Brahman were often given in short formulas also known as Upanishads. 'Its secret name (Upanishad) is *Satyasya Satyam*, "the Truth of truth".'[7] 'Now, therefore, the instruction [about Brahman]: *Neti, neti*—"Not this, not this".' 'That Brahman is called *Tadvana*, the Adorable of all; It should be worshipped by the name of *Tadvana*.' The books which contained the above-mentioned secret teachings and formulas were also called Upanishads.

QUALIFICATIONS OF STUDENTS

The Vedānta teachers formulated the qualifications of the pupil entitled to study Vedānta. He had to know, in a general way, the Vedas and their auxiliaries; must have attained purity of heart by freeing himself from sin, through an avoidance of selfish and forbidden actions as well as by the practice of daily devotions and obligatory duties, particular religious observances on special occasions, and the customary penances prescribed by religion. Further, he had to discriminate between the Real and the unreal, and renounce the unreal. He had to cultivate inner calmness and control of the senses, preserve the serenity of the mind and organs after they had been controlled, acquire such virtues as forbearance and concentration, and finally, possess an intense

[7] The quotations in the two introductory chapters, if not specified otherwise, are from the Upanishads. The exact references are given in the regular four-volume edition of the Upanishads translated by the present author.

yearning for liberation from the bondages of worldly life. Such a one, and such a one alone, was qualified to receive from the teacher the profound knowledge of the Upanishads.

'This highest mystery of Vedānta,' we read, 'should not be given to one whose passions have not been completely subdued, nor to one who is not a son or is not a pupil.' 'A father may therefore tell that doctrine of Brahman to his eldest son or to a worthy pupil. But it should not be imparted to anybody else, even if he give the teacher the whole sea-girt earth full of treasure, for this doctrine is worth more than that. Yea, it is worth more.'

The custodians of the Vedic culture were the members of the brāhmin, or priestly, caste. That is why the brāhmins were held in the highest esteem by every section of Hindu society.

TESTS BY TEACHERS

Aspirants desiring the knowledge of the Upanishads were subjected to severe ordeals by their preceptors. The *Katha Upanishad* describes the case of Nachiketā, who was tested in various ways by Yama, the god of death, to ascertain his fitness for the Knowledge of Brahman. He was offered horses, elephants, and cattle; children and grandchildren; rulership of the earth and many years of life; heavenly damsels and their music; and numerous other desirable things which do not fall to the lot of an ordinary mortal. But he spurned them all, understanding their transitory nature, and persisted in his prayer for the Knowledge of the Self. Pratardana was tested by Indra,[8] Jānaśruti Pautrāyana by Raikva,[9] Āruni by Pravāhana,[10] Janaka by Yājnavalkya,[11] and Brihadratha by Śākāyanya.[12]

In the *Praśna Upanishad* the teacher Pippalāda demanded of his six disciples that they should spend one year practising austerities, continence, and faith. 'Afterwards you may ask me any question you like; if I know the answer I shall give it to you.' The *Chhāndogya Upanishad*,[13] in a celebrated passage, tells how the teacher Prajāpati required Indra and Virochana to practise spiritual disciplines for thirty-two years. Even after that, Virochana, the king of the demons, who had not acquired the necessary purity of heart, went away satisfied with the erroneous idea that the Self was identical with the body, while Indra, the king of the gods, had to continue in the austere life of a brahmachāri for another seventy-three years (one hundred and five in all) before he could realize the true knowledge of the Self.

---

[8] *Kau. Up.* III. 1.
[9] *Chh. Up.* IV. i.
[10] *Br. Up.* VI. ii. 6.
[11] *Br. Up.* IV. iii. 1.
[12] *Mai. Up.* I. 2.
[13] VIII. vii. 3; VIII. xi. 3.

RECONCILING THE TEACHINGS OF THE UPANISHADS

One finds in the Upanishads various strands of thought: Dualism (Dvaita)¦ Qualified Non-dualism (Viśishtādvaita), and Non-dualism (Advaita). Further, the Upanishads describe both the Brahman with attributes (Saguna Brahman) and the attributeless Brahman (Nirguna Brahman). They also deal with the disciplines of philosophical knowledge (jnāna), divine love (bhakti), action (karma), and yoga. Sometimes contradictions appear. Hence the question arises as to whether the Upanishads present a single, consistent, co-ordinated system of knowledge or a mere conglomeration of unrelated ideas. The orthodox Hindu view is that the Upanishads are consistent, that they describe a single truth, namely, the reality of the non-dual Brahman, and furthermore, that this same truth is rendered in the Bhagavad Gitā and the *Brahma Sutras*. The Vedāntic philosophers support this conclusion by certain accepted means of proof.

The subject matter of the Upanishads is Brahman, the Absolute, which transcends time, space, and causality and cannot be comprehended by human thought or rendered in words. Human language and reasoning can describe and interpret sense-perceived phenomena; but Brahman is beyond their grasp. Any presentation of this subject in finite and relative human terms cannot but contain seeming contradictions. This does not, however, vitiate the Absolute Itself. Further, the Hindu philosophers admit different degrees of power of comprehension on the part of various pupils and they formulate their instructions accordingly. But such differences do not affect Brahman Itself, which is the final object of Upanishadic knowledge.

According to Śankarāchārya, the sole purpose of the Upanishads is to prove the reality of Brahman and the phenomenality or unreality of the universe of names and forms, and to establish the absolute oneness of the embodied soul and Brahman. This Vedic truth is not a product of the human mind and cannot be comprehended by the unaided human intellect. Only a competent teacher, through direct experience, can reveal to the qualified student the true significance of the Vedas and the fullness of their absolutely consistent truth.

THE KSHATRIYA INFLUENCE

A striking feature of the Upanishads is the part played in them by the kshatriyas, the members of the royal military caste. This fact has given rise to certain interesting speculations. The Mantra and Brāhmana portions of the Vedas treat of sacrifices in which the brāhmins serve as priests. They deal with ritualistic works, in which a diversity of the actor, the instruments of action, and the result is recognized, while the sacrifices themselves are performed with a view to reaping results either here on earth or in the afterworld. This multiplicity of elements and ends stands in contrast to the central theme of the Upanishads, which is Brahmavidyā, the unitive knowledge of Brahman, and to the Vedāntic condemnation of sacrifices as barriers to this unitive knowledge. Therefore several Western writers have contended that the Upanishads represent a protest of the kshatriyas against the influence of the brāhmins.[14] They contend also that the Knowledge of Ātman, whatever its origin, was cultivated primarily by the kshatriyas and accepted by the brāhmins only later on. Hindu scholars, however, do not accept this view.

In reviewing the problem, let us first point out a few of the references to kshatriyas in the Upanishads. Among those teachers who are spoken of as having given instruction to brāhmin disciples are the following: Pravāhana Jaivali (*Br. Up.* VI. ii; *Chh. Up.* I. viii; V. iii), Kaikeyi Aśvapati (*Chh. Up.* V. xi), and Chitra (*Kau. Up.* I). These teachers were versed in rituals, in the mysteries of rebirth, in the identity of the jiva and Brahman, and in the Knowledge of the Infinite. And this fact, as we have said, has led certain Vedic scholars of the West to conclude that the Upanishads, containing the Knowledge of the Self, must be a later development by the kshatriyas in reaction against the rituals and sacrifices of the Mantra and Brāhmana portions of the Vedas: the brāhmins, occupied solely with the details and paraphernalia of sacrifice, were ignorant of the philosophy of the Self and so had to learn Self-Knowledge from the teachers of the military caste.

Such a conclusion, however, is hardly valid. Undoubtedly, according to Advaita Vedānta, the Knowledge of Brahman and the performance of sacrifices are incompatible: he who contemplates the oneness of the jiva and Brahman and the unreality of the relative world cannot participate in Vedic sacrifices. However—and this is the great point—sacrifices and the Knowledge of Brahman are meant for *two different classes of aspirants*. A sannyāsin, who has experienced the transitory nature of enjoyment, is qualified for Self-Knowledge; but such enlightened ones do not constitute the major portion of society. It is the duty of others, who belong to the first three stages of life and seek material happiness, to engage in sacrificial action. This is a basic principle, understood and taken for granted by every member of Hindu society. It is neither necessary nor possible for a sannyāsin to perform sacrifices. To suppose that there were among the brāhmins no sannyāsins who were endowed with Self-Knowledge would be wrong. The fact is that as there were both illumined and unillumined persons among the kshatriyas, so there were among the brāhmins those who were devoted to sacrifices and also

[14] P. Deussen, *The Philosophy of the Upanishads*, p. 19. Clark, Edinburgh, 1908.

those who cultivated the Knowledge of Brahman. The passages of the Upanishads that condemn sacrifices and other actions cannot possibly apply to the performers of sacrifices; for they are still householders. Such passages were directed to, and can apply to, sannyāsins alone.

As already stated, according to the Vedic tradition, the Lord is the source of the Vedic knowledge. As time goes on, the Vedic knowledge is disseminated through a succession of competent teachers. The *Brihadāranyaka Upanishad* supplies several genealogical tables of such Vedic seers. There were a number of kshatriyas among the rishis, and the brāhmins, eager to acquire their knowledge, accepted discipleship under them, in accordance with the well-known Hindu maxim that superior knowledge should be learnt even from a person of inferior rank.

According to the *Mundaka Upanishad*, one should acquire two forms of knowledge: the aparā (lower) and the Parā (Higher). The lower consists of the four Vedas (that is to say, their ritualistic portions) and their six auxiliaries. It deals with the phenomenal universe. The importance of the lower knowledge was admitted by the rishis. Most of the Upanishads exhibit stark realism in describing how to obtain wealth, fame, power, a long life on earth, a healthy body, and worthy children. Many of the prayers are directed to this end. The rishis' understanding of man and the universe, though it may appear crude and naïve in the light of modern science, was derived from observation of nature. Such knowledge, they repeatedly stated, is conducive to human welfare and provides the foundation for spiritual wisdom. But both the universe and material enjoyments, they taught, are impermanent.

The Higher Knowledge is that by which the Imperishable Substance is known. To this Imperishable Substance the Indo-Āryan seers gave the name of Brahman; hence the Higher Knowledge was also called Brahmavidyā, the Knowledge of Brahman. Brahmavidyā was regarded as the foundation of all other forms of knowledge—*sarvavidyāpratishthā*. Highly treasured by the rishis, it was zealously guarded by them; for they regarded it as more precious than the earth filled with riches. The secret of Brahman could be transmitted only to a qualified disciple.

The actual experience of Brahman, which is the culmination of the Higher Knowledge, requires extremely austere disciplines. Only the great renouncers known as paramahamsas, belonging to the highest order of sannyāsins, can gain this cómplete Knowledge of Brahman. It is yoga that gives a man the subtle depth of understanding by which the supramental truths can be apprehended. The rishis were adept in yoga. That is why their hearts were open to the secrets of creation and the universe.

The methods of the modern physical sciences for the discovery of truth are based upon a different notion of how to search than that which directed the rishis in their realization of Brahman. A scientist seeks to understand the universe through reason based on knowledge derived from the sense-organs. The rishis, on the other hand, did not entirely depend upon reason, as this word is usually understood. They developed another faculty of understanding, which is called bodhi, or deeper consciousness. The seeker of Brahmavidyā wakened the subtle power of the mind and senses by means of concentration and self-control. By withdrawing the senses from outer objects, he made the scattered mind one-pointed. This practice of concentration presently endowed it with keenness, depth, and a new intensity, and as the power of concentration increased, the seeker became aware of deeper phases of existence. Instinct, reason, and intuition, or higher consciousness—the three instruments of knowledge—all are differing states of one and the same mind. Hence a lower state can be developed into a higher. The means to this end, however, are not external instruments but appropriate disciplines directed within.

The Vedic teacher prepared the soil of his disciple's mind before giving him any instruction regarding Brahman. Moreover, there were occasions when the instruction given was not oral. A pupil would often be asked to meditate on a problem and seek the answer from within his own self. And so we read in the *Taittiriya Upanishad* that Bhrigu came to his father Varuna and asked: 'Revered sir, teach me Brahman.' Varuna did not give him a direct reply; he asked the boy to practise meditation and austerities. Bhrigu followed this advice and came to the conclusion that food alone was Brahman. He was asked to meditate again. This time he realized that prāna alone was Brahman. His father exhorted him to concentrate further. At last the nature of Brahman was revealed in Bhrigu's heart and he realized that Brahman is Ānandam, Bliss Absolute.

The Upanishads teach the truth—unknown to the sense-organs—regarding living beings (jivas), the universe (jagat), and God (Iśvara). They describe the nature and attributes of Brahman, Its reality and manifestations, Its powers and aspects. They also describe the creation, preservation, and ultimate dissolution of the universe, and the changes and modifications of nature (prakriti). Furthermore, the Upanishads deal with the development of the individual soul (jiva), its evolution and its destiny, its bondage and its freedom. The relationship between matter and Spirit, between God, the universe, and living beings, also belongs to the subject matter of the Upanishads. These concerns relate to a supersensuous realm unknowable to a man's everyday state of consciousness. Yet the weal and woe and the good and evil of a man depend, in a special manner, upon his knowledge of these things. For man is rooted in a reality far deeper than is apparent to the senses. Just as only a small portion of an iceberg is visible, so only a small portion of man is available to the senses, no matter how their powers may be magnified. The solution of many of our most vital problems must come, therefore, from regions beyond the scope of the ordinary faculty of reason.

Is there a soul apart from the body? What happens to the soul after the death of the body? If a soul survives the destruction of the body, does it ever return to earth? Is a man responsible for his good and bad deeds? What is the goal and purpose of human life? Our conduct and work depend upon our answers to these questions. And yet we cannot answer them intelligently with an intellect aided only by the senses.

Or again: Does God exist? Is God just and compassionate? Is He unconcerned about man, regarding him with indifferent eyes? Is God endowed with a form or is He formless? Has He attributes or is He attributeless? Is He immanent in the universe, or transcendent, or is He both? Is the universe real or unreal? Does it exist outside a man's mind or is it a product of his imagination? Is the universe beginningless or has it a beginning? Has the Godhead become the universe or has He made it, like a watch, or is the universe a mere appearance superimposed upon the Godhead through an inscrutable illusion of some kind, like a mirage upon a desert?

An inquiring mind longs to find satisfactory answers to these philosophical questions; but there is no logical method to satisfy such a longing. Only the Knowledge of Brahman can break the 'fetters of the heart' and solve all doubts. This is the Hindu view. The more a man's intelligence deepens, the more his heart is made pure and his mental horizon widens, the more will he understand and appreciate the teaching of the rishis, as preserved in the Vedas and Upanishads.

One can hardly exaggerate the influence of the Vedas upon the individual and collective life of the Hindus. Since the days of their greatness, both the political and the religious life of India have undergone tremendous changes. Many aggressive races have entered the country from outside and been absorbed in this melting-pot; other powerful cultures, like the ingredients in a salad-bowl, have retained their individual traits. Foreign conquerors have sought, by various means, to impose their customs and ideals upon Hindu society. Nevertheless, through all these vicissitudes, the Hindu world as a whole has retained its loyalty to the Vedas and still recognizes them as the highest authority in religious matters.

The outer forms of the Hindu religion have certainly changed. Modern Hindus do not, like their ancestors, perform sacrifices. The worship in the temples has been influenced by the Smritis and the Purānas. Tantra has also left its impression upon the worship in many parts of the country. Yet underlying all of this there are certain fundamental truths, taught in the Upanishads, to which the Hindus have always adhered. It is this flexibility of the Hindu mind in adapting itself to the demands of changing circumstances while remaining true to the immutable ideals of religion, that accounts for the marvellous vitality and the enduring character of the spiritual culture of India. Even now the Vedic rituals are observed at the time of birth, marriage, death, and other important occasions of a man's life. Every orthodox Hindu belonging to the three upper castes recites, three times a day during his prayers, the same selections from the Vedas which his forbears repeated five thousand years ago, while his daily obligatory religious devotions are the remnants of similar obligatory sacrifices of the Vedic period.

Indian philosophy is divided into two classes: orthodox and heterodox. The orthodox philosophy is, again, subdivided into six groups. These groups are called orthodox because they rest upon the Vedas, not because they accept the idea of a Creator God. The Sāmkhya philosophy, one of the orthodox systems, does not accept God as the Creator of the universe. Jainism and Buddhism, on the other hand, are called unorthodox because they do not accept the Vedas as their authority. Yet they, too, have incorporated in their systems many of the Vedic doctrines. Thus the Vedas have influenced every vital phase of Hindu life. The Smritis and other canonical law-books, which govern the life of a Hindu, derive their validity from the Vedas. The laws that regulate the inheritance of property, adoption of children, and other social, legal, domestic, and religious customs, claim their authority from the Vedas. Hindu society has always drawn its power and vision from the spiritual experiences of its ancient seers. Under the crust of the many superstitions of present-day society, a penetrating eye can still discern the shining core of the Vedic wisdom.

Yet this wisdom, the Knowledge of Brahman, is not the monopoly of any country, sect, or race. It was developed in a special manner on the banks of the Ganges and the Indus by the Indo-Āryan seers; nevertheless, like Brahman Itself, Brahmavidyā is universal. It belongs to all peoples and all times. It is the universal truth that is the common essence of all religions and faiths.

DISCUSSION OF BRAHMAN IN THE UPANISHADS

THE INDO-ĀRYAN THINKERS, as early as the times of the Rig-Veda, recognized the eternal Unity of Existence which 'holds in Its embrace all that has come to be.' This seamless Unity, which they have described in poetic language, pervades the universe and yet remains beyond it. All objects, animate and inanimate, are included in It. Gods, men, and subhuman beings are parts of It. As the unchanging Reality behind the universe, It is called Brahman by the Hindu philosophers; and as the indestructible Spirit in man, It is called Ātman. Brahman and Ātman, identical in nature, are the First Principle.[1]

Derived from a root which means 'to expand', the word *Brahman* denotes the Entity to whose greatness, magnitude, or expansion no one can put a limit or measure. The word *Ātman* is used to denote the immutable inner Consciousness, which experiences gross objects during the waking state, subtle objects during the dream state, and during dreamless sleep, when the subject-object relationship ceases to exist, remains as a witness. This is the unchanging and transcendental Consciousness in man, present in his every act of cognition, no matter what the level or state of the experience.

Bādarāyana Vyāsa, in the *Brahma Sutras*, describes Brahman as that 'from which proceed the origin, the sustenance, and the dissolution' of the universe. He further states that the Vedas are the source of this knowledge of Brahman, and that in Brahman all Vedāntic texts find their agreement and harmony. It is Brahman alone that appears as the universe. We read in the Upanishads: 'All is, indeed, Brahman'; 'The soul is Brahman'; 'Brahman is Consciousness and Bliss'; 'There is no multiplicity whatsoever.'

THE TWO ASPECTS OF BRAHMAN

The Upanishads describe Brahman as having two aspects: the one devoid of any qualifying characteristics (nirviśesha) and the other endowed with qualities (saviśesha). The former is called also the Supreme Brahman (Parā Brahman), while the latter is called the Inferior Brahman (Aparā Brahman). When Brahman is said to be devoid of qualifying characteristics, what is meant is that the Supreme Brahman cannot be pointed out or described by any characteristic

---

[1] The Upanishads discuss Brahman from three standpoints: as a theological dogma based upon the Vedas, as a mystical experience which transcends the senses, and as a metaphysical reality established by universally accepted reasoning.

signs; It is not to be comprehended by means of any attributes or indicative marks. For this reason It is called the unqualified (Nirguna) and unconditioned (Nirvikalpa) Brahman; It is devoid of any limiting adjunct (nirupādhi). The Inferior Brahman, on the other hand, can be described by certain characteristic signs and recognized by virtue of His attributes and proper marks.

'Brahman,' states Śankarāchārya in his commentary on *Brahma Sutras* I. i. 2, 'is apprehended under two forms: in the first place, as qualified by limiting conditions owing to the multiformity of the evolutions of name and form; in the second place, as being the opposite of this, that is to say, as being free from all limiting conditions whatever.' A striking passage regarding the attributeless Brahman declares: 'It is neither gross nor minute, neither short nor long, neither redness nor moisture, neither shadow nor darkness, neither air nor ākāśa, unattached, without savour or odour, without eyes or ears, without vocal organ or mind, non-luminous, without vital force or mouth, without measure, and without interior or exterior.' The Inferior Brahman, Brahman with positive attributes, on the other hand, has been described as He 'whose body is spirit, whose form is light, whose thoughts are true, whose nature is like ākāśa, from whom all works, all desires, all odours, and all tastes proceed.' The Inferior Brahman is often called Saguna Brahman. The Upanishads tend to designate Brahman with attributes by the masculine 'He', and the attributeless Brahman by the neuter 'It'.

But what is the final conclusion of the Upanishads concerning the ultimate nature of Brahman? Is the ultimate Brahman devoid of attributes or is It endowed with them? Śankarāchārya affirms that the purpose of Vedānta is to establish the attributeless Brahman as Ultimate Reality.

Rāmānuja, the chief exponent of the Qualified Non-dualistic School of Vedānta, declares, on the other hand, that the goal of the scriptures is to demonstrate the ultimate reality of Brahman as endowed with benign qualities only and free from all blemish. Śankarāchārya, therefore, stands as the upholder of an unconditioned and attributeless Brahman, while Rāmānuja represents the belief in a Brahman abounding in blessed attributes.[2]

Which is the true purport of Vedānta? We shall attempt to show, in the following pages, that Brahman is one and without a second and that the same Brahman has been described in two ways from two points of view. The one may be called the empirical or ordinary (vyāvahārika) point of view, and the other, the real or transcendental (pāramārthika).

[2] There are other schools of Vedānta. One, for example, propounded by Nimbārka, says that there are in Brahman both non-duality and duality (dvaitādvaita), and that the two aspects are equally real.

The first is upheld by those who regard the world as real and therefore describe Brahman as its omnipotent and omnipresent Creator, Sustainer, and Destroyer; such a Brahman is, to be sure, Saguna, endowed with attributes. But according to the opposite opinion, the world of names and forms is finally unreal and only Brahman exists. All that is perceived anywhere is Brahman alone, and this Brahman is unconditioned, free from all qualities or attributes. Thus the same indefinable Reality is described in two different ways according to the point of view of the perceiver.

What we shall see is that Brahman, in association with māyā, which is Its own inscrutable power, becomes the Creator of the universe and is then called Saguna Brahman. It is then also known as the Great Lord (Maheśvara) and Bhagavān.

NIRGUNA BRAHMAN

Nirguna Brahman, as has already been stated, cannot be characterized by any indicative marks, qualities, or attributes. Therefore It is not describable by words. 'From whence all speech, with the mind, turns away, unable to reach It.' That is why the attributeless Brahman is explained sometimes by silence. Śankara declares, in his commentary on *Brahma Sutras* III. ii. 17, that Bāhva, being questioned about Brahman by Bāshkalin, explained It to him by silence. 'He said to Bāshkalin: "Learn Brahman, O friend," and became silent. Then, on a second and third questioning, Bādhva replied: "I am teaching you indeed, but you do not understand. Silence is that Self." '

The impossibility of knowing Brahman by any human means has been most emphatically expressed in the famous formula employed by Yājnavalkya: *Neti, neti*—'Not this, not this.' 'He, this Self, is that which has been described as "Not this, not this".'

In describing the attributeless Brahman, the Upanishads usually employ the technique of negation: 'Turiya (the attributeless Brahman) is not that which is conscious of the internal (subjective) world, nor that which is conscious of the external (objective) world, nor that which is conscious of both, nor that which is a mass of sentiency, nor that which is simple consciousness, nor that which is insentient. It is unperceived [by any sense-organ], not related [to anything], incomprehensible [to the mind], uninferable, unthinkable, indescribable.' The Upanishads abound in passages like this.

Though unknown and unknowable, Brahman is yet the eternal 'Knower of knowing' and also the goal of all knowledge. It is the Consciousness that functions through the senses but cannot be known by them. 'How can you know the eternal Knower?' 'It is different from the known; It is above the unknown.' Brahman is neither the subject nor the object; It is neither the knower nor knowledge nor what is known. Nothing whatsoever can be predicated of It. Yet the search for Brahman is not futile. The Upanishads reiterate that Its realization is the supreme purpose of life: 'Having realized Ātman . . . one is freed from the jaws of death.' It is the Supreme Unity of all contradictions: in It alone all differences are harmonized.

Sometimes the Upanishads ascribe to Brahman irreconcilable attributes in order to deny in It all empirical predicates and to show that It is totally other than anything we know. 'That non-dual Ātman, though never stirring, is swifter than the mind. The devas cannot reach It, for It moves ever in front. Though standing still, It overtakes others who are running.' Brahman is often described as 'subtler than an atom and greater than the great'. The two attributes, though opposed to each other, are valid from the relative standpoint: Brahman is the essence of a subtle as well as of a gross substance. But these attributes do not apply to the Absolute Brahman. Pure Consciousness in association with material upādhis appears to possess empirical qualities such as nearness and distance, or rest and movement, like a transparent crystal that assumes different colours in the presence of flowers of differing hue.

The entire phenomenal universe is subject to the categories of space, time, and causation; but Brahman, the Supreme Reality, is beyond. 'That which is not destroyed when the upādhis of time, space, and causation are destroyed, is Brahman, the immortal Reality.' In describing Brahman as omnipresent, all-pervading, unlimited, infinitely great, and infinitely small, the Upanishads only point out that It is absolutely spaceless. 'That, O Gārgi, which is above heaven and below the earth, which is this heaven and earth as well as what is between them, and which they say was, is, and will be, is pervaded by the unmanifested ākāśa (Brahman).' 'In the beginning Brahman was all this. He was one and infinite: infinite in the east, infinite in the south, infinite in the west, infinite in the north, above and below and everywhere infinite. East and the other regions do not exist for Him—no athwart, no beneath, no above. The Supreme Self is not to be fixed; He is unlimited, unborn, not to be reasoned about, not to be conceived.' Brahman, which is spaceless and immeasurable, is also indivisible. For the same reason Brahman is incorporeal and partless. 'Who is without parts, without actions, tranquil, faultless, taintless, the highest bridge to Immortality—like a fire that has consumed its fuel.' 'What is here, the same is there; and what is there, the same is here. He goes from death to death who sees any difference here.'

The timelessness of Brahman is indicated by the statement that It is free from the limitations of past, present, and future. Sometimes It is described as eternal, without beginning or end; sometimes as momentary, involving no time at all. 'Other than what has been and what is to be.' 'At whose feet, rolling on, the year with its days passes by—upon that immortal Light of all lights, the gods meditate as longevity.' Brahman is described as instantaneous duration, through the illustration of lightning: 'It is like a flash of lightning; It is like a wink of the eye.'

Brahman is independent of causation. Causality is operative only in the realm of becoming and cannot affect Pure Being. Brahman is not the Creator of the universe in the sense that a potter is the creator of a pot, nor the cause of the universe in the sense that milk is the cause of curds. No change is possible in Brahman; It is Itself—causeless. Therefore It is called the Imperishable (Aksharam). 'The Self is not born; It does not die. It has not sprung from anything; nothing has sprung from It. Birthless, eternal, everlasting, and ancient, It is not killed when the body is killed.'

Brahman is declared to be indescribable in words and unknowable to the mind. To be known, a thing must be made an object. Brahman, as Pure Consciousness, is the eternal Subject; It cannot be made an object. One must presuppose Brahman in order to know objects; therefore one cannot know It as an object. Brahman, the substratum of all experience, cannot Itself be an object of experience. But, more properly, one cannot even say that Brahman is a subject; for a subject must have an object that it perceives. Nothing is real, however, except Brahman. All that can be said, then, of Brahman is that *It is*. 'He by whom Brahman is not known, knows It; he by whom It is known, knows It not. It is not known by those who know It; It is known by those who do not know It.' Since Brahman, as the 'Knower of knowing', can never become an object, It is called unknowable. 'You cannot see That which is the Witness of vision; you cannot hear That which is the Hearer of hearing; you cannot think of That which is the Thinker of thought; you cannot know That which is the Knower of knowledge.' 'He is never seen, but is the Witness; He is never heard, but is the Hearer; He is never thought of, but is the Thinker; He is never known, but is the Knower. There is no other witness but Him, no other hearer but Him, no other thinker but Him, no other knower but Him.'

Brahman is unknowable for still another reason: It is bhumā, infinite. What is the Infinite? This is how It is described in the Upanishads: 'Where one sees nothing else, hears nothing else, understands nothing else—that is the Infinite. Where one sees something else, hears something else, understands something else—that is the finite. The Infinite is immortal; the finite, mortal.'

Brahman is 'one and without a second'—*ekamevādvitiyam*. The second part of this phrase ('and without a second'), qualifying the first ('one'), is important; for what it means is that Brahman is not one in the sense that the sun or the moon is one, or in the sense that the God of the monotheist is one. In such a case there is a perceiver of the oneness—which implies duality. When the non-duality of Brahman is completely realized, there is absolutely no consciousness of subject and object; the distinction between perceiver and perceived is annihilated and they become one.

SACHCHIDĀNANDA (EXISTENCE–KNOWLEDGE–BLISS ABSOLUTE)

The Vedānta philosophy often describes Brahman by the term Sachchidānanda, a compound consisting of three words: Sat (Existence, Reality, or Being), Chit (Consciousness, or Knowledge), and Ānandam (Bliss). This term, however, does not appear in any of the principal Upanishads, though Brahman is often described in them by such separate terms as Reality, Consciousness, and Bliss. According to some, the words Sat, Chit, and Ānandam refer to Saguna Brahman; according to others, to Nirguna Brahman. The former group contends that the words are positive characterizing terms, and therefore cannot be employed in connexion with the Supreme Brahman, which is to be described, as we have already seen, only by negation. But according to the other view, Sat, Chit, and Ānandam can very well refer to the attributeless Brahman; for these words are used, it is declared, in a negative sense. Sat indicates that Brahman is not non-being; Chit, that Brahman is not nescient; and Ānandam, that Brahman is not a mere absence of pain. By such denial the positive nature of Brahman as the Absolute is affirmed.

Brahman does not exist as an empirical object—for instance, like a pot or a tree—but as Absolute Existence, without which material objects would not be perceived to exist. Just as a mirage cannot be seen without the desert, which is its unrelated substratum, so also the universe cannot exist without Brahman. Further, when the Vedāntic process of negation is followed, step by step, to its conclusion, there remains a residuum of existence, or being. No object, illusory or otherwise, could exist without the foundation of an immutable Existence; and that is Brahman. Therefore the term Sat, or Existence, as applied to Brahman, is to be understood as the negation of both empirical reality and its correlative unreality.

There are, to be sure, passages in the Upanishads which state that *non*-being was in the beginning: 'In the beginning all this was non-existent. It became existent; it grew. It turned into an egg.' As early as the Rig-Veda, it is said of the primeval condition of things that at that time there was *na asat, na u sat*, neither non-being nor being. But in these texts 'non-being' is used in the sense of 'non-manifestation'. That is to say, before the creation of names and forms, these things existed only in an unmanifested state. The word *sat* (being) in the Rig-Veda signifies *empirical* being.

The word *beginning* (*agrē*) in the text quoted above does not denote time. It indicates Brahman in Its purest essence, unassociated with the upādhis of creation, preservation, and destruction. Brahman is beyond time. Time, space, and causality belong to māyā. Not only before creation, but always, Brahman is Pure Consciousness, one and without a second.

The universe is not, in reality, other than Brahman. In the *Chhāndogya Upanishad* there is a celebrated scene in which the sage Āruni gives instruction to his son. 'Śvetaketu,' says the father, 'since you are so conceited, considering yourself so well read, and so stern, my dear, have you ever asked for that instruction by which we hear what cannot be heard, by which we perceive what cannot be perceived, by which we know what cannot be known?' 'What is that instruction, sir?' asks the son. Āruni replies: 'My dear, just as by one clod of clay all that is made of clay may be known, the difference (vikāra) being only a name, arising from speech, but the truth being that all is clay; and just as, my dear, by one nugget of gold all that is made of gold may be known, the difference being only a name arising from speech, but the truth being that all is gold . . . even so, my dear, is that instruction.'

The effect, apart from the cause, is nothing but a name, a mere matter of words; it is, in essence, the same as the cause. We distinguish the effect from the cause by superimposing upon the latter a name and a form to serve a practical purpose of life in the empirical world. This name and form, apart from the substratum, is māyā. Practically, one may see a gold bracelet or a gold earring and the difference between them, but in truth they are only gold. It is the same with the ocean and its waves, which are identical in essence. Likewise, the non-dual Brahman alone appears as the universe and its objects. Just as, from the standpoint of name and form, one distinguishes between a bracelet and an earring, so also, from the standpoint of name and form, one makes distinctions between the various objects of the world; yet all are, in reality, Brahman. For nothing whatsoever exists but Brahman. If a man believes that he sees something other than Brahman, he is being deceived by an illusion. What an ignorant person, a victim of māyā, regards as the universe, endowed with names and forms and characterized by the interplay of the pairs of opposites, is realized by the illumined soul to be the non-dual Brahman, just as the water of a mirage, which is seen by a deluded man, is realized by a knowing person to be dry sand. But samsāra, or the relative world, as such, the Upanishad warns, is not Brahman, or Ultimate Reality.

Brahman is Chit, or Consciousness. Many philosophers in the East and the West have come to the conclusion that the soul is to be conceived of as something similar to reason, spirit, thought, or intelligence. The very conception of Ātman in the Upanishads implies that the First Principle of things must above all be sought in man's inmost self. The core of Yājnavalkya's teachings in the *Brihadāranyaka Upanishad* is that Brahman, or Ātman, is the knowing subject within us. 'You cannot see That which is the Seer of seeing; you cannot hear That which is the Hearer of hearing; you cannot think of That which is the Thinker of thought; you cannot know That which is the Knower of knowledge. This is your Self, that is within all; everything else but This is perishable.' It is the inner Consciousness, the Self, that is the real agent of perception; the senses are mere instruments. 'He who knows: "Let me smell this"—he is Ātman; the nose is the instrument of smelling. He who knows: "Let me say this"—he is Ātman; the tongue is the instrument of saying. He who knows: "Let me hear this"—he is Ātman; the ear is the instrument of hearing. He who knows: "Let me think this"—he is Ātman; the mind is his divine eye.' As Brahman is the essence of Being, so It is the essence of Consciousness or Light. Brahman needs no other light to illumine Itself. It is self-luminous. 'It is pure; It is the Light of lights; It is That which they know who know the Self.' All material objects, such as trees, rivers, houses, forests, are illumined by the sun; but the light that illumines the sun is the light of Brahman. 'The sun does not shine there, nor the moon and the stars, nor these lightnings, not to speak of this fire. When He shines, everything shines after Him; by His light everything is lighted.'

Brahman is Bliss, or Ānandam. Brahman as Bliss means that Bliss is Its very being, as is Consciousness. Brahman is the immeasurable ocean of Bliss—the Bliss that knows no change. It is important to remember that no real Bliss is possible without Knowledge or Consciousness—*natu jnānād bhinnam sukhamasti.*

Needless to say, the Bliss that is the very substance of Brahman is not to be confused with the happiness that a man experiences when in contact with an agreeable sense-object. Worldly bliss is but an infinitesimal part of the Bliss of Brahman, the Bliss of Brahman coming through an earthly medium. The Bliss of Brahman pervades all objects. Without it a man could not live. 'He who is self-created is Bliss. A man experiences happiness by tasting that Bliss. Who could breathe, who could live, if that Bliss did not exist in his heart?' For a more vivid description: 'It is not for the sake of the husband, my dear, that the husband is loved, but for the sake of the Self that he is loved. It is not for the sake of the wife, my dear, that the wife is loved, but for the sake of the Self that she is loved. It is not for the sake of the sons, my dear, that the sons are loved, but for the sake of the Self that they are loved. It is not for the sake of wealth, my dear, that wealth is loved, but for the sake of the Self that it is loved.' The same formula is repeated in reference to the brāhmin and kshatriya castes, the worlds, the gods, created beings, and all things. Then the magnificent passage concludes with the following exhortation: 'The Self, my dear Maitreyi, should be realized—should be heard about, reflected on, and meditated upon. By the realization of the Self, my dear, through hearing, reflection, and meditation, all this [world] is known.'

To summarize the description of Nirguna Brahman: Nirguna Brahman is the negation of all attributes and relations. It is beyond time, space, and causality. Though It is spaceless, yet without It space could not exist; though It is timeless, yet without It time could not exist; though It is causelsss, yet without It the universe, bound by the law of cause and effect, could not exist. Only if one admits the existence of Nirguna Brahman as an unchanging substratum can one understand proximity in space, succession in time, and interdependence in the chain of causality. Without the unchanging white screen, one cannot relate in time or space the disjoined pictures in 'a cinema film. No description of It is possible except by the denial of all empirical attributes, definitions, and relations: *Neti, neti*—'Not this, not this.'

Obviously Nirguna Brahman cannot be worshipped, prayed to, or meditated upon. No relationship whatsoever can be established with It. Yet It is not altogether detached; for It is the very foundation of relative existence. It is 'the setu (dike) that keeps asunder these worlds to prevent their clashing together.' It is the intangible Unity that pervades all relative existence and gives a strong metaphysical foundation to fellowship, love, unselfishness, and other ethical disciplines. Being the immortal Essence of every man, It compels us to show respect to all, in spite of their illusory masks. Though It cannot be an object of formal devotion, yet It gives reality to the gods, being their inner substance, and thus binds together all worshippers in the common quest of Truth.

SAGUNA BRAHMAN

When Brahman becomes conditioned by the upādhi of māyā and shrinks, as it were, because of that māyā, It is called Saguna Brahman, the conditioned Brahman. Saguna Brahman is the Personal God. Without compulsion from outside, Brahman imposes upon Itself, as it were, a limit and thus becomes manifest as God, soul, and world. Creation, preservation, and destruction are the activities of Saguna Brahman. But Nirguna Brahman and Saguna Brahman are not two realities. The sea is the same, whether it is peaceful or agitated. Māyā, as we shall presently see, has no independent reality. It inheres in Brahman, as the power of Brahman. Fire's power of burning cannot be conceived of as in essence different from fire.

MĀYĀ

The Upanishads reveal a systematic search, on the part of the seers, to discover the essential nature, or First Principle, of the universe. They came to the decision that the essence of things is not given in the objects as they present themselves to our senses in space and time. The entire aggregate of experience, external and internal, shows us merely how things appear to us, not how they are in themselves. Like the Greek philosophers Parmenides and Plato, who asserted the empirical object to be a mere show, or shadow of reality, the Upanishads declared that the world is only māyā and that empirical knowledge does not give true Knowledge, or Vidyā, but belongs to the realm of ignorance, or avidyā. The Upanishadic philosophers, through a process of rigorous discrimination, analysed both the individual and the universe. All that does not belong to the inalienable substance of things they considered as non-Self and stripped away. The conclusion arrived at was that the 'great, omnipresent Ātman', which is 'greater than heaven, space, and earth', is, at the same time, present—whole and undivided—in man's own self. The Universal Self is identical with the individual self.

The crux of the philosophy of Yājnavalkya, as presented in the *Brihadāranyaka Upanishad*, is the sole reality of Ātman and the unreality of the universe independent of Ātman.

All objects and relationships in the universe exist for us, and are known and loved by us, only in so far as they enter into our consciousness, which comprehends in itself all the objects and relationships, knowing nothing that is absolutely alien to itself. 'Just as all the spokes are fixed in the nave and the felloe of a chariot wheel, so are all beings, all gods, all worlds, all organs, and all these [individual selves] fixed in this Self.' If Ātman, the knowing subject in us, is the only reality, there can be no universe outside consciousness. Therefore the duality perceived in the universe, independent of Ātman, is māyā. This idea is reiterated in the Upanishads again and again.

A well-known prayer in the *Brihadāranyaka Upanishad* begs the Lord to lead the devotee from the unreal to the Real, from darkness to Light, from death to Immortality. What is referred to here as unreality, darkness, and death is duality, which is māyā. Non-duality, Ātman, alone is Reality, Light, and Immortality.

The *Iśa Upanishad* states that the 'door of the Truth' is veiled with a 'golden disc'. This veil must be removed that the seeker may behold the Truth. The figure of a veil or curtain has often been used by Vedāntic philosophers to describe māyā. But it must be understood that Brahman, or Ātman, is not to be sought *on the other side* of māyā; for there is no such thing as space beyond the sphere of māyā. Nor is It to be realized *after* the veil is removed; for beyond māyā there is no time. Nor, finally, is It to be known as the *cause* of the universe; for Brahman is beyond the causal law. Rather, Brahman becomes real to us to the extent that the universe, with its time, space, and causal principle, is realized as unreal. That is to say, Brahman becomes real to the extent that we can shake off from our minds the world of appearance.

The doctrine of māyā was developed in the Vedānta philosophy, in a systematic form, by later thinkers. The implications of the doctrine have been distorted and misunderstood by its critics, Indian as well as Western. They tell us that if one accepts the concept of māyā one must believe that life on earth is meaningless, and that Liberation consists in turning away from it; that human values are totally worthless, and that to seek happiness on earth is to pursue a will-o'-the-wisp.

Proper understanding of the philosophy of Non-dualistic Vedānta depends upon the recognition of the two standpoints from which Truth can be observed. The one is the standpoint of the Relative; the other, the standpoint of the Absolute.

From the standpoint of the Relative the field of multiplicity is real. Good and evil exist, and so also pleasure and pain; the gods, heaven, and the after-life all are real. The Indo-Āryans sought celestial happiness by propitiating the deities through sacrifice, according to the directions of the Vedas. Admitting the empirical reality of the individual ego and the manifold universe, the Vedic seers developed an elaborate system of theology, cosmology, ethics, spiritual disciplines, and methods of worship. Their division of Hindu society into four castes, and of the individual life into four stages, shows that they did not explain away the relative world. Their acknowledgement of the ideals of righteousness (dharma), wealth (artha), sense pleasure (kāma), and final Liberation (moksha) as worthy human pursuits (purushārtha) shows that they appreciated human values and were solicitous for human happiness. Had they considered the world to be non-existent or unreal, like a 'barren woman's son', such injunctions as they laid down for these four ends of life would have been meaningless.

Nevertheless, from the standpoint of the Absolute, or Brahman, this world is not real; for duality disappears when the absolute Truth is known, and all the activities and thoughts associated with duality drop away.

Non-dualists describe the creation as the illusory superimposition (adhyāropa or vivarta), through māyā, of names and forms upon Brahman. They explain this subtle concept by means of various illustrations. One may be cited here.

A lion cub was born as its mother was attacking a flock of sheep. In giving birth to the cub, the mother died and so the cub grew up with the sheep. It bleated, ate grass, and regarded itself in all respects as a sheep. One day it was pounced upon by a lion from the forest and dragged to the water. There it was shown its reflection and a piece of meat was pressed into its mouth. Then suddenly the veil dropped off and the sheep-lion discovered itself to be a real lion.

Through the power of māyā, or ignorance, names and forms are attributed to Brahman and the relative universe comes into existence. Through the negation (apavāda) of the illusory manifold, Brahman, or Pure Consciousness, is revealed again. The true nature of Brahman is not in the least affected by the superimposition of illusory notions.

Relativity is māyā. The fact that the One appears as the many, the Absolute as the relative, the Infinite as the finite, is māyā. The doctrine of māyā recognizes the reality of multiplicity from the relative standpoint—and simply states that the relationship of this relative reality with the Absolute cannot be described or known. The very limitations of the mind preclude such knowledge. In fact, there is no relationship between the One and the many, since there can be a relationship only between two existing entities. The One and the many do not exist in the same sense. When a man sees the One, he does not see the many; when he sees the non-dual Brahman, he does not see the universe. When anyone, seeing the manifold universe, establishes a relationship of any kind between it and the non-dual Brahman, the Non-dualists call that notion of relationship māyā.

Śankara described māyā as the 'power of the Lord'—parameśa śakti. It is the inscrutable power of Brahman, resting in Brahman and having no existence independent of Brahman. Māyā makes possible the appearance of the manifold universe, and it endows names and forms with apparent reality. Non-dualists ascribe creation, preservation, and destruction to Saguna Brahman, or Brahman associated with māyā. Māyā and also its effect, the universe, have a positive existence and cannot be called absolutely unreal, like the 'horns of a hare'. They are seen to exist from the relative standpoint but are non-existent from the standpoint of Brahman. Māyā and its manifestations disappear with the dawn of the Knowledge of Brahman.

Māyā has three components, namely, sattva, rajas, and tamas. They are called gunas. The word *guna* is generally translated—though incorrectly—as 'quality'. Essentially the gunas are the very substance of māyā. Everything in nature consists of these three gunas, which are combined in varying proportions. Rajas and tamas have opposing characteristics, while sattva strikes the balance between the two. The principal trait of rajas is energy, which is responsible for the 'primal flow of activity'; the power of rajas moves the universe. Tamas is lassitude, dullness, inertia, and stupidity; while sattva, which is characterized by harmony, is manifest, on the human level, in such spiritual virtues as tranquillity, self-control, and contentment.

Māyā functions in the world through its two powers: the power of concealment and the power of projection. The former, as in the case of a sleeping person, obscures the knowledge of the observer; it conceals, as it were, the true nature of Brahman. Next the projecting power of māyā creates the universe and all the objects seen in it, just as, after a man's consciousness is obscured by sleep, he begins to dream. In actuality, however, the two powers of māyā function practically simultaneously. Māyā, ajnāna (ignorance), avidyā (nescience), and prakriti (nature) are practically synonymous. Māyā generally signifies the cosmic illusion on account of which Brahman, or Pure Consciousness, appears as the Creator, Preserver, and Destroyer of the universe. It is under the influence of avidyā that Ātman, or Pure Consciousness, appears as the jiva, or individual self. Prakriti is the stuff out of which the universe is evolved. But Vedāntic writers do not always strictly maintain these distinctions.

Māyā is used by Brahman as the material of creation; that is to say, Brahman creates the universe and its various objects out of māyā. Māyā has no existence independent of the Lord; therefore, from the standpoint of māyā, Brahman is the material cause of the universe. But, as Pure Consciousness, It is the efficient cause. This causal relation is often explained by the illustration of the spider and its web. When the spider wants to weave a web, it uses the silk which belongs to it and without which it cannot weave. Therefore the spider, as a conscious creature, is the efficient cause of the web, while from the standpoint of the silk it is the material cause.

The first element to evolve from Saguna Brahman is ākāśa, which is usually translated as 'space' or 'sky', and sometimes as 'ether'. The creation, or evolution, of ākāśa really means that Brahman, in association with māyā, appears as ākāśa. From ākāśa evolves air (vāyu); that is to say, Brahman, in association with māyā, appearing as ākāśa, further appears as air. From air evolves fire (agni); from fire, water (ap); from water, earth (prithivi). The five elements thus evolved are not the gross elements that we see, but they are subtle, rudimentary, and unmixed. Out of these subtle elements are produced the subtle bodies of all created beings and also the gross elements. From the gross elements is produced the gross universe, with all the various physical objects contained therein. Both the totality of the subtle bodies and the gross universe are upādhis of Brahman and appear to limit It. In association with them, Pure Consciousness descends, as it were, into the realm of relativity and is known by such epithets as Hiranyagarbha and Virāt.

Māyā exercises its bewitching power upon the unillumined; but sages, whose minds are enlightened by the Knowledge of Brahman, see in the relative universe, created of māyā, the manifestation of Brahman. To them everything—even māyā—is Brahman. They do not deny the forms of God and the creation. Whether contemplating the Absolute or participating in the Relative, they see Brahman alone everywhere—in the undifferentiated Absolute and in names and forms as well. Māyā cannot delude them. Śri Ramakrishna used to say that to accept names and forms divorced from the reality of Brahman is ajnāna, ignorance; to see Brahman alone, and deny the world, is philosphical knowledge, jnāna; but to see Brahman everywhere—in names and forms, in good and evil, pain and pleasure, life and death, as well as in the depths of meditation—is vijnāna, a supremely rich knowledge. Endowed with vijnāna, blessed souls commune with Brahman in meditation and devote themselves, when not meditating, to the service of the world.

ASPECTS OF SAGUNA BRAHMAN

With reference to the three activities of creation, preservation, and destruction, Saguna Brahman is known, respectively, as Brahmā, Vishnu, and Rudra, or Śiva. These form the Trimurti, the Trinity of Hinduism, any one being incomplete without the other two. The influence of rajas is seen in creation, of sattva in preservation, and of tamas in destruction.

Nirguna Brahman, as already remarked, cannot be the object of prayer or meditation, but Saguna Brahman can. 'By the yogins He is realized through worship.' Many sublime passages are found in the Upanishads and other writings of the Hindu seers, describing the glories of Saguna Brahman. 'He is the Lord of all; He is the knower of all; He is the controller within; He is the source of all; and He is that from which all things originate and in which they finally disappear.' 'He is the fountain of all blessed qualities and the consummation of such divine attributes as power, strength, glory, knowledge, and virility. By a fraction of His power He upholds all beings. He is the Supreme Lord, greater than the Great, and free from the least trace of suffering.' 'Everywhere are His eyes, everywhere is His mouth, everywhere are His arms, everywhere His feet. He has endowed men with arms, and birds with wings. He is the Creator of earth and heaven. He is one and without a second.' 'He who is the supreme Lord of lords, the supreme Deity of deities, the supreme Ruler of rulers—Him let us know as God, adorable and paramount, the Lord of the world.' Saguna Brahman was later worshipped under various personifications—as Śiva, Vishnu, Rāma, and so on, the ideal deities (ishta devatās) of various Hindu sects. In the Upanishads He is described as Maheśvara, the Great Lord, and also as Iśa, Iśāna, and Iśvara—all meaning the Lord.

Saguna Brahman is called Iśvara because He is all-powerful, the Lord of all, the Ruler of the entire universe. 'He rules over all two-footed and four-footed beings.' 'He does not increase by a good action nor does He decrease by a bad action.' He is the source of all powers. All created objects, and the all-powerful māyā as well, are under His control. 'The non-dual Lord of māyā rules alone by His powers . . . There is one Rudra only—they do not allow a second—who rules all the worlds by His powers.' He is the Supreme Ruler of the universe. Under His control the sun, the moon, and the planets perform their allotted functions. Because of His power a moral order controls the universe as well as man's life.

This Brahman can inspire great terror, 'like a thunderbolt ready to be hurled.' 'From terror of Him the wind blows; from terror of Him the sun rises; from terror of Him fire, Indra, and death perform their respective duties.' The different gods, the powerful cosmic forces, are His manifestations through māyā. They are entirely dependent upon Him.

Brahman as Antaryāmin, the Inner Ruler, has been elaborately described in the seventh section of the third chapter of the *Brihadāranyaka Upanishad*. 'He who inhabits the earth, but is within it, whom the earth does not know, whose body is the earth, and who controls the earth from within, is the Internal Ruler, your own immortal Self.' What is true of the earth is also true, as one learns from the continued repetition of the same formula, of water, fire, the atmosphere, the wind, the sky, the sun, and other objects. All these are bodies of Brahman, who dwells within them but is distinct from them, whom they do not know, and yet who rules them all from within.

The seers of the Upanishads felt that the Personal God was an important factor in man's spiritual development. A man attached to the body, and influenced by love and hate, cannot meditate on the Impersonal Absolute. For his benefit, therefore, the Upanishads describe Saguna Brahman as the Providence who determines the course of the universe.

The *Śvetāśvatara Upanishad*, with its theistic inclination, contains many passages depicting this aspect of Brahman: 'The source of all, who determines the gunas, who brings to maturity whatever can be ripened, and who engages the gunas in their respective functions—over the whole world rules the One.' 'The one who, Himself without colour (differentiation), by the manifold application of His power produces [at the time of creation] many colours according to His hidden purpose, and in whom the whole universe, during its continuance, subsists, and in the end dissolves—He is the Lord. May He endow us with right intellect.'

The *Kaushitaki Upanishad* says that if the Lord wishes to lead a man up from these worlds, He makes him do a good deed, and that if the Lord wishes to lead him down from these worlds, He makes him do a bad deed. This is not to be confused with the doctrine of predestination. The text only means that no action, good or bad, is possible without the power of the Lord. Brahman is like a light: with its help a good man performs righteous action, an evil man the reverse, but the light is impartial, though without it no action can be performed. Man reaps the result of his own action. He chooses a good or an evil action according to his inner tendencies created by his past works.

It has already been stated that Brahman, without any external compulsion, assumes the upādhi of māyā and appears as the universe and its Creator. Thus He becomes immanent in the universe, from the relative standpoint.

The Upanishads contain descriptions of both the transcendent and the immanent aspect of Brahman. The Immanent Brahman dwells in the universe and is to be sought therein. 'Having created the universe, He entered into it.' He is lost, as it were, in the universe, as when 'a lump of salt, dropped into water, dissolves in the water, so that no one is able to grasp it.' But just as wheresoever one tastes the water, it tastes salt, so also Brahman is to be felt everywhere in the universe as life and consciousness.

The Upanishadic passages describing the Immanent Brahman show a pantheistic trend of thought. Brahman has become the universe, like milk transformed into curds, or clouds into rainwater. But does Brahman exhaust Himself in the universe? The texts contain passages supporting realism, theism, and pantheism, according to the different stages of an aspirant's understanding; but the fundamental thought that runs through the whole body of the Upanishads is the *sole reality* of Brahman, or Ātman. Even when the reality of the universe is conceded, the purpose is to maintain that the manifold world is not different from Brahman. But the reality of the universe is denied when it is reiterated that with the Knowledge of Brahman everything is known. Therefore, though perceived to be immanent, Brahman remains transcendent. 'It is inside all this and It is outside all this.' The Rig-Veda states that Brahman covers the whole universe and yet transcends it by the measure of 'ten fingers'.

The *Katha Upanishad* very clearly describes both the immanent and the transcendent aspect of Brahman: 'As the same non-dual fire, after it has entered the world, becomes different according to whatever it burns, so also the same non-dual Ātman, dwelling in all beings, becomes different according to whatever It enters. And It exists also without . . . As the sun, which helps all eyes to see, is not affected by the blemishes of the eyes or of the external things revealed by it, so also the one Ātman, dwelling in all beings, is never contaminated by the misery of the world, being outside it.'

The very definition of Brahman (Saguna Brahman is understood) in the *Vedānta Sutras* is, as we have stated: 'Whence is the origin, continuance, and dissolution of the universe.' The *Taittiriya Upanishad* puts it this way: 'That whence these beings are born, That by which, when born, they live, That into which at death they enter—try to know That. That is Brahman.' The *Chhāndogya Upanishad* reveals 'Tajjalān' as a secret name of Brahman by which He should be worshipped. The meaning of the formula is this: From this (*tad*) Brahman the universe has arisen (*ja*). So, on the reverse path to that by which it has arisen, it disappears (*li*) into this identical Brahman. And in the same way, finally, it is Brahman in whom the universe, after it is created, breathes (*an*), lives, and moves. Therefore in the three periods (past, present, and future) the universe is not distinct from Brahman.

Brahman alone, as the inmost essence of things, preserves them all. 'He is the sun dwelling in the bright heavens. He is the air dwelling in the mid-region. He is the fire dwelling on earth. He is the guest dwelling in the house. He dwells in men, in the gods, in truth, in the sky. He is born in the water, on earth, in the sacrifice, on the mountains. He is the True and the Great.'

Brahman is the womb into which the universe again returns. Hence He is called the Destroyer. The Vedāntists have formulated a doctrine of cycles, by which is described the unceasing process of creation and destruction, or, more precisely, manifestation and non-manifestation. The actions of one's present life find their recompense in the next life. Again, the present life is the result of the preceding one. Therefore each existence presupposes an earlier one and consequently no existence can be the first. The rebirth of the soul (jiva) has been going on from all eternity; and so samsāra, or the relative universe, is without beginning. Indeed, it is absurd to speak of the beginning of a causal chain. When the Upanishads speak of a beginning or creation, they mean, really, the beginning of the present cycle. At the conclusion of each cycle the universe and all those living beings that have not been liberated from māyā return to Brahman, that is to say, to His prakriti, or primordial nature. The Rig-Veda says: 'The Lord creates in this cycle the sun and moon as they existed in the previous cycle.' So creation is a never-ending process, following an invariable, monotonous pattern.

Some of the oft-repeated epithets of Saguna Brahman in the Upanishads are Brahmā, Prajāpati, Hiranyagarbha, Virāt, Prāna, Sutra, and Sutrātmā. They all in a general way denote the World Soul, the Cosmic Soul, the Cosmic Mind, or the Cosmic Person. According to Vedāntists, when Brahman becomes conditioned by the upādhi of the gross universe, It is called Virāt; when conditioned by that of the subtle universe, It is called Hiranyagarbha; and when conditioned by that of the causal universe, It is called Prāna or Sutrātmā. In the writings of Vedāntists, however, these terms are often interchanged. Hiranyagarbha, or Brahmā, is mentioned in the Rig-Veda as the first-born when Brahman becomes conditioned by māyā. He is the first entity endowed with the consciousness of individuality. He is the 'Golden Egg', containing in potential form the future manifold universe. In contrast with the jiva, the individualized consciousness, who is conscious only of his own soul, Brahmā is conscious of all souls. The totality of all beings is His individuality (sarvābhimāni).

It is implicit in the Upanishadic teachings that the entire objective universe can be known only in so far as it is sustained by a knowing subject. Though this knowing subject is manifested in all individual subjects, yet it is not, by any means, identified with them. Individual subjects come into existence and die, but the universe continues to exist. Who, then, is its perceiver or knower? It is Brahmā, or Hiranya-garbha, who is the Knowing Subject by which the universe is sustained. All living beings respond in a more or less like manner to the outside world, and experience the same sensations, because their individual minds are controlled by the cosmic mind of Brahmā, and also because they are part and parcel of Him. When, at the end of a cycle, Brahmā dies, the universe dies with Him. Though identified with all minds and the entire universe, Brahmā is also described as the presiding deity or governor of a special plane, or heaven, known as Brahmaloka, the Plane of Brahmā. This is the most exalted realm in the relative universe and may be compared, in a general way, to the heaven of the dualistic religions. Those fortunate mortals who, while living on earth, worship Saguna Brahman with whole-souled devotion, meditating on their identity with Him, proceed after death to Brahmaloka, where they dwell absorbed in contemplation of Saguna Brahman. There they experience uninterrupted peace and blessedness and take part in the cosmic life of Brahmā. They are not affected by any of the shortcomings of the other relative planes, such as disease, pain, thirst, or hunger. These inhabitants of Brahmaloka do not come back to earth, but at the end of the cycle become absorbed, together with Brahmā, in the attributeless Brahman and thus attain final Liberation. This is described as kramamukti, or Liberation attained by stages. There is another class of devotees who also attain to Brahmaloka after death but come back to earth for a new embodiment after reaping the results of their meritorious actions. They are those who have performed one hundred Horse-sacrifices and also those who have lived, according to the scriptural injunctions, the life of a brahmachāri until their death.

The path to Brahmaloka lies through what has been described in the Upanishads as the Devayāna, or Way of the Gods, which is characterized by various luminous stages, such as flame, day, the bright fortnight of the moon, the bright half of the year (when the sun travels northward), the sun, and lightning. It is also called the Northern Path. There is another path, called the Pitriyāna, the Way of the Fathers, or the Southern Path, which leads to Chandraloka, the Plane of the Moon.

To it go, after death, those householders who have performed their daily obligatory duties and worshipped the gods, following the scriptural rules, with a view to enjoying the results of their meritorious actions in this lower heaven. The path leading to Chandraloka is characterized by dark stages, such as smoke, night, the dark fortnight of the moon, and the dark half of the year, and not, as in the Devayāna, by flame, day, the bright fortnight of the moon, and the bright half of the year. After enjoying the results of their meritorious actions in this lower heaven, souls come back to earth and are born as ordinary mortals. What happens to those who have attained complete Self-Knowledge while living here on earth, and also to those who have committed extremely vile actions, will be discussed later.

Brahman's universal form, known as Virāt, has been described in sublime language in the Hindu scriptures. 'The Purusha (the Cosmic Person) has a thousand heads, a thousand eyes, and a thousand feet. He covers the universe on all sides and transcends it "by the measure of ten fingers".' 'The heavens are His head; the sun and moon, His eyes; the quarters, His ears; the revealed Vedas, His speech; the wind is His breath; the universe, His heart. From his feet is produced the earth. He is, indeed, the Inner Self of all beings.' This universal form comprises not only our earth and the galactic system to which it belongs, but all the fourteen worlds of Hindu mythology—the seven above and the seven below—and all the animate and inanimate creatures dwelling therein, including gods and angels, men and animals, birds and insects, trees, plants, shrubs, and creepers. This totality is the Lord's universal form.

There is an aspect of Saguna Brahman which is tender, gentle, and redemptive. 'He is Bliss.' The *Chhāndogya Upanishad* describes Him as the 'Refuge of love' and the 'Lord of love'. 'O Rudra, let Thy gracious face protect me for ever.' 'The Lord, the Giver of blessings, the Adorable God—by revering Him one attains eternal peace.' The seers of the Upanishads addressed Him as their Father and prayed to Him to lead them to the other side of māyā. The various forms which Saguna Brahman assumes for the welfare of the devotees have been known and worshipped all over the world—as the Father in Heaven, Āllāh, Jehovah, Vishnu, Śiva, and Brahmā—emphasizing the different aspects of the Great Lord.

MICROCOSM AND MACROCOSM

One of the most significant symbols of Brahman, both Personal and Impersonal, is Aum, often written Om (to be pronounced as in *home*). 'The goal which all the Vedas declare, which all austerities aim at, and which men desire when they lead the life of continence, I will tell you briefly: it is Om. This syllable Om is indeed Brahman. This syllable is the Highest. Whoso knows this syllable obtains whatever he desires. This is the best support; this is the highest support. Whoso knows this support is adored in the world of Brahmā.' The *Māndukya Upanishad* discusses Brahman through Om. 'Om, the syllable, is all this.'

The word as written in Sanskrit consists of three letters: *A*, *U*, and *M*. These are called the three quarters, or letters, of Om. There is a fourth quarter, denoted by the prolonged undifferentiated sound *M*, which comes at the end, as the word is pronounced. This is the symbol of Nirguna Brahman, or Pure Consciousness. 'That which is partless, incomprehensible, non-dual, all bliss, and which brings about the cessation of the phenomenal world, is Om, the Fourth, and verily the same as Ātman. He who knows this merges his self in the Self.' The first three quarters, or letters, of Om apply to the relative universe. *A* is the first quarter; it functions in the waking state. *U* is the second quarter; it functions in the dream state. And *M* is the third quarter; it functions in the state of dreamless sleep. The fourth quarter—which in reality is indescribable in terms of relations, but is called the fourth only with reference to the other three—is Turiya, or Pure Consciousness, which permeates all the states and is also transcendent.

All our relative experiences are included in the waking state, the dream state, and the state of deep sleep. In the waking state we experience, through the gross body and the sense-organs, the gross world. In dreams we experience subtle objects through mind, or the subtle body. The causal world we experience in dreamless sleep, when the mind and the sense-organs do not function. One uses the gross body to experience the gross world, the subtle body to experience the subtle world, and the causal body to experience the causal world. Corresponding to the three worlds—the gross, the subtle, and the causal—there are three states, namely, waking, dreaming, and deep sleep, and also three bodies, namely, the gross, the subtle, and the causal. But it must not be forgotten that Consciousness is Ātman, which is always present in the three states and forms their substratum. When Ātman uses the gross body for the experience of the gross world, It is given the technical name of Viśva. When It uses the subtle body for the experience of the subtle world, It is called Taijasa. And when the same Ātman uses the causal body for the experience of the causal world, It is called Prājna. Ātman is one and without a second. When associated with these three upādhis It is given three different names. Free from any upādhi, It is Brahman, the Absolute.

The above is a description of the microcosm, or individual soul. The same is true of the macrocosm, or totality of souls. As in the individual soul, so in the universe, Brahman functions in three states, in association with three upādhis, and is known by three technical names. With reference to the gross upādhi, Brahman is called Virāt; with reference to the subtle upādhi, Hiranyagarbha or Prajāpati; and with reference to the causal upādhi, Sutrātmā or Prāna. But, as has already been stated, all these terms are often interchanged in the earlier Vedānta books.

Though there is no intrinsic difference between the microcosm and the macrocosm, both possess their own distinctive individuality. The macrocosm, though an aggregate of individual units, is not a mere abstraction. This can be better explained by the illustration of bodily cells. A living body consists of innumerable cells, each of which possesses a distinctive individuality. The totality of cells, the body, has however its own independent individuality. Each cell has a distinct life and purpose of its own. It lives by extracting from its immediate environment what is necessary for its growth and nutrition. But this work has, for its end, the ultimate nutrition and building-up of the whole body, of which each individual cell forms a very small, though necessary, distinct unit. As the aggregate of its living cells constitutes the gross living body, so the aggregate of all individual gross bodies constitutes Virāt; the aggregate of all individual subtle bodies, Hiranyagarbha; and the aggregate of all individual causal bodies, Sutrātmā, or Prāna. Brahman uses the gross upādhi as Its instrument to function in the gross world, the subtle upādhi to function in the subtle world, and the causal upādhi to function in the causal world.

It has been stated before that the Lord, when associated with the upādhi of the causal bodies, is called Sutrātmā. The word means, literally, the 'Thread Soul'—that is to say, the thread-like, subtle substance that joins together all the different individuals—men, gods, animals, and inorganic beings. It is like the protoplasmic substance which, by its minute threads, passing through the cell-walls, unites the cells in a living organism. 'It is He who pervades all.'

The Upanishads often say that only when a man feels dispassion for experience through all forms of life, from the blade of grass to Brahmā, is he qualified to be a seeker of Liberation. From the standpoint of the Absolute, all manifestations are impermanent and transitory. Brahman alone is the immutable Witness of the births and deaths in the creation. And that Brahman dwells in each man's heart as his inmost Soul.

METHODS OF INSTRUCTION: SYMBOLS

The seventh chapter of the *Chhāndogya Upanishad* narrates the story of Sanatkumāra's instructing Nārada in the Knowledge of Brahman. The pupil had studied the different branches of the lower knowledge, such as the Vedic rituals, the Purānas, grammar, ethics, and the other sciences; but with all that, he knew that he could not overcome grief.

He therefore asked the teacher for that knowledge which would carry him beyond grief. Sanatkumāra told Nārada that all he had studied was only a name. He taught Nārada about Brahman through such symbols as vāk (speech), manas (mind), sankalpa (desire), chittam (mind-stuff), and dhyānam (meditation). Through these Nārada was instructed finally in Bhumā, the Infinite, beyond which there is nothing, which comprehends all, fills all space, and yet is identical with Ātman.

The Upanishads abound in symbolic representations of Brahman and Ātman. What is the meaning of a symbol? It is a visible sign of an invisible entity. The Sanskrit words generally used for symbol are pratika and pratimā. Some of the important symbols of Brahman are prāna (the vital breath), vāyu (wind), ākāśa (space), manas (mind), āditya (the sun), and Om. A pratimā, or image, as found in the popular religions, is also a symbol of the Godhead. Beginners, with their restricted understanding, need a symbol in order to contemplate the Highest. Thus a Cross, an Ark, a Crescent, a statue, a book, fire, and a temple have all been used as symbols. In the minds of the unworthy a symbol often degenerates into an idol which is worshipped. To worship a symbol as God is idolatry. But to worship God through a symbol is a legitimate means of divine communion. In the one case the Godhead is brought down to the level of a material object; in the other case, the image itself is spiritualized.

Two frequently used symbols of Brahman in the Upanishads are prāna and vāyu. The word *prāna*, often inadequately translated as 'breath', is used in a variety of ways. It denotes the vital organs, the breathing, and also the life principle which animates the vital organs. Of vāyu, the cosmic breath, the breath of the individual is a partial manifestation. As in the case of the fly-shuttle in a textile mill, when the prāna begins to work, all the organs work. The body of an organic being lives as long as the prāna inhabits it. All the organs are dependent upon the prāna. 'As bees go out when their queen goes out and return when she returns, even so did speech, mind, eye, and ear [follow the prāna].' 'As the spokes of a wheel hold to the nave, so does all this hold to the prāna.' Relinquished by the prāna, a living being is reduced to a corpse, without value or significance. The *Chhāndogya Upanishad* says that a man must not treat roughly his father or mother, or sister or brother or teacher; if he does so he is condemned by all. But after the prāna has left them, their bodies, now corpses, may be struck even with a spear, as is done to a burning body on a funeral pyre.

Prāna is not only the life principle in the individual; it is also a cosmic principle. On account of its pervasiveness it is identified with vāyu, the wind. Regarding vāyu it is declared: 'From which the sun rises and in which it sets.' Prāna, as vāyu, is identified with Hiranyagarbha, or

Sutrātmā. 'Through this Sutra, or Vāyu, this and the next life and all beings are held together.' The senses, at the time of deep sleep, enter into the prāna, and the deities, at the end of a cycle, into Sutrātmā, or the cosmic prāna.

Thus we find that in the Upanishads one of the most important symbols of Brahman is prāna, the life principle that pervades and sustains the universe and the individual body. 'Prāna is verily Brahman'— prāno vai Brahma.

The Upanishads have used the mind as a symbol of Brahman. 'Let a man meditate on the mind as Brahman.' Mano vai Brahma—'The mind is verily Brahman.' The mind is the inner organ. It is the instrument of deliberation. The mind deliberates on the sensations gathered through the outer organs and determines what is right and what is wrong. Though an untrained mind is a cause of attachment and bondage, a purified mind is the means by which one realizes Brahman. 'May He stimulate our understanding' is the most ancient prayer of the Vedas.

Ākāsa, generally translated as sky, space, ether, or heaven, has no real equivalent in English. It is an intangible substance, the finest form of matter, just as prāna is the subtlest form of energy. Ākāsa is that all-pervading and all-penetrating substance found everywhere in the universe, of which tangible objects are gross manifestations. It is the first material element to be evolved from Brahman. On account of its omnipresence and all-pervasiveness, ākāsa is often used as a symbol of Brahman. 'It is ākāsa from which all these creatures take their rise and into which they again return. Ākāsa is older than these; ākāsa is their ultimate end.' 'Brahman . . . is the same as the ākāsa which is around us; and the ākāsa which is around us is the same as the ākāsa which is within us; and the ākāsa which is within us is the same as the ākāsa which is within the heart. That ākāsa which is within the heart is omnipresent and unchanging.' The ākāsa 'within the lotus of the heart' is to be meditated upon as Brahman.

Of all phenomenal objects, the sun was regarded with the greatest wonder and admiration by the ancients everywhere. Its rays dispel darkness, and the daytime is generally filled with men's various activities. The Upanishads describe the sun as a symbol of Brahman. The Gāyatri mantra is directed to the Purusha dwelling in the sun. The natural sunlight is a symbol of spiritual light. Brahman is the real Sun of the universe; and the natural sun is the phenomenal form of Brahman. A dying man prays to the sun: 'The door of the Truth is covered by a golden disc. Open it, O Nourisher! Remove it so that I who have been worshipping the Truth may behold It. O Nourisher, lone Traveller of the sky! Controller! O Sun, Offspring of Prajāpati! Gather Your rays; withdraw Your light. I would see, through Your grace, that form of

Yours which is the fairest. I am indeed He, that Purusha, who dwells there.'

But the most important symbol of Brahman is Om. It is, as stated before, the symbol of both Nirguna Brahman and Brahman with attributes. Ordinary worshippers cannot disregard symbols. Only the highest man, in the depths of his meditation, sees Truth face to face and gives up symbols. As the times change, so do the symbols. Most of the Vedic symbols are out of date; their places have been taken by other and newer ones.

BRAHMAN AND ĀTMAN[3] (PSYCHOLOGY)

The Vedānta philosophy admits the existence of a multitude of individual souls, jivātmās, and distinguishes these from the Supreme Soul, Paramātmā. The individual soul is identified with a body, and is the victim of hunger and thirst, pain and pleasure, good and evil, and the other pairs of opposites. Limited in power and wisdom, it is entangled in the eternal round of samsāra and seeks deliverance from it. Scriptural study, instruction from a teacher, and practice of ethical and spiritual disciplines are all meant for the benefit of bound, individual souls. The Supreme Soul, or Brahman, is eternally free, illumined, and pure. When a man realizes Brahman, he transcends the scriptures, ethics, and the injunctions of religion; but until that moment the experiences of the embodied individual soul are real to him. As long as he sees good and evil he must cultivate the former and shun the latter. The individual soul takes māyā to be real. The Upanishads admit the empirical reality (vyavahārika sattvā) of the jiva and deal with its characteristics, wanderings, and final deliverance.

Ātman, through māyā, has projected material forms from Itself and then entered into them as their living self—anena jivena ātmanā anupraviśya. Thus the Upanishads speak of two souls, as it were, dwelling side by side in a man: the Real Soul and the apparent soul. The contrast between the two is made vivid in the following text: 'Two birds, inseparable friends, cling to the same tree. One of them eats the sweet

[3] The Sanskrit word ātman has been translated in this book as soul and self. Ātman has been used in the Vedānta philosophy to denote both the individual being and the Supreme Being; the individual being has been expressed by ātman, soul, and self (with small letter); the Supreme Being, by Ātman, Soul, and Self (with capital letter). The Sanskrit word purusha has been translated as person. This word, too, signifies both the individual being and the Universal Being. We have indicated the difference by the use of small and capital letters. The word means, literally, the one who dwells in the body or who pervades the body, which may be the individual physical body or the universe. According to the Non-dualists, the Purusha, the Supreme Person, is Pure Consciousness, pervading the individual body and the universe; but the Dualists describe It as a Person endowed with a form and attributes.

fruit; the other looks on without eating. On the same tree the purusha sits, immersed in grief, bewildered by his own impotence. But when he sees the other, the Lord, contented, and knows His glory, then his grief passes away.' The whole fifth chapter of the *Śvetāśvatara Upanishad* is devoted to the contrast between the Supreme Soul and the individual soul. The individual soul, endowed with desire, ego, and mind, enjoys the fruits of its actions; it is limited and insignificant. But it wins Immortality after ridding itself of its upādhis. Then it is recognized as identical with the infinitely great Supreme Soul. 'It is not woman, it is not man, nor is it neuter. Whatever body it takes, with that it is joined. By means of thoughts, touching, seeing, and passions, the jiva assumes successively, in various places, various forms in accordance with his deeds . . . The jiva assumes many shapes, coarse or refined, in accordance with his virtue, and having himself caused his union with them, is seen as different beings, through the qualities of his acts and the qualities of his body.' But even while subjected to all the limitations and sufferings of the relative world, Ātman does not in reality lose, even in the slightest degree, Its perfect nature. While the jiva, compelled by the bright and dark fruits of its actions, enters on a good or a bad birth, follows a course upwards or downwards, and roams about overcome by the pairs of opposites, 'his immortal Self remains like a drop of water on a lotus leaf. He himself is overcome by the gunas of nature. Then, because he is thus overcome, he becomes bewildered, and because he is bewildered he does not see the Creator, the holy Lord, abiding within himself. Carried along by the waves of the gunas, darkened in his imagination, unstable, fickle, crippled, full of desires, vacillating, sensual, disordered, and a prey to delusion, he fancies: "This is I", "This is mine", and fetters himself by his own action, as a bird by its nest.'

'From Ātman are born prāna, mind, and all the sense-organs.' After creating the body, Ātman enters into it as the living soul. 'Right to the tips of the fingers,' He fills the body and is hidden in it like a knife in its sheath or fire in fuel. 'When It performs the function of living, It is called the prāna; when It speaks, the organ of speech; when It sees, the eye; when It hears, the ear; and when It thinks, the mind. These are merely Its names according to Its functions.'

There are ten indriyas, sense-organs, all subordinate to the mind as the central organ: five of perception, five of action. The former comprise the ears, nose, tongue, skin, and eyes; the latter, the hands, feet, tongue, and the organs of procreation and evacuation. A sense-organ— the eye, for instance—is not the outer instrument that one sees, nor the optic nerve, but its subtle counterpart, which accompanies the subtle body after death. As the rays of the sun are gathered in the sunset, 'so also [on a man's falling asleep] is all this gathered in the manas, the supreme deity. Therefore at that time the man does not hear, see, smell, taste, or touch; he does not speak, grasp, beget, evacuate or move about. He sleeps—that is what people say.'

The mind is the inner organ, the antahkarana. 'Desire, deliberation, doubt, faith, want of faith, patience, impatience, shame, intelligence, and fear—all these are but the mind.' The mind is the central organ of the entire conscious life. The impressions carried by the sense-organs are shaped by the mind into ideas; for 'we see only with the mind, hear with the mind.' Further, the mind changes the ideas into resolutions of the will (sankalpa). 'When a man directs his manas to the study of the sacred hymns and sayings, he then *studies* them; when to the accomplishment of works, he then *accomplishes* them; when to the desire for sons and cattle, he then *desires* them; when to the desire for the present and the future worlds, he then *desires* them.'

Prāna means, primarily, that vital force in a living being which is incessantly active in waking and sleep. In sleep the organs of sense enter into the mind and 'the fires of the prāna keep watch, as it were, in the city of the body.' According to its different functions, the prāna is given five names: prāna, apāna, vyāna, udāna, and samāna. 'Now the air which rises upwards is prāna; that which moves downwards is apāna.' Vyāna 'sweeps like a flame through all the limbs'; it is what sustains life when, for instance, in drawing a stiff bow, a man neither breathes in nor breathes out. Udāna conducts the soul from the body at death. By virtue of samāna, food is assimilated.

According to later Vedāntists the five organs of action, the five organs of perception, the five prānas, the manas, and the buddhi constitute the 'subtle body', which accompanies the soul at the time of rebirth. The gross body is dissolved at death; the subtle body departs with the organs. The relation between the subtle body and the gross body is like that between seed and plant. According to some Vedāntists another entity, called the 'shelter of karma' (karma-āśraya), which determines the character of the new body and life, accompanies the subtle body. This entity is formed of impressions created by the actions performed in the course of life.

Vedāntists analyse the material body into five kośas, or sheaths, namely, the gross physical sheath (annamayakośa), the sheath of the prāna (prānamayakośa), the sheath of the mind (manomayakośa), the sheath of the buddhi or intellect (vijnānamayakośa), and the sheath of bliss (ānandamayakośa). They are called sheaths because they conceal Ātman, as a sheath conceals a sword. They are described as being one inside another—the physical sheath being the outermost and the sheath of bliss the innermost. Each succeeding sheath is finer than the preceding one. As a fine substance permeates a gross one, so the finer sheath permeates the grosser sheath. Ātman is unattached to the sheaths. Its light and consciousness permeate them all, though in varying degrees according to their density. By cultivating detachment toward these sheaths, one by one, and gradually penetrating deeper, a man realizes Ātman as Pure Consciousness.[4]

The body is often described as the 'city of Brahman'. The gates of the body are sometimes described as eleven, and sometimes as nine. The nine gates consist of the eyes, the ears, the nostrils, the mouth, and the organs of evacuation and generation. Two additional gates are the navel and the aperture at the top of the head (Brahmarandhra). Without the soul, the body is absolutely valueless—a mere corpse. 'This ill-smelling, unsubstantial body: a mere mass of bones, skin, sinews, marrow, flesh, seed, blood, mucus, tears, eye-gum, ordure, urine, gall, and phlegm. What is the use of enjoying pleasures in this body, which is assailed by lust, hatred, greed, delusion, fear, anguish, jealousy, separation from what is loved, union with what is not loved, hunger, thirst, old age, death, illness, grief, and other evils?'

The heart has received much attention from the seers of the Upanishads. It is the resting-place of the prānas, the senses, and the mind. It is the abode of Brahman. 'That great birthless Self, which is identified with the intellect and is in the midst of the organs, lies in the ākāśa that is within the heart. It is the controller of all, the lord of all, the ruler of all.' Its physical shape is often compared to a lotus bud. The aspirant is asked to meditate on Brahman dwelling in the heart.

REBIRTH

The question of a man's hereafter was perhaps raised even at the dawn of human thinking. Vedic philosophy has dealt with the subject, and the conclusion arrived at is very significant. Its doctrine of karma and the rebirth of the soul has exercised a profound practical influence upon millions of Hindus from the most ancient times. Even now its influence on their daily lives is great. All the good and evil that befall a man during one lifetime cannot be explained if we confine our attention to this life alone. What does he know of life who only one life knows? In the narrow span of a single life we cannot possibly reap the fruit of all that we do. It is reasonable to admit the existence of a transmigrating soul in order to substantiate the general belief in moral requital. 'A mortal ripens like corn, and like corn he springs up again.' But the seed is left. We are all born with a blue-print of our life, as it were, mainly prepared by our actions in the previous life. Our present acts and thoughts are the result of our past and create our future. Man is the architect of his own fate and the builder of his own future destiny.

[4] For a detailed description of the sheaths, see *Self-Knowledge*, by Swami Nikhilananda, p. 81 ff.

This conviction makes the believer in the doctrine of rebirth responsible for his present suffering and also gives him an incentive for habitual right conduct to build up a happy future. As he accepts with serenity his present ill fortune, he can also look forward to the future with joy and courage. If present suffering is the result of a past wicked action, then, in order to avoid suffering in a future existence, a thoughtful man should desire to sin no more.

What happens after death is, to the rational mind, a mere matter of conjecture. The experiences of the hereafter cannot be demonstrated in public. Time, space, and other conditions would certainly be different on the two sides of the grave. Therefore a living man would not understand the accounts of the dead even if they were to return to earth to tell him of their experiences. For this reason a scientific mind can only accept a plausible theory regarding after-death experiences. The theory of total annihilation is not satisfactory. It gives only a partial picture of existence. This theory is not only inconsistent with the self-love we all possess, but also with the intuitive and direct experience of the seers regarding the indestructibility of the Soul. The rishis of the Upanishads were not impressed by the theory of eternal retribution in heaven or hell. That theory reveals a total disproportion between cause and effect. Life on earth is short, exposed to error, and bristling with temptations. Many of our wrong actions are the result of faulty upbringing and environment. To inflict upon the soul eternal punishment for the errors of a few years, or even of a whole lifetime, is to throw to the winds all sense of proportion. It is also inconsistent with God's love for His created beings.

The Hindus have therefore developed the doctrine of rebirth. According to this view, it is desire that is responsible for a person's embodiment. Desires are of many kinds: some can be fulfilled in a human body, some in a subhuman body, and others in a superhuman body. When a man has fulfilled every desire through repeated births, without deriving abiding satisfaction, and finds the relative world to be bound by the law of cause and effect, he longs for communion with Brahman, which alone is untouched by the causal law. In most cases—barring those souls who attain Liberation from Brahmaloka—a human body is the best instrument for the attainment of Knowledge and Freedom; for in a god's body or in a subhuman body one experiences only the fruits of one's past action. Neither a god nor an animal can perform action which will bear new fruit.

According to the theory of rebirth, a soul is born again and again, high or low, depending on the merit or demerit of his actions. This theory is in conformity with the law of cause and effect, which is the very basis of the physical universe. It is also in agreement with the spiritual experiences of the mystics regarding man's ultimate end, which is the attainment of the knowledge of the Soul's Immortality. Rebirth is the inevitable corollary of the Soul's indestructibility and explains the *raison d'être* of its embodiment in the relative universe.

The teachings of the *Katha Upanishad* begin with a direct question regarding the soul's hereafter. 'There is this doubt about a man when he is dead: Some say that he exists; others, that he does not. This I should like to know, taught by you.' The teacher, the god of death, first gives, in reply, a striking discourse on the Soul's indestructibility. Then he states the doctrine of rebirth: 'Some jivas enter the womb to be embodied as organic beings and some go into non-organic matter—according to their work and according to their knowledge.'

The *Brihadāranyaka Upanishad* gives a more vivid description of rebirth: 'When the soul departs, the prāna follows; when the prāna departs, all the organs follow. Then the soul has specific consciousness and goes to the body which is related to that consciousness. It is followed by knowledge, works, and past experience. Just as a leech supported on a straw goes to the end of it, takes hold of another support, and contracts itself, so does the self throw this body aside—make it senseless—take hold of another support, and contract itself. Just as a goldsmith takes a little quantity of gold and fashions another—a newer and better—form, so does the soul throw this body away, or make it senseless, and make another—a newer and better—form, suited to the Manes, or the celestial minstrels, or the gods, or Virāt, or Hiranyagarbha, or other beings . . . As it does and acts, so it becomes; by doing good it becomes good, and by doing evil it becomes evil—it becomes virtuous through good acts and vicious through evil acts. Others, however, say: "The self is identified with desire alone. What it desires, it resolves; what it resolves, it works out; what it works out, it attains." '

The *Brihadāranyaka Upanishad* describes the 'doctrine of the Five Fires' in connexion with rebirth. According to this teaching, as the body is cremated, the soul ascends heavenward through the flame and smoke and goes to the Plane of the Moon, whence it falls to earth in the form of rain. With the rain it is absorbed by plants that bear cereal; with the food it is eaten by man and is transformed into semen, and, entering a woman's womb, is born as a human being. Thus people are born again and again on earth and lead their merry-go-round existence. But those wretched souls who do not follow either of the two ways—the Way of the Gods (Devayāna) or the Way of the Fathers (Pitriyāna)—become insects: moths or biting creatures like gnats and mosquitoes.

The assurance of rebirth may bring happiness to those who are afraid of annihilation after death or of the boredom of heaven, or who are eager to return to earth for fresh experience; but life on earth in any form cannot escape old age, disease, and death. The law of karma is inexorable here and in heaven, or, as a matter of fact, anywhere in time and space. The individual soul is bound by this chain of cause and effect. The seeker of Liberation, therefore, resolves upon 'cutting the knot' by turning away from the entire phenomenal existence of time, space, and causality. True, the destruction of individuality and the suppression of the natural cravings are regarded by many as the severest punishment; but these are the supreme reward for the spiritual endeavour of those who aspire after true Immortality.

What impelled the rishis of the Upanishads to regard the whole of phenomenal existence as evil and the absorption of individuality in Brahman as the Highest Good? It was not their desire to escape the sufferings of existence, well known to all; it was not their unwillingness to face the problems of life. Nor was it the result of frustration, which, it is often stated, was experienced by the majority of the Hindus because they were always exploited by a handful of brāhmin priests and kshatriya rulers. Life on the banks of the Ganges and the Indus was happy, affluent, and colourful. It was filled with the joy of adventure, as evidenced by the many-sided development of Hindu society at that time. Moreover, the longing for Liberation was not cultivated by the less fortunate masses, but by reflective minds belonging to the upper castes. The brāhmin boy Nachiketā spurned all the happiness of earth and heaven in order to attain Liberation. Maitreyi refused to accept from her brāhmin husband her share of wealth, which makes a worldly person happy, because she wanted to know the secret of Immortality.

The Vedas and the books dealing with Hindu dharma ask a Hindu to cultivate a warm love of life. One must enjoy, on earth, one hundred years—the life-span allotted to man by God. Marriage is compulsory for Hindu men and women, except in a few specified cases. One without progeny goes, after death, to the abode of suffering. Without money all-round happiness cannot be enjoyed. One must heighten the power of the senses so that, through enjoyment of material pleasures, one may relieve the drabness of everyday existence.

And yet the three worlds—earth, heaven, and the mid-region—will one day disappear. Brahmā, the Creator God, with all the dwellers in the highest heaven, will also perish. The Vedic sacrifices bring rewards that are contaminated by māyā and the three gunas. The inquirer after Immortality must transcend the Vedas. He is required to cut at the very foundation of the attachment that supports phenomenal existence here and hereafter. He must relinquish the longing for wealth, progeny, and the heavenly world. These make one forgetful of Ātman. The forgetfulness of one's true Self is the greatest suffering for a man. Everything that is not Ātman is trivial.

Why, then, did the Vedas lay down injunctions for a religious and ethical life and the propitiation of the gods through sacrifices? The earthbound soul must learn through actual experience the futility of attachment to material things. Only then will it cultivate dispassion for māyā and its effects. Those alone who have renounced all longings for the pleasures found on earth, and also for the felicity in heaven described in the Vedas, can cultivate vairāgyam, dispassion, and become entitled to the Knowledge of Ātman.

ETHICS

One of the cardinal disciplines for the Knowledge of Ātman is the practice of ethical virtues. Self-Knowledge is denied to him 'who has not first turned away from wickedness, who is not tranquil and subdued, and whose mind is not at peace.' The *Katha Upanishad* states that the sense-organs are created with an inclination toward material pleasures and hence embodied souls are entangled in the phenomenal life of unceasing birth and death, but that calm sages turn their sense-organs inward in order to attain freedom and immortality. It does not allow any compromise, for the advanced seeker, between the ideal of pleasure and the ideal of the good. The two are as sharply distinguished as darkness and light. 'He who chooses the pleasant misses the end.' 'The fool chooses the pleasant out of greed and avarice.' In the *Taittiriya Upanishad* the boy Bhrigu is repeatedly asked by his father to seek Brahman by means of tapas, or austerities. Mere mental austerities are not enough; these must be accompanied by appropriate external conduct. The practice of austerities does not, however, mean the mere mortification of the flesh or the sense-organs. This is explained in the *Katha Upanishad* by the illustration of a chariot. The body is compared to the chariot, the senses to the horses, the intellect to the charioteer, the mind to the reins, the sense-objects to the road, and the embodied soul to the master of the chariot, who is desirous of reaching the goal of Self-Knowledge. The chariot can take the master to his destination only when the vehicle is well built, when the driver knows the way, and when the reins are strong, the horses held firmly under control, and the roads well chosen. What is emphasized here is the need of a healthy body, vigorous sense-organs, a strong mind, and an intellect which will choose only those material objects conducive to a man's spiritual life. Some of the ethical virtues especially extolled by Hindu philosophers are: truthfulness, non-injury, forgiveness, good conduct, non-appropriation of others' property, control of the senses, absence of anger, equanimity, detachment from the world, charity, and continence. Through the practice of these virtues the heart becomes pure and the mind tranquil, and a mood is created for the proper contemplation of God or of Brahman.

The virtues mentioned above may be called subjective or personal. Objective ethics, dealing with social welfare with a view to creating an ideal environment for the peaceful pursuit of the spiritual life, is also mentioned in the Upanishads. A good action is thus extolled in the *Mahānārāyana Upanishad*: 'As the scent is wafted afar from a tree laden with flowers, so also is wafted afar the scent of a good deed.' The *Brihadāranyaka Upanishad* exhorts the gods, that is to say, the refined and wealthy men of society, to cultivate control of body and mind; average greedy men to practise liberality; and cruel men to cultivate compassion.

Objective ethics is based upon the conception of the duties (dharma) determined by a man's position in society and his stage of life. Progressive renunciation is the goal of both. These four stages have already been described.[5] Caste duties, too, are included in objective morality: morality as represented in a code of external acts requiring conformity with others. It is the duty of a brāhmin to officiate at religious ceremonies and to study and teach the Vedas. He leads a simple life, supporting himself on gifts from others. It is the duty of a kshatriya, or military man, to protect people from external aggression and internal anarchy, to guarantee peace and prosperity to them through wise administration of justice, to chastise the wicked, to reward the righteous, and never to turn away from an enemy on the battlefield. His code of ethics demands that he be always ready to sacrifice his life, if necessary, in the performance of his duties. The duties of a vaiśya are trade, agriculture, and the breeding and rearing of cattle. He should increase the wealth of the country for the welfare of all. The śudra should engage in manual labour and serve the three upper castes, receiving protection from them in return.

According to the Rig-Veda, the four castes are the four principal parts of society, which is conceived of as a person. They form its head, arms, thighs, and feet. The welfare of one depends upon the welfare of all. The higher caste must be gentle and compassionate toward the lower. Through the caste system, as formulated in the Vedas, India stressed the superiority of intellect and spirituality over military valour, the power of wealth, and the tyranny of organized labour. The general moral tone of the people of Upanishadic times is indicated in the *Chhāndogya Upanishad* by the following statement of King Aśvapati Kaikeya: 'In my kingdom there is no thief, no miser, no drunkard, no man without an altar in his house, no ignorant person, no adulterer, much less adulteress.'

The non-dualistic philosophy of the Upanishads points out that ethics, both subjective and objective, belongs to the phenomenal world, where one finds such pairs of opposites as good and evil. As a person transcends his identification with the body and the physical world, and realizes the oneness of existence, he is no longer troubled by the idea

[5] See p. 15ff.

of good and evil. But an illumined person can never perform an action injurious to others. Though he no longer consciously strives for moral perfection, virtues like humility, love, compassion, self-control, and humility become his natural attributes. In the words of the *Brihadāranyaka Upanishad*: 'Evil does not overtake him, but he transcends all evil. Evil does not trouble him, but he consumes all evil. He becomes sinless, stainless, and free from doubts.'

LIBERATION (MOKSHA)

The knowledge of Ātman is to be attained now and here, and not elsewhere after death. 'If a man knows Ātman here, he then attains the true goal of life. If he does not know It here, a great destruction awaits him.' Moksha, or Liberation, is not, however, the result of Knowledge. It is not a new acquisition. Causation applies to the realm of becoming and not to Ātman. It is inconceivable in Ātman, which is one and without a second. If Moksha were the result of Knowledge and were therefore endowed with a beginning, it would then come to an end. It would not be eternal. Arising from non-existence, it would again dissolve into nothingness. 'Liberation cannot have a beginning and be eternal.' Liberation is therefore not something which is created, but is the realization of what has existed from eternity but has hitherto been concealed. 'All jivas are ever free from bondage and pure by nature. They are ever illumined and liberated from the very beginning.'

He who knows the Self is liberated; even the gods cannot prevent his being so, because he has realized himself to be the very Soul (Ātman) of the gods. 'He who knows the Supreme Brahman verily becomes Brahman.' He has attained the true Immortality, that is to say, indestructibility without a continued existence, and not the state of non-dying-ness in heaven. Thus, according to the Upanishads, Liberation is not the *result* of the Knowledge of Ātman; it *is* that Knowledge. It is not affected by the Knowledge of Ātman; but this Knowledge is itself Liberation in its fullness. Desire is death; desirelessness is Liberation. He who has realized himself as Brahman, infinite and all-pervading, he who sees the whole universe in himself and himself in the universe, cannot desire anything. 'What can he crave who has attained the fulfilment of all desires?'

What happens to a knower of the Self after death? He finds himself everywhere in the whole universe. For him 'the east is the eastern prāna; the south, the southern prāna; the west, the western prāna; the north, the northern prāna; the direction above, the upper prāna; the direction below, the nether prāna; and all the quarters, the different prānas.' Whither will the soul of the knower of Ātman go? There is no place where it has not been from the very beginning, nor does it become anything other than what it has always been—that is to say, Brahman, Pure Consciousness.

He who desires is reborn. 'But the man who does not desire is not reborn. Of him who is without desires, who is free from desires, the objects of whose desire have been attained, and to whom all objects of desire are but the Self—the prānas do not depart. Being but Brahman, he is merged in Brahman. Regarding this there is the following verse: "When all the desires that dwell in his heart are gone, then he, having been mortal, becomes immortal and attains Brahman in this very body." Just as the lifeless slough of a snake is cast off and lies on an ant-hill, so does his body lie. Then the self becomes disembodied and immortal; it becomes the Supreme Brahman, the Light.'

The knower of Ātman is like a man who is awakened from sleep and dreams no more of empty things. He is like a man who, having been sick, is now whole again; he is like a man who, having been blind, has received back his eyesight. The Knowledge of the Self liberates a man from desire, fear, and death.

A liberated man is not given to inactivity, which is a characteristic of tamas. He sees action in non-action and non-action in action. Actions do not cling to him. Even while performing actions through his body and senses, he knows his inner Self to be actionless and detached. He knows that the Self is not the doer, but the Witness. He can never perform an evil action. All his evil instincts were destroyed when he practised spiritual discipline prior to attaining Self-Knowledge. Only good comes out of him—and that, too, without any effort. 'This is the eternal glory of a knower of Brahman: it never increases or decreases by work. [Therefore] one should know the nature of That alone. Knowing It one is not touched by evil action. Therefore he who knows It as such becomes self-controlled, calm, withdrawn into himself, enduring, and concentrated, and sees the Self in his own body; he sees all as the Self.'

A jivanmukta, or liberated soul, is no longer concerned about bondage or Liberation; for these do not really belong to Ātman. Bondage and Liberation are characteristics of the mind. On account of māyā an ignorant person thinks of himself as bound and then strives for Liberation; but Ātman is always free. In the words of Gauḍapāda: 'There is neither death nor birth, neither a struggling nor a bound soul, neither a seeker after Liberation nor a liberated one—this, indeed, is the ultimate truth.'

KATHA UPANISHAD

INTRODUCTION

THE *KATHA UPANISHAD* is widely read both in the East and in the West. The Knowledge of the Self is here described in a lucid style almost unparalleled in the Hindu scriptures. Max Müller has said that the French, German, and English translators of the Upanishads regard this treatise as 'one of the most perfect specimens of the mystic philosophy and poetry of the ancient Hindus.'

The exact relationship of the *Katha Upanishad* to the Vedas is a controversial subject, some associating it with the Sāma-Veda, some with the Yajur-Veda, and others with the Atharva-Veda. The Brāhmana of the Taittiriya Yajur-Veda contains a story of Nachiketā very similar to the one found in the *Katha Upanishad.*

Like all the Upanishads, the *Katha Upanishad* aims at inculcating the Knowledge of Brahman. As the subject is profound and difficult to grasp, the Upanishad, following an ancient Hindu method, begins with an illustrative story.

There once lived a rishi named Vājaśravasa, who performed a sacrifice that required, among other things, the giving away by the sacrificer of all his wealth. He had a son named Nachiketā, who, though young, cherished a reverence for spiritual ideals. When the cows were brought for distribution among the brāhmins and priests who were to conduct the sacrifice, Nachiketā found them to be old and unfit for any use. Such an unworthy gift, the boy realized, would only bring misery to his father after death. And so, since he was eager to save his father from this impending calamity, he said to him that a son was also property and should be included among the things for distribution. He wished to know, therefore, to whom he was going to be given. Three times he asked the question. But Vājaśravasa was annoyed by what he regarded as impudence on the part of his son, and he answered angrily that he would give him to Yama, the King of Death.

Nachiketā obeyed his father and proceeded to the abode of Yama. The latter, as the arbiter of man's final destiny and the bestower of punishments and rewards, held a high position among the gods. He was reputed, moreover, to be a teacher of the Knowledge of Brahman.

Yama was away when Nachiketā arrived, and only returned after three days. He sought to make amends for not having been there to receive his worthy guest, and for any discourtesy that might have been shown to him during his absence, by allowing him three boons, one for each night. Nachiketā asked, as the first boon, the allaying both of his father's anger and of his anxiety on account of his son's absence from home. As the second boon, he desired to know the Fire-sacrifice, by

67

which one goes to Brahmaloka and enjoys there a long life of felicity, free from disease and old age, sorrow and fear. Both boons were granted. The first two boons represent all the happiness one expects to enjoy on earth, through the fulfilment of social duties, and in heaven, through the propitiation of Saguna Brahman, the most exalted divinity. Being associated with the phenomenal universe, such happiness is transitory. Self-Knowledge alone bestows the Highest Good, and it is this that is the subject matter of the Upanishad.

With the asking of the third boon, the teaching of the *Katha Upanishad* begins. Nachiketā wished to know whether or not there was an immortal substance in a man that survived the death of the body. He asked, in other words, about the Ātman: Its nature, Its origin, and Its destiny.

INVOCATION[1]

OM. MAY BRAHMAN protect us both! May Brahman bestow
upon us both the fruit of Knowledge! May we both obtain the
energy to acquire Knowledge! May what we both study reveal
the Truth! May we cherish no ill feeling toward each other!
Om. Peace! Peace! Peace!

[1] The Supreme Lord is invoked at the commencement and the termination of
the study of the Vedas and other scriptures for the removal of all faults committed intentionally, unintentionally, carelessly, or through excitement, oversight,
or non-observance of the proper rules. Here the blessings are supplicated for both
the teacher and the disciple.

I

NACHIKETĀ SAID: THERE is doubt about a man when he is dead: Some say that he exists; others, that he does not. This I should like to know, taught by you. This is the third of my boons. (I. i. 20)

Yama said: On this subject even the gods formerly had their doubts. It is not easy to understand: the nature of Ātman is subtle. Choose another boon, O Nachiketā! Do not press me. Release me from that boon. (I. i. 21)

Nachiketā said: O Death, even the gods have their doubts about this subject; and you have declared it to be not easy to understand. But another teacher like you cannot be found, and surely no other boon is comparable to this. (I. i. 22)

Yama said: Choose sons and grandsons who shall live a hundred years; choose elephants, horses, herds of cattle, and gold. Choose a vast domain on earth; live here as many years as you desire. (I. i. 23)

If you deem any other boon equal to that, choose it; choose wealth and a long life. Be the king, O Nachiketā, of the wide earth. I will make you the enjoyer of all desires. (I. i. 24)

Whatever desires are difficult to satisfy in this world of mortals, choose them as you wish: these fair maidens, with their chariots and musical instruments—men cannot obtain them. I give them to you and they shall wait upon you. But do not ask me about death. (I. i. 25)

Nachiketā said: But, O Death, these endure only till tomorrow. Furthermore, they exhaust the vigour of all the sense-organs. Even the longest life[2] is short indeed. Keep your horses, dances, and songs for yourself. (I. i. 26)

Wealth can never make a man happy. Moreover, since I have beheld you, I shall certainly obtain wealth; I shall also live as long as you rule. Therefore no boon will be accepted by me but the one that I have asked. (I. i. 27)

Who among decaying mortals here below, having approached the undecaying immortals and coming to know that his higher needs may

[2] Refers to the life of relative immortality enjoyed in Brahmaloka. Everything that exists in time and space is subject to birth, growth, decay, and death.

be fulfilled by them, would exult in a life over long, after he had pondered on the pleasures arising from beauty and song? (I. i. 28)

Tell me, O Death, of that Great Hereafter about which a man has his doubts.
Nachiketā will surely not choose any other boon but the one so wrapped in mystery. (I. i. 29)

Yama said: The good is one thing; the pleasant, another. Both of these, serving different needs, bind a man.[3] It goes well with him who, of the two, takes the good; but he who chooses the pleasant misses the end. (I. ii. 1)

Both the good and the pleasant present themselves to a man. The calm soul examines them well and discriminates. Yea, he prefers the good to the pleasant; but the fool chooses the pleasant out of greed and avarice. (I. ii. 2)

O Nachiketā, after pondering well the pleasures that are or seem to be delightful, you have renounced them all. You have not taken the road abounding in wealth, where many men sink. (I. ii. 3)

Wide apart and leading to different ends are these two: ignorance and what is known as Knowledge. I regard you, O Nachiketā, to be one who desires Knowledge; for even many pleasures could not tempt you away. (I. ii. 4)

Fools dwelling in darkness, but thinking themselves wise and erudite, go round and round,[4] by various tortuous paths, like the blind led by the blind. (I. ii. 5)

The Hereafter[5] never reveals itself to a person devoid of discrimination, heedless, and perplexed by the delusion of wealth. 'This world alone exists,' he thinks, 'and there is no other.' Again and again he comes under my sway. (I. ii. 6)

Many there are who do not even hear of Ātman; though hearing of Him, many do not comprehend. Wonderful is the expounder and rare

---

[3] Refers to unillumined persons, of whom some seek pleasure, and some, the Highest Good, or Liberation, according to their respective spiritual evolution. The former pursue the lower knowledge, and the latter, the Higher Knowledge. So both are said to be bound by their respective sense of duty. Even the striving after Liberation indicates a state of bondage.

[4] That is to say, after death they are forced to assume different bodies, good and evil, all resulting from their ignorance.

[5] The knowledge of the soul's existence after the destruction of the body.

the hearer; rare indeed is the experiencer of Ātman taught by an able preceptor. (I. ii. 7)

Ātman, when taught by an inferior person, is not easily comprehended, because It is diversely regarded by disputants. But when It is taught by him who has become one with Ātman, there can remain no more doubt about It.[6] Ātman is subtler than the subtlest and not to be known through argument. (I. ii. 8)

This Knowledge cannot be attained by reasoning. Ātman becomes easy of comprehension, O dearest, when taught by another. You have attained this Knowledge now. You are, indeed, a man of true resolve. May we always have an inquirer like you! (I. ii. 9)

The fulfilment of desires,[7] the foundation of the universe,[8] the endless rewards of sacrifices, the shore where there is no fear,[9] that which is adorable and great, the wide abode, and the goal—all this you have seen; and being wise, you have with firm resolve discarded everything. (I. ii. 11)

The wise man who, by means of concentration on the Self, realizes that ancient, effulgent One, who is hard to be seen, unmanifest, hidden, and who dwells in the buddhi and rests in the body[10]—he, indeed, leaves joy and sorrow far behind. (I. ii. 12)

The mortal who has heard this and comprehended it well, who has separated that Ātman, the very soul of dharma,[11] from all physical objects and has realized the subtle essence, rejoices because he has obtained that which is the cause of rejoicing. The Abode of Brahman, I believe, is open for Nachiketā. (I. ii. 13)

[6] The following is an adaptation of Śankara's commentary regarding the meaning of the sentence:

'How is Ātman well comprehended? The answer is as follows: If Ātman is taught by a preceptor who himself is free from the illusion of duality and who has become one with Brahman, then all doubts—such as whether Ātman exists or not and whether or not It is the doer—disappear. It is the very nature of the Knowledge of Ātman to put an end to all doubts.'

[7] All the relative desires of a man find their fulfilment in the happiness of Brahmaloka.

[8] Brahmā, the controlling deity of Brahmaloka.

[9] One who has attained to Brahmaloka is free from the fear of old age, disease, and death, which are the lot of mortals on earth. Yet this is not real Freedom.

[10] Though Ātman is all-pervading Pure Consciousness, yet Its presence is directly felt in the body, in the heart.

[11] The word *dharma* denotes the inner foundation of all beings, without which they can neither exist nor further evolve.

Nachiketā said: That which you see as other than righteousness and unrighteousness, other than all this cause and effect, other than what has been and what is to be—tell me That. (I. ii. 14)

Yama said: The goal which all the Vedas declare, which all austerities aim at, and which men desire when they lead the life of continence,[12] I will tell you briefly: it is Om. (I. ii. 15)

This syllable *Om* is indeed Brahman. This syllable is the Highest. Whosoever knows this syllable obtains all that he desires. (I. ii. 16)

This is the best support; this is the highest support. Whosoever knows this support is adored in the world of Brahmā. (I. ii. 17)

The knowing Self[13] is not born; It does not die. It has not sprung from anything; nothing has sprung from It. Birthless, eternal, everlasting, and ancient, It is not killed when the body is killed. (I. ii. 18)

If the killer thinks he kills and if the killed man thinks he is killed, neither of these apprehends aright. The Self kills not, nor is It killed.[14] (I. ii. 19)

Ātman, smaller than the small, greater than the great, is hidden in the hearts of all living creatures. A man who is free from desires beholds the majesty[15] of the Self through tranquillity of the senses and the mind and becomes free from grief.[16] (I. ii. 20)

Though sitting still, It travels far; though lying down, It goes everywhere. Who but myself can know that luminous Ātman who rejoices and rejoices not? (I. ii. 21)

[12] The reference is to the religious students known as brahmachārins, who live with their teacher, observing the vows of continence and celibacy and practising other spiritual disciplines.

[13] That is to say, the knower of Ātman.

[14] The agent of killing is the ego (I-consciousness), and the object is the body. The ego identified with the mind, the senses, and the body—known as the phenomenal being—kills another body. The real Self, Pure Consciousness, is the detached witness. As Ātman does not kill, neither does It participate in any other action.

[15] The unique greatness of the Self consists in the fact that It undergoes neither expansion nor contraction by Its association with objects imposed upon It through illusion. It does not become holy through good action or sinful through evil action. But evil action creates a barrier and hinders a man from beholding the vision of the effulgent Self, whereas good action destroys the barrier.

[16] Commentators who uphold Dualism explain the compound word *dhātu-prasādāt* ('tranquillity of the senses and the mind') in the text as 'by the grace (prasādāt) of the Creator (dhātu).' One does not feel the grace of God without desirelessness, inner calmness, and purity.

The wise man, having realized Ātman as dwelling within imperma-nent bodies but Itself bodiless, vast, and all-pervading, does not grieve. (I. ii. 22)

This Ātman cannot be attained by the study of the Vedas, or by intelligence, or by much hearing of sacred books. It is attained by him alone whom It chooses.[17] To such a one Ātman reveals Its own form. (I. ii. 23)

He who has not first turned away from wickedness, who is not tran-quil and subdued, and whose mind is not at peace, cannot attain Ātman. It is realized only through the Knowledge of Reality. (I. ii. 24)

Who, then, knows where He is—He to whom brāhmins and kshat-triyas are mere food, and death itself a condiment? (I. ii. 25)

Two[18] there are who dwell within the body, in the buddhi, the supreme ākāśa of the heart, enjoying the sure rewards of their own actions.[19] The knowers of Brahman describe them as light and shade, as do those householders who have offered oblations in the Five Fires[20] and also those who have thrice performed the Nachiketā sacrifice. (I. iii. 1)

Know the ātman[21] to be the master of the chariot; the body, the chariot; the buddhi, the charioteer; and the mind, the reins. (I. iii. 3)

The senses, they say, are the horses; the objects, the roads. The wise call the ātman—united with the body, the senses, and the mind—the enjoyer. (I. iii. 4)

[17] According to Dualistic interpreters, the words mean: 'whom the Supreme Lord chooses'. Obviously this emphasizes the divine grace. But according to the Non-dualist Śankara, it is the self, that is to say, the lower, phenomenal self, that seeks and worships the Supreme Self, or Brahman. There is, however, no real contradiction between the two interpretations. Both self-effort and divine grace are necessary for the realization of Ātman. Through self-effort the seeker removes obstacles and prepares the ground; next there is the spontaneous revelation of Ātman.

[18] The jivātmā, or individual soul, and the Paramātmā, or Supreme Self.

[19] Though both the individual soul and the Supreme Self are described in the text as enjoying the fruits of action, in reality it is the individual soul that does so. The Supreme Self is the detached Witness of the activities of the individual soul.

[20] Every householder belonging to the three upper castes was required, in Vedic times, to offer daily oblations in the five kinds of sacrificial fire. Or the words may refer to the Five Fires described in the *Chhāndogya Upanishad* (V. 4–8).

[21] Here the word signifies the embodied self.

If the buddhi, being related to a mind that is always distracted, loses its discrimination, then the senses become uncontrolled, like the vicious horses of a charioteer. (I. iii. 5)

But if the buddhi, being related to a mind that is always restrained, possesses discrimination, then the senses come under control, like the good horses of a charioteer. (I. iii. 6)

If the buddhi, being related to a distracted mind, loses its discrimination and therefore always remains impure, then the embodied soul never attains the goal, but enters into the round of births. (I. iii. 7)

But if the buddhi, being related to a mind that is restrained, possesses discrimination and therefore always remains pure, then the embodied soul attains that goal from which he is not born again.[22] (I. iii. 8)

A man who has discrimination for his charioteer, and holds the reins of the mind firmly, reaches the end of the road; and that is the supreme position of Vishnu.[23] (I. iii. 9)

Beyond[24] the senses are the objects;[25] beyond the objects is the mind; beyond the mind, the intellect; beyond the intellect, the Great Ātman;[26] beyond the Great Ātman, the Unmanifest;[27] beyond the Unmanifest, the Purusha. Beyond the Purusha there is nothing: this is the end, the Supreme Goal. (I. iii. 10–11)

That Self hidden[28] in all beings does not shine forth; but It is seen by subtle seers through their one-pointed and subtle intellects. (I. iii. 12)

[22] He who has realized Brahman is not born again in the world of ignorance. But this does not, by any means, indicate that such a person ceases to exist. On the contrary, he becomes one with Brahman, Absolute Existence. All that can be said of him is that he is free from ignorance and delusion. He is awakened from the dream of illusory individuality.

[23] That is to say, Brahman, which is the all-pervading Consciousness.

[24] The word in the text is *para*, which Śankarāchārya explains as subtler, greater, and more inward. Thus the objects are subtler, greater, and more inward than the senses. They are the inner stuff of the senses.

[25] The word means here the subtle rudimentary elements. They are beyond the senses, because the senses are produced from them. Śankarāchārya says in his commentary that the objects create the senses so that they (the objects) may be apprehended.

[26] Hiranyagarbha.

[27] That is to say, Brahman, or the Absolute, associated with undifferentiated ajnāna, or ignorance. The Absolute Itself is beyond causal relations. The Unmanifest is the cause of all the causes and effects perceived in the material universe.

[28] Like fire in fire-wood, or oil in oil-seed, or butter in milk.

The wise man should merge his speech in his mind, and his mind in his intellect. He should merge his intellect in the Cosmic Mind, and the Cosmic Mind in the Tranquil Self.[29] (I. iii. 13)

Arise! Awake! Approach the great[30] and learn. Like the sharp edge of a razor is that path, so the wise say—hard to tread and difficult to cross. (I. iii. 14)

Having realized Ātman, which is soundless, intangible, formless, un-decaying, and likewise tasteless, eternal, and odourless; having realized That which is without beginning and end, beyond the Great, and unchanging—one is freed from the jaws of death. (I. iii. 15)

[29] The reference is to the practice of yoga. The activities of the senses should be stopped and the attention directed to the mind. Then the mind should be drawn into the buddhi, or discriminative faculty. Next the aspirant should sink the buddhi into the Cosmic Mind, or Hiranyagarbha. In other words, he should make his mind as pure as the Cosmic Mind, which is free from all notions of discrete individuality. Last, the thin veil of the Cosmic Mind should be rent, and the seeker should merge in the Absolute, which is calm because of an utter absence of any distinction or difference either with regard to others or within Itself. The method of absorption into Brahman is the reverse of the process of manifestation.

[30] Illumined teachers.

Yama said: The self-existent[31] Supreme Lord inflicted an injury upon the sense-organs in creating them with outgoing tendencies;[32] therefore a man perceives only outer objects with them, and not the inner Self. But a calm person, wishing for Immortality, beholds the inner Self with his eyes closed. (II. i. 1)

Children pursue outer pleasures and fall into the net of widespread death; but calm souls, having known what is unshakeable Immortality, do not covet any uncertain thing in this world. (II. i. 2)

It is through Ātman that one knows form, taste, smell, sounds, touches, and carnal pleasures. Is there anything that remains unknown to Ātman? This, verily, is That.[33] (II. i. 3)

It is through Ātman that one perceives all objects in sleep or in the waking state.[34] Having realized the vast, all-pervading Ātman, the calm soul does not grieve. (II. i. 4)

He who knows the individual soul, the experiencer of the fruits of action, as Ātman, always near, and the Lord of the past and the future, will not conceal himself from others.[35] This, verily, is That. (II. i. 5)

He verily knows Brahman who knows the First-born,[36] the offspring of austerity,[37] created prior to the waters,[38] and dwelling, with the elements, in the cave of the heart. This, verily, is That. (II. i. 6)

He verily knows Brahman who knows Aditi, the soul of all deities, who was born in the form of Prāna,[39] who was created with the elements,

[31] The Lord, who exists by Himself, is not accountable to anyone for His action.

[32] The experience of outer objects, and not the inmost Self, by the sense-organs is a kind of injury done to them by the Lord Himself when He created them and turned them outward.

[33] That is to say, what Nachiketā asked of the King of Death as his third boon is nothing but Ātman.

[34] Ātman is the Witness of the activities of the waking and dream states and of their absence in dreamless sleep.

[35] The desire for concealment is the outcome of fear, which results from the perception of duality.

[36] That is to say, Hiranyagarbha.

[37] Desirous of creation, the Lord (Saguna Brahman) practised austerity, which consisted of intense thinking or brooding.

[38] That is to say, the five elements.

[39] The word refers to Hiranyagarbha.

and who, entering into the heart, abides therein. This, verily, is That. (II. i. 7)

Whence[40] the sun rises and whither it goes to set, in whom all the devas are contained, and whom none can ever pass beyond—This, verily, is That. (II. i. 9)

What is here,[41] the same is there; and what is there,[42] the same is here. He goes from death to death who sees any difference here. (II. i. 10)

By the mind alone is Brahman to be realized; then one does not see in It any multiplicity whatsoever. He goes from death to death who sees multiplicity in It. This, verily, is That. (II. i. 11)

The Purusha, of the size of a thumb,[43] dwells in the body. He is the Lord of the past and the future. After knowing Him, one does not conceal oneself any more. This, verily, is That. (II. i. 12)

The Purusha, of the size of a thumb, is like a flame without smoke. The Lord of the past and the future, He is the same today and tomorrow. This, verily, is That. (II. i. 13)

As rainwater falling on a mountain peak runs down the rocks in all directions, even so he who sees the attributes[44] as different from Brahman verily runs after them in all directions. (II. i. 14)

As pure water poured into pure water becomes one with it, so also, O Gautama,[45] does the Self of the sage who knows.[46] (II. i. 15)

[40] Refers to Prāna, which is the seed of all the tangible objects in the universe.
[41] That is to say, what appears to non-discriminating persons as a phenomenal being subject to the laws of time, space, and causation, but, from the standpoint of Truth, is nothing but pure Brahman.
[42] Refers to Brahman, which is absolute and immutable Consciousness, free from all relativity.
[43] The Vedāntic mystics conceive of the heart as a lotus bud of the size of a thumb, within which there is a luminous space where Brahman, or the Purusha, is manifest.
[44] That is to say, the multiple phenomenal beings created by ignorance.
[45] A term of endearment by which a disciple is often addressed by his teacher.
[46] 'One should give up false pride and haughtiness, discard the fallacious advice of the misguided logicians who proclaim the multiplicity of Ātman, and the erroneous counsel of the heretics who teach Its non-existence, and should realize Ātman's non-duality as taught by the Vedas, which are more solicitous of our welfare than a thousand fathers and mothers.' (Śankarāchārya.)

There is a city with eleven gates[47] belonging to the unborn Ātman of undistorted Consciousness. He who meditates on Him grieves no more; liberated [from the bonds of ignorance], he becomes free. This, verily, is That. (II. ii. 1)

He is the sun dwelling in the bright heavens. He is the air dwelling in the mid-region. He is the fire dwelling on earth. He is the guest dwelling in the house. He dwells in men, in the gods, in truth, in the sky. He is born in the water, on earth, in the sacrifice, on the mountains. He is the True and the Great. (II. ii. 2)

He it is who sends prāna upward and who leads apāna downward. All the devas[48] worship that adorable One seated in the middle.[49] (II. ii. 3)

When the soul, identified with the body and dwelling in it, is torn away from the body, is freed from it, what then remains? This, verily, is That. (II. ii. 4)

No mortal ever lives by prāna, which goes up, nor by apāna, which goes down. Men live by something different, on which these two depend. (II. ii. 5)

Well then, Gautama, I shall tell you about this profound and eternal Brahman, and also about what happens to the ātman after meeting death. (II. ii. 6)

Some jivas enter the womb for the purpose of [new] embodiment, and some enter into stationary objects—according to their work and according to their knowledge.[50] (II. ii. 7)

He, the Purusha, who remains awake while the sense-organs are asleep, shaping one lovely form after another,[51] is indeed the Pure; He is Brahman, and He alone is called the Immortal. All worlds are

[47] That is to say, the body. The eleven gates are the eleven apertures: the two eyes, the two ears, the two nostrils, the mouth, the navel, the two lower organs, and the aperture at the top of the head through which the life-breath of a yogin goes out at the time of death.

[48] Here the word means the sense-organs.

[49] That is to say, in the heart.

[50] According to the doctrine of karma and rebirth, the future of the embodied soul is determined by its present action and knowledge. By good action it becomes good, and by evil action it becomes evil. One can assume any body in the relative universe, from that of a god to that of a plant.

[51] The materials of dream objects are the impressions of the waking state, which are revealed by the light of the Self.

contained in Him, and none can pass beyond. This, verily, is That. (II. ii. 8)

As the same non-dual fire, after it has entered the world, becomes different according to whatever it burns, so also the same non-dual Ātman, dwelling in all beings, becomes different according to whatever It enters. And It exists also without.[52] (II. ii. 9)

As the same non-dual air, after it has entered the world, becomes different according to whatever it enters, so also the same non-dual Ātman, dwelling in all beings, becomes different according to whatever It enters. And It exists also without. (II. ii. 10)

As the sun, which helps all eyes to see, is not affected by the blemishes of the eyes or of the external things revealed by it, so also the one Ātman, dwelling in all beings, is never contaminated by the misery of the world, being outside it. (II. ii. 11)

There is one Supreme Ruler, the inmost Self of all beings, who makes His one form manifold. Eternal happiness belongs to the wise, who perceive Him within themselves—not to others. (II. ii. 12)

There is One who is the eternal Reality among non-eternal objects, the one [truly] conscious Entity among conscious objects,[53] and who, though non-dual, fulfils the desires of many. Eternal peace belongs to the wise, who perceive Him within themselves—not to others. (II. ii. 13)

The sages realize that indescribable Supreme Joy as 'This is That.'[54] How can I realize It? Is It self-luminous? Does it shine brightly, or not? (II. ii. 14)

The sun does not shine there, nor the moon and the stars, nor these lightnings—not to speak of this fire. He shining, everything shines after Him. By His light all this is lighted. (II. ii. 15)

This is that eternal Aśvattha Tree[55] with its root above[56] and branches

[52] Though phenomenal objects are many, and endowed with different attributes, yet Ātman remains non-dual and stainless because It is transcendental.
[53] The deities and other living beings derive their intelligence and consciousness from the Supreme Self, as a piece of hot iron derives its power of burning from fire.
[54] That is to say, as a direct and immediate experience distinct from indirect knowledge through inference or verbal testimony.
[55] The well-known banyan tree of India, which sends down its branches so that they strike root and form new stems, one tree growing into a sort of forest.
[56] Brahman conditioned by māyā (Saguna Brahman) is the root of the universe.

below.[57] That root, indeed, is called the Bright; That is Brahman, and That alone is the Immortal. In That all worlds are contained, and none can pass beyond. This, verily, is That. (II. iii. 1)

Whatever there is—the whole universe—vibrates because it has gone forth from Brahman, which exists as its Ground. That Brahman is a great terror, like a poised thunderbolt. Those who know It become immortal. (II. iii. 2)

From terror of Brahman, fire burns; from terror of It, the sun shines; from terror of It, Indra and Vāyu, and Death, the fifth, run. (II. iii. 3)

If a man is able to realize Brahman here, before the falling asunder of his body, then he is liberated; if not, he is embodied again in the created worlds. (II. iii. 4)

As in a mirror, so in the buddhi;[58] as in a dream, so in the World of the Fathers;[59] as in water, so Brahman is seen in the World of the Gandharvas; as in light and shade, so in the World of Brahmā. (II. iii. 5)

Having understood that the senses have their separate origin and that they are distinct from Ātman, and also that their rising and setting[60] belong to them alone, a wise man grieves no more. (II. iii. 6)

Beyond the senses is the mind, beyond the mind is the intellect, higher than the intellect is the Great Ātman[60a], higher than the Great Ātman is the Unmanifest. (II. iii. 7)

Beyond the Unmanifest is the Person, all-pervading and imperceptible. Having realized Him, the embodied self becomes liberated and attains Immortality. (II. iii. 8)

His form is not an object of vision; no one beholds Him with the eye. One can know Him when He is revealed by the intellect free from doubt and by constant meditation. Those who know this become immortal. (II. iii. 9)

[57] Heaven, earth, the nether worlds, and all other spheres of relative existence inhabited by either embodied or disembodied souls are described here as the downward-spreading branches of the Tree of the Universe.

[58] As one sees one's reflection clearly in a clean mirror, so one sees Brahman clearly in the buddhi, that is to say, in the intellect purified by self-control and contemplation.

[59] The vision of Ātman is indistinct in the World of the Fathers (Pitriloka), since one is engrossed there in the enjoyment of the fruits of past karma.

[60] Activity and non-activity.

[60a] Hiranyagarbha, which is the totality of all minds.

When the five instruments of knowledge stand still, together with the mind, and when the intellect does not move, that is called the Supreme State. (II. iii. 10)

This, the firm control of the senses, is what is called yoga. One must then be vigilant; for yoga can be both beneficial and injurious.[61] (II. iii. 11)

Ātman cannot be attained by speech, by the mind, or by the eye. How can It be realized in any other way than by the affirmation of him who says: 'He is'? (II. iii. 12)

He is to be realized [first] as Existence [limited by upādhis], and [then] in His true transcendental nature. Of these two aspects, Ātman realized as Existence leads [the knower] to the realization of His true nature. (II. iii. 13)

When all the desires that dwell in the heart fall away, then the mortal becomes immortal and here attains Brahman. (II. iii. 14)

When all the ties of the heart are severed here on earth, then the mortal becomes immortal. This much alone is the teaching. (II. iii. 15)

There are one hundred and one arteries of the heart, one of which[62] pierces the crown of the head. Going upward by it, a man[63] [at death] attains immortality.[64] But when his prāna passes out by other arteries,[65] going in different directions, then he is reborn in the world. (II. iii. 16)

The Purusha, not larger than a thumb, the inner Self, always dwells in the hearts of men. Let a man separate Him from his body with steadiness, as one separates the tender stalk from a blade of grass. Let him know that Self as the Bright, as the Immortal—yea, as the Bright, as the Immortal. (II. iii. 17)

Having received this wisdom taught by the King of Death, and the entire process of yoga, Nachiketā became free from impurities and death and attained Brahman. Thus it will be also with any other who knows, in this manner, the inmost Self. (II. iii. 18)

[61] When yogic disciplines are not properly practised, one may fall a victim to deep sleep, laziness, or other obstacles.
[62] Called the Sushumnā by the yogins.
[63] Refers to the worshipper of Saguna Brahman, who at the time of death controls the ātman in the heart by the power of yoga and makes it go upward through the Sushumnā artery.
[64] The relative immortality enjoyed by the dwellers in Brahmaloka.
[65] Refers to those who are attached to the world and come back to earth after experiencing the results of their past actions.

PEACE CHANT

OM. MAY BRAHMAN protect us both! May Brahman bestow upon us both the fruit of Knowledge! May we both obtain the energy to acquire Knowledge! May what we both study reveal the Truth! May we cherish no ill feeling toward each other! Om. Peace! Peace! Peace!

IŚA UPANISHAD

INTRODUCTION

THE *IŚA UPANISHAD* forms the fortieth chapter of the *Vājasaneyi Samhitā* of the Śukla Yajur-Veda. The Upanishad generally forms the concluding section of the Āranyaka, which, in turn, belongs to the Brāhmana portion of the Vedas. The *Iśa Upanishad*, however, is an exception, forming a part of the Samhitā, or Mantra. It derives its name from the opening word of the book: *Iśāvāsyam*. A short treatise consisting of only eighteen mantras, or verses, it appears to be a very ancient Upanishad, as is evidenced by its versification and literary style.

The book contains many obscure passages, which are explained differently by different commentators to suit their particular theories and systems. According to Śankarāchārya, the path of action and the path of knowledge cannot be pursued by a person at one and the same time.[1] The goal of the former is the attainment of happiness in the relative world, here or hereafter, and the goal of the latter, the realization of Immortality through the knowledge of the identity of Brahman and Ātman. But action, if performed following the instructions of the Vedas, ultimately prepares one for the cultivation of knowledge. The *Iśa Upanishad* refers to both the discipline of action and the discipline of knowledge.

The first verse speaks of the ultimate unreality of the sense-perceived world. But for those who are attached to earthly life, the second verse prescribes the performance of duties in accordance with the directions of the scriptures. Verses three to eight are meant for sannyāsins, who have renounced the world in order to attain the Knowledge of Brahman.

---

[1] 'Ātman cannot be connected with an action, because It is not something that is attained, created, or produced through the process of purification or transformation; and also because It is not of the nature of a doer or an enjoyer. The sole purpose of all the Upanishads is to determine the true nature of Ātman; the Bhagavad Gitā and other treatises dealing with man's Liberation have the same end in view. Action has been prescribed in the scriptures to suit the understanding of worldly people, who associate with Ātman such characteristics as multiplicity, agency, enjoyment, impurity, sinfulness, and so on. According to those competent to determine who should perform work and who should not, he who seeks the result of action—a result visible on earth, such as the glories of a brāhmin's life, or a result not so visible, such as enjoyment in heaven—is entitled to perform work. Thus the mantras of the *Iśa Upanishad* reveal the true nature of Ātman and thereby destroy the natural ignorance regarding It. Further, they produce in us the knowledge of the oneness of Ātman by means of which we can uproot grief, delusion, and other characteristics of samsāra. One who is eager to rid himself of the suffering and delusion of samsāra, created by ignorance, and attain Supreme Bliss, is competent to read this Upanishad.' (*From Śankarāchārya's Introduction to the* Iśa Upanishad.)

Verses nine to fourteen apply to those who cannot ascend the steep path of total renunciation. Some among them engage in the mechanical performance of sacrifices and rituals without understanding the deities behind such action; and some devote themselves to meditation on the deities without the performance of appropriate rituals.

According to the author of the *Iśa Upanishad*, the two disciplines should be harmonized. Likewise, the aspirant should harmonize devotion to the unmanifest (prakriti) and to the World Soul (Hiranyagarbha, or Brahmā). Thus alone can he reap the desired result, which is the attainment of Brahmaloka.

The last four verses deal with the prayer of the aspirant on his deathbed. He prays to the sun, a vivid symbol of Brahman, to withdraw the outer physical light so that the inner effulgence of Truth may be revealed. As the hour of death approaches, he fills his mind with the memories of his good deeds; the thought at the final moment determines the course of the soul hereafter. And lastly he prays to Fire, which will soon consume his physical body, to lead his soul through the Way of the Gods to Brahmaloka, from which he will attain final Liberation.

INVOCATION

OM. THAT[2] IS full;[3] this[4] is full. This fullness has been projected[5] from that fullness. When this fullness merges[6] in that fullness, all that remains is fullness.
    Om. Peace! Peace! Peace!

[2] Pure Consciousness.

[3] Perfect.

[4] Hiranyagarbha. The word *this* in the text also means the manifest universe, which, like Pure Consciousness, is perfect, names and forms being māyā.

[5] On account of māyā.

[6] That is to say when, by means of Knowledge, the universe is realized as Brahman.

ALL THIS—WHATEVER exists in this changing universe—should be covered by the Lord.[7] Protect the Self[8] by renunciation. Lust not after any man's wealth. (1)

If a man wishes to live a hundred years[9] on this earth, he should live performing action.[10] For you, who cherish such a desire and regard yourself as a man,[11] there is no other way by which you can keep work from clinging to you.[12] (2)

Verily, those worlds of the asuras are enveloped in blind darkness; and thereto they all repair after death who are slayers of Ātman.[13] (3)

That non-dual Ātman, though never stirring, is swifter than the mind.[14] The devas (the senses) cannot reach It, for It moves ever in front. Though standing still, It overtakes others who are running. Because of Ātman, Vāyu[15] apportions the activities of all. (4)

It moves and moves not; It is far and likewise near. It is inside all this and It is outside all this. (5)

The wise man beholds all beings in the Self, and the Self in all beings; for that reason he does not hate anyone. (6)

To the seer, all things have verily become the Self: what delusion, what sorrow, can there be for him who beholds that oneness? (7)

[7] One should view the universe, through the knowledge of non-duality, as Ātman alone.

[8] That is to say, liberate the Self from the grief, delusion, and other evil traits of samsāra in which It has been entangled on account of ignorance.

[9] According to Vedic tradition, the span of life allotted to a man is one hundred years.

[10] That is to say, the daily devotions and other moral duties prescribed by the scriptures.

[11] One who is identified with his body and conscious of his human duties and responsibilities.

[12] A person attached to his human body and desirous of enjoying on earth his full span of life should devote himself to religious duties and other unselfish actions; if not, he will engage in evil action.

[13] A person clinging to ignorance is described as a slayer of Ātman.

[14] It is well known that the mind, though encased in a body, can travel in the twinkling of an eye, and by its mere will, to such a distant place as the farthest heaven. But what does the mind find on reaching its destination? It finds the Self, or Ātman already there. The drift of the text is that before one is conscious of any object one must be conscious of oneself. Self-Knowledge must be admitted before the knowledge of any object. Further, the mind is a material thing. It cannot know an object without the light of Ātman.

[15] The first manifestation of the Absolute in the relative universe, also known by such epithets as Hiranyagarbha and Prāna. He sustains the whole universe by apportioning to the other deities their respective functions.

It is He who pervades all—He who is bright and bodiless, without scar or sinews, pure and by evil unpierced; who is the Seer, omniscient, transcendent and uncreated. He has duly allotted to the eternal World-Creators[16] their respective duties. (8)

Into a blind darkness they enter who are devoted to ignorance (rituals); but into a greater darkness they enter who engage in knowledge [of a deity] alone.[17] (9)

One thing,[18] they say, is obtained from knowledge; another,[19] they say, from ignorance. Thus we have heard from the wise who have taught us this. (10)

He who is aware that both knowledge and ignorance should be pursued together, overcomes death[20] through ignorance[21] and obtains immortality[22] through knowledge. (11)

Into a blind darkness they enter who worship only the unmanifested prakriti;[23] but into a greater darkness they enter who worship the manifested Hiranyagarbha. (12)

One thing,[24] they say, is obtained from the worship of the manifested; another,[25] they say, from the worship of the unmanifested. Thus we have heard from the wise who taught us this.[26] (13)

[16] Various exalted cosmic beings, such as Brahmā, Vishnu, and Śiva; or the word may mean the Creators of different universes. They endure as long as the universe lasts, but are not absolutely eternal, like Brahman, which transcends time.

[17] According to Śankarāchārya, the gist of this verse is that one should combine rituals with meditation on a deity; it is not a condemnation of either of these. The result of combining the two is the attainment of a heavenly world.

[18] That is to say, the Plane of the Deities (Devaloka).

[19] The Plane of the Fathers (Pitriloka).

[20] Action and thought not related to rituals and the gods are here called death. The agent of such action and thought does not see anything beyond the sense-perceived world.

[21] That is to say, ritualistic actions which reveal to their performers the other planes of existence not perceived by the senses.

[22] The relative immortality enjoyed by the gods with whom devotees become identified through meditation.

[23] That is to say, prakriti, or nature, prior to the manifestation of names and forms. Some people assert that prakriti itself is the self-creating, self-preserving, and self-destroying principle, and that it is not necessary to admit the existence of a Creator God.

[24] As a result of worshipping Hiranyagarbha, the devotee obtains such supernatural powers as the ability to reduce himself to the size of an atom, to make himself light as a feather, and to pervade the entire universe. These are characteristics of Hiranyagarbha.

[25] According to the Purānas, the result of such worship is absorption in prakriti.

[26] The scriptures say that whatever a person worships he becomes after death. He who worships prakriti, characterized by nescience, remains merged in prakriti

He who knows that both the unmanifested prakriti and the manifested Hiranyagarbha should be worshipped together, overcomes death by the worship of Hiranyagarbha and obtains immortality[27] through devotion to prakriti.[28] (14)

The door of the Truth[29] is covered[30] by a golden disc. Open it, O Nourisher! Remove it so that I who have been worshipping the Truth may behold It.[31] (15)

O Nourisher, lone Traveller of the sky! Controller! O Sun, Offspring of Prajāpati! Gather Your rays; withdraw Your light. I would see, through Your grace, that form of Yours which is the fairest. I am indeed He, that Purusha, who dwells there. (16)

Now may my breath return to the all-pervading, immortal Prāna! May this body be burnt to ashes! Om. O mind, remember, remember all that I have done.[32] (17)

O Fire,[33] lead us by the good path for the enjoyment of the fruit of our action. You know, O god, all our deeds. Destroy our sin of deceit. We offer, by words,[34] our salutations to you. (18)

---

for untold years. And he who worships Hiranyagarbha, who is only a manifestation of prakriti, obtains a corresponding result.

[27] The result of this worship is, as stated above, absorption in prakriti. The devotee remains so merged till the next creation.

[28] The result of combining the two kinds of worship described in the text is, first, the attainment of supernatural powers through devotion to Hiranyagarbha, and second, the attainment of immortality (relative) by merging in prakriti. The attainment of this immortality is the culmination of the efforts of a man or a god. It is the highest achievement in the relative universe.

[29] Refers to the manifestation of Brahman in the sun.

[30] It is hidden from the view of people who are without self-control.

[31] See the last paragraph of the introduction to this Upanishad.

[32] That is to say, a man should think only of his good deeds at the time of death. The thought occupying the mind in the hour of death determines the course of the soul after death.

[33] During Vedic times fire was considered as the intermediary god through whom oblations to the other gods were made.

[34] At the time of death the devotee cannot offer any other worship to the god. As his limbs become inert, he cannot prostrate himself; hence the salutations through words alone.

THE PEACE CHANT

OM. THAT IS full; this is full. This fullness has been projected from that fullness. When this fullness merges in that fullness, all that remains is fullness.

Om. Peace! Peace! Peace!

KENA UPANISHAD

INTRODUCTION

THE *KENA UPANISHAD*—so called because it begins with the word *Kena*—is also known as the *Talavakāra Upanishad* because it forms the ninth chapter of the *Talavakāra Brāhmana* of the Sāma-Veda. The preceding eight chapters of the Brāhmana deal with rites, sacrifices, meditation on the deities, and such cognate matters as are necessary for the purification of the aspirant's heart and also for the practice of concentration. The aim of the *Kena Upanishad*, like that of all the other Upanishads, is to teach the knowledge of the oneness of Ātman and Brahman.

INVOCATION

OM. MAY BRAHMAN protect us both (the preceptor and the disciple)! May Brahman bestow upon us both the fruit of Knowledge! May we both obtain the energy to acquire Knowledge! May what we both study reveal the Truth! May we cherish no ill feeling toward each other!

Om. Peace! Peace! Peace!

Om. May the different parts of my body, my tongue, prāna, eyes, ears, and my strength, and also all the other sense-organs, be nourished! All, indeed, is Brahman, as is declared in the Upanishads. May I never deny Brahman! May Brahman never deny me! May there never be denial on the part of Brahman! May there never be denial on my part! May all the virtues described in the Upanishads belong to me who am devoted to Brahman! Yea, may they all belong to me!

Om. Peace! Peace! Peace!

THE DISCIPLE ASKED: Om. By whose will directed does the mind proceed to its object? At whose command does the prāna, the foremost, do its duty? At whose will do men utter speech? Who is the god that directs the eyes and ears? (I. 1)

The teacher replied: It is the Ear of the ear, the Mind of the mind, the Speech of speech, the Life of life, and the Eye of the eye. Having detached the Self [from the sense-organs] and renounced the world,[1] the wise attain to Immortality. (I. 2)

The eye does not go thither, nor speech, nor the mind. We do not know It; we do not understand how anyone can teach It.[2] It is different from the known;[3] It is above the unknown. Thus we have heard from the preceptors of old who taught It to us. (I. 3–4)

That which cannot be expressed by speech, but by which speech is expressed—That alone know as Brahman, and not that[4] which people here worship. (I. 5)

That which cannot be apprehended by the mind, but by which, they say, the mind is apprehended—That alone know as Brahman, and not that which people here worship. (I. 6)

That which cannot be perceived by the eye, but by which the eye is perceived—That alone know as Brahman, and not that which people here worship. (I. 7)

That which cannot be heard by the ear, but by which the hearing is perceived—That alone know as Brahman, and not that which people here worship. (I. 8)

That which cannot be smelt by the breath, but by which the breath smells an object—That alone know as Brahman, and not that which people here worship. (I. 9)

[1] Or the phrase in the text may mean 'after the discarding of the body.'

[2] 'It is no doubt true that one cannot be made to believe in Brahman by the evidence of the sense-organs; yet one can cultivate faith in It from the evidence of the scriptures.' (Śankarāchārya.)

[3] Brahman is different from the known, that is to say, from the tangible world of name and form. Lest the disciple should misunderstand the statement of the teacher and conclude that Brahman is altogether unknown, the preceptor says that It is above the unknown. The word *unknown* refers to undifferentiated primal matter, which is the seed of the gross universe. By describing Brahman as both distinct from the known and above the unknown, the text indicates that Brahman is Ātman, or the inmost Self of the knower.

[4] Refers to the deities endowed with positive attributes. They are not the real Brahman, but Brahman limited by specific names and forms.

The teacher said: If you think: 'I know Brahman well,' then surely you know but little of Its form; you know only Its form as conditioned by man or by the gods.[5] Therefore Brahman, even now, is worthy of your inquiry.

The disciple said: I think I know Brahman. (II. 1)

The disciple said: I do not think I know It well, nor do I think I do not know It.[6] He among us who knows the meaning of 'Neither do I not know, nor do I know'—knows Brahman. (II. 2)

He by whom Brahman is not known, knows It; he by whom It is known, knows It not. It is not known by those who know It; It is known by those who do not know it. (II. 3)

Brahman is known when It is realized in every state of mind;[7] for by such Knowledge one attains Immortality. By Ātman one obtains strength; by Knowledge, Immortality. (II. 4)

If a man knows Ātman here, he then attains the true goal of life. If he does not know It here, a great destruction awaits him. Having realized the Self in every being, the wise relinquish the world and become immortal. (II. 5)

Brahman, according to the story, obtained a victory for the gods;[8] and by that victory of Brahman the gods became elated. They said to themselves: 'Verily, this victory is ours; verily, this glory is ours only.'[9] (III. 1)

Brahman, to be sure, understood it all and appeared before them. But they did not know who that adorable Spirit was. (III. 2)

[5] The forms of Brahman conditioned by the bodies and minds of men and gods are only insignificant manifestations of It in time and space. The gist of the passage is that Brahman, free from all limitations, is infinite, non-dual, sublime, and eternal and therefore cannot be described as well known by anyone.

[6] Brahman cannot be known as a pot or a jar or any other external object can be known. On the other hand, Brahman exists in all beings as their inmost Self. No one can deny the Self. Even a doubter or negator of the Self thinks only in the light of the Self. So it is not altogether unknown.

[7] The word bodha in the text means mental experience. That by which all states of the mind are illumined and also perceived like objects is Ātman.

[8] In ancient times, according to the story, there was a fight between the gods and the demons. It was Brahman who won the victory for the gods; He gave them the fruit of victory for the preservation of the world.

[9] The gods, because of their ignorance, did not know that all power and glory belong to Brahman.

They said to Agni (Fire): 'O Agni! Find out who this great Spirit is.' 'Yes,' he said, and hastened to It. Brahman asked him: 'Who are you?' He replied: 'I am known as Agni; I am also called Jātavedā.' Brahman said: 'What power is in you, who are so well known?' Fire replied: 'I can burn all—whatever there is on earth.' Brahman put a straw before him and said: 'Burn this.' He rushed toward it with all his ardour but could not burn it. Then he returned from the Spirit and said to the gods: 'I could not find out who this Spirit is.' (III. 3–6)

Then they said to Vāyu (Air): 'O Vāyu! Find out who this great Spirit is.' 'Yes,' he said, and hastened to It. Brahman asked him: 'Who are you?' He replied: 'I am known as Vāyu; I am also called Mātariśvā.' Brahman said: 'What power is in you, who are so well known?' Vāyu replied: 'I can carry off all—whatever there is on earth.' Brahman put a straw before him and said: 'Carry this.' He rushed toward it with all his ardour but could not move it. Then he returned from the Spirit and said to the gods: 'I could not find out who this Spirit is.' (III. 7–10)

Then the gods said to Indra: 'O Maghavan! Find out who this great Spirit is.' 'Yes,' he said and hastened to It. But the Spirit disappeared from him. Then Indra beheld in that very region of the sky a Woman[10] highly adorned. She was Umā,[11] the daughter of the Himālayas. He approached Her and said: 'Who is this great Spirit?' (III. 11–12)

She replied: 'It is, indeed, Brahman. Through the victory of Brahman alone have you attained glory.' After that Indra understood that It was Brahman. (IV. 1)

Since they approached very near Brahman and were the first to know that It was Brahman, these devas, namely, Agni, Vāyu, and Indra, excelled the other gods. (IV. 2)

Since Indra approached Brahman nearest, and since he was the first to know that It was Brahman, Indra excelled the other gods. (IV. 3)

This is the instruction about Brahman with regard to the gods:[12]

[10] The word refers to the Knowledge of Brahman (Brahmavidyā) or the Power (Śakti) of Brahman personified as a woman.

[11] Known as Durgā in later mythology. She is the inseparable consort of Śiva, or the Absolute. The Absolute is inactive, but Its power, Umā, is the active principle in creation. One finds that in Vedic symbolism the power of a god is represented by his consort. For example, the power of Indra is Indrāni; the power of Brahmā is Brahmāni.

[12] Brahman is often explained in the Upanishads from the point of view of the individual self, and also from the point of view of the gods. From the first point of view, Brahman is the true experiencer in every being. From the second, It is the World Soul, known as Virāt, who, according to Vedāntic mystics, is conceived of as dwelling in the solar orb, being the effulgent Lord of all the gods, who are parts of It.

It is like a flash of lightning;[13] It is like a wink of the eye.[14] (IV. 4)

Now the instruction about Brahman with regard to the individual self: The mind, as it were, goes to Brahman.[15] The seeker, by means of the mind, communes with It intimately again and again. This should be the volition of his mind. (IV. 5)

That Brahman is called Tadvana,[16] the Adorable of all; It should be worshipped by the name of Tadvana. All creatures desire him who worships Brahman thus. (IV. 6)

The disciple said: 'Teach me, sir, the Upanishad.'[17]
The preceptor replied: 'I have already told you the Upanishad. I have certainly told you the Upanishad about Brahman.' (IV. 7)

Austerities, self-restraint, and sacrificial rites are Its feet,[18] and the Vedas[19] are all Its limbs. Truth is Its abode. (IV. 8)

He who thus knows this Upanishad shakes off all sins and becomes firmly established in the infinite and the highest Heaven,[20] yea, the highest Heaven. (IV. 9)

---

[13] The brilliance of lightning illumines the universe all at once. Brahman, likewise, is endowed with indescribable radiance.

[14] It takes no more time than a wink of the eye for Brahman to create, maintain, and destroy the universe.

[15] While meditating on Brahman, the aspirant should think that his mind has attained to the luminous Brahman and is established in It.

[16] One of the mystical epithets which the Vedic seers used in worshipping Brahman.

[17] The word denotes here the secret and profound wisdom regarding Brahman, which one can obtain only from a qualified preceptor.

[18] The virtues mentioned in this verse are the means for the attainment of the Knowledge of Brahman.

[19] That is to say, the four Vedas and their six auxiliary members. The latter comprise the science of proper articulation and pronunciation (śikshā), the science of prosody (chhandas), grammar (vyākaranam), etymological explanation of difficult Vedic words (nirukta), astronomy (jyotis), and ritual (kalpa). They help in the correct pronunciation and interpretation of the text and the right use of the mantras in the rituals; therefore they are called the limbs, or protectors, of the Vedic wisdom.

[20] This word, according to Śankarāchārya, denotes Brahman, or the Absolute, and not any celestial abode. He mentions as his reason the two qualifying words *infinite* and *highest*.

THE PEACE CHANT

OM. MAY BRAHMAN protect us both (the preceptor and the disciple)! May Brahman bestow upon us both the fruit of Knowledge! May we both obtain the energy to acquire Knowledge! May what we both study reveal the Truth! May we cherish no ill feeling toward each other!

Om. Peace! Peace! Peace!

Om. May the different parts of my body, my tongue, prāna, eyes, ears, and my strength, and also all the other sense-organs be nourished! All, indeed, is Brahman, as is declared in the Upanishads. May I never deny Brahman! May Brahman never deny me! May there never be denial on the part of Brahman! May there never be denial on my part! May all the virtues described in the Upanishads belong to me, who am devoted to Brahman! Yea, may they all belong to me!

Om. Peace! Peace! Peace!

MUNDAKA UPANISHAD

INTRODUCTION

THE *MUNDAKA UPANISHAD* belongs to the Atharva-Veda. It is called a Mantra Upanishad because it is written in verse. But it is not, like the Mantra section of the Vedas, intended to be used in the sacrifices or rituals. The *Mundaka Upanishad* teaches the Knowledge of Brahman.

The word *mundaka* is derived from a root that signifies shaving. The instruction given in this Upanishad has the sharpness of a razor; it cuts off a man's error and ignorance, like a razor. The name also suggests that this Upanishad is meant only for the shaven-headed sannyāsins, who renounce all the actions prescribed for householders and devote themselves to the cultivation of Brahmavidyā, or the Knowledge of Brahman.[1]

The *Mundaka Upanishad* and the *Praśna Upanishad*, both belonging to the Atharva-Veda, are said to be complementary. The topics that are briefly stated in the one are elaborated in the other. The importance of the *Mundaka Upanishad* can be recognized from the fact that this is the only Upanishad of the Atharva-Veda which contains a verse (I. i. 6) directly used by Bādarāyana Vyāsa in constructing an aphorism (I. ii. 11) of the *Vedānta Sutras*, the most authoritative book on the Vedānta philosophy. Like some other Upanishads, the *Mundaka Upanishad* gives its instruction in the form of a dialogue between a disciple and his preceptor.

---

[1] 'Although people belonging to all stages of life (āśramas) are equally entitled to the Knowledge of Brahman, yet knowledge culminating in complete renunciation (sannyāsa) becomes the means to Liberation (Moksha), and not knowledge combined with action. This is shown by such passages as: "Who live in the forests on alms" (I. ii. 11) and "Having purified their minds through the practice of sannyāsa" (III. ii. 6). The Knowledge of Brahman is incompatible with action. One who has realized the identity of Ātman and Brahman cannot perform action even in a dream. Knowledge is independent of the time factor; it is not the effect of any definite cause. Therefore it is not reasonable to consider the Knowledge of Brahman to be conditioned by time. If it be suggested that Knowledge and action are compatible, as *indicated* by the fact that the teachers among the householders handed down the Knowledge of Brahman to their disciples, it may be replied that this mere *indication* cannot override a well established truth. The co-existence of darkness and light cannot be made possible even by a hundred rules—much less by mere indications.' (*From the introduction by Śankarāchārya.*)

INVOCATION

OM. MAY WE, O gods, hear with our ears what is auspicious!
May we, O worshipful gods, see with our eyes what is good!
May we, strong in limbs and body, sing your praise and enjoy
the life allotted to us by Prajāpati!
Om. Peace! Peace! Peace!

I

OM. BRAHMĀ, THE Maker of the universe and the Preserver of the world, was the first among the devas. He told His eldest son Atharva about the Knowledge of Brahman, the foundation of all knowledge. (I. i. 1)

The Knowledge of Brahman about which Brahmā told Atharva, Atharva in olden times told Angir. Angir taught it to Satyavaha, belonging to the clan of Bharadvāja, and the latter taught it, in succession, to Angiras. (I. i. 2)

Śaunaka, the great householder, approached Angiras in the proper manner and said: Revered sir, what is that by the knowing of which all this[2] becomes known? (I. i. 3)

To him he said: Two kinds of knowledge must be known—that is what the knowers of Brahman tell us. They are the Higher Knowledge[3] and the lower knowledge.[4] (I. i. 4)

Of these two, the lower knowledge is the Rig-Veda, the Yajur-Veda, the Sāma-Veda, the Atharva-Veda, śikshā (phonetics), kalpa (rituals), vyākaranam (grammar), nirukta (etymology), chhandas (metre), and jyotis (astronomy); and the Higher Knowledge is that by which the Imperishable Brahman is attained. (I. i. 5)

By means of the Higher Knowledge the wise behold everywhere Brahman, which otherwise cannot be seen or seized, which has no root or attributes, no eyes or ears, no hands or feet; which is eternal and omnipresent, all-pervading and extremely subtle; which is imperishable and the source of all beings. (I. i. 6)

As the spider sends forth and draws in its thread, as plants grow on the earth, as hair grows on the head and the body of a living man—so does everything in the universe arise from the Imperishable. (I. i. 7)

Brahman expands by means of austerity,[5] and from It primal matter is produced; from matter, Prāna; from Prāna, mind; from mind, the

[2] All the sense-perceived objects of the world.
[3] The Knowledge of the Supreme Self, which is beyond duality.
[4] The knowledge of righteous actions (dharma) and unrighteous actions (adharma) and their results; that is to say, the knowledge of the phenomenal world.
[5] The word *tapas* in the text also denotes the intense thinking which precedes any creative act. Here the word means knowledge regarding the future creation. When there arises in Brahman the desire for creation, forthwith It becomes en-

elements; from the elements, the worlds; thence works,[6] and from the works, their immortal fruits. (I. i. 8)

From him who knows all and understands everything, whose austerity consists of knowledge—from Him, the Imperishable Brahman, are born Brahmā, name, form,[7] and food. (I. i. 9)

This is the truth: The sacrificial works which were revealed to the rishis in the hymns have been described in many ways in the three Vedas. Practise them, being desirous to attain their true results. This is your path leading to the fruits of your works.[8] (I. ii. 1)

When the fire is well lighted and the flames flicker, let a man offer his oblations in the space between the two portions of melted butter. (I. ii. 2)

Kāli,[9] Karāli,[10] Manojavā,[11] Sulohitā,[12] Sudhumravarnā,[13] Sphu-lingini,[14] and the luminous Viśvaruchi[15]—these seven, flickering about, form the seven tongues of the fire. (I. ii. 4)

A man who performs the sacrifices when these flames are shining, and offers oblations at the right time, is carried by these oblations on the rays of the sun to where dwells the sole sovereign of the gods. (I. ii. 5)

The luminous oblations say to the sacrificer: 'Come hither! Come hither!' and lead him on the rays of the sun, worshipping him all the while and greeting him with the pleasant words: 'This is the holy heaven of Brahmā, earned by your good deeds.' (I. ii. 6)

dowed with omniscience, that is to say, with the knowledge and capacity of creating, preserving, and destroying the universe. Thus Brahman appears to increase in size, like a seed before it splits and the sprout comes out; or like a father dilating with joy before begetting a son. In this stage the attributeless Absolute becomes known as Saguna Brahman.

[6] Work (karma) creates desire, and the desire again impels one to action. Thus in the relative universe the stream of work never comes to an end.

[7] Name and form stand for the modern term *individuality*.

[8] The second chapter begins with a description of the lower knowledge, dealing with sacrifices and other meritorious deeds. It will be shown that their results are ephemeral. Only when a man understands this does he desire to cultivate the Higher Knowledge, which leads to Liberation.

[9] Lit., black.

[10] Terrific.

[11] Swift as thought.

[12] Very red.

[13] Of the colour of bright smoke; purple.

[14] Scintillating.

[15] All-gleaming, all-formed.

But frail indeed are those rafts of sacrifices, conducted by eighteen persons,[16] upon whom rests the inferior work;[17] therefore they are destructible.[18] Fools who rejoice in them as the Highest Good fall victims again and again to old age and death. (I. ii. 7)

Fools, dwelling in darkness, but wise in their own conceit and puffed up with vain scholarship, wander about, being afflicted by many ills, like blind men led by the blind. (I. ii. 8)

Children, immersed in ignorance in various ways, flatter themselves, saying: We have accomplished life's purpose. Because these performers of karma do not know the Truth owing to their attachment, they fall from heaven, misery-stricken, when the fruit of their work is exhausted. (I. ii. 9)

Ignorant fools, regarding sacrifices and humanitarian works as the highest, do not know any higher good. Having enjoyed their reward on the heights of heaven, gained by good works, they enter again this world or a lower one. (I. ii. 10)

But those wise men[19] of tranquil minds who live in the forest on alms, practising penances appropriate to their stations of life and contemplating such deities as Hiranyagarbha, depart, freed from impurities, by the Path of the Sun,[20] to the place[21] where that immortal Person dwells whose nature is imperishable.[22]   (I. ii. 11)

Let a brāhmin, after having examined all these worlds that are gained by works, acquire freedom from desires: nothing that is eternal can be produced by what is not eternal. In order that he may understand that

[16] Sixteen priests, the sacrificer, and his wife.

[17] Refers to the sacrifices performed without knowledge of, or meditation on, the deities.

[18] It is because the eighteen persons who conduct the sacrifice are themselves liable to destruction. 'As curds or milk kept in a pot are destroyed when the pot is destroyed, so also the results of the sacrifices come to an end because the eighteen persons who perform them are mortal.' (*Śankarāchārya.*)

[19] The text refers to the worshippers of Saguna Brahman: pious householders and those who, having retired from the world after the completion of the householder's life, go to the forest to lead the life of contemplation.

[20] Known as the Devayāna, or Way of the Gods.

[21] That is to say, Brahmaloka.

[22] This verse describes what is known as kramamukti, gradual liberation. Those who worship Saguna Brahman with whole-souled devotion do not return to earth or go to any other lower plane. They dwell in Brahmaloka, absorbed in contemplation of Hiranyagarbha, and attain final Liberation at the end of the cycle, when Hiranyagarbha Himself merges in the Absolute.

Eternal, let him, fuel in hand,[23] approach a guru who is well versed in the Vedas and always devoted to Brahman. (I. ii. 12)

To that pupil who has duly approached him, whose mind is completely serene, and whose senses are controlled, the wise teacher should indeed rightly impart the Knowledge of Brahman,[24] through which one knows the immutable and the true Purusha. (I. ii. 13)

---

[23] The pupil approaches the teacher, carrying fuel for the sacrificial fire; this indicates his humility and desire for service.

[24] 'The duty of the preceptor is to help the qualified pupil who has duly approached him to cross the great ocean of ignorance.' (*Śankarāchārya*.)

II

THIS IS THE Truth:[25] As, from a blazing fire, sparks essentially akin to it fly forth by the thousand, so also, my good friend, do various beings come forth from the imperishable Brahman and unto Him again return. (II. i. 1)

He is the self-luminous and formless Purusha, uncreated and existing both within and without. He is devoid of prāna, devoid of mind, pure, and higher than the supreme Imperishable.[26] (II. i. 2)

Of Him are born prāna, mind, all the sense-organs, ākāśa, air, fire, water, and earth, which supports all. (II. i. 3)

The heavens are His head; the sun and moon, His eyes; the quarters, His ears; the revealed Vedas, His speech; the wind is His breath; the universe, His heart. From His feet is produced the earth. He is, indeed, the inner Self of all beings. (II. i. 4)

From Him comes the Fire (i.e. the heavens) whose fuel is the sun; from the moon comes rain; from rain, the herbs that grow on the earth; from the herbs, the seminal fluid which a man pours into a woman. Thus many living beings are born of the Purusha.[27] (II. i. 5)

From Him have come the Rik, the Sāman, the Yajus, the Dikshā, all sacrifices, the Kratus, gifts, the year, the sacrificer, and the worlds which the moon sanctifies and the sun illumines. (II. i. 6)

By Him are begotten the various devas, the sādhyas, men, cattle, birds, and also prāna and apāna, rice and corn, penance, faith, truth, continence, and law. (II. i. 7)

From Him come all the oceans and the mountains; from Him flow rivers of every kind; from Him have come, as well, all plants and flavours, by which the inner self[28] subsists surrounded by the elements. (II. i. 9)

The Purusha alone is verily the universe, which consists of work and austerity.[29] O my good friend, he who knows this Brahman—the

[25] The truth here referred to is the ultimate Truth, in contrast to the truth mentioned in I. ii. 1.

[26] That is to say, Saguna Brahman.

[27] This verse refers to the Five Fires described in *Chh. Up.* V. 4–8.

[28] Refers to the subtle body.

[29] *Work* signifies sacrifices and their results; *austerity*, knowledge and its result.

Supreme and the Immortal, hidden in the cave of the heart—cuts asunder even here the knot of ignorance. (II. i. 10)

The radiant Brahman dwells in the cave of the heart and is known to move there. It is the great support of all; for in It is centred everything that moves, breathes, and blinks. O disciples, know that to be your Self—that which is both gross and subtle, which is adorable, supreme, and beyond the understanding of creatures. (II. ii. 1)

That which is radiant, subtler than the subtle, That by which all the worlds and their inhabitants are supported—That, verily, is the indestructible Brahman; That is the prāna, speech, and the mind; That is the True and That is the Immortal. That alone is to be struck.[30] Strike It, my good friend. (II. ii. 2)

Take the Upanishad as the bow, the great weapon, and place upon it the arrow sharpened by meditation. Then, having drawn it back with a mind directed to the thought of Brahman, strike that mark, O my good friend—that which is the Imperishable. (II. ii. 3)

Om is the bow; the ātman is the arrow; Brahman is said to be the mark. It is to be struck by an undistracted mind. Then the ātman becomes one with Brahman, as the arrow with the target. (II. ii. 4)

In Him are woven heaven, earth, and the space between, and the mind with all the sense-organs. Know that non-dual Ātman alone and give up all other talk. He is the bridge to Immortality. (II. ii. 5)

He moves about, becoming manifold,[31] within the heart, where the arteries meet, like the spokes fastened in the nave of a chariot wheel. Meditate on Ātman as Om. Hail to you! May you cross beyond the sea of darkness! (II. ii. 7)

He who knows all and understands all, and to whom belongs all the glory in the world—He, Ātman, is placed in the space in the effulgent abode of Brahman. He assumes the forms of the mind and leads the body and the senses.[32] He dwells in the body, inside the heart. By the knowledge of That which shines as the blissful and immortal Ātman, the wise behold Him fully in all things.

---

[30] That is to say, to be known or penetrated by the mind.
[31] The individual self reflected in the mind identifies itself with pleasure, pain, anger, love, and other states of mind.
[32] He leads the subtle body, after death, to the future gross body.

The fetters of the heart are broken, all doubts are resolved, and all works cease to bear fruit, when He is beheld who is both high and low. (II. ii. 8)

There the stainless and indivisible Brahman shines in the highest, golden sheath.[33] It is pure; It is the Light of lights; It is That which they know who know the Self. (II. ii. 9)

The sun does not shine there, nor the moon and the stars, nor these lightnings, not to speak of this fire. When He shines, everything shines after Him; by His light everything is lighted. (II. ii. 10)

That immortal Brahman alone is before, that Brahman is behind, that Brahman is to the right and left. Brahman alone pervades everything above and below; this universe is that Supreme Brahman alone. (II. ii. 11)

[33] The sheath referred to here is the buddhi, or intellect. Brahman is most vividly manifest in the buddhi, which is described as golden because it is endowed with reason and knowledge and is therefore superior to the other organs.

III

TWO BIRDS,[34] UNITED always[35] and known by the same name,[36] closely cling to the same tree.[37] One of them eats the sweet fruit; the other looks on without eating. (III. i. 1)

Seated on the same tree, the jiva moans,[38] bewildered by his impotence. But when he beholds the other, the Lord worshipped by all, and His glory, he then becomes free from grief. (III. i. 2)

When the seer beholds the self-luminous Creator, the Lord, the Purusha, the progenitor of Brahmā, then he, the wise seer, shakes off good and evil, becomes stainless, and reaches the supreme unity. (III. i. 3)

He indeed is Prāna; He shines forth variously in all beings. The wise man who knows Him does not babble. Revelling in the Self, delighting in the Self, performing actions,[39] he is the foremost among the knowers of Brahman. (III. i. 4)

This Ātman, resplendent and pure, whom the sinless sannyāsins behold residing within the body, is attained by unceasing practice of truthfulness, austerity, right knowledge, and continence. (III. i. 5)

Truth alone triumphs, not falsehood. By truth the path is laid out, the Way of the Gods, on which the seers, whose every desire is satisfied, proceed to the Highest Abode of the True. (III. i. 6)

That Brahman shines forth, vast, self-luminous, inconceivable, subtler than the subtle. He is far beyond what is far, and yet here very near at hand. Verily, He is seen here, dwelling in the cave of the heart of conscious beings. (III. i. 7)

Brahman is not grasped by the eye, nor by speech, nor by the other senses, nor by penance or good works. A man becomes pure through

---

[34] The two birds signify the individual soul and the Supreme Self.
[35] The two are inseparable companions, like an object and its reflection.
[36] That is to say, Ātman.
[37] Refers to the body.
[38] The grief of the jiva is the result of his identification with the body.
[39] Such as meditation and teaching. The word does not refer to any rite or ceremony of worship. The knower of Brahman is not by any means lazy or inert.

serenity of intellect;[40] thereupon, in meditation, he beholds Him who is without parts. (III. i. 8)

That subtle Ātman is to be known by the intellect here in the body where the prāna has entered fivefold.[41] By Ātman the intellects of men are pervaded, together with the senses. When the intellect is purified, Ātman shines forth. (III. i. 9)

Whatever world a man of pure understanding envisages in his mind and whatever desires he cherishes, that world he conquers and those desires he obtains. Therefore let everyone who wants prosperity worship the man who knows the Self. (III. i. 10)

He, the knower of the Self, knows that Supreme Abode of Brahman, which shines brightly and in which the universe rests. Those wise men who, free from desires, worship such a person transcend the seed of birth. (III. ii. 1)

He who, cherishing objects, desires them, is born again here or there through his desires. But for him whose desires are satisfied and who is established in the Self, all desires vanish even here on earth. (III. ii. 2)

This Ātman cannot be attained through study of the Vedas, nor through intelligence, nor through much learning.[42] He who chooses Ātman—by him alone is Ātman attained. It is Ātman that reveals to the seeker Its true nature. (III. ii. 3)

This Ātman cannot be attained by one who is without strength or earnestness or who is without knowledge accompanied by renunciation. But if a wise man strives by means of these aids, his soul enters the Abode of Brahman. (III. ii. 4)

Having realized Ātman, the seers become satisfied with that Knowledge. Their souls are established in the Supreme Self, they are free from passions, and they are tranquil in mind. Such calm souls, ever

---

[40] 'The buddhi of every man is by nature pure, like a clean mirror or water, and therefore capable of Self-Knowledge. But, being polluted by attachment to external objects, it becomes unclean, like a stained mirror or like muddy water. That is why the buddhi does not know Ātman, which is the inmost Self of all. But when the taint caused by attachment and desire is removed, then the buddhi becomes clear and serene, like a clean mirror and clear water. Through the pure intellect one realizes Ātman.' (*Adapted from Śankarāchārya's commentary.*)

[41] The reference is to the five divisions of the prāna.

[42] See *Ka. Up.* I. ii. 23, p. 74.

devoted to the Self, behold everywhere the omnipresent Brahman and in the end enter into It, which is all this. (III. ii. 5)

Having well ascertained the Self, the goal of the Vedāntic knowledge, and having purified their minds through the practice of sannyāsa, the seers, never relaxing their efforts, enjoy here supreme Immortality[43] and at the time of the great end attain complete freedom in Brahman. (III. ii. 6)

As flowing rivers disappear in the sea, losing their names and forms, so a wise man, freed from name and form, attains the Purusha, who is greater than the Great.[44] (III. ii. 8)

He who knows the Supreme Brahman verily becomes Brahman. In his family no one is born ignorant of Brahman. He overcomes grief; he overcomes evil; free from the fetters of the heart, he becomes immortal. (III. ii. 9)

A Rik-verse declares: This Knowledge of Brahman should be told to those only who have performed the necessary duties, who are versed in the Vedas and devoted to Brahman, and who, full of faith, have offered oblations in the Ekarshi Fire and performed, according to rule, the rite of carrying fire on the head.[45] (III. ii. 10)

Thus the seer Angiras declared this truth in olden times. A man who has not performed the vow should not read it. Salutation to the great seers! Salutation to the great seers! (III. ii. 11)

---

[43] This experience is called jivanmukti, or Liberation in life.

[44] The word *Great* refers to Saguna Brahman.

[45] The text mentions the sacrifice known as the Ekarshi and the penance of the Śirovrata, in which one is required to carry fire on one's head. This penance (Śirovrata) is described in the Atharva-Veda. By means of the sacrifice and the penance the aspirant acquires concentration of mind and purity of heart.

THE PEACE CHANT

**OM. MAY WE, O gods, hear with our ears what is auspicious!
May we, O worshipful gods, see with our eyes what is good!
May we, strong in limbs and body, sing your praise and enjoy
the life allotted to us by Prajāpati!**

Om. Peace! Peace! Peace!

ŚVETĀŚVATARA UPANISHAD

INTRODUCTION

THE *ŚVETĀŚVATARA UPANISHAD*, which belongs to the Taittiriya or Black Yajur-Veda, may be regarded as one of the authoritative Upanishads. Its verses are quoted profusely in all Vedāntic treatises. The name seems to have been derived from the sage Śvetāśvatara, who, as we read at the end of the last chapter, imparted the Upanishad to a company of world-renouncing hermits.

That the *Śvetāśvatara* ranks high among the Upanishads may be inferred from the fact that the non-dualist Śankarāchārya, the qualified non-dualist Rāmānujāchārya, and the teachers of many other schools of Hindu philosophy have quoted from it to support their respective views. The Upanishad contains passages which can be interpreted to support dualism, qualified non-dualism, non-dualism, and even other systems of thought. Certain verses can be related to the Sāmkhya philosophy of Kapila.

It is apparent that the *Śvetāśvatara Upanishad*, unlike most of the major Upanishads, contains a strong theistic strain. Names like Hara (I. 10), Rudra (III. 2, 4; IV. 12, 21, 22), Śiva (III. 11; IV. 14), Bhagavān (III. 11), Agni, Āditya, Vāyu (IV. 2), etc., which appear in the *Śvetāśvatara Upanishad*, are generally used as epithets of the Personal God. Devotion, or bhakti, moreover, is mentioned as a means of realizing the Supreme Spirit, though the word *bhakti* actually occurs only once, and that in the very last verse. The word *deva* is used frequently. All this, according to Rāmānuja and other theistic interpreters, establishes the Personal God as Ultimate Reality. But Śankarāchārya adroitly gives these words a non-dualistic meaning and emphasizes that the goal of this, as of the other major Upanishads, is to prove the sole reality of the non-dual Brahman.

Even if a theistic interpretation be given to certain passages in the Upanishad, this need not invalidate its non-dualistic aim. Theism can be accepted as a step toward non-dualism. Non-dualists do not deny the Personal God. He is the highest manifestation of Brahman in the phenomenal universe. He is the Creator, Preserver, and Destroyer of the universe. But the whole creation is māyā, a 'power belonging to the Lord Himself and hidden in its own gunas.' (*Śvet. Up.* I. 3) Non-dualists also speak of bhakti, or love of God, as one of the chief disciplines for the attainment of the non-dual Brahman. The worship of the Personal God with devotion purifies the mind and helps in the cultivation of concentration. Śankarāchārya has written many devotional hymns to the Personal God.

The Sāmkhya philosophers quote the fifth verse of the fourth chapter of the *Śvetāśvatara Upanishad* to show its relationship with the Sāmkhya philosophy. According to them, the red, white, and black colours mentioned in this verse refer to the three gunas: rajas, sattva, and tamas, whereas the word *aja*, meaning 'unborn', signifies prakriti. But Śankarāchārya gives a different interpretation.

The second chapter of the Upanishad gives suggestions for the practice of concentration and other disciplines of yoga, which have been accepted, in some form or other, by all the systems of Hindu philosophy. A careful study of the entire *Śvetāśvatara Upanishad* will show that, like the other principal Upanishads, it affirms the non-dual Brahman as Ultimate Reality.

INVOCATION

OM. THAT IS full; this is full. This fullness has been projected from that fullness. When this fullness merges in that
fullness, all that remains is fullness.
Om. Peace! Peace! Peace!

Om. May Brahman protect us both! May Brahman bestow
upon us both the fruit of Knowledge! May we both obtain the
energy to acquire Knowledge! May what we both study reveal
the Truth! May we cherish no ill feeling toward each other!
Om. Peace! Peace! Peace!

RISHIS, DISCOURSING ON Brahman, ask: Is Brahman the cause? Whence are we born? By what do we live? Where do we dwell at the end (after death)? Please tell us, O ye who know Brahman, under whose guidance we abide, whether in pleasure or in pain. (I. 1)

Should time, or nature,[1] or necessity,[2] or chance, or the elements be regarded as the cause? Or he who is called the purusha,[3] the living self? The cause cannot be the combination of these entities, since there is a living self, ātman, for whose sake the combination has been made; yet neither is the ātman the cause, for it, in turn, is dependent upon good and evil. (I. 2)

The sages, absorbed in meditation through one-pointedness of mind,[4] discovered the [creative] power (i.e. māyā) belonging to the Lord Himself and hidden in its own gunas. That non-dual Lord rules over all those causes—time, the self, and the rest. (I. 3)

The sages saw the Wheel of Brahman,[5] which has one felly,[6] a triple tire,[7] sixteen end-parts,[8] fifty spokes[9] with twenty counter-spokes,[10]

[1] The inalienable characteristic of an entity; for instance, the heat of fire.

[2] The law of cause and effect, which unfailingly determines good and evil.

[3] The individual living self, associated with body, senses, mind, and ego.

[4] It is not possible to discover the final cause of the universe by means of reason based upon sense experience. Therefore the seers pursued the path of yoga, and came to the conclusion that the Supreme Lord evolved the world with the help of His own māyā.

[5] Refers to the universe, which is non-different from the Creator, who, again, is essentially the same as Brahman.

[6] The outer circumference of a wheel, which is its support. With regard to the universe, the word signifies the power of māyā in its causal aspect. At the time of the cosmic dissolution, names and forms return to the seed state; this is called the causal state of māyā.

[7] That is to say, three bonds or hoops, which form the tire. These are the three gunas: sattva, rajas, and tamas.

[8] Refers to the five elements, the five organs of perception, the five organs of action, and the mind. Or they may refer to the sixteen parts (kalās) mentioned in *Pr. Up.* VI. 1. These sixteen parts form the utmost extent of the universe.

[9] Which support the motion of the wheel of the universe. They are as follows: the five misconceptions, or different kinds of ignorance or doubt, described by Patanjali as ignorance, self-love, attachment, hatred, and clinging to life (*Yog. Su.* II. 3); the twenty-eight disabilities, or aśaktis, which are causes of misconception (*Sām. Su.* III. 38); the nine inversions of satisfactions, or tustis (*Sām. Su.* III. 39); the eight inversions of perfections, or siddhis (*Sām. Su.* III. 40). Detailed descriptions of these terms will be found in *Sām. Su.* III. 37–45; *Sām. Kā.* 47 ff; *Yog. Su.* II. 3 ff.

[10] Refers to the ten organs (of perception and action) and their ten corresponding objects. They are the wedges to strengthen the spokes.

and six sets of eight;[11] whose one rope[12] is manifold; which moves on three different roads;[13] and whose illusion arises from two causes.[14] (I. 4)

We meditate on the River[15] whose five currents are the five organs of perception, which is made impetuous and winding by the five elements, whose waves are the five organs of action, and whose fountain-head is the mind,[16] the source of the five forms of perception. This River has five whirlpools[17] and its rapids are the fivefold misery;[18] and lastly, it has fifty branches[19] and five pain-bearing obstructions.[20] (I. 5)

In this great Brahma-Wheel, in which all things abide and finally rest, the swan (jiva) wanders about so long as it thinks the self is different from the Controller. When blessed by Him the self attains Immortality. (I. 6)

It is the Supreme Brahman alone [untouched by phenomena] that is proclaimed [in the Upanishads]. In It is established the triad [of the enjoyer, the object, and the Lord who is the Controller]. This Brahman is the immutable foundation; It is imperishable. The sages, having realized Brahman to be the essence of phenomena, become

[11] These octads are explained as the octad of prakriti (namely, ākāśa, air, fire, water, and earth, mind, buddhi, and I-consciousness); that of the dhatu, or bodily substance (skin, cuticle, flesh, blood, fat, bone, marrow, and semen); the eight supernatural powers, endowed with which a man can be small as an atom, huge as a mountain, light as air, all-pervasive can reach any object, rule everything he wants, conquer everything, and fulfil all desires; the octad of the bhavas, or states (righteousness, or dharma, knowledge, or jnāna, renunciation, majesty, unrighteousness, ignorance, non-renunciation, and poverty); the octad of gods and incorporeal beings (Brahmā, Prajāpati, deities, gandharvas, yakshas, rākshasas, pitris, fiends); and the octad of virtues (compassion, forgiveness, absence of malice, purity, absence of effort, goodness, liberality, and absence of longing).

[12] The rope of love, which manifests itself as love for children, food, and the heavenly world.

[13] These are the roads of righteousness, unrighteousness, and knowledge.

[14] This deception arises from two causes: virtuous action and sinful. On account of it one regards the body, or non-Self, as the Self.

[15] The Causal Brahman, or Iśvara, appearing, in association with māyā, as the phenomenal universe, is also described as a river.

[16] The whole universe, consisting of animate and inanimate objects, is but the states of the mind; when the mind stops functioning the multiple universe is not perceived.

[17] The objects of the five senses.

[18] This consists in resting in the womb, being born, growing old, becoming ill, and dying.

[19] The fifty branches mentioned in the text are not clear. They are not adequately explained by the commentators.

[20] The five pain-bearing obstructions are ignorance, egoism, attachment, aversion, and clinging to life. (See Yog. Su. II. 3.)

devoted to It. Completely merged in Brahman, they attain freedom from rebirth. (I. 7)

The Lord, Iśa,[21] supports all this which has been joined together— the perishable and the imperishable, the manifest (the effect) and the unmanifest (the cause). The same Lord (the Supreme Self), devoid of Lordship [i.e. as the jiva], becomes bound because of assuming the attitude of the enjoyer. The jiva again realizes the Supreme Self and is freed from all fetters. (I. 8)

The Supreme Lord appears as Iśvara, omniscient and omnipotent, and as the jiva, of limited knowledge and power, both unborn.[22] [But this does not deny the phenomenal universe;] for there exists further the unborn prakriti, which creates [the ideas of] the enjoyer, enjoyment, and the object. Ātman is infinite and all-pervading, and therefore devoid of agency. When the seeker knows all these three to be Brahman, he is freed from his fetters. (I. 9)

Prakriti is perishable. Hara,[23] the Lord, is immortal and imperishable. The non-dual Supreme Self rules both prakriti and the individual soul. Through constant meditation on Him, by union with Him, by the knowledge of identity with Him, one attains, in the end, cessation of the illusion of phenomena. (I. 10)

When the Lord is known all fetters fall off; with the cessation of miseries, birth and death come to an end. From meditation on Him there arises, after the dissolution of the body, the third state,[24] that of universal lordship. And lastly, the aspirant, transcending that state also, abides in the complete Bliss of Brahman. (I. 11)

The enjoyer (jiva), the objects of enjoyment, and the Ruler (Iśvara)— the triad described by the knowers of Brahman—all this is nothing but Brahman. This Brahman alone, which abides eternally within the self, should be known. Beyond It, truly, there is nothing else to be known. (I. 12)

The [visible] form of fire, while it lies latent in its source [the firewood], is not perceived; yet there is no destruction of its subtle form.

[21] Brahman, or Pure Consciousness.
[22] Both Iśvara and the jiva are, in reality, Brahman; therefore they are called unborn.
[23] Lit., the Destroyer of ignorance. The word also signifies Śiva, or Rudra, one of the divine manifestations of Brahman in the phenomenal world. In this verse the word stands for the Supreme Lord.
[24] The first state represents the destruction of bondage; the second, the cessation of miseries; and the third, the attainment of supernatural powers in the highest heaven, or Brahmaloka.

That very fire can be brought out again by means of [persistent] rubbing of the wood, its source. In like manner, Ātman, which exists in two states,[25] like fire, can be grasped in this very body by means of Om. (I. 13)

By making the body the lower piece of wood, and Om the upper piece, and through the practice of the friction of meditation, one perceives the luminous Self, hidden like the fire in the wood. (I. 14)

As oil [exists] in sesame seeds, butter in milk, water in river-beds, and fire in wood, so the Self is realized [as existing] within the self, when a man looks for It by means of truthfulness and austerity—when he looks for the Self, which pervades all things as butter [pervades] milk, and whose roots are Self-Knowledge and austerity. That is the Brahman taught by the Upanishad; yea, that is the Brahman taught by the Upanishad. (I. 15–16)

May the Sun,[26] at the commencement of yoga, join our minds and other organs to the Supreme Self so that we may attain the Knowledge of Reality. May He, also, support the body, the highest material entity, through the powers of the deities who control the senses.[27] (II. 1)

Having received the blessings of the divine Sun, and with minds joined to the Supreme Self, we exert ourselves, to the best of our power, toward meditation, by which we shall attain Heaven (Brahman). (II. 2)

May the Sun bestow favour upon the senses and the mind by joining them with the Self, so that the senses may be directed toward the Blissful Brahman and may reveal, by means of Knowledge, the mighty and radiant Brahman. (II. 3)

It is the duty of those brāhmins who fix their minds and senses on the Supreme Self to utter such lofty invocations to the divine Sun, omnipresent, mighty, and omniscient. For He, all-witnessing and non-dual, is the dispenser of sacrifices. (II. 4)

[25] Namely, manifested and unmanifested.

[26] In the Vedas the sun is described as the chief symbol of Brahman. The Gāyatri prayer is directed to the Purusha dwelling in the sun.

[27] 'May the Sun take our thoughts away from external things in order to concentrate them on the Supreme Self, and transmit to our organ of speech and other organs that power which lightens all objects and which inheres in Agni (Fire) and the other deities who control the various organs. Through the grace of the Sun we shall attain success in yoga.' (*From the commentary of Śankarāchārya.*)

O senses, and O deities who favour them! Through salutations I unite myself with the eternal Brahman, who is your source. Let this prayer sung by me, who follow the right path of the Sun, go forth in all directions. May the sons of the Immortal,[28] who occupy celestial positions, hear it! (II. 5)

[If sacrifices are performed without first propitiating the Sun,] then the mind becomes attached to sacrifices in which fire is kindled by the rubbing [of the pieces of fire-wood], the oblations are offered to the deity Vāyu, and the soma juice is drunk excessively.[29]

Serve the eternal Brahman with the blessings of the Sun, the cause of the universe. Be absorbed, through samādhi, in the eternal Brahman. Thus your work will not bind you. (II. 7)

The wise man should hold his body steady, with the three [upper] parts[30] erect, turn his senses, with the help of the mind, toward the heart, and by means of the raft of Brahman[31] cross the fearful torrents of the world.[32] (II. 8)

The yogi of well regulated endeavours should control the prānas;[33] when they are quieted he should breathe out through the nostrils. Then let him undistractedly restrain his mind, as a charioteer restrains his vicious horses. (II. 9)

Let yoga be practised within a cave protected from the high wind, or in a place which is level, pure, and free from pebbles, gravel, and fire, undisturbed by the noise of water or of market-booths, and which is delightful to the mind and not offensive to the eye. (II. 10)

When yoga is practised, the forms which appear first and which gradually manifest Brahman are those of snow-flakes, smoke, sun, wind, fire, fire-flies, lightning, crystal, and the moon. (II. 11)

[28] Refers to Hiranyagarbha.
[29] Which has an intoxicating effect. Those participating in such sacrifices may forget their real significance and indulge in excessive drinking.
[30] The chest, neck, and head.
[31] The word *Brahman* here signifies Om. Repetition of the word and meditation on its meaning are prescribed.
[32] The teachers of the Upanishads recommend the disciplines of Patanjali's yoga for the attainment of samādhi, in which the Knowledge of Brahman is directly realized.
[33] 'First close your right nostril with a finger and breathe in through the left nostril as much as possible. Then breathe out by the right nostril, closing the left nostril. Next breathe in again by the right nostril and breathe out by the left. This process should be repeated three or five times.' (*Śankarāchārya.*) Afterwards the yogi should practise prānāyāma, which consists in the inhalation, exhalation, and retention of the breath, under the guidance of a qualified teacher.

When earth, water, fire, air, and ākāśa arise, that is to say, when the five attributes of the elements,[34] mentioned in the books on yoga, become manifest, then the yogi's body becomes purified by the fire of yoga and he is free from illness, old age, and death. (II. 12)

The precursors of perfection in yoga, they say, are lightness and healthiness of the body, absence of desire, clear complexion, pleasantness of voice, sweet odour, and slight excretions. (II. 13)

As gold covered by earth shines bright after it has been purified, so also the yogi, realizing the truth of Ātman, becomes one [with the non-dual Ātman], attains the goal, and is free from grief. (II. 14)

And when the yogi beholds the real nature of Brahman, through the Knowledge of the Self, radiant as a lamp, then, having known the unborn and immutable Lord, who is untouched by ignorance and its effects, he is freed from all fetters. (II. 15)

He indeed, the Lord, who pervades all regions, was the first to be born,[35] and it is He who dwells in the womb [of the universe].[36] It is He, again, who is born [as a child], and He will be born in the future. He stands behind all persons, and His face is everywhere. (II. 16)

The self-luminous Lord, who is in fire, who is in water, who has entered into the whole world, who is in plants, who is in trees—to that Lord let there be adoration! Yea, let there be adoration! (II. 17)

The non-dual Ensnarer[37] rules by His powers.[38] Remaining one and and the same, He rules by His powers all the worlds during their manifestation and continued existence. They who know this become immortal. (III. 1)

Rudra is truly one; for the knowers of Brahman do not admit the existence of a second. He alone rules all the worlds by His powers. He dwells as the inner Self of every living being. After having created all the worlds, He, their Protector, takes them back into Himself at the end of time. (III. 2)

His eyes are everywhere, His faces everywhere, His arms everywhere, everywhere His feet. He it is who endows men with arms, birds with

[34] Each of the five subtle elements is endowed with its unique characteristic: earth with smell, water with taste, fire with form, air with touch, and ākāśa with sound. Through concentration the yogi can experience these attributes.
[35] That is to say, as Hiranyagarbha.
[36] As Virāt, or the personified totality of all bodies.
[37] The word *jāla*, in the text, means snare or net and refers to māyā.
[38] Māyā is endowed with the powers of concealment and projection.

feet and wings, and men likewise with feet. Having produced heaven and earth, He remains as their non-dual manifester. (III. 3)

He, the omniscient Rudra, the creator of the gods and the bestower of their powers, the support of the universe, He who, in the beginning, gave birth to Hiranyagarbha—may He endow us with clear intellect! (III. 4)

O Rudra, Thou who dwellest in the body[39] and bestowest happiness! Look upon us with that most blessed form of Thine, which is auspicious, unterrifying, and all good. (III. 5)

O Dweller in the body and Bestower of happiness, make benign that arrow[40] which Thou holdest in Thy hand ready to shoot, O Protector of the body! Do not injure man or the world![41] (III. 6)

The Supreme Lord is higher than Virāt, beyond Hiranyagarbha. He is vast and is hidden in the bodies of all living beings. By knowing Him who alone pervades the universe, men become immortal. (III. 7)

I know the great Purusha, who is luminous, like the sun, and beyond darkness. Only by knowing Him does one pass over death; there is no other way to the Supreme Goal. (III. 8)

The whole universe is filled by the Purusha, to whom there is nothing superior, from whom there is nothing different, than whom there is nothing either smaller or greater; who stands alone, motionless as a tree, established in His own glory. (III. 9)

That which is farthest from this world is without form and without affliction. They who know It become immortal; but others, indeed, suffer pain. (III. 10)

All faces are His faces; all heads, His heads; all necks, His necks. He dwells in the heart of all beings. He is the all-pervading Bhagavān. Therefore He is the omnipresent and benign Lord. (III. 11)

He, indeed, is the great Purusha, the Lord [of creation, preservation, and destruction], who inspires the mind to attain the state of stainlessness. He is the Ruler and the Light that is imperishable. (III. 12)

[39] The word *Girisanta*, in the text, is translated by theistic interpreters of the Upanishad as 'dweller in the mountains'. The deity Siva is described in the Purānas as dwelling in the Himālayas.
[40] Refers to the terrible aspect of the Godhead.
[41] Or the passage may mean: 'Do not hide from us Brahman with form, who manifests Himself as the phenomenal universe.'

The Purusha, no bigger than a thumb, is the inner Self, ever seated in the heart of man. He is known by the mind, which controls knowledge,[42] and is perceived in the heart. They who know Him become immortal. (III. 13)

The Purusha with a thousand heads, a thousand eyes, a thousand feet, compasses the earth on all sides and extends beyond it by ten fingers' breadth.[43] (III. 14)

The Purusha alone is all this—what has been and what will be. He is also the Lord of Immortality and of whatever grows by food. (III. 15)

His hands and feet are everywhere; His eyes, heads, and faces are everywhere; His ears are everywhere; He exists compassing all. (III. 16)

Himself devoid of senses, He shines through the functions of the senses. He is the capable ruler of all; He is the refuge of all. He is great. (III. 17)

The Swan, the ruler of the whole world, of all that is moving and all that is motionless, becomes the embodied self, and dwelling in the city of nine gates, flies outward.[44] (III. 18)

Grasping without hands, hasting without feet, It sees without eyes, It hears without ears. It knows what is to be known, but no one knows It. They call It the First, the Great, the Full.[45] (III. 19)

The Self, smaller than the small, greater than the great, is hidden in the hearts of creatures. The wise, by the grace of the Creator,[46] behold the Lord, majestic and desireless, and become free from grief. (III. 20)

I know this undecaying, primeval One, the Self of all things, which exists everywhere, being all-pervading, and which the wise declare to be free from birth. The teachers of Brahman, indeed, speak of It as eternal. (III. 21)

[42] Refers to the process of reflection by which one discriminates between the Self and the non-Self.

[43] Śankara explains 'ten fingers' breadth' to mean infinity. Brahman permeates the universe and extends into the boundless beyond.

[44] That is to say, becomes active for the experiencing of external objects.

[45] After describing the cosmic aspect of Brahman, the Upanishad shows Its acosmic aspect.

[46] Or the passage may mean 'through the tranquillity of the senses and the mind'.

He, the One and Undifferentiated,[47] who by the manifold application of His powers produces, in the beginning, different objects[48] for a hidden purpose,[49] and, in the end, withdraws the universe into Himself, is indeed the self-luminous [Supreme Self]. May He endow us with clear intellect! (IV. 1)

That [Supreme Self] is Agni (Fire); It is Āditya (Sun); It is Vāyu (Wind); It is Chandramā (Moon). That Self is the luminous stars; It is Hiranyagarbha; It is water; It is Virāt. (IV. 2)

Thou art woman, Thou art man; Thou art youth and maiden too. Thou as an old man totterest along on a staff; it is Thou alone who, when born, assumest diverse forms. (IV. 3)

Thou art the dark-blue bee; Thou art the green parrot with red eyes; Thou art the thunder-cloud, the seasons, and the seas. Thou art beginningless and all-pervading. From Thee all the worlds are born. (IV. 4)

There is one unborn [prakriti][50]—red, white, and black[51]—which gives birth to many creatures like itself.[52] An unborn [individual soul][53] becomes attached to it and enjoys it, while another unborn [individual soul] leaves it after his enjoyment is completed. (IV. 5)

Two birds,[54] united always and known by the same name, closely cling to the same tree. One of them eats the sweet fruit; the other looks on without eating.[55] (IV. 6)

Seated on the same tree, the jiva moans, bewildered by its impotence. But when it beholds the other, the Lord worshipped by all, and His glory, it becomes free from grief. (IV. 7)

[47] Or the word *avarna*, in the text, may mean 'without colour or caste'. In ancient India caste was primarily determined by the colour or complexion of the individual.

[48] Or the words *varnān anekān*, in the text, may refer to the various castes of Hindu society, based upon the psychological and physical differences observed among human beings.

[49] Or the phrase *nihitārtho*, in the text, may mean 'without any personal purpose'. The purpose of the creation, whether it is considered as illusory or as real, will ever remain unknown to the finite mind.

[50] From the relative standpoint, prakriti, or nature, is without beginning.

[51] The passage denotes the three gunas—rajas, sattva, and tamas—which constitute prakriti.

[52] All physical objects, like prakriti, their cause, consist of the three gunas.

[53] The individual soul is beginningless.

[54] The individual self and the Supreme Self.

[55] This and the following verse also appear in the *Mundaka Upanishad* (III. i. 1–2).

Of what use are the Vedas to him who does not know that indestructible Substance, that ākāśa-like Brahman, which is greater than the unmanifest and wherein the Vedas and all the gods are sheltered? Only those who know It attain bliss. (IV. 8)

The sacred verses, the offerings (yajna), the sacrifices (kratu), the penances (vrata), the past, the future, and all that the Vedas declare, have been produced from the imperishable Brahman. Brahman projects the universe through the power of Its māyā. Again, in that universe Brahman [as the jiva] is entangled through māyā. (IV. 9)

Know, then, that prakriti is māyā and that the Great God is the Lord of māyā. The whole universe is filled with objects which are parts of His being. (IV. 10)

By truly realizing Him who, though non-dual, dwells in prakriti, both in its primary and in its secondary aspect,[56] and in whom this whole world comes together and dissolves—by truly realizing Him who is the Lord, the bestower of blessings, the Adorable God, one attains the supreme peace. (IV. 11)

He, the creator of the gods and the bestower of their powers, the Support of the universe, Rudra the omniscient, who at the beginning gave birth to Hiranyagarbha—may He endow us with clear intellect! (IV. 12)

He who is the sovereign of the gods, in whom the worlds find their support, who rules over all two-footed and four-footed beings—let us serve that God, radiant and blissful, with an oblation. (IV. 13)

By realizing Him who is subtler than the subtlest, who dwells in the midst of the chaos [of the world],[57] who is the Creator of all things and is endowed with many forms, who is the non-dual Pervader of the universe, and all good—by realizing Him one attains the supreme peace. (IV. 14)

It is He who, in proper time,[58] becomes the custodian of the universe and the sovereign of all; who conceals Himself in all beings [as their

---

[56] The primary aspect of prakriti is called mulāvidyā, or primary ignorance, which, at the beginning of the creation, veils Brahman and obscures Its true nature. Its secondary aspect consists of the various elements—ākāśa, air, fire, water, and earth—which form, as it were, the bricks of the universe.

[57] The universe, being the product of avidyā, presents a state of indescribable confusion.

[58] That is to say, at the beginning of a cycle.

inner Witness]; and in whom the sages and the deities are united. Verily, by knowing Him one cuts asunder the fetters of death. (IV. 15)

He who knows Brahman, who is all Bliss, extremely subtle, like the film that rises to the surface of clarified butter,[59] and is hidden in all beings—he who knows the radiant Deity, the sole Pervader of the universe, is released from all his fetters. (IV. 16)

The Maker of all things, self-illumined and all-pervading, He dwells always in the hearts of men. He is revealed by the negative teachings [of the Vedānta],[60] discriminative wisdom, and the Knowledge of Unity based upon reflection. They who know Him become immortal. (IV. 17)

When there is no darkness [of ignorance], there is no day or night, neither being nor non-being; the pure Brahman alone exists. That immutable Reality is the meaning of 'That';[61] It is adored by the Sun. From It has proceeded the ancient wisdom.[62] (IV. 18)

No one can grasp Him above, across, or in the middle. There is no likeness of Him. His name is Great Glory (Mahad Yaśah). (IV. 19)

His form is not an object of vision; no one beholds Him with the eyes. They who, through pure intellect and the Knowledge of Unity based upon reflection, realize Him as abiding in the heart become immortal. (IV. 20)

It is because Thou, O Lord, art birthless, that some rare souls, frightened [by birth and death], take refuge in Thee. O Rudra, may Thy benign face protect me for ever! (IV. 21)

O Rudra, do not, in Thy wrath, destroy our children and grandchildren. Do not destroy our lives; do not destroy our cows or horses; do not destroy our strong servants. For we invoke Thee always, with oblations, for our protection. (IV. 22)

In the immutable, infinite Supreme Brahman remain hidden the two: knowledge and ignorance.[63] Ignorance leads to worldliness, and knowl-

[59] When butter, which is the subtle part of milk, is boiled, a thin film forms on the surface which is extremely fine and tasty.
[60] Refers to the well-known Vedāntic method of Neti, neti—'Not this, not this.'
[61] Refers to the well-known Vedic statement 'That thou art'—Tattvamasi. (Chh. Up. VI. viii. 7)
[62] The knowledge of the identity of the individual soul and Brahman, as expressed by the Vedic statement 'That thou art'.
[63] Ignorance and knowledge, both belonging to māyā, are two categories of the phenomenal universe, of which Brahman is the unattached support.

edge, to Immortality. Brahman, who controls both knowledge and ignorance, is different from both. (V. 1)

He, the non-dual Brahman, who rules over every position [by dwelling in each as its inner Guide]; who controls all forms and all sources; who, in the beginning, filled with knowledge the omniscient Hiranyagarbha, His own creation, whom He beheld when He (Hiranyagarbha) was produced—He is other than both knowledge and ignorance. (V. 2)

[At the time of the creation] the Lord spreads out individual nets[64] in various ways, and then [at the time of the cosmic dissolution] withdraws them into the great prakriti. Again the all-pervading Deity creates the aggregates of body and senses, both individual and collective, and their controllers also, and thus exercises His overlordship. (V. 3)

As the sun shines, illumining all the quarters—above, below, and across—so also God, self-resplendent, adorable, and non-dual, controls all objects, which themselves possess the nature of a cause.[65] (V. 4)

He who is the cause of all and who enables all things to function according to their nature; who brings to maturity all that can be ripened; who, being non-dual, rules over the whole universe and engages the gunas in their respective functions—He is concealed in the Upanishads, the secret part of the Vedas. Brahmā knew Him who can be known only from the evidence of the Vedas. The gods and seers of olden times who knew Him became Brahman and attained Immortality. (V. 5–6)

Endowed with gunas, the jiva performs action, seeking its fruit; and again, it reaps the fruit of what it has done. Assuming all forms and led by the three gunas, the jiva, ruler of the pranas, roams about following the three paths,[66] according to its deeds. (V. 7)

Of the size of a thumb, but brilliant, like the sun, the jiva possesses both volition and egoism. It is endowed with the qualities of both buddhi and Ātman.[67] Therefore it is seen as another entity, inferior, and small as the point of a goad. (V. 8)

[64] The non-Self, or physical element, consisting of body, mind, senses, and prāna is called a net because it entraps the soul and entangles it in the world.

[65] Every entity in the phenomenal world functions both as a cause and as an effect.

[66] The paths of righteousness, unrighteousness, and knowledge. Or the paths may mean the Way of the Gods (Devayāna), the Way of the Fathers (Pitriyāna), and the path leading to rebirth as a worm or insect.

[67] The jiva reveals both ignorance and Knowledge, the former being the quality of the buddhi, and the latter its own nature.

Know the embodied soul to be a part of the hundredth part of the point of a hair divided a hundred times; and yet it is infinite. (V. 9)

It is not female, it is not male, nor is it neuter. Whatever body it takes, with that it becomes united. (V. 10)

By means of desires, contact, attachment, and delusion, the embodied soul assumes, successively, diverse forms in various places, according to its deeds, just as the body grows when food and drink are poured into it. (V. 11)

The embodied soul, by means of good and evil deeds committed by itself, assumes many forms, coarse and fine. By virtue of its actions and also of such characteristics of the mind as knowledge and desire, it assumes another body for the enjoyment of [suitable] objects. (V. 12)

He who knows the Lord, who is without beginning or end, who stands in the midst of the chaos [of the world], who is the Creator of all things and is endowed with many forms—he who knows the radiant Deity, the sole Pervader of the universe, is released from all his fetters. (V. 13)

Those who know Him who can be realized by the pure heart, who is called incorporeal, who is the cause of creation and destruction, who is all good and the creator of the [sixteen] parts[68]—those who know the luminous Lord are freed from embodiment. (V. 14)

Some learned men speak of the inherent nature of things, and some speak of time, [as the cause of the universe]. They all, indeed, are deluded. It is the greatness of the self-luminous Lord that causes the Wheel of Brahman to revolve. (VI. 1)

He by whom the whole universe is constantly pervaded is the Knower, the Author of time. He is sinless and omniscient. It is at His command that the work which is called earth, water, fire, air, and ākāśa appears as the universe. All this should be reflected upon [by the wise]. (VI. 2)

The yogi who first performs actions[69] and then turns away from them,[70] and who practises one,[71] two,[72] three,[73] or eight[74] [disciplines], unites

[68] For the sixteen parts, which constitute the embodied being, see *Pr. Up.* VI. 4.
[69] For the purification of his heart.
[70] That is to say, embraces the monastic life.
[71] Service of the guru.
[72] Love of God and love of the guru.
[73] The Vedāntic disciplines of learning the truths of the scriptures with the help of a guru, reasoning about them, and finally meditating on them.
[74] The eight disciplines of yoga laid down by Patanjali. (*Yog. Su.* II. 29–30.)

one principle[75] with another principle[76] and with the help of virtues cultivated by the self and of subtle tendencies [acquired from actions in previous lives] attains Liberation in course of time. (VI. 3)

He who attains purity of heart by performing actions as an offering to the Lord, and merges prakriti and all its effects in Brahman, realizes his true Self and thereby transcends phenomena. In the absence of māyā, both collective and individual, all his past actions [except the prārabdha] are destroyed [and he becomes liberated though still dwelling in the body]. After the destruction of the prārabdha karma he attains final Liberation. (VI. 4)

The Great Lord is the beginning, the cause which unites [the soul with the body]; He is above the three kinds of time and is seen to be without parts. After having worshipped that adorable God dwelling in the heart, who is of many forms and is the true source of all things, [one attains final Liberation]. (VI. 5)

He from whom this universe proceeds is higher and other than all forms of the Tree [of the World] and of time. When one knows Him who is the indweller, the bringer of good, the destroyer of evil, the Lord of powers,[77] the immortal support of all, [one attains final Liberation]. (VI. 6)

We know Him who is the Supreme Lord of lords, the Supreme Deity of deities, the Ruler of rulers; who is higher than the imperishable prakriti and is the self-luminous, adorable Lord of the world. (VI. 7)

He is without a body or organs; none like unto Him is seen, or better [than He]. The Vedas speak of His exalted power, which is innate and capable of producing diverse effects, and also of His omniscience and might. (VI. 8)

He has no master in the world, no ruler, nor is there even a sign of Him [by which He can be inferred]. He is the cause, the Lord of the lord of the organs; and He is without progenitor or controller. (VI. 9)

May the non-dual Lord, who, by the power of His māyā, covered Himself, like a spider, with threads drawn from primal matter (pradhāna),[78] merge us in Brahman! (VI. 10)

[75] A reference to 'thou' in the Vedic statement 'That thou art'.

[76] Refers to 'That' in the statement 'That thou art'.

[77] The six great powers, namely, total power, dharma, glory, affluence, knowledge, and renunciation. They are the characteristics of the Lord.

[78] The word *pradhāna* refers to primal matter in its undifferentiated state, the first entity to be evolved from the contact of Purusha with prakriti, which is the

The non-dual and resplendent Lord is hidden in all beings. All-pervading, the inmost Self of all creatures, the impeller to actions, abiding in all things, He is the Witness, the Animator, and the Absolute, free from gunas. (VI. 11)

There is a non-dual Ruler of the actionless many;[79] He makes the one seed manifold. Eternal happiness belongs to the wise, who perceive Him within themselves—and not to others. (VI. 12)

He is the Eternal among the eternal,[80] the Conscious among the conscious, and though non-dual, fulfils the desires of many. He who has known Him, the luminous Lord, the Great Cause, to be realized by Sāmkhya (Knowledge) and yoga,[81] is freed from all fetters. (VI. 13)

The sun does not shine there, nor the moon and the stars, nor these lightnings—much less this fire. He shining, everything shines after Him. By his light all this is lighted. (VI. 14)

In this universe the Swan (the Supreme Self) alone exists. It is He who, as fire,[82] abides in the water.[83] Only by knowing Him does one pass over death. There is no other way to reach [the Supreme Goal]. (VI. 15)

He who is the support of both the unmanifested prakriti and the jiva, who is the Lord of the three gunas, and who is the cause of bondage, existence, and Liberation from samsāra, is verily the Creator of the universe, the Knower, the inmost Self of all things, and their Source— the omniscient Lord, the Author of time, the Possessor of virtues, the Knower of everything. (VI. 16)

He who constantly rules the world is verily the cause of bondage and Liberation. Established in His own glory, He is the Immortal, the Embodiment of Consciousness, the omnipresent Protector of the universe. There is no one else able to rule it. (VI. 17)

germ of all material appearances. The word *threads* signifies the manifestations of matter in the phenomenal world, such as name, form, and action.

[79] Refers both to the embodied soul (jiva) and to its body, senses, mind, prāna, etc., which are modifications of matter and hence inert. In essence, however, the jiva is Brahman and therefore is free from activity.

[80] The word *eternal* signifies the jivas.

[81] The word refers here to the following spiritual disciplines: receiving instruction from a qualified teacher, reasoning about them, and contemplating their meaning.

[82] The word *agni*, or *fire*, also denotes the Supreme Self.

[83] Used here to denote the body, which contains a preponderance of the element water. Or the word may indicate the heart.

Seeking Liberation, I take refuge in the Lord, the revealer of Self-Knowledge, who in the beginning created Brahmā and delivered the Vedas to Him. (VI. 18)

When men shall roll up space (ākāśa) as if it were a piece of hide,[84] then there will be an end of misery without one's cultivating the Knowledge of the Lord, who is without parts, without actions, tranquil, blameless, unattached, the supreme bridge to Immortality, and like a fire that has consumed all its fuel. (VI. 19–20)

Through the power of austerity and through the grace of the Lord, the sage Śvetāśvatara realized Brahman and proclaimed the highly sacred Knowledge, supremely cherished by the company of seers, to sannyāsins of the most advanced stage. (VI. 21)

The profound mystery in the Vedānta[85] was taught in the previous cycle.[86] It should not be given to one whose passions have not been subdued, nor to one who is not a son or a disciple. (VI. 22)

If these truths have been told to a high-minded person who feels the highest devotion for God, and for his guru as for God, then they will surely shine forth [as inner experiences]—then, indeed, they will shine forth. (VI. 23)

---

[84] Just as it is impossible to roll up the ākāśa as one does a piece of hide, so it is impossible to put an end to misery without the Knowledge of the Lord.

[85] The word refers here to the Upanishads, which form the essence and the concluding part (anta) of the Vedas.

[86] The teachings of the Vedas are eternal and immutable. They are revealed in the same form in every cycle. (See *Br. Su.* I. iii. 29.)

THE PEACE CHANT

OM. THAT IS full; this is full. This fullness has been projected from that fullness. When this fullness merges in that
fullness, all that remains is fullness.
   Om. Peace! Peace! Peace!

   Om. May we, O gods, hear with our ears what is auspicious!
May we, O worshipful gods, see with our eyes what is good!
May we, strong in limbs and body, sing your praise and
enjoy the life allotted to us by Prajāpati!
   Om. Peace! Peace! Peace!

PRAŚNA UPANISHAD

INTRODUCTION

IT HAS BEEN stated in the Introduction to the *Mundaka Upanishad* that both the *Mundaka Upanishad* and the *Praśna Upanishad* belong to the Atharva-Veda. They are complementary in their teachings: what is briefly taught in the one is expanded in the other.

The *Mundaka Upanishad* deals with the lower knowledge and the Higher Knowledge; the *Praśna Upanishad*, with prāna, the symbol of Saguna, or the Lower, Brahman and the goal of the lower knowledge.

As in some other Upanishads, the instructions in the *Praśna Upanishad* are given in the form of questions and answers between a teacher and his disciples; hence the title of the Upanishad (the word *praśna* means *question*). The practice of austerity, faith, and chastity of body and mind are emphasized as special qualifications on the part of pupils seeking deep spiritual knowledge.

INVOCATION

OM. MAY WE, O gods, hear with our ears what is auspicious! May we, O worshipful gods, see with our eyes what is good! May we, strong in limbs and body, sing your praise and enjoy the life allotted to us by Prajāpati!

Om. Peace! Peace! Peace!

OM. SUKEŚĀ, THE son of Bharadvāja, and Satyakāma, the son of Śibi, and Sauryāyani, belonging to the family of Garga, and Kausalya, the son of Aśvala, and Vaidarbhi, belonging to the family of Bhrigu, and Kabandhi, the son of Katya—all these, devoted to Brahman[1] and firm in Brahman, and seeking the Supreme Brahman, approached, fuel in hand, the venerable Pippalāda with the thought that he would tell them everything about Brahman. (I. 1)

The rishi said to them: Stay with me a year more, practising austerities, chastity, and faith. Then you may ask questions according to your desire. If we know we shall tell you all. (I. 2)

Then Kabandhi, the son of Katya, came to him and asked: Sir, whence are these creatures born? (I. 3)

To him the teacher said: Prajāpati,[2] the Creator, was desirous of progeny. He performed austerities, and having performed austerities, created the pair, the moon (rayi)[3] and the sun (prāna).[4] He said to Himself: 'These two should produce creatures for Me in manifold ways.'[5] (I. 4)

The sun is, indeed, prāna, life; the moon is rayi, food. Food is, indeed, all this[6]—what has form and what is formless. Therefore everything having form is, indeed, food.[7] (I. 5)

[1] That is to say, Saguna Brahman. These seekers regarded the Lower Brahman as the Supreme Brahman and worshipped Him.

[2] According to the Vedas, a highly developed rishi cherishes the desire to become Prajāpati, and with that end in view contemplates his identity with the Creator and performs a special sacrifice. At the beginning of the next cycle he is born as the Creator and becomes known as Prajāpati. Then through intense contemplation He awakens in His mind the subtle impressions of the Vedic knowledge acquired in His previous birth. With the help of that knowledge He sets about the task of creation. First He creates the sun (Surya) and the moon (Soma), which stand for the eater and the food respectively. Without them the creation cannot be preserved.

[3] The Sanskrit word *rayi* in the text, means both food and wealth. Cereals, or food, which are acquired through wealth, are nourished by the moisture, or dew, coming through the moon's rays. (See *B. G.* XV. 13.)

[4] The Sanskrit word *prāna* means both the life principle and the eater. The sun, in one of its aspects (i.e. the gastric fire), digests food. (See *B. G.* XV. 14.)

[5] The words *moon* and *sun*, in the text, may also mean matter and life, or energy. At the beginning of creation the undifferentiated Cosmic Principle evolves matter and energy, which, in turn, evolve the various material entities.

[6] Food, or matter, being all-pervading, is the same as the all-pervading Prajāpati. Prajāpati manifests Himself as food and eater, the moon and the sun, and pervades them.

[7] Energy and matter are the first two manifestations of the Cosmic Mind. The sun, being the centre of energy, is identified with prāna, or the cosmic energy. The

147

Now the sun, when it rises, enters the eastern quarter and thereby enfolds the living beings of the east in its rays. And when it illuminates the southern, the western, the northern, the lower, the upper, and the intermediate quarters—when it illuminates everything—it thus enfolds all living beings in its rays.[8] (I. 6)

That sun rises every day—the sun, which is the soul of all creatures, the soul of all forms, which is life and fire. This has been described by the following rik:

'[The wise know him who] is in all forms, full of rays, all-knowing, non-dual, the support of all life, the eye of all beings, the giver of heat. There rises the sun, the thousand-rayed, existing in a hundred forms, the life of all creatures.' (I. 7–8)

The year, verily, is Prajāpati,[9] and there are two paths thereof: the Southern and the Northern. Those who perform sacrifices and engage in pious actions, as duties to be done, win only the World of the Moon; verily they return hither again. Therefore the rishis who desire offspring travel by the Southern Path. This Path of the Fathers is rayi, food.[10] (I. 9)

But those who seek the Self through austerity, chastity, faith, and knowledge travel by the Northern Path and win the Sun. The Sun, verily, is the support of all lives. He is immortal and fearless; He is the final goal. Thence they do not return. This path is blocked [for the ignorant]. Concerning it there is the following verse: (I. 10)

'Some call Him the father with five feet[11] and with twelve forms,[12] the giver of rain, and the dweller in the region above the sky. Others,

---

moon, devoid of heat and light, is identified with inert matter. Whatever object is perceived to exist in the universe—gross or subtle, with form or without form—is matter. Even the subtlest substance is a form of matter.

[8] The foregoing verse describes rayi, food, as Prajāpati, because Prajāpati manifests Himself as food. Because He is everything, food is said to be everything. The same is true of intangible prāna, the sun or eater. Prāna, likewise, is everything.

[9] The next manifestation of Prajāpati is the year, or time, brought into being by the moon and the sun and consisting of night and day. The year may consist of solar or lunar months, determined by the rising and setting of either the sun or the moon. Prajāpati manifests Himself as the pair, the sun and the moon; and this pair constitutes the year. Therefore the year is none other than Prajāpati.

[10] The Southern Path and the Northern Path have been elaborated in *Br. Up.* VI. ii. 15–16; *Chh. Up.* V. 10; *B. G.* VIII. 24–26.

[11] Refers to the six seasons: summer, the rainy season, autumn, fall, winter, and spring—fall and winter being here counted as one. As a man walks by the help of his feet, so the sun, by means of the seasons, moves along its orbit.

[12] The twelve months of the year.

again, say that the world is fixed in the omniscient Sun, endowed with seven wheels[13] and six spokes.'[14] [15] (I. 11)

The month, verily, is Prajāpati. Its dark half, verily, is food, rayi; its bright half, the eater, prāna. Therefore some rishis perform sacrifice in the bright half, some in the other half.[16] (I. 12)

Day and night, verily, are Prajāpati. Of these, day is the eater, prāna, and night, the food, rayi. Those who join in sexual enjoyment by day verily dissipate life; but to join in sexual enjoyment by night[17] is, verily, chastity.[18] (I. 13)

Food, verily, is Prajāpati. From that comes semen; from semen are all these creatures born.[19] (I. 14)

Those, therefore, who practise this rule of Prajāpati[20] beget a pair.[21] But Brahmaloka[22] belongs to those who observe austerity and chastity and in whom truth is firmly established. (I. 15)

The stainless World of Brahmā belongs to those in whom there is no crookedness, no falsehood, no deception. (I. 16)

Then Vaidarbhi, belonging to the family of Bhrigu, asked him: Sir, how many gods support the body of the created being? How many of

[13] Seven rays or colours. They are described by the Vedic seers as the seven horses of the sun's chariot.

[14] The six seasons.

[15] The gist of the text is that Prajāpati, manifesting Himself as the sun and moon, next as time or the year, further manifests Himself as the universe. The verse occurs in *Ri.* I. I. clxiv. 12.

[16] The whole universe rests in Prajāpati, who manifests Himself as the year and who further evolves as the month. Therefore the moon, or food (rayi), and the sun, or the eater (prāna), are the component parts of the month, as they are of the year.

[17] This kind of self-control is prescribed for the householder.

[18] Prajāpati further manifests Himself as day and night, of which the eater, prāna, and the food, rayi, are component parts.

[19] The Upanishads teach that life has not evolved from matter, but is implicit in it. The first projection of Prajāpati consists of a pair: matter and energy. He then further evolves as the year, or time, and its subdivisions of month and day. Lastly He evolves as edible food and semen; from the latter are directly born the created beings. Therefore life is present in all stages of creation, though its tangible manifestation is seen in living creatures.

[20] As laid down in verse 13, referring to sexual intercourse at night and in the proper period.

[21] That is to say, a son and a daughter.

[22] The word here means Chandraloka, or the Plane of the Moon, reached by the Southern Path. The moon is also a manifestation of Brahmā, or Prajāpati.

these manifest their power through it? And which one, furthermore, is paramount? (II. 1)

To the disciple, he said: Space, ākāśa, verily is that god[23]—the wind, fire, water, earth, speech, mind, eye, and ear, as well. These, having manifested their glory, said boastfully: 'We [each of us] support this body and uphold it.' (II. 2)

To them prāna, the chiefmost said: 'Do not fall into delusion. I alone, dividing myself into five parts, support this body and uphold it.'[24] But they were incredulous. (II. 3)

Prāna, out of pride, rose upward, as it were, from the body. Now, when it rose upward all the others rose upward also, and when it settled down they all settled down with it. As bees go out when their queen goes out and return when she returns, even so did speech, mind, eye, and ear. They, being satisfied, praised prāna. (II. 4)

It burns as fire, it is the sun, it is the rain; it is Indra, it is the wind, it is the earth, it is food. It is the radiant god. It is being[25] and non-being;[26] it is immortality.[27] (II. 5)

As spokes in the hub of a wheel, all are fixed in prāna, including the Rig-Veda, the Yajur-Veda, the Sāma-Veda, the kshatriyas, and the brāhmins. (II. 6)

As Prajāpati thou movest about in the womb; it is thou, indeed, who art born again.[28] To thee, O Prāna, creatures bring offerings,[29] to thee who dwellest in the body with the organs. (II. 7)

Thou art the chief bearer of oblations to the gods[30] and the first offering[31]

[23] Consciousness permeates matter; all elements and organs are controlled by a portion of Consciousness called a god, or deva.
[24] The powers by which the elements and the organs uphold the body are not their own, but the expression of prāna functioning through them. This prāna is the same as Prajāpati. The same energy manifests itself through both microcosm and macrocosm. This fact is stated in the two following verses.
[25] That is to say, the gross elements.
[26] The subtle elements.
[27] Refers to the heavenly nectar by which the gods are nourished.
[28] The father and mother are reborn as the son.
[29] The sensations gathered by the senses are the tributes they offer to prāna.
[30] Refers to Agni, who carries the sacrificial oblations to the gods.
[31] At the beginning of a sacrifice the first offering is made to the departed fathers. It is performed while uttering the word svadhā. Therefore this word has here been translated as 'first offering'.

to the departed fathers; thou art the true activities[32] of the rishis,[33] of the Atharvāngiras. (II. 8)

Indra[34] thou art, O Prāna, and Rudra,[35] too, in prowess. Thou art the Protector.[36] Thou movest in the sky; thou art the sun, the lord of lights. (II. 9)

When, O Prāna, thou showerest down rain, these creatures of thine are delighted, thinking there will be as much food as they desire. (II. 10)

Thou art vrātya,[37] O Prāna, and the Ekarshi Fire that devours the butter. Thou art the Supreme Lord of all. We are the givers of the butter that thou consumest, O Mātariśvā! Thou art our father. (II. 11)

That form of thine which abides in speech, which abides in the ear, which abides in the eye, and which pervades the mind, make propitious. Go not away! (II. 12)

All that exists here is under the control of Prāna, and also what exists in heaven. Protect us as a mother her sons; bestow upon us prosperity and wisdom. (II. 13)

Then Kausalya the son of Aśvala asked Pippalāda: Sir, whence is this prāna[38] born? How does it come into this body? How does it abide in the body after it has divided itself? How does it depart? How does it support the external[39] and how the internal?[40] (III. 1)

To him the teacher replied: You are asking difficult questions; you must be exceedingly devoted to Brahman. Therefore I will answer you. (III. 2)

[32] By which the body is upheld.
[33] Refers to the sense-organs, including the prānas. The sense-organs are often called prānas in the Upanishads.
[34] The word here means the Supreme Lord.
[35] The Destroyer of the universe.
[36] That is to say, Vishnu.
[37] Refers to persons, from any of the three higher castes, for whom the samskāras, or sacramental initiatory rites, have not been performed. They are unclean sinners. Since prāna was the first born, there was no one to perform the rites for it. Therefore it is called vrātya. But prāna is pure by nature and needs no sacramental rites in order to purify itself. In Sanskrit rhetoric such an expression is called byangastuti, that is to say, praise through the pointing out of a blemish.
[38] The word here denotes the vital breath which sustains the body. This prāna is a manifestation of the cosmic prāna, or Prajāpati.
[39] Refers to the created beings (adhibhuta) and the gods (adhidaiva).
[40] The body, senses, and mind (adhyātma).

This prāna is born of Ātman. As a shadow is cast by a person, so this prāna is, by Ātman.[41] Through the activity of the mind it comes into this body.[42] (III. 3)

As an emperor commands his officials, saying: 'Rule these villages or those,' so this prāna employs the other prānas,[43] each in its separate place. (III. 4)

Prāna engages apāna in the organs of excretion and generation; he himself moves through the mouth and nose and dwells in the eye and ear. In the middle is samāna; it distributes equally what has been offered as food [in the fire in the stomach]. From this prāna fire arise the seven flames.[44] (III. 5)

The ātman dwells in the heart, where there are one hundred and one arteries (nādi); for each of these there are one hundred branches, and for each of these branches, again, there are seventy-two thousand sub-sidiary vessels.[45] Vyāna moves in these. (III. 6)

And then udāna, ascending upward through one of them, conducts the departing soul to the virtuous world, for its virtuous deeds; to the sinful world, for its sinful deeds; and to the world of men, for both. (III. 7)

The sun, verily, is the external prāna; for it rises, favouring the prāna in the eye.[46] The deity that exists in the earth controls the apāna of man. The space, ākāśa, between heaven and earth is samāna. The air is vyāna. (III. 8)

Fire, verily, is udāna; therefore he whose fire has been extinguished goes out for rebirth, with the senses absorbed in the mind. (III. 9)

Whatever one's thinking [at the time of death], with that one enters into prāna. Prāna joined with fire,[47] together with the soul, leads to whatever world has been fashioned by thought. (III. 10)

[41] As a shadow cannot exist independent of the body, so the prāna cannot exist independent of Ātman.

[42] Here the text refers to the doctrine of rebirth: A man's present life is the sure and appropriate result of his thoughts in a previous existence.

[43] The secondary prānas, or the sense-organs, which are modifications of the chief prāna.

[44] Namely, the two eyes, the two ears, the two nostrils, and the organ of speech. It is prāna that enables the seven organs to perform the irrespective functions: hearing, seeing, smelling, and speaking.

[45] This ancient enumeration is intended to include the nervous system as well.

[46] Without the sun, the eye could not see.

[47] That is to say, udāna, which keeps the body warm.

The wise man who thus knows prāna does not lose his offspring and becomes immortal. As to this there is the following verse: (III. 11)

'He who knows the origin of prāna, its entry, its place, its fivefold distribution, its internal aspect and also its external, obtains immortality; yea, he obtains immortality.' (III. 12)

Next Sauryāyani, belonging to the family of Garga, asked: Sir, what are they that sleep in man, and what are they that remain awake in him? Which deity is it that sees dreams? Whose is the happiness [of deep sleep]? In whom, again, are all these gathered together?[48] (IV. 1)

To him Pippalāda replied: O Gārgya, as the rays of the sun, when it sets, are gathered in that luminous orb, and again go forth when it rises, even so, verily, all these—the objects and the senses—become one in the superior god, the mind. Therefore at that time a man hears not, sees not, smells not, tastes not, touches not, speaks not, grasps not, enjoys not, emits not, and does not move about. He sleeps—that is what people say. (IV. 2)

The prāna fires remain awake in this city.[49] Apāna is the Gārhapatya Fire, and vyāna, the Anvāhāryapachana Fire. And prāna is the Āhavaniya Fire, so called from being taken—since it is taken from the Gārhapatya Fire.[50] (IV. 3)

[48] All that belongs to samsāra, or the phenomenal universe, has been dealt with in the first three questions. The next three questions deal with the Purusha, the Supreme Person, which is unborn and is both inside and outside of everything.

[49] That is to say, the body.

[50] Lifelong performance of the Agnihotra sacrifice was enjoined upon householders belonging to the three upper castes. Three fires were necessary for this sacrifice: The Gārhapatya Fire, the Āhavaniya Fire, and the Anvāhāryapachana Fire, commonly called the Dakshina or Southern Fire. The Gārhapatya or Householder's Fire was never allowed to go out; it had to be fed by the offering of daily oblations. At the time of the Agnihotra sacrifice, fires were taken from the Gārhapatya Fire, and the Āhavaniya and the Southern Fires were lighted. The Āhavaniya Fire, placed to the east, was used for offering oblations to the gods. The Anvāhāryapachana or Southern Fire, placed in the south, was used for offering oblations to the departed ancestors. In the Āhavaniya Fire two oblations were offered every morning and evening, as mentioned in the next verse. In this manner the Hindus communed, in olden times, with the gods and the souls of their ancestors. These external fires and oblations have their counterparts in a man himself. The sacrifices can also be made mentally, through meditation. In the text the various prānas are identified with the various fires. Vyāna is identified with the Southern Fire because it issues from the heart through an artery on the right side. Apāna, functioning in the lower part of the body, remains always active and hence is compared to the Gārhapatya Fire, which is never allowed to go out. The prāna of a sleeping person issues from the apāna and functions through his mouth and

Samāna is so called because it distributes *equally* the two oblations,[51] namely, the out-breathing and the in-breathing; it is the priest. The mind, verily, is the sacrificer. Udāna is the fruit of the sacrifice,[52] because it leads the sacrificer every day, in deep sleep, to Brahman.[53] (IV. 4)

There, in dreams, that god, the mind, experiences glory. Whatever has been seen he sees again;[54] whatever has been heard he hears again; whatever has been experienced in different countries and quarters, he experiences again. Whatever has been seen or not seen,[55] heard or not heard, and whatever is real or not real[56]—he sees it all. He sees all, himself being all. (IV. 5)

When the jiva is overcome by light[57] he sees no dreams; at that time, in this body, arises this happiness. (IV. 6)

As a bird goes to a tree to roost, even so, O friend, all this rests in the Supreme Ātman:
Earth and its subtle counterpart, water and its subtle counterpart, fire and its subtle counterpart, air and its subtle counterpart, ākāśa and its subtle counterpart, the eye and what can be seen, the ear and what can be heard, the nose and what can be smelt, the taste (tongue) and what can be tasted, the skin and what can be touched, the organ of speech and what can be spoken, the hands and what can be grasped, the organ of generation and what can be enjoyed, the organ of excretion and what can be excreted, the feet and what is their destination, the

nostrils. Because it is *taken from* apāna, prāna is compared to the Āhavaniya Fire, which is also taken from the Gārhapatya Fire. Even when all the other senses remain inactive in sleep, the different prānas keep watch over the body. Therefore they are compared to the sacrificial fires.

[51] The priest carries the two oblations and distributes them *equally* into the Āhavaniya Fire; samāna, likewise, equally distributes the two breaths, inhalation and exhalation, for the protection of the body.

[52] At the time of death the sacrificer leaves the body through udāna and reaps the fruit of the sacrifice in heaven. The same udāna leads the mind (the sacrificer) away from the dream state to dreamless sleep and enables it to attain Brahman. Therefore udāna is called the fruit of the sacrifice.

[53] Often the Upanishads compare the Consciousness of Brahman to the consciousness experienced in deep sleep. Both are characterized by an absence of pain and of the subject-object relationship. But the state of dreamless sleep, which is mechanically attained, is impermanent, and the consciousness experienced during it is covered by a thin layer of ignorance.

[54] An object experienced in the waking state leaves its impression on the mind. When the same object is dreamt of, it is only the mental impression that appears as the object.

[55] That is to say, not seen in this life, but in a previous one.

[56] A mirage, for instance.

[57] The light of Brahman.

mind (manas) and what can be thought, the intellect (buddhi) and what can be comprehended, the ego (ahamkāra) and the object of egoism, the memory (chitta) and its object, knowledge (tejah) and its object, prāna and what is to be supported.[58] (IV. 7–8)

He,[59] verily, it is who sees, feels, hears, smells, tastes, thinks, and knows. He is the doer, the intelligent self, the purusha. He is established in the Highest, the imperishable Ātman. (IV. 9)

He who knows that imperishable Being, bright, without shadow, without body, without colour, verily attains the Supreme, the undecaying Purusha. O my good friend, he who knows Ātman becomes all-knowing, becomes all. About it there is the following verse: (IV. 10)

'He, O friend, who knows that imperishable Being wherein rests the intelligent self, together with the gods, the prānas, and the elements— he becomes all-knowing and enters into all.' (IV. 11)

Then Satyakāma the son of Śibi asked Pippalāda: Sir, if among men someone should here meditate on the syllable Aum until death, which world, verily, would he win thereby? (V. 1)

He replied: O Satyakāma, the syllable Aum is the Supreme Brahman and also the other Brahman.[60] Therefore he who knows it attains, with its support, the one or the other. (V. 2)

If he meditates on one letter (mātrā),[61] then, being enlightened by that alone, he quickly comes back to earth after death. The rik verses lead him to the world of men.[62] By practising austerity, chastity, and faith he enjoys greatness. (V. 3)

[58] In deep sleep the subtle and gross elements, the sense-organs and their objects, and the mind and its various parts all remain inactive and are absorbed in Ātman. At that time the jiva, or embodied soul, dwells in the causal body (kārana śarira), which is covered by the veiling-power of māyā but unaffected by its projecting-power. Thus in deep sleep the jiva approaches nearest to Ātman and experiences Its glory.

[59] It is the jiva, or embodied soul, which, owing to its association with various upādhis of the mind, senses, etc., becomes the seer, feeler, hearer, etc.

[60] That is to say, Saguna Brahman.

[61] The letter A.

[62] It is said in the Vedas that the letter A in the syllable Aum is the very soul of the Rig-Veda and of the earth. One who meditates on A realizes his identity with it and through it attains the earthly plane.

If, again, he meditates on the second letter, he attains the mind and is led up by the yajur verses to the intermediate space, to the Plane of the Moon. Having enjoyed greatness in the Plane of the Moon, he returns hither again. (V. 4)

Again, he who meditates on the Highest Person through this syllable *Aum* consisting of three letters, becomes united with the effulgent sun. As a snake is freed from its skin, even so he is freed from sin. He is led up by the sāma verses to the World of Brahmā. From this, which is the aggregate of all lives, he beholds the Supreme Purusha, higher than the High and pervading all bodies.
As to this there are these two verses: (V. 5)

[The first verse:] 'The three letters of Aum [if employed separately] are mortal; but when joined together in meditation on the total Reality and used properly on the activities of the external, internal, and inter-mediate states, the knower trembles not.' (V. 6)

[The second verse:] 'The wise man, meditating on Aum, attains this world by means of the rik verses; the intermediate world by means of the yajur verses; and that which is known to the seers by means of the sāma verses. And also through the syllable Aum he realizes that which is tranquil, free from decay, death, and fear, and which is the Highest.'[63] (V. 7)

Then Sukeśā the son of Bharadvāja said to Pippalāda: Sir, Hiran-yābha, the prince of Kosala, once came to me and asked this question: 'O son of Bharadvāja, do you know the Person with sixteen parts?' I said to the prince: 'I do not know Him; if I knew Him, why should I not tell you? Surely he who speaks what is not true withers away to the very root; therefore I should not speak untruth.' Then he silently mounted his chariot and went away. Now I ask you: Where does that Person dwell?[64] (VI. 1)

Pippalāda said to him: 'That Person—He from whom these sixteen parts[65] arise—is verily here within the body.' (VI. 2)

[63] The three letters of Aum, associated with three sounds, have been described above. There is another aspect of Aum, known as the ardhamātrā, or half letter, an undifferentiated sound which lingers after the three differentiated sounds die away. This is called the Fourth and is used as the symbol of Turiya, or Pure Consciousness, the attributeless Brahman. (See *Mā. Up.* 12.)

[64] The aim of the sixth question is to elaborate what is said in *Mu. Up.* III. ii, 7–8.

[65] These will be enumerated in the fourth verse.

The Purusha reflected: 'What is it by whose departure I shall depart, and by whose staying I shall stay?' (VI. 3)

He created prāna; from prāna faith, space, air, fire, water, earth, the organs, mind, food; from food virility, austerity, the Vedic hymns, sacrifice, the worlds; and in the worlds He created names. (VI. 4)

As these flowing rivers, bound for the ocean,[66] disappear into the ocean after having reached it, their names and forms being destroyed, and are called simply the ocean[67]—even so, these sixteen parts of the seer, whose goal is the Purusha, disappear into the Purusha after having reached Him, their names and forms being destroyed, and are called simply the Purusha. He becomes free of parts and immortal.

On this there is the following verse: (VI. 5)

'Know Him, the Purusha, who alone is to be known and in whom the parts rest firm, like the spokes in the nave of a wheel, that death may not affect you.' (VI. 6)

Pippalāda said to them: Thus far, indeed, I know the Supreme Brahman; there is nothing higher than this. (VI. 7)

And they, worshipping him, said: Thou, indeed, art our father—thou who hast taken us across our ignorance to the other shore.

Adoration to the supreme rishis! Adoration to the supreme rishis! (VI. 8)

---

[66] The rivers have their origin in the ocean and therefore are irresistibly drawn toward it. (Compare *Mu. Up.* III. ii. 8.)

[67] It is the name and form that distinguish the water of the river from that of the ocean. After the destruction of the name and form, what remains is only the ocean.

THE PEACE CHANT

OM. MAY WE, O gods, hear with our ears what is auspicious!
May we, O worshipful gods, see with our eyes what is good!
May we, strong in limbs and body, sing your praise and enjoy
the life allotted to us by Prajāpati!
  Om. Peace! Peace! Peace!

MĀNDUKYA UPANISHAD

INTRODUCTION

THE *MĀNDUKYA UPANISHAD*, like the *Mundaka* and the *Praśna* and several minor Upanishads, forms part of the Atharva-Veda. It is the shortest of the major Upanishads, containing only twelve verses. Āchārya Gauḍapāda, the teacher of Śankarāchārya's teacher, has explained the Upanishad in two hundred and fifty verses, arranged in four chapters and known as the *Kārikā*, which constitute the first systematic exposition of non-dualistic, or Advaita, Vedānta. Śankarāchārya has written a highly philosophical commentary on both the Upanishadic text and the *Kārikā*, which has been further elucidated by Ānandagiri in his notes. A translation of the entire Kārikā, with explanatory notes, is given in the unabridged edition of *The Upanishads*.

Unlike the other Upanishads, the *Māndukya Upanishad* does not relate any anecdote or imaginary dialogue to illustrate its teachings. It is also silent about rituals or concrete forms of worship, since they are irrelevant to the metaphysical discussion of Reality. It plunges at once into a discussion of Brahman and Ātman, the inmost essence of the universe and of man, and proclaims that they are non-different.

The word *Aum* is used in the *Māndukya Upanishad* as the most effective symbol of Brahman. This word consists of three letters, *A*, *U*, and *M*, which are symbols of the ordinary states of waking, dreaming, and dreamless sleep. The knowledge of Brahman covers not only these three states of phenomenal experience, but also a transcendental experience, called Turiya, which is that of undifferentiated Pure Consciousness. The word *Aum*, likewise, includes an undifferentiated sound which comes at the end of the word. *Aum* therefore stands for Brahman in both aspects. Hence it is said that the study of the *Māndukya Upanishad* is sufficient to enable a man to realize his ultimate goal.[1]

[1] 'What is the goal? As a man stricken with disease regains his normal health when the disease is removed, so Ātman, having identified Itself with misery, recovers Its normal state when the duality manifesting itself as the phenomenal universe is destroyed. The realization of Non-duality is the goal to be achieved.' (*From the commentary of Śankarāchārya.*)

INVOCATION

**OM. MAY WE, O gods, hear with our ears what is auspicious!
May we, O worshipful gods, see with our eyes what is good!
May we, strong in limbs and body, sing your praise and enjoy
the life allotted to us by Prajāpati!**
   Om. Peace! Peace! Peace!

ŚRI ŚANKARĀCHĀRYA'S INVOCATION

I BOW TO Brahman, which experiences (during the waking state) gross objects by covering the universe with the tendril-like rays of Its consciousness, enfolding all movable and immovable entities; which, further, experiences during the dream state the objects produced by the mind due to desires; and which, again, in deep sleep, absorbs the various particulars and enjoys bliss, and makes us also experience, through māyā, the same bliss—I bow to the supreme, immortal and, birthless Brahman, designated, in terms of māyā, as Turiya, the Fourth.

May that Turiya, which, as the World Soul, experiences in the waking state gross objects, good and evil; which, again, experiences in the dream state other and subtle objects produced by Its own mind and illumined by Its own light; and which, lastly, in dreamless sleep withdraws all objects and remains devoid of distinctions—may that attributeless Turiya protect us!

HARIH AUM! AUM, the word, is all this.[2] A clear explanation of it is as follows: All that is past, present, and future is, indeed, Aum. And whatever else there is, beyond the threefold division of time[3]—that also is truly Aum. (1)

All this is, indeed, Brahman. This Ātman is Brahman. This same Ātman has four quarters (pādas). (2)

The first quarter (pāda) is called Vaiśvānara, whose sphere of activity is the waking state, who is conscious of external objects, who has seven limbs[4] and nineteen mouths,[5] and who is the experiencer of gross objects. (3)

The second quarter (pāda) is Taijasa, whose sphere of activity is the dream state, who is conscious of internal objects, who is endowed with seven limbs and nineteen mouths, and who is the experiencer of subtle objects.[6] (4)

That is the state of deep sleep wherein one asleep neither desires any object nor sees any dream.[7] The third quarter is Prājna,[8] whose sphere

[2] Diversified objects, designated by names, constitute the universe, and the objects are not different from their respective names.

[3] Refers to the state of non-manifestation (avyākrita), which is free from the concept of time. The existence of such a state can be inferred from the existence of the manifest world.

[4] Namely, the head, the eyes, the mouth, the breath, the middle part of the body, the kidney, and the feet. They have their counterparts in the universe, namely, the heavens, the sun, fire, air, ākāśa, water, and earth. (Compare *Chh. Up.* V. xviii. 2.)

[5] Namely, the five organs of perception, the five organs of action, the five prānas, the mind, the intellect, I-consciousness, and the mind-stuff. These are, as it were, the mouths or organs by means of which the waking person (Vaiśvānara) experiences gross objects. The etymological meaning of the word *Vaiśvānara* is 'common to all men'.

[6] 'Waking experience is associated with many factors, such as the subject-object relationship, the idea of agency, and the idea of instrumentality. In the waking state one feels that the objects of perception are external, though in reality they are nothing but states of the mind. The external objects perceived by the sense-organs have no independent reality. Their reality cannot be proved for the simple reason that they become non-existent when one inquires into their essential character. These external objects appear to be real on account of avidyā. We take our mental states to be external objects. Again, those who seek the cause of these mental states, which are seen as external objects, are led into a logical *regressus*. From the standpoint of reality, the whole idea of causality is unreal.' (*From Ānandagiri's commentary on Śaṅkarāchārya.*)

[7] All three states have a common feature, namely, absence of the Knowledge of Reality. But deep sleep differs from waking and dreaming in that it is associated

is deep sleep, in whom all experiences become unified,[9] who is, verily, a mass of consciousness, who is full of bliss and experiences bliss,[10] and who is the door leading to the knowledge [of dreaming and waking].[11] (5)

He[12] is the Lord of all.[13] He is the knower of all. He is the inner controller. He is the source of all; for from him all beings originate and in him they finally disappear. (6)

Turiya is not that which is conscious of the inner (subjective) world, nor that which is conscious of the outer (objective) world, nor that which is conscious of both, nor that which is a mass of consciousness. It is not simple consciousness nor is It unconsciousness. It is unperceived, unrelated, incomprehensible, uninferable, unthinkable, and indescribable. The essence of the Consciousness manifesting as the self [in the three states], It is the cessation of all phenomena; It is all peace, all bliss, and non-dual. This is what is known as the Fourth (Turiya).[14] This is Ātman, and this has to be realized.[15] (7)

neither with gross objects nor with subtle impressions, which are the characteristics of the other two.

[8] That is to say, the knower *par excellence*. This state is characterized only by general consciousness. The other two states are associated with the knowledge of particulars.

[9] In deep sleep all the diversified experiences of waking and dreaming, which are nothing but the activities of the mind, reach the state of non-discrimination, without, however, losing their peculiar characteristics—just as the various objects perceived during the day lose their diverse appearances when enveloped by the darkness of night. (*Adapted from Śankarāchārya.*)

[10] It is because of the absence of conflict caused by the subject-object relationship. All effort disappears. Hence a person in deep sleep experiences bliss, in the sense that one who is free from effort is said to be happy. This bliss is quite different from the Bliss of Brahman.

[11] The unified consciousness of deep sleep is antecedent to the waking and dream experiences.

[12] Refers to Prājna. In this state, Consciousness, free from the diversities of waking and dreaming, manifests in a marked degree its natural purity.

[13] That is to say, of the physical and the supraphysical universe. But this lordship does not refer to an extra-cosmic Creator, as some schools hold. (Compare *Br. Up.* IV. iv. 22.)

[14] This does not signify a numerical relationship with the three states of waking, dreaming, and deep sleep. Turiya is called the Fourth because It occupies the fourth place in the order of exposition of Brahman.

[15] Turiya, or Pure Consciousness, is described in the text by the negation of all attributes. No language can directly express It, either by affirmative or by negative words. But It is not therefore a void or utter non-existence; for one cannot imagine the illusory universe without a positive substratum. It may, however, be contended that Turiya should be described as the substratum of the universe, and not in a negative way. Such a contention has no force; for the universe is unreal. No relation between real and unreal can be imagined, much less expressed, since

The same Ātman [explained before as being endowed with four quarters] is now described from the standpoint of the syllable *Aum*.[16] Aum, too, divided into parts, is viewed from the standpoint of letters. The quarters [of Ātman] are the same as the letters of Aum, and the letters are the same as the quarters. The letters are *A*, *U*, and *M*. (8)

Vaiśvānara Ātman, whose sphere of activity is the waking state, is *A*, the first letter [of Aum], on account of his all-pervasiveness[17] or on account of his being the first.[18] He who knows this obtains all desires and becomes first [among the great]. (9)

Taijasa Ātman, whose sphere of activity is the dream state, is *U*, the second letter [of Aum], on account of his superiority[19] or intermediateness.[20] He who knows this attains a superior knowledge, receives equal treatment from all, and finds in his family no one ignorant of Brahman. (10)

Prājna Ātman, whose sphere is deep sleep, is *M*, the third letter [of Aum], because both are the measure[21] and also because in them all

the relationship itself is non-existent. Turiya cannot be described by any instrument of empirical knowledge, because of Its unique nature. It is devoid of all characteristics, specific or generic, being one and without a second. Then, it may be asked, what purpose is served by the Knowledge of Turiya? Is Turiya not something non-existent like the son of a barren woman? Not at all. When a person realizes his self to be Turiya, he is freed from craving for outer objects. The realization of the self as Turiya destroys ignorance, desire, attachment, aversion, etc. The gist of the teachings of the Upanishads is the identity of the self and Turiya.

[16] Aum is pronounced Om. 'In Sanskrit the vowel *o* is constitutionally a diphthong, contracted from *a+u*. *Om* therefore may be analyzed into the elements *a+u+m*.' (R. E. Hume, *The Thirteen Principal Upanishads*, Oxford University Press, fn. p. 393.)

[17] When a man wants to utter any sound, the very opening of his mouth produces (audibly or inaudibly) the sound *A*; therefore *A* is said to pervade all sounds. Likewise, the entire universe is pervaded by Vaiśvānara Ātman, whose symbol is the waking state, when alone a man can think about the dream state and deep sleep. Since the three states constitute our entire experience of the universe, the waking state pervades the whole universe.

[18] Another point of resemblance between *A* and Vaiśvānara is that just as *A* is the beginning, or first, of the three letters constituting Aum, so also Vaiśvānara, or the waking state, may be said to be the beginning, or first, of the three states.

[19] Taijasa, or Ātman functioning through the dream state, is said to be superior to Vaiśvānara because he perceives ideas, whereas the latter sees only gross objects.

[20] As the letter *U* is between *A* and *M*, so the dream state is between waking and deep sleep.

[21] Both the waking state and the dream state emerge from (during manifestation) and disappear into (during non-manifestation) the dreamless state. Therefore both Vaiśvānara and Taijasa are said to be contained in Prājna, which may be compared to the container. The word *measure* in the text is used in the sense of a container.

become one.[22] He who knows this is able to measure all and also comprehends all within himself. (11)

The Fourth (Turiya) is without parts[23] and without relationship; It is the cessation of phenomena; It is all good and non-dual. This Aum is verily Ātman. He who knows this merges his self in Ātman—yea, he who knows this.[24] (12)

[22] When the word *Aum* is repeated quickly several times, the sound actually heard is *maum*. That is why it is said that the letters *A* and *U* become one with *M*. Likewise, Visva and Taijasa become one with, or merge in, Prājna in deep sleep.

[23] That is to say, without sound. This aspect of Aum cannot be expressed by any sound. Being non-dual, it cannot even be described as the substratum of the three other sounds. The Aum uttered through sounds points, by contrast, to the soundless Aum. All sounds must some time or other merge in silence or soundlessness. The soundless Aum is the same as Turiya.

[24] Those who have realized Brahman, the Highest Reality, merge the self in Turiya because they have transcended the notion of cause and effect, which inheres in the third quarter of Ātman. They are not born again; for they have realized their identity with the causeless Turiya. The illusory snake which has merged in the rope as a result of discrimination between the snake and the rope, does not reappear. Students of dull or mediocre mind who have renounced the world and are endowed with spiritual virtues should meditate on the common features of the sounds of Aum and the quarters of Ātman, as explained before. Thus, proceeding step by step, they ultimately realize Turiya, devoid of any state or sound, and attain the Highest Goal. (*Adapted from Śankarāchārya's commentary.*)

THE PEACE CHANT

OM. MAY WE, O gods, hear with our ears what is auspicious!
May we, O worshipful gods, see with our eyes what is good!
May we, strong in limbs and body, sing your praise and enjoy
the life allotted to us by Prajāpati!

Om. Peace! Peace! Peace!

FINAL SALUTATION
BY ŚRI ŚANKARĀCHĀRYA

I SALUTE BRAHMAN, the destroyer of the fear of those who take refuge in It—which, though unborn, appears to be associated with birth through Its own majestic powers; which, though motionless, appears to be moving; and which, though non-dual, appears to have assumed many forms to those whose vision is deluded by the perception of diverse objects and their attributes.

I prostrate myself at the feet of the teacher of my teacher,[25] the most adored among the adorable, who—out of sheer compassion for the beings drowned in the deep ocean of the world, infested by the terrible sharks of incessant births and deaths —rescued, for the benefit of all, this nectar, hardly attainable even by the immortals, from the inmost depths of the ocean of the Vedas by churning it with the rod of his illumined wisdom.

I make obeisance with my whole being to those holy feet— the dispellers of the fear of the chain of births and deaths—of my own great teacher, who, through the light of his illumined wisdom, destroyed the darkness of delusion enveloping my mind; who put an end, for ever, to my appearance and disappearance in this terrible ocean of innumerable births and deaths; and who enables all others, too, that take shelter at his feet, to attain unfailing knowledge of the scriptures, peace, and the state of perfect non-differentiation.

Aum Tat Sat

[25] A reference to Gaudapāda, who was the teacher of Śankarāchārya's teacher, Govindapāda.

AITAREYA UPANISHAD

INTRODUCTION

THE *AITAREYA UPANISHAD* belongs to the *Aitareya Āranyaka* and is a part of the Rig-Veda. Consisting of three parts, the Upanishad proper begins with the fourth section of the second part of the Āranyaka and comprises sections four, five, and six. The preceding part of the Āranyaka prescribes rituals for the attainment of oneness with Prāna, or Saguna Brahman. According to some, the attainment of this oneness through rituals and meditation is the goal of human endeavour and the ultimate teaching of the Vedas. Śankarāchārya, however, refutes this view and asserts that Self-Knowledge is the goal. This Knowledge is taught in the *Aitareya Upanishad*.

The Upanishad, as already noted, is divided into three parts. The method by which Self-Knowledge is taught is twofold. First is shown the illusory superimposition of names and forms (adhyāropa) upon Brahman, or Ātman, and next, through their refutation (apavāda), is revealed the sole reality of Ātman. The verses up to the first sentence of I. ii. 13 deal with illusory superimposition, and then follows the refutation.

INVOCATION

MAY MY SPEECH be fixed in my mind, may my mind be fixed in my speech![1] O self-luminous Brahman, be manifest to me. O mind and speech, may you bring me the meaning of the Vedas! May what I study from the Vedas not leave me! I shall unite day and night through this study.[2] I shall think of the right; I shall speak the right. May Brahman protect me, may Brahman protect the teacher! May Brahman protect me, may Brahman protect the teacher!

Om. Peace! Peace! Peace!

[1] The meaning is that while the student studies the Upanishad his mind and speech should help each other so that he may understand its significance.

[2] i.e. I shall devote the whole day and night to the study of the Upanishad.

I

IN THE BEGINNING [all] this verily was Ātman only, one and without a second. There was nothing else that winked. He bethought Himself: 'Let Me now create the worlds.' (I. i. 1)

He created these worlds: Ambhah (the world of water-bearing clouds), Marichi (the world of the solar rays), Mara (the world of mortals), and Ap (the world of waters). Yon is Ambhah, above heaven; heaven is its support. The Marichis are the mid-region. Mara is the earth. What is underneath is Ap.[3] (I. i. 2)

He bethought Himself: 'Here now are the worlds. Let Me now create world-guardians.' Right from the waters[4] He drew forth the Person [in the form of a lump] and gave Him a shape.[5] (I. i. 3)

He brooded over Him (the lump). From Him, so brooded over, the mouth was separated out, as with an egg [when it is hatched]; from the mouth,[6] [the organ of] speech; from speech, fire (the controlling deity of the organ).

Then the nostrils were separated out; from the nostrils, [the organ of] breath (prāna); from breath, air (the controlling deity of the organ).

Then the eyes were separated out; from the eyes, [the organ of] sight (chakshu); from sight, the sun (the controlling deity of the organ).

Then the ears were separated out; from the ears, [the organ of] hearing (śrotra); from hearing, the quarters of space (the controlling deity of the organ).

Then the skin was separated out; from the skin, hairs (i.e. the organ of touch); from the hairs, plants and trees (i.e. air, the controlling deity of the organ).

Then the heart was separated out; from the heart, [the organ of] the mind (manas); from the mind, the moon (the controlling deity of the organ).

Then the navel was separated out; from the navel, the [organ of the] apāna; from the apāna, Death (i.e. Varuna, the controlling deity of the organ).

[3] Refers to the nether worlds, which are frequented by inferior beings.
[4] Though the worlds contain all five elements, yet they preponderate in water.
[5] Refers to Virāt, the gross form of the Cosmic Person.
[6] It will be seen that first the visible instrument is formed, next the subtle organ (indriya) which is the real instrument of perception, and last the controlling deity (devatā) or conscious element which animates the organ.

Then the virile member was separated out; from the virile member, semen (the organ of generation); from semen, the waters (the controlling deity of the organ). (I. i. 4)

These deities, thus created, fell into this great ocean.[7] He (the Creator)[8] subjected that Person (i.e. Virāt in the form of a lump) to hunger and thirst. They (the deities) said to Him (the Creator): 'Find out for us an abode wherein being established we may eat food.' (I. ii. 1)

He (the Creator) brought them a cow.[9] They said: 'But this is not enough for us.' He brought them a horse. They said: 'This, too, is not enough for us.'
He brought them a person. The deities said: 'Ah, this is well done, indeed.' Therefore a person is verily something well done.
He said to the deities: 'Now enter your respective abodes.' (I. ii. 2-3)

[The deity] fire became [the organ of] speech and entered the mouth. Air became breath and entered the nostrils. The sun became sight and entered the eyes. The quarters of space became hearing and entered the ears. Plants and trees (i.e. the deity air) became hairs and entered the skin. The moon became the mind and entered the heart. Death became the apāna and entered the navel. The waters became semen and entered the virile member.[10] (I. ii. 4)

Hunger and thirst said to the Creator: 'For the two of us find an abode also.' He said to them: 'I assign the two of you to these deities; I make you co-sharers with them.'
Therefore to whatsoever deity an oblation is made, hunger and thirst become sharers in it. (I. ii. 5)

He (the Creator) bethought Himself: 'Here now are the worlds and the world-guardians. Let Me create food for them.' (I. iii. 1)

He brooded over the waters.[11] From the waters, thus brooded over, there emerged a [condensed] form. The form that so emerged is indeed food. (I. iii. 2)

The food so created wished to flee away. He sought to grasp it with speech. But He was not able to grasp it with speech. If, indeed, He had

[7] That is to say, samsāra, or the phenomenal world.
[8] From now on the word *Creator* will be used for *Ātman*.
[9] A tangible body in the shape of a cow, produced like the other beings, from the waters.
[10] The text indicates an interrelationship and continuity between man and nature, and the various cosmic forces which control them.
[11] That is to say, the five elements.

grasped it with speech, one would then have been satisfied by merely uttering [the word] *food*. (I. iii. 3)

[The Creator] sought to grasp it with the breath. But He was not able to grasp it with the breath. If, indeed, He had grasped it with the breath, one would then have been satisfied by merely smelling food.

He sought to grasp it with the eye. But He was not able to grasp it with the eye. If, indeed, He had grasped it with the eye, one would then have been satisfied by merely seeing food.

He sought to grasp it with the ear. But He was not able to grasp it with the ear. If, indeed, He had grasped it with the ear, one would then have been satisfied by merely hearing of food.

He sought to grasp it with the skin. But He was not able to grasp it with the skin. If, indeed, He had grasped it with the skin, one would then have been satisfied by merely touching food.

He sought to grasp it with the mind. But He was not able to grasp it with the mind. If, indeed, He had grasped it with the mind, one would then have been satisfied by merely thinking of food.

He sought to grasp it with the virile member. But He was not able to grasp it with the virile member. If, indeed, He had grasped it with the virile member, one would then have been satisfied by merely emitting food.[12]

He sought to grasp it with the apāna, and He grasped it. This grasper of food is what vāyu (air, or prāna) is. This vāyu is what lives on food. (I. iii. 4–10)

He (the Creator) bethought Himself: 'How could this [aggregate of body and organs] exist without Me?' Then He said to Himself: 'Which way shall I enter it?' He said to Himself further: 'If speech is uttered by the organ of speech, if smelling is done by the breath (prāna), seeing by the eyes, hearing by the ears, touching by the skin, thinking by the mind, eating by the apāna, and the emission [of semen] by the virile member, then who am I?'[13] (I. iii. 11)

So, piercing the end (i.e. the place where the parting of the hair ends), the Lord entered through that door. That door is known as the vidriti, the cleft. This is the place of bliss.

Ātman [thus embodied] has three abodes, three conditions of sleep. This is one abode, this is another, this is the third. (I. iii. 12)

---

[12] That is to say, emitting semen, which is the essence of food.

[13] An aggregate serves the purpose of someone else. A house, for instance, consisting of such parts as pillars, floor, and roof, serves the purpose of its occupant. If the actions of the tongue, eyes, ears, etc., are not performed consciously for someone other than themselves, then these actions are meaningless. In reality, the organs function in different ways so that through their action a man may realize the true nature of Ātman, the Master of the body.

Having been born as the jiva, He realized the elements (bhutas) as one with Himself [and expressed this in words]. What else here would one desire to speak about?

He perceived this very person as the all-pervading Brahman. He said: 'Ah, I have seen It.' (I. iii. 13)

Therefore He (the Supreme Self) is called Idandra.[14] Idandra, indeed, is His name. Him who is Idandra they call indirectly Indra. For the gods appear to be fond of cryptic epithets; yea, the gods appear to be fond of cryptic epithets. (I. iii. 14)

[14] Lit., the perceiver of this. The Supreme Self is called Idandra because He is directly perceived as Brahman and is not perceived through the sense-organs.

II

THIS [PERSON] IS, at first, the germ in a man. That which is the semen is here called the germ. This semen is the vigour (tejas) drawn from all the limbs. The man bears the self (i.e. the semen) in the self (i.e. the body). When he pours the semen into a woman, he gives it a birth. This, indeed, is the first birth of the embodied soul. (II. i. 1)

That semen becomes one with the woman—just like a limb of her own. That is why it does not hurt her. She nourishes this self of his that has come into her. (II. i. 2)

She, being the nourisher, should be nourished [by her husband]. The woman nourishes the embryo. Immediately after its birth he (the father) nourishes [with natal ceremonies] the child, which in the beginning was already born [as the embryo]. Nourishing the child from birth onward, he thus nourishes himself for the continuation of these worlds. For thus alone are these worlds perpetuated. This is one's second birth. (II. i. 3)

He (the son) who is the one self (body) of his [father's] is made his [father's] substitute for [performing] virtuous deeds. Then the other self (body) of his [father's], having accomplished his duties and reached his age departs [from this world]. So departing hence, he is born again. This is his third birth. (II. i. 4)

About this a rishi has said:
'While still lying in the womb, I came to know all the births of the gods. A hundred strongholds,[15] as if made of iron, confined me, yet I burst through them all swiftly, like a hawk.'
Vāmadeva spoke, in this wise, even while lying in the womb. (II. i. 5)

Thus endowed with Knowledge, he, becoming one with the Supreme Self and soaring aloft on the dissolution of the body, obtained all desires in the heavenly world and became immortal—yea, became immortal. (II. i. 6)

---

[15] Physical bodies.

III

WHO IS HE whom we worship, thinking: 'This is the Self (Ātman)'? [Of the two mentioned in the scriptures,] which one[16] is the Self? Is it He by whom one sees form, by whom one hears sound, and by whom one tastes the sweet and the unsweet? (III. i. 1)

It[17] is the heart and the mind. It is [known, in accordance with its different functions, as] consciousness, lordship, knowledge [of arts], wisdom, retentive power of mind, sense knowledge, steadfastness, thought, thoughtfulness, sorrow, memory, concepts, purpose, life, desire, longing [for sense-objects]: all these are but various names of Consciousness (Prajnānam). (III. i. 2)

He is Brahman, He is Indra, He is Prajāpati; He is all these gods; He is the five great elements—earth, air, ākāśa, water, light; He is all these small creatures and the others which are mixed [with them]; He is the origin [of the moving and the unmoving]—those born of an egg, of a womb, of sweat, and of a sprout; He is horses, cows, human beings, elephants—whatever breathes here, whether moving on legs or flying in the air or unmoving. All this is guided by Consciousness (Prajnānam), is supported by Consciousness. The basis [of the universe] is Consciousness. Consciousness is Brahman. (III. i. 3)

He,[18] [having realized oneness with Pure Consciousness,] soared from this world, and having obtained all desires in yonder heavenly world, became immortal—yea, became immortal. (III. i. 4)

---

[16] Two selves have been mentioned in the Upanishads: One is the prāna, or vital breath, which is transformed into the various sense-organs and through them experiences various objects. The other is that which witnesses these sensations and remembers them.

[17] Refers to the Higher Self, which enters the body through the top of the head.

[18] That is to say, Vāmadeva, mentioned in II. i. 5–6. The result of the knowledge described in this verse may apply to any other illumined soul.

THE PEACE CHANT

MAY MY SPEECH be fixed in my mind, may my mind be fixed in my speech! O self-luminous Brahman, be manifest to me. O mind and speech, may you bring me the meaning of the Vedas! May what I study from the Vedas not leave me! I shall unite day and night through this study. I shall think of the right; I shall speak the right. May Brahman protect me, may Brahman protect the teacher! May Brahman protect me, may Brahman protect the teacher!

Om. Peace! Peace! Peace!

BRIHADĀRANYAKA UPANISHAD

INTRODUCTION

THE *BRIHADĀRANYAKA UPANISHAD* forms an important part of the philosophical and religious literature of the Vedas. It belongs to the *Śatapatha Brāhmana* of the Śukla Yajur-Veda. The literal meaning of the term *Brihadāranyaka Upanishad* is 'Great Forest Upanishad'. Śankarāchārya, in the Introduction to his commentary, says that this Upanishad, consisting of six parts, is called 'Great' (Brihat) because of its length and profundity, and 'Forest' (Āranyaka) because of its having been taught in à forest. It contains both teaching and reasoning in support of the teaching. The theme of the book, as of all Vedāntic treatises, is the absolute identity of Ātman and Brahman. This identity has been established by the well-known logical method of jalpa (argument repudiating the views of opponents) and vāda (reasoning for the purpose of discovering Reality). Throughout his commentary Śankarāchārya reveals himself not only as exegete and philosopher, but also as mystic.

It is sometimes asked whether the *Brihadāranyaka Upanishad* develops a single theme or is a mere conglomeration of unrelated views. Traditional Hindu interpreters uphold the former view, while some Western Orientalists uphold the latter. Sureśvarāchārya, in his illuminating explanation (vārttika) of Śankara's commentary, has pointed out the harmony between the different parts of the Upanishad. He has arranged the book in three divisions (kāndas): the Madhukānda, the Yājnavalkyakānda or Munikānda, and the Khilakānda. The first kānda contains the revelation of the principal Advaita doctrines and is called upadeśa (teaching); the second furnishes logical arguments (upapatti) showing the soundness of the upadeśa, and the third deals with certain forms of meditation (upāsanā), by means of which the aspirant experiences what is laid down in the upadeśa.

There exists an apparently unbridgeable gap between the ritualistic section (Karmakānda) of the Vedas and the philosophical section (Jnānakānda), describing the Knowledge of Brahman. The section of the Upanishads dealing with upāsanā, however, supplies the bridge. It shows the way to direct the mind from the performance of rituals to the philosophical contemplation of Brahman.

In the *Brihadāranyaka Upanishad* one meets with certain noble characters of ancient India—ideal women, ideal kings, and an ideal monk. Maitreyi, Yājnavalkya's second wife, indifferent to worldly happiness attainable through wealth and possessions, seeks to know that Reality which enables one to conquer death. Gārgi engages Yājnavalkya in an erudite discussion about Brahman and shows the superiority of

her intelligence to that of the other Vedic scholars. Janaka is both king
and sage, being known by the well deserved title of rājarshi, or 'royal
sage'. He is called Vaideha, signifying his total detachment from the
body; and by a strange coincidence he is the ruler of Videha (north-east
of modern Patna). Janaka is the centre of the intellectual life of the court
that surrounds him. The Upanishad also speaks of the court of Ajātaśatru, King of Kāśi (which lay about Benares), and the court of Jivala,
King of the Panchālas, where learned discussions about Brahman and
the soul took place.

Yājnavalkya dominates the teachings of the *Brihadāranyaka Upanishad*. His contribution to the philosophy of Ātman and Brahman is the
essence of Advaita Vedānta. He is a great ritualist, a subtle debater, an
expert in Vedic exegesis, and at the same time a man with a delicate
sense of humour. Yājnavalkya has two wives and owns land, wealth,
and cattle. Wishing to put into practice his own teaching, given in the
Upanishad, that one who has gained the Knowledge of the Self abstains
from the desire for children, wealth, and the world, and wanders about
as a religious mendicant—for what need has he of offspring whose Self
is this universe?—Yājnavalkya renounces the worldly life, after having
fulfilled the obligations of a householder by making provision for his
wives, and becomes a sannyāsin. In Janaka's court he teaches the
nature of Ātman and Brahman.

The utter oneness of Ātman and Brahman is the most significant
contribution of Yājnavalkya to the philosophic thought of India.
Brahman is the Reality behind the universe, and Ātman the Reality
behind the individual. Though the Reality underlying the universe may
be unlimited, It may appear to be something vague; It may also appear
to be material in nature. The self, conversely, is clear, directly perceived,
and spiritual in nature, though it may appear to be limited by other
selves. The realization of the identity of the self and Brahman in a
mystical experience establishes the existence of a Reality which is
infinite, directly perceived, unlimited, and spiritual. Neither reasoning
nor philosophical speculation can soar higher or penetrate deeper than
this metaphysical Reality—the non-duality of Existence.

INVOCATION

OM. THAT IS full; this is full. This fullness has been projected from that fullness. When this fullness merges in that fullness, all that remains is fullness.

Om. Peace! Peace! Peace!

I

THERE WERE TWO classes of Prajāpati's sons: the gods (devas) and the demons (asuras).[1] Naturally, the gods were few and the demons many. They struggled with one another for [mastery of] these worlds. [Being overwhelmed by the demons,] the gods said: 'Well, let us overcome the demons at the sacrifice (jyotishtoma) by means of the Udgitha.'[2] (I. iii. 1)

They said to the organ[3] of speech: 'Chant [the Udgitha] for us.' 'So be it,' said speech and chanted for them. Whatever enjoyment common to all comes from the organ of speech, it secured for the gods by chanting, while [the enjoyment derived from] the fine utterance [of the words] it utilized for itself. Now, the demons knew that through this chanter the gods would overcome them. They charged[4] at it (speech) and pierced it with evil. That evil is what is found today when one speaks improperly; that is that evil. (I. iii. 2)

Then they said to the organ of smell: 'Chant [the Udgitha] for us.' 'So be it,' said the organ and chanted for them. Whatever enjoyment common to all comes from the nose, it secured for the gods by chanting, while [the enjoyment derived from] fine smelling it utilized for itself. Now, the demons knew that through this chanter the gods would overcome them. They charged at it and pierced it with evil. That evil is what is found today when one smells improper things; that is that evil. (I. iii. 3)

Then they said to the organ of seeing: 'Chant [the Udgitha] for us.' 'So be it,' said the organ and chanted for them. Whatever enjoyment common to all comes from the eye, it secured for the gods by chanting, while [the enjoyment derived from] fine seeing it utilized for itself. Now, the demons knew that through this chanter the gods would over-

---

[1] By the word *sons* are meant the organs of speech, hearing, etc. They signify both gods and demons. 'When the organs think and act according to the scriptural injunctions to gain spiritual ends, they are called gods. But those very organs become demons when their actions and thoughts are guided only by se nse perception and inference and are directed to secular ends.' (*Adapted from Śankarāchārya's commentary*.)

[2] A part of the Sāma-Veda chanted at the sacrifice. The gods intended to defeat the demons through the Udgitha, that is to say, by identifying themselves with the chanter (prāna, or the vital breath) of the Udgitha.

[3] In this and the succeeding verses the organ refers to that deity which controls and regulates the organ by identifying itself with it.

[4] Evil entered through the fault furnished by the attachment of the organ of speech to its own enjoyment.

come them. They charged at it and pierced it with evil. That evil is what is found today when one sees improper things; that is that evil. (I. iii. 4)

Then they said to the organ of hearing: 'Chant [the Udgitha] for us.' 'So be it,' said the organ and chanted for them. Whatever enjoyment common to all comes from the ear, it secured for the gods by chanting, while [the enjoyment derived from] fine hearing it utilized for itself. Now, the demons knew that through this chanter the gods would overcome them. They charged at it and pierced it with evil. That evil is what is found today when one hears improper things; that is that evil. (I. iii. 5)

Then they said to the mind: 'Chant [the Udgitha] for us.' 'So be it,' said the mind and chanted for them. Whatever enjoyment common to all comes from the mind, it secured for the gods by chanting, while [the enjoyment derived from] fine thinking it utilized for itself. Now, the demons knew that through this chanter the gods would overcome them. They charged at it and pierced it with evil. That evil is what is found today when one thinks improperly; that is that evil.

Likewise they also touched these [other] deities with evil—smote them with evil. (I. iii. 6)

Then they said to the vital breath in the mouth: 'Chant [the Udgitha] for us.' 'So be it,' said the vital breath and chanted for them. The demons knew that through this chanter the gods would overcome them. They charged at it, intending to pierce it with evil. But as a clod of earth, hitting a stone, is scattered, even so they were scattered in all directions, crushed, and completely destroyed. Thereupon the gods became established [in their true selves] and the demons perished. He who knows this becomes his true self, and his spiteful kinsman[5] perishes (I. iii. 7)

'Lead me from the unreal to the real. From darkness lead me to light. From death lead me to immortality.'
When the mantra (verse) says: 'Lead me from the unreal to the real,' 'the unreal' means death, and the 'real', immortality; so it says, 'From death lead me to immortality,' that is to say, 'Make me immortal.'
When it says: 'From darkness lead me to light,' 'darkness' means death, and 'light', immortality; so it says: 'From death lead me to immortality,' that is to say, 'Make me immortal.'

[5] That is to say, the power of evil, which obstructs spiritual progress.

In the verse: 'From death lead me to immortality,' there is nothing that is hidden. (I. iii. 28)

In the beginning, this [universe] was the self (Virāj) alone, in the shape of a person. He reflected and saw nothing else but His self. He first said: 'I am He.' Therefore He came to be known by the name *I* (*Aham*). Hence, even now, when a person is addressed, he first says: 'It is I,' and then says whatever other name he may have. And because He, prior to (purva)[6] the whole group [of aspirants], burnt (aushat) all evils, therefore He is called Purusha. He who knows this verily burns up him who wishes to be [Virāj] in advance of him. (I. iv. 1)

He was afraid. Therefore people [still] are afraid when alone. He thought: 'Since there is nothing else but Myself, what am I afraid of?' Thereupon His fears were gone; for what was there to fear? Assuredly, it is from a second [entity] that fear arises. (I. iv. 2)

He was not at all happy. Therefore a person [even today] is not happy when alone. He desired a mate. He became the size of a man and wife in close embrace.[7] He divided this body into two. From that [division] arose husband (pati) and wife (patni). Therefore, as Yājnavalkya said, the body [before one accepts a wife] is one half of oneself, like the half of a split pea. Therefore this space is indeed filled by the wife. He was united with her. From that [union] human beings were born. (I. iv. 3)

She reflected: 'How can he unite with me after having produced me from himself? Well, let me hide myself.' She became a cow, the other became a bull and was united with her; from that [union] cows were born. The one became a mare, the other became a stallion; the one became a she-ass, the other became a he-ass and was united with her; from that [union] one-hoofed animals were born. The one became a she-goat, the other became a he-goat; the one became a ewe, the other became a ram and was united with her; from that [union] goats and sheep were born. Thus, indeed, he produced everything that exists in pairs, down to the ants. (I. iv. 4)

---

[6] In a previous incarnation, when, as a religious student, he was the first of all the candidates who wanted to attain the status of Virāj and practised adequately the rites and meditation laid down in the Vedas for this purpose.

[7] It should be remembered that Virāj did not wipe out His former self in order to assume this new form. He remained as He was. But, being a person of true resolve, He projected another body of the size of a man and wife united in close embrace. Such a phenomenon is called māyā.

He (Virāj) realized: 'Indeed, I am the creation, for I produced all this.' Therefore He became the creation. He who knows this becomes a creator in this creation of Virāj. (I. iv. 5)

Now, all this [universe] was then undifferentiated. It became differentiated by name and form: it was known by such and such a name, and such and such a form.[8] Thus to this day this [universe] is differentiated by name and form; [so it is said:] 'He has such a name and such a form.'

This Self has entered into these bodies up to the very tips of the nails, as a razor lies [hidden] in its case, or as fire, which sustains the world, [lies hidden] in its source. People do not see the Self, for [when viewed in parts] It is incomplete: when breathing, It is called the vital breath (prāna); when speaking, the organ of speech; when seeing, the eye; when hearing, the ear; when thinking, the mind. These are merely Its names according to Its functions. He who meditates on one or another of Its aspects does not know, for It is then incomplete: the Self is separated from Its totality by being associated with a single characteristic.

The Self alone is to be meditated upon, for in It all these become unified. Of all these, this Self alone should be known, for one knows all these through It, just as one may find [an animal which is lost] through its footprints. He who thus knows the Self obtains fame and association [with dear ones]. (I. iv. 7)

This [Self] is dearer than a son, dearer than wealth, dearer than everything else, [because] It is innermost. If one [holding the Self dear] were to say to a person who speaks of anything other than the Self as dear, that he, the latter, will lose what he holds dear—and the former is certainly competent to do so—it will indeed come true.

One should meditate upon the Self alone as dear. He who meditates upon the Self alone as dear—what he holds dear will not perish. (I. iv. 8)

They say: 'Since men think that by the Knowledge of Brahman they become all, what, pray, was it that Brahman knew by which It became all?' (I. iv. 9)

This [self] was indeed Brahman in the beginning.[9] It knew itself only as 'I am Brahman'. Therefore it became all. And whoever among the

---

[8] Name and form constitute individuality in the relative universe.

[9] Even before the realization of its true nature, the self is Brahman and identical with all; 'but owing to ignorance it superimposes upon itself the notion that it is not Brahman and that it is not all, and consequently thinks, through mistake, that

gods had this enlightenment, also became That [Brahman]. It is the same with the seers (rishis), the same with men. The seer Vāmadeva, having realized this [self] as That, came to know: 'I was Manu and the sun.' And to this day, whoever in a like manner knows the self as 'I am Brahman', becomes all this [universe]. Even the gods cannot prevent his becoming this,[10] for he has become their Self.

Now, if a man[11] worships another deity, thinking: 'He is one and I am another,'[12] he does not know. He is like an animal to the gods.[13] As many animals serve a man, so does each man serve the gods. Even if one animal is taken away, it causes anguish [to the owner]; how much more so when many [are taken away]! Therefore it is not pleasing to the gods that men should know this.[14] (I. iv. 10)

In the beginning this (the kshatriya and other castes) was indeed Brahman,[15] one only without a second. He, being one,[16] did not flourish.[17] He projected, further, an excellent form, kshatriyahood—those kshatriyas (rulers) among the gods: Indra, Varuna, Soma (Moon), Rudra, Parjanya, Yama, Mrityu (Death),[18] and Iśāna. Therefore there is none higher than the kshatriyas. Thus at the Rājasuya sacrifice, the brāhmin sits below and worships the kshatriya. He confers that glory on kshatriyahood alone. But brāhminhood is [nevertheless] the source of kshatriyahood. Therefore even though the king is exalted [in the

---

it is a performer of action and the experiencer of its fruits, that it is happy or miserable, and that it transmigrates. But really it is Brahman, different from all these, and is all.' (*Śankarāchārya*.)

[10] The gods are sustained by the oblations offered in the rites and sacrifices performed by men. Therefore they do not want men to pursue the Knowledge of Brahman, in which case the latter would not be interested in propitiating the gods through sacrifices. Thus the gods are said to put obstacles in the way of men's attaining the Knowledge of Brahman.

[11] Refers to an ignorant person who worships a god 'different from himself and approaches him in a subordinate position, offering him praise, salutations, sacrifices, presents, self-surrender, etc.' (*Śankarāchārya*.)

[12] That is to say, his subordinate. The ignorant man must serve the god like a debtor. The god is regarded as a creditor because the ignorant man, seeking worldly prosperity, owes him worship, sacrifice, etc.

[13] As cows or other animals are used for various services, such as carrying loads or giving milk, so is an ignorant man used by the gods for many services, such as the performance of sacrifices.

[14] The gods do not wish men to know the ultimate truth, for then they realize the subordinate position the gods hold, and give up making offerings to them. 'The world of the gods, O Arjuna, is filled with those who perform rites. And the gods do not want mortals to surpass them.' (*Mahābhārata* XIV. xx. 59.)

[15] In the beginning there was only one caste or class, the brāhmin; there was no differentiation in society.

[16] Being without protectors, such as the kshatriyas.

[17] That is to say, the brāhmins could not discharge their task properly.

[18] The king of diseases.

sacrifice], at the end of it he resorts to brāhminhood as his source. He who slights a brāhmin strikes at his own source. He becomes more evil, as one who slights his superior. (I. iv. 11)

Yet He (Virāj) did not flourish.[19] He projected the vaiśya caste—those classes of gods who are designated in groups:[20] the Vasus, Rudras, Ādityas, Viśve-devas, and Maruts. (I. iv. 12)

Still He did not flourish. He projected the śudra caste—Pushan. This [earth] is verily Pushan (the nourisher); for it nourishes all that exists. (I. iv. 13)

Yet He did not flourish. He projected, further, that excellent form, justice (dharma). This justice is the controller of the kshatriya. Therefore there is nothing higher than justice. So even a weak man hopes [to defeat] a stronger man through justice, as one does with the help of a king. Verily, that which is justice is truth. Therefore if a man speaks the truth, they say he speaks what is just, and if he speaks what is just, they say he speaks the truth; for justice alone is both these. (I. iv. 14)

So these [four castes were projected]: the brāhmin, the kshatriya, the vaiśya, and the śudra. Among the gods Prajāpati became a brāhmin as fire, and among men [He became] the brāhmin.[21] He became a kshatriya [among men] through the [divine] kshatriyas, a vaiśya through the [divine] vaiśyas, and a śudra through the [divine] śudras. Therefore people desire to attain the results of their rites among the gods through fire, and among men as a brāhmin.[22] For Prajāpati [directly] projected Himself as these two forms.

Now, if a man departs from this world without realizing his own World (the Self), It, being unknown, does not protect him—as the Vedas, unrecited, or as a deed unaccomplished, do not [protect him]. Nay, even if one who does not know It (the Self) should perform here on earth a great many meritorious acts, those acts will in the end surely perish for him. One should meditate only upon the World called the Self. He who meditates upon the World called the Self—his work does not perish; for from this very Self he projects whatever he desires. (I. iv. 15)

[19] Still He lacked someone who could earn wealth.

[20] The vaiśyas abound in groups, for they succeed in acquiring wealth mostly in combination, not singly.

[21] Prajāpati directly manifested Himself, among the gods, as a brāhmin in the form of fire, and among men, as the brāhmin.

[22] If a person wishes to obtain the highest goal in the world of men, he does not have to perform rites depending on fire. He can obtain it simply by being born as a brāhmin, who is a projection of Prajāpati. A brāhmin may attain perfection through the repetition of sacred formulas, whether or not he performs rites depending on fire.

Now, this self (the ignorant person) is an object of enjoyment (lokah) to all beings.[23] In so far as he offers oblations in the fire and performs sacrifices, he becomes an object of enjoyment to the gods. In so far as he studies the Vedas, he becomes an object of enjoyment to the rishis. In so far as he makes offerings to the Manes and desires children, he becomes an object of enjoyment to the Manes. In so far as he gives shelter and food to men, he becomes an object of enjoyment to men. In so far as he gives fodder and water to the animals, he becomes an object of enjoyment to the animals. In so far as beasts and birds and even ants find a living in his home, he becomes an object of enjoyment to these. Just as one wishes no injury to one's body, so do all beings wish no injury to him who has this knowledge.[24] All this, indeed, has been known and well investigated. (I. iv. 16)

In the beginning[25] this [aggregate of desirable objects] was but the self,[26] one only. He cherished the desire: 'Let me have a wife,[27] so that I may be born [as the child]; and let me have wealth, so that I may perform rites.' This much, indeed, is [the range of] desire; even if one wishes, one cannot get more than this. Therefore, to this day, a man who is single desires: 'Let me have a wife, so that I may be born [as the child]; and let me have wealth, so that I may perform rites.' So long as he does not obtain each one of these, he thinks he is incomplete.

Now, his completeness[28] [can also come in this way]: The mind is his self, speech his wife, the vital breath his child, the eye his human wealth, for he finds it with the eye; the ear his divine wealth, for he hears it with the ear; the body his [instrument of] rites, for he performs rites through the body. [So] this sacrifice has five factors—the animals have five factors, men have five factors, and all this that exists has five factors. He who knows this obtains all this. (I. iv. 17)

[23] The ignorant person is dependent upon various beings, from the gods to the ants, for the fulfilment of his desires. Thus, through what is known as his caste duties, he serves these beings. He is a debtor to them and makes himself an object of enjoyment to them. They help him in the fulfilment of his desires.

[24] All beings in the relative universe, from the gods to the ants, are slaves of desires which are satisfied through the fulfilment of their duties to one another. Duties to men are discharged through the giving of shelter to guests and strangers; to the gods, through the offering of oblations; to the rishis, through study of the scriptures; to the Manes, through the begetting of children; to the animals, by offering them fodder and water. And the gods, the rishis, the Manes, etc., protect men from injury.

[25] Before marriage.

[26] Here the word *self* means a man identified with the body and the organs.

[27] A wife qualifies a man belonging to the three upper castes for the Vedic rites. Without her they cannot be performed.

[28] If he cannot make himself complete in any other way, he may pursue the following instruction of the scripture to bring about his completeness.

Now, these are, verily, the three worlds: the world of men, the world of the Manes, and the world of the gods. The world of men can be gained through a son only, and by no other rite; the world of the Manes through rites; and the world of the gods through meditation.[29] The world of the gods is the best of worlds. Therefore they praise meditation. (I. v. 16)

Prajāpati projected the organs. They, when they were projected, quarrelled with one another. The organ of speech resolved: 'I will go on speaking'; the eye: 'I will go on seeing'; the ear: 'I will go on hearing.' So did the other organs, according to their functions. Death, having taken the form of weariness, laid hold of them—it overtook them, and having overtaken them restrained them. Therefore does the organ of speech become tired, and so do the eye and the ear. But death did not overtake the vital breath (prāna) in the body. The other organs resolved to know it and said: 'This is verily the greatest among us; whether moving or not moving, it neither feels pain nor is injured. Well then, let us assume its form.' They all assumed its form. Therefore they are called prānas after it. (I. v. 21)

Now with regard to the gods. Fire resolved: 'I will go on burning'; the sun: 'I will go on giving heat'; the moon: 'I will go on shining.' And so did the other gods, according to their functions. As is the vital breath in the body among the organs, so is air (vāyu) among the gods. The other gods fade, but not air. Air is the deity that never sets. (I. v. 22)

---

[29] The Sanskrit word *upāsanā* means a form of worship in which meditation on the deity plays an important part. The word *rites* (*karma*) refers to ritualistic worship without meditation.

II

OM. THERE LIVED of yore a man of the Garga family called proud Bālāki, who was [an eloquent] speaker. He said to Ajātaśatru, the king of Kāśi: 'I will tell you about Brahman.' Ajātaśatru said: 'For this proposal I give you a thousand [cows]. People indeed rush, saying: "Janaka, Janaka."[30] [I too have some of his virtues.]' (II. i. 1)

Gārgya said: 'That being (purusha)[31] who is in the sun, I meditate upon as Brahman.' Ajātaśatru said: 'No, no! Please do not talk to me about him. I meditate upon him as all-surpassing, as the head of all beings, and as resplendent.' Whosoever thus meditates upon him becomes all-surpassing, the head of all beings, and resplendent.[32] (II. i. 2)

Gārgya said: 'That being (purusha) who is in the moon, I meditate upon as Brahman.' Ajātaśatru said: 'No, no! Please do not talk to me about him. I meditate upon him as the great, white-robed, radiant Soma.' Whosoever thus meditates upon him has, every day, abundant soma pressed for him in his principal and auxiliary sacrifices, and his food never runs short. (II. i. 3)

Gārgya said: 'That being (purusha) who is in lightning, I meditate upon as Brahman.' Ajātaśatru said: 'No, no! Please do not talk about him. I meditate upon him as luminous.' Whosoever thus meditates upon him becomes luminous, and his progeny too becomes luminous. (II. i. 4)

Gārgya said: 'This being (purusha) who is in the ākāśa, I meditate upon as Brahman.' Ajātaśatru said: 'No, no! Please do not talk about him. I meditate upon him as full and unmoving.' Whosoever thus meditates upon him is filled with progeny and cattle, and his progeny is never extinct from this world. (II. i. 5)

[30] People who want to hear or speak about Brahman or want some present rush to Janaka. Bālāki, also known as Gārgya because he belonged to the Garga family, through his proposal gave the king a chance to prove that he too had those qualities.

[31] 'The being who identifies himself both with the sun and with the eye, and who, having entered the body through the eye, resides in the heart as the ego, the experiencer, and the agent.' (*Śankarāchārya*.) Gārgya worshipped Brahman in the aggregate of the body and organs and asked the king to do so.

[32] Gārgya, though a brāhmin, regarded the conditioned Brahman as the Self. But Ajātaśatru, though a kshatriya, knew the Supreme Brahman as the Self. The one represents imperfect knowledge of Brahman, and the other, perfect knowledge.

Gārgya said: 'This being (purusha) who is in the air, I meditate upon as Brahman.' Ajātaśatru said: 'No, no! Please do not talk about him. I meditate upon him as the Lord (Indra), as irresistible, and as the unvanquished army.' Whosoever thus meditates upon him becomes ever victorious, invincible, and a conqueror of enemies. (II. i. 6)

Gārgya said: 'This being (purusha) who is in fire, I meditate upon as Brahman.' Ajātaśatru said: 'No, no! Please do not talk about him. I meditate upon him as forbearing.' Whosoever thus meditates upon him becomes forbearing, and his progeny becomes forbearing. (II. i. 7)

Gārgya said: 'This being (purusha) who is in water, I meditate upon as Brahman.' Ajātaśatru said: 'No, no! Please do not talk about him. I meditate upon him as agreeable.' Whosoever thus meditates upon him—to him comes what is agreeable, not what is disagreeable, and to him are born children who are agreeable. (II. i. 8)

Gārgya said: 'This being (purusha) who is in the mirror, I meditate upon as Brahman.' Ajātaśatru said: 'No, no! Please do not talk about him. I meditate upon him as shining.' Whosoever thus meditates upon him becomes shining, and his progeny too becomes shining, and he outshines all those with whom he comes in contact. (II. i. 9)

Gārgya said: 'The sound that arises behind a man while he walks, I meditate upon as Brahman.' Ajātaśatru said: 'No, no! Please do not talk about him. I meditate upon him as life.' Whosoever thus meditates upon him reaches his full age on this earth, and life does not depart from him before the completion of that time. (II. i. 10)

Gārgya said: 'This being (purusha) who is in the quarters, I meditate upon as Brahman.' Ajātaśatru said: 'No, no! Please do not talk about him. I meditate upon him as second and as inseparable.' Whosoever thus meditates upon him gets companions, and his followers never part with him. (II. i. 11)

Gārgya said: 'This being (purusha) who consists of shadow, I meditate upon as Brahman.' Ajātaśatru said: 'No, no! Please do not talk about him. I meditate upon him as death.' Whosoever thus meditates upon him reaches his full age on this earth, and death does not overtake him before the completion of that time. (II. i. 12)

Gārgya said: 'This being (purusha) who is in the self, I meditate upon as Brahman.' Ajātaśatru said: 'No, no! Please do not talk about him. I meditate upon him as self-possessed.' Whosoever thus meditates upon him becomes self-possessed, and his progeny too becomes self-possessed.

Gārgya remained silent. (II. i. 13)

Ajātaśatru said: 'Is this all?'
'That is all.'
'By knowing that much one cannot know Brahman.'
'Let me approach you as a student,' said Gārgya. (II. i. 14)

Ajātaśatru said: 'It is contrary to usual practice that a brāhmin should approach a kshatriya, thinking: "He will teach me about Brahman." Nevertheless, I will instruct you.' [So saying,] he took Gārgya by the hand and rose. They came to a sleeping man. [Ajātaśatru] addressed him by these names: Great, White-robed, Radiant, Soma.[33] The man did not get up.[34] [The king] pushed him again and again with his hand till he awoke. Then he got up. (II. i. 15)

Ajātaśatru said: 'When this being full of consciousness (identified with the intellect) was thus asleep, where was it then[35] and whence did it thus come back?'[36] Gārgya did not know the answer. (II. i. 16)

Ajātaśatru said: 'When this being full of consciousness (vijnānamaya) is thus asleep, it absorbs, at that time, the functions of the organs through its own consciousness and rests in the Supreme Self (ākāśa) that is in the heart. When this being absorbs them, it is called svapiti.[37] Then the organ of smell is absorbed, the organ of speech is absorbed, the eye is absorbed, the ear is absorbed, and the mind is absorbed.' (II. i. 17)

When the self remains in the dream state, these are its achievements (results of past action): It then becomes a great king, as it were; or a noble brāhmin, as it were; or attains, as it were, high or low states. Even as a great king, taking with him his [retinue of] citizens, moves about, according to his pleasure, within his own domain, so does the self, taking with it the organs, move about according to its pleasure, in the body. (II. i. 18)

[33] These are epithets of the prāna.

[34] The fact that the sleeping man did not awake when addressed by the epithets mentioned in the text shows that the being described by Gārgya was not Brahman. Two different beings were referred to as Brahman by Gārgya and Ajātaśatru. According to Gārgya, the Prāna was Brahman. Prāna, or the vital breath which sustains the universe and the individual body, is the Saguna or conditioned Brahman. The Brahman referred to by Ajātaśatru is the jiva, or soul, which in reality is the Nirguna or attributeless Brahman.

[35] The question implies that Ātman, in Its true nature, is free from the attributes of action, agency, and result. These attributes, which are the results of past action, are not experienced in deep sleep. At that time Ātman remains in a transcendental state.

[36] The implication of the question is that when the jiva awakes it deviates from its true nature and becomes conscious of action, agency, and result.

[37] The literal meaning of the word is 'merged (apiti) in its own self (svam)'.

Next, when the self goes into deep sleep—when it does not know any-thing—it returns along the seventy-two thousand nerves called hitā,[38] which extend from the heart throughout the whole body, and remains in the body. As a baby or an emperor or a noble brāhmin lives, having reached the summit of happiness, so does the self rest. (II. i. 19)

As the spider moves along the thread [it produces], or as from a fire tiny sparks fly in all directions, even so from this Ātman come forth all organs, all worlds, all gods, all beings. Its secret name (Upanishad) is 'the Truth of truth'. The vital breaths are the truth, and their truth is Ātman. (II. i. 20)

Verily, there are two forms of Brahman: gross and subtle, mortal and immortal, limited and unlimited, definite and indefinite. (II. iii. 1)

The gross form is that which is other than air and ākāśa. It is mortal, limited, and definite. The essence of that which is gross, which is mortal, which is limited, and which is definite is the sun that shines, for it (the sun) is the essence of the three elements. (II. iii. 2)

Now the subtle: It is air and ākāśa. It is immortal, it is unlimited, and it is indefinite. The essence of that which is subtle, which is im-mortal, which is unlimited, and which is indefinite is the Person (Hiranyagarbha) in the solar orb, for that [Person] is the essence of the two elements. This is with reference to the gods. (II. iii. 3)

Now with reference to the body: The gross form is that which is other than the air and the ākāśa that is in the body. It is mortal, it is limited, and it is definite. The essence of that which is gross, which is mortal, which is limited, and which is definite is the eye; for it (the eye)[39] is the essence of the three elements. (II. iii. 4)

---

[38] The heart is the seat of the intellect (buddhi). The external organs are subject to the intellect. During the waking state, the intellect extends along the nerves, interwoven like a fish-net, to the periphery of the body and directs the organs in accordance with the individual's past actions. The individual self (jīvātmā) per-vades the intellect with a reflection of consciousness. When the intellect contracts, the self, too, contracts; this is called the sleep of the individual. When the intellect expands, the self, too, expands; this is called the waking state. The self follows the nature of the intellect, as the reflection of the moon follows the nature of the water or other medium in which it is reflected.

[39] The eye is the essence of the three gross materials that build up the body, for it is that which lends importance to the three gross elements; another reason is the priority of the eye in point of time: in the embryo it is the eyes that are first formed. (Śa. Br. IV. ii. 1.) Furthermore, the sun enters the body as the eye. (Ai. Br. I. ii. 4.)

Now the subtle: It is the air and the ākāśa that is in the body. It is immortal, it is unlimited, and it is indefinite. The essence of that which is subtle, which is immortal, which is unlimited, and which is indefinite is the person (purusha) that is in the right eye,[40] for that [person] is the essence of the two elements. (II. iii. 5)

The form of that person[41] is like a cloth dyed with turmeric,[42] or like grey sheep's wool, or like the [scarlet] insect called Indragopa, or like a tongue of fire, or like a white lotus, or like a flash of lightning. He who knows this—his splendour is like a flash of lightning.

Now, therefore, the description of Brahman: 'Not this, not this'; for there is no other and more appropriate description than this 'Not this'. Now the designation of Brahman: 'The truth of truth.' The vital breath is truth, and It (Brahman) is the Truth of that. (II. iii. 6)

'Maitreyi, my dear,' said Yājnavalkya, 'I am going to renounce this life.[43] Let me make a final settlement between you and Kātyāyani (his other wife).' (II. iv. 1)

Thereupon Maitreyi said: 'Venerable Sir, if indeed the whole earth, full of wealth, belonged to me, would I be immortal through that?' 'No,' replied Yājnavalkya, 'your life would be just like that of people who have plenty. Of Immortality, however, there is no hope through wealth.' (II. iv. 2)

Then Maitreyi said: 'What should I do with that which would not make me immortal? Tell me, venerable Sir, of that alone which you know [to be the only means of attaining Immortality].' (II. iv. 3)

Yājnavalkya replied: 'My dear, you have been my beloved [even before], and [now] you say what is after my heart. Come, sit down; I will explain it to you. As I explain it, meditate [on what I say].' (II. iv. 4)

---

[40] That is to say, the subtle body. This is stated on the evidence of the scriptures.
[41] That is to say, the subtle body. It is produced by the union of the intellect (vijnāna) and the impressions of gross and subtle objects, and consists of the impressions.
[42] In the presence of the objects of enjoyment the mind receives a corresponding tinge of impressions, as a cloth, for instance, is said to be dyed. The colouring varies sometimes according to the objects presented to the mind, and sometimes according to the tendencies of the mind itself.
[43] The householder's life. He intended to embrace the life of renunciation, which is the highest stage of life.

Then Yājnavalkya said: 'Verily, not for the sake of the husband, my dear, is the husband loved, but he is loved for the sake of the self[44] [which, in its true nature, is one with the Supreme Self].

'Verily, not for the sake of the wife, my dear, is the wife loved, but she is loved for the sake of the self.

'Verily, not for the sake of the sons, my dear, are the sons loved, but they are loved for the sake of the self.

'Verily, not for the sake of wealth, my dear, is wealth loved, but it is loved for the sake of the self.

'Verily, not for the sake of the brāhmin, my dear, is the brāhmin loved, but he is loved for the sake of the self.

'Verily, not for the sake of the kshatriya, my dear, is the kshatriya loved, but he is loved for the sake of the self.

'Verily, not for the sake of the worlds, my dear, are the worlds loved, but they are loved for the sake of the self.

'Verily, not for the sake of the gods, my dear, are the gods loved, but they are loved for the sake of the self.

'Verily, not for the sake of the beings, my dear, are the beings loved, but they are loved for the sake of the self.

'Verily, not for the sake of the All, my dear, is the All loved, but it is loved for the sake of the self.

'Verily, my dear Maitreyi, it is the Self that should be realized— should be heard of, reflected on, and meditated upon. By the realization of the Self, my dear—through hearing, reflection, and meditation—all this is known. (II. iv. 5)

'The brāhmin rejects one who knows him as different from the Self. The kshatriya rejects one who knows him as different from the Self. The worlds reject one who knows them as different from the Self. The gods reject one who knows them as different from the Self. The beings reject one who knows them as different from the Self. The All rejects one who knows it as different from the Self. This brāhmin, this kshatriya, these worlds, these gods, these beings, and this All—are that Self. (II. iv. 6)

'As the various particular [kinds of] notes of a drum, when it is beaten, cannot be grasped by themselves, but are grasped only when the general note[45] of the drum or the general sound produced by different kinds of strokes is grasped;

'And as the various particular notes of a conch, when it is blown, cannot be grasped by themselves, but are grasped only when the general

---

[44] The real attraction of things for a man is the attraction of the Spirit, or Brahman, which is the indwelling essence of all.

[45] The particular kinds of notes are modifications of the general note; they have no existence apart from the general note.

note of the conch or the general sound produced by different kinds of blowing is grasped;

'And as the various particular notes of a vīnā, when it is played, cannot be grasped by themselves, but are grasped only when the general note of the vīnā or the general sound produced by different kinds of playing is grasped;

[Similarly, no particular objects are perceived in the waking and dream states apart from Pure Intelligence.] (II. iv. 7–9)

'As from a fire kindled with wet fuel various [kinds of] smoke issue forth, even so, my dear, the Rig-Veda, the Yajur-Veda, the Sāma-Veda, the Atharvāṅgirasa, history (itihāsa), mythology (purāṇa), the arts (vidyā), the Upanishads, verses (ślokas), aphorisms (sutras), elucidations (anuvyākhyānas), and explanations (vyākhyānas) are [like] the breath of this infinite Reality. From this [Supreme Self] are all these, indeed, breathed forth. (II. iv. 10)

'As the ocean is the one goal of all waters (i.e. the place where they merge), so the skin is the one goal of all kinds of touch,[46] the nostrils are the one goal of all smells, the tongue is the one goal of all savours, the ear is the one goal of all sounds, the mind is the one goal of all deliberations, the intellect is the one goal of all [forms of] knowledge, the hands are the one goal of all actions, the organ of generation is the one goal of all [kinds of] enjoyment, the excretory organ is the one goal of all excretions, the feet are the one goal of all [kinds of] walking, the organ of speech is the one goal of all the Vedas. (II. iv. 11)

'As a lump of salt dropped into water becomes dissolved in water and cannot be taken out again, but wherever we taste [the water] it tastes salt, even so, my dear, this great, endless, infinite Reality is Pure Intelligence alone. [This self] comes out [as a separate entity] from these elements and with their destruction [this separate existence] also is destroyed. After attaining [oneness] it has no more consciousness.[47] This is what I say, my dear.'

So said Yājnavalkya. (II. iv. 12)

[46] In the general sensation of touch all the different kinds of touch are merged; they have no separate existence apart from the general sensation of touch. The general sensation of touch merges in the general deliberation of the mind, which, in its turn, merges in the general cognition of the intellect: the former is a nonentity without the latter. Finally, the general cognition of the intellect merges in Pure Intelligence, the Supreme Brahman, like different kinds of water in the ocean. This applies to all the organs of perception. When, through these successive steps, sound and the rest, together with their organs, merge in Pure Intelligence, there are no more limiting adjuncts, and Brahman, which is Pure Intelligence, alone remains. Therefore Brahman alone must be regarded as one and without a second.

[47] That is to say, no more specific consciousness.

Then Maitreyi said: 'Just here you have bewildered me,[48] venerable Sir, by saying that after attaining [oneness] the self has no more consciousness.'

Yājnavalkya replied: 'Certainly I am not saying anything bewildering, my dear. This [Reality] is enough for knowledge, O Maitreyi.' (II. iv. 13)

'For when there is duality, as it were,[49] then one smells another, one sees another, one hears another, one speaks to another, one thinks of another, one knows another. But when everything has become the Self, then what should one smell and through what, what should one see and through what, what should one hear and through what, what should one speak and through what, what should one think and through what, what should one know and through what? Through what should one know That owing to which all this is known—through what, my dear, should one know the Knower?' (II. iv. 14)

[48] Maitreyi thought that Yājnavalkya attributed contradictory qualities to Brahman by saying at first that Brahman is Pure Consciousness and then that the self attaining It loses consciousness.

[49] From the standpoint of Brahman duality is an appearance. Whenever the scriptures speak of the universe, the individual soul, created objects, etc., the words 'as it were' are implied.

III

OM. JANAKA, EMPEROR of Videha, performed a sacrifice in which gifts were freely distributed [among the priests]. Brāhmin scholars from [the countries of] Kuru and Panchāla were assembled there. Emperor Janaka of Videha wished to know which of these brāhmins was the most erudite Vedic scholar. So he confined a thousand cows in a pen and fastened on the horns of each ten pādas of gold. (III. i. 1)

He said to them: 'Venerable brāhmins, let him among you who is the best Vedic scholar drive these cows home.'

None of the brāhmins dared. Then Yājnavalkya said to one of his pupils: 'Dear Sāmśravā, drive these cows [home].' He drove them away.

The brāhmins were furious and said: 'How does he dare to call himself the best Vedic scholar among us?'

Now [among them] there was Aśvala, the hotri priest of Emperor Janaka of Videha. He asked Yājnavalkya: 'Are you indeed the best Vedic scholar among us, O Yājnavalkya?'

He replied: 'I bow to the best Vedic scholar, but I just wish to have these cows.'

Thereupon the hotri Aśvala determined to question him. (III. i. 2)

'Yājnavalkya,' said he, 'since everything[50] here (i.e. connected with the sacrifice) is overtaken by death,[51] since everything is overcome by death, by what means does the sacrificer free himself from the reach of death?'

'Through the hotri priest and the organ of speech looked upon as fire. The sacrificer's organ of speech is the hotri. This organ of speech is fire; this fire is the hotri; this [fire] is [the means to] liberation;[52] this is complete liberation.'[53] (III. i. 3)

---

[50] That is to say, the accessories of this rite, such as the priests and the fire.

[51] Because the ritualistic sacrifice is attended by natural attachment to the result, which brings about new birth to be followed in turn by death.

[52] The two auxiliaries of a sacrifice, namely, the priest called hotri and the organ of speech, being finite, are overcome by death, that is to say, are subject to incessant change. If the sacrificer regards these two auxiliaries as finite, he is subject to repeated deaths. But if he looks upon them as fire, which is their divine (adhidaiva) aspect, he is liberated from death. Therefore, the text says: 'This is liberation'. In other words, looking upon the hotri priest and the organ of speech as fire is liberation.

[53] It is called complete liberation because it leads to the attainment of the status of Virāj. Neither 'liberation' nor 'complete liberation' refers to the Liberation which results from the Knowledge of Brahman.

'Yājnavalkya,' said he, 'since everything here is overtaken by day and night, since everything is overcome by day and night, by what means does the sacrificer free himself from the reach of day and night?'

'Through the adhvaryu priest and the eye looked upon as the sun. The sacrificer's eye is the adhvaryu. This eye is the sun. This sun is the adhvaryu; this [sun] is [the means to] liberation; this is complete liberation.' (III. i. 4)

'Yājnavalkya,' said he, 'since everything here is overtaken by the bright and dark fortnights, since everything is overcome by the bright and dark fortnights, by what means does the sacrificer free himself from the reach of the bright and dark fortnights?'

'Through the udgātri priest and the vital breath looked upon as the air. This vital breath is the udgātri. This vital breath is the air; this air is the udgātri; this [air] is [the means to] liberation; this is complete liberation.' (III. i. 5)

'Yājnavalkya,' said he, 'since the sky is, as it were, without a support, by means of what support does the sacrificer go to heaven?'

'Through the Brahmā priest and the mind looked upon as the moon. The sacrificer's mind is the Brahmā. The mind is the moon; this moon is the Brahmā; this [moon] is [the means to] liberation; this is complete liberation.'

So far about the ways of liberation; now about the meditation based upon resemblance. (III. i. 6)

'Yājnavalkya,' said he, 'how many [kinds of] rik verses will the hotri priest use today in this sacrifice?'

'Three kinds.'

'And which are these three?'

'The introductory,[54] the sacrificial,[55] and the eulogistic[56] as the third.'

'What does he (the sacrificer) win through them?'

'All this that has life.' (III. i. 7)

'Yājnavalkya,' said he, 'how many [kinds of] oblations will the adhvaryu priest offer today in this sacrifice?'

'Three.'

'And which are these three?'

'Those which, when offered, blaze upward; those which, when offered, make a great noise; and those which, when offered, sink down.'

'What does he (the sacrificer) win through them?'

---

[54] Those hymns which are used before the sacrifice starts.
[55] Those hymns which are chanted at the time of offering the oblation.
[56] Those hymns which are used in praise of the deity.

'By those which, when offered, blaze upward, he wins the world of the gods; for the world of the gods shines bright, as it were. By those which, when offered, make a great noise, he wins the world of the Manes; for this world of the Manes is excessively noisy. By those which, when offered, sink down, he wins the world of men; for the world of men is down below.' (III. i. 8)

'Yājnavalkya,' said he, 'with how many gods does the Brahmā priest [seated] on the right protect the sacrifice today?'
'With one.'
'Which is that one?'
'The mind. The mind is indeed infinite, and infinite are the Viśve-devas.[57] An infinite world he (the sacrificer) wins thereby.' (III. i. 9)

'Yājnavalkya,' said he, 'how many [kinds of] hymns of praise will the udgātri priest chant today in this sacrifice?'
'Three.'
'And which are these three?'
'The introductory, the sacrificial, and the eulogistic as the third.'
'Which are those that have reference to the body?'
'The prāna is the introductory hymn, the apāna is the sacrificial hymn, and the vyāna is the eulogistic hymn.'
'What does he (the sacrificer) win through them?'
'Through the introductory hymn he wins the earth, through the sacrificial hymn he wins the sky, and through the eulogistic hymn he wins heaven.'
Thereupon the priest Aśvala held his peace. (III. i. 10)

Then Ārtabhāga, of the line of Jaratkāru, questioned him.[58] (III. ii. 1)

'Yājnavalkya,' said he, 'when this [liberated] person dies, do his organs depart from him or not?'
'No,' replied Yājnavalkya, 'they merge in him[59] only. The body swells, is inflated, and in that state the dead [body] lies at rest.' (III. ii. 11)

---

[57] The particular deities known as the Viśve-devas are in reality ten in number; but etymologically the word embraces all the gods. They possess an infinity of names. He who knows this teaching becomes identified with the Viśve-devas, who possess an infinity of names, and through this identification wins an infinite world. This is a eulogy of the teaching.
[58] Here a number of technical questions have been omitted.
[59] That is to say, in Brahman.

'Yājnavalkya,' said he, 'when such a man dies, what is it that does not leave him?'

'The name. For the name is infinite,[60] and infinite are the Viśve-devas. He [who knows this] wins thereby an infinite world.' (III. ii. 12)

'Yājnavalkya,' said he, 'when the vocal organ of this dead person merges in fire, the nose in air, the eye in the sun, the mind in the moon, the ear in the quarters, the body in the earth, the ākāśa (space) in the heart in the external ākāśa, the hair on the body in the herbs, the hair on the head in the trees, and the blood and semen are deposited in water, where is that person then?'[61]

Yājnavalkya said: 'Give me your hand, dear Ārtabhāga. We shall decide this between ourselves; we cannot do it in a crowd.'

Then they went out and deliberated, and what they talked about was karma (work),[62] and what they praised was karma: one becomes good through good karma and evil through evil karma.

Thereupon Ārtabhāga, of the line of Jaratkāru, held his peace. (III. ii. 13)

Next Bhujyu, the grandson of Lahya, questioned him.[63]

'Yājnavalkya,' said he, 'we were travelling in [the country of] Madra as [religious] students, when we came to the house of Patanchala, of the line of Kapi. His daughter was possessed by a gandharva. We asked him (the gandharva): "Who are you?" He said: "I am Sudhanvan, of the line of Angiras." While asking him about the limits of the world, we said: "Where were the descendants of Parikshit?" And likewise I ask you, Yājnavalkya, where were the descendants of Parikshit? [Tell me,] where were the descendants of Parikshit?' (III. iii. 1)

Yājnavalkya said: 'The gandharva, I suppose, told you that they went where those who perform the Horse-sacrifice go.'

'And where do they go who have performed the Horse-sacrifice?'

[60] The name is called infinite because it is cherished for a long time.

[61] That is to say, What is that support resting on which he again takes a body and organs?

[62] They concluded that karma is the support which causes the repeated taking up of the physical body. Nature, chance, and the rest may, however, be indirect causes.

[63] It was stated at the very beginning of the Upanishad that the Horse-sacrifice, whether performed along with meditation or without meditation, produces the highest result. But that result falls within the realm of the relative universe. Now will be stated the range and the extent of the universe, so that one may understand the entire world of bondage.

'Thirty-two times the space traversed by the sun's chariot in a day makes this plane (loka); around it, covering twice the area, is the world (prithivi); around the world, covering twice the area, is the ocean. Now, as is the edge of a razor or the wing of a fly, so is there just that much space [between the two halves of the cosmic shell. Through that opening they go out].

'Fire, in the form of a falcon, delivered them to Vāyu (Hiranya-garbha). Vāyu, placing them in itself, took them where [previous] per-formers of the Horse-sacrifice were.'

Thus did the gandharva praise Vāyu. Therefore Vāyu alone is the aggregate of all individuals. He who knows this, as stated above, conquers further death.

Thereupon Bhujyu, the grandson of Lahya, held his peace. (III. iii. 2)

Then Ushasta, the son of Chakra, questioned him.

'Yājnavalkya,' said he, 'explain to me the Brahman that is im-mediately and directly perceived—the self that is within all.'

'This is your self that is within all.'

'Which [self] is within all, Yājnavalkya?'

'That which breathes through the prāna is your self that is within all. That which moves downward through the apāna is your self that is within all. That which pervades through the vyāna is your self that is within all. That which goes out with the udāna is your self that is within all. This is your self that is within all.'[64] (III. iv. 1)

Ushasta, the son of Chakra, said: 'You have explained it as one might say: "Such is a cow," "Such is a horse." Tell me precisely the Brahman that is immediate and direct—the self that is within all.'

'This is your self that is within all.'

'Which [self] is within all, Yājnavalkya?'

'You cannot see the seer of seeing; you cannot hear the hearer of hearing; you cannot think of the thinker of thinking; you cannot know the knower of knowing. This is your self that is within all; everything else but this is perishable.'

Thereupon Ushasta, the son of Chakra, held his peace. (III. iv. 2)

---

[64] It has already been stated that a man attached to the organs and objects is reborn. Birth is controlled by merit and demerit. The result of the highest merit is identification with Hiranyagarbha. Now the question arises as to whether or not there exists an entity which assumes repeated births and if it exists, then what it is like. If a man realizes it as the unconditioned Self, free from actions and their accessories, he is freed from rebirth.

Next Kahola, the son of Kushitaka, questioned him.[65]

'Yājnavalkya,' said he, 'explain to me the Brahman that is directly and immediately perceived—the self that is within all.'

'This is your self that is within all.'

'Which [self] is within all, Yājnavalkya?'

'It is that which transcends hunger and thirst, grief, delusion, old age, and death. Having realized this Self, brāhmins give up the desire for sons, the desire for wealth, and the desire for the worlds, and lead the life of [religious] mendicants. That which is the desire for sons is the desire for wealth, and that which is the desire for wealth is the desire for the worlds; for both these are but desires. Therefore a brāhmin, after he is done with scholarship, should try to live on that strength which comes of scholarship. After he is done with that strength and scholarship, he becomes meditative, and after he is done with both meditativeness and non-meditativeness, he becomes a knower of Brahman.

'How does the knower of Brahman behave? Howsoever he may behave, he is such indeed. Everything else but this is perishable.'

Thereupon Kahola, the son of Kushitaka, held his peace. (III. v. 1)

Then Gārgi, the daughter of Vachaknu, questioned him.

'Yājnavalkya,' said she, 'if all this is pervaded by water, by what, pray, is water pervaded?'[66]

'By air, O Gārgi.'

'By what, pray, is air pervaded?'

'By the sky, O Gārgi.'

'By what is the sky pervaded?'

'By the world of the gandharvas, O Gārgi.'

'By what is the world of the gandharvas pervaded?'

'By the world of the sun, O Gārgi.'

'By what is the world of the sun pervaded?'

'By the world of the moon, O Gārgi.'

'By what is the world of the moon pervaded?'

'By the world of the stars, O Gārgi.'

---

[65] Now Self-Knowledge together with renunciation, which is the means of Liberation, will be discussed. That is why Kahola's question is introduced.

[66] Gārgi's question presupposes an inference: the effect is pervaded by the cause, the limited by the (relatively speaking) unlimited, and the gross by the subtle, just as a pot is pervaded by clay. The form of the inference is that the cause, the subtle, and the unlimited are woven, like the warp and woof of a cloth, in the effect, the gross, and the limited. Each preceding element, in the questions asked by Gārgi, is pervaded by the succeeding one, till we come to the Self which is within all.

'By what is the world of the stars pervaded?'
'By the world of the gods, O Gārgi.'
'By what is the world of the gods pervaded?'
'By the world of Indra, O Gārgi.'
'By what is the world of Indra pervaded?'
'By the World of Virāj, O Gārgi.'
'By what is the World of Virāj pervaded?'
'By the World of Hiranyagarbha, O Gārgi.'
'By what, pray, is the World of Hiranyagarbha pervaded?'
'Do not, O Gārgi,' said he, 'question too much, lest your head should fall off.[67] You are questioning too much about a deity about whom we should not ask too much. Do not ask too much, O Gārgi.'

Thereupon Gārgi, the daughter of Vachaknu, held her peace. (III. vi. 1)

Then Uddālaka, the son of Aruna, questioned him.

'Yājnavalkya,' said he, 'in [the country of] Madra we lived in the house of Patanchala, of the line of Kapi, studying the scriptures on the sacrifices. His wife was possessed by a gandharva. We asked him (the gandharva): "Who are you?" He said: "I am Kabandha, the son of Atharvan." He said to Patanchala Kāpya and those studying the scriptures on the sacrifices: 'O descendant of Kapi, do you know that Sutra by which this world, the other world, and all beings are held together?" Patanchala Kāpya said: "I do not know it, venerable Sir." [Then] he (the gandharva) said to Patanchala Kāpya and those studying the scriptures on the sacrifices: "O descendant of Kapi, do you know that Inner Controller who controls this world, the next world, and all beings?" Patanchala Kāpya said: "I do not know him, venerable Sir." [Then] he (the gandharva) said to Patanchala Kāpya and those studying the scriptures on the sacrifices: "O descendant of Kapi, he who knows that Sutra and that Inner Controller indeed knows Brahman; he knows the worlds, he knows the gods, he knows the Vedas, he knows the beings, he knows the self, he knows everything." He (the gandharva) explained it all to them, and I know it. If you, Yājnavalkya, do not know that Sutra and that Inner Controller, and still take away the cows that belong only to the knowers of Brahman, your head will fall off.'

'I know, O Gautama, that Sutra and that Inner Controller.'

'Anyone might say: "I know, I know." Tell us what you know.' (III. vii. 1)

[67] The cause of Hiranyagarbha, or the Sutra, cannot be ascertained by inference. This cause is Brahman, which is known only through direct experience and the evidence of the scriptures. Therefore Yājnavalkya warns Gārgi against pushing her inquiry too far.

Yājnavalkya said: 'Vāyu (Hiranyagarbha), O Gautama, is that Sutra. By Vāyu, as by a thread, O Gautama, are this world, the other world, and all beings held together. Therefore, O Gautama, they say of a person who dies that his limbs have been loosened; for they are held together by Vāyu as by a thread.'

'Quite so, Yājnavalkya. Now describe the Inner Controller.' (III. vii. 2)

[Yājnavalkya said:] 'He who inhabits the earth, yet is within the earth, whom the earth does not know, whose body the earth is, and who controls the earth from within—He is your Self, the Inner Controller, the Immortal. (III. vii. 3)

'He who inhabits water, yet is within water, whom water does not know, whose body water is, and who controls water from within—He is your Self, the Inner Controller, the Immortal.

'He who inhabits fire, yet is within fire, whom fire does not know, whose body fire is, and who controls fire from within—He is your Self, the Inner Controller, the Immortal.

'He who inhabits the sky, yet is within the sky, whom the sky does not know, whose body the sky is, and who controls the sky from within —He is your Self, the Inner Controller, the Immortal.

'He who inhabits the air, yet is within the air, whom the air does not know, whose body the air is, and who controls the air from within—He is your Self, the Inner Controller, the Immortal.

'He who inhabits heaven, yet is within heaven, whom heaven does not know, whose body heaven is, and who controls heaven from within— He is your Self, the Inner Controller, the Immortal.

'He who inhabits the sun, yet is within the sun, whom the sun does not know, whose body the sun is, and who controls the sun from within —He is your Self, the Inner Controller, the Immortal.

'He who inhabits the quarters [of space], yet is within them, whom the quarters do not know, whose body the quarters are, and who controls the quarters from within—He is your Self, the Inner Controller, the Immortal.

'He who inhabits the moon and stars, yet is within the moon and stars, whom the moon and stars do not know, whose body the moon and stars are, and who controls the moon and stars from within—He is your Self, the Inner Controller, the Immortal.

'He who inhabits the ākāśa, yet is within the ākāśa, whom the ākāśa does not know, whose body the ākāśa is, and who controls the ākāśa from within—He is your Self, the Inner Controller, the Immortal.

'He who inhabits darkness, yet is within darkness, whom darkness does not know, whose body darkness is, and who controls darkness from within—He is your Self, the Inner Controller, the Immortal.

'He who inhabits light, yet is within light, whom light does not know, whose body light is, and who controls light from within—He is your Self, the Inner Controller, the Immortal.'

This much with reference to the gods (adhidaivatam). Now with reference to beings (adhibhutam). (III. vii. 4–14)

[Yājnavalkya said:] 'He who inhabits all beings, yet is within all beings, whom no beings know, whose body all beings are, and who controls all beings from within—He is your Self, the Inner Controller, the Immortal.'

This much with reference to the beings. Now with reference to the body. (III. vii. 15)

[Yājnavalkya said:] 'He who inhabits the nose (prāna), yet is within the nose, whom the nose does not know, whose body the nose is, and who controls the nose from within—He is your Self, the Inner Controller, the Immortal.

'He who inhabits [the organ of] speech, yet is within speech, whom speech does not know, whose body speech is, and who controls speech from within—He is your Self, the Inner Controller, the Immortal.

'He who inhabits the eye, yet is within the eye, whom the eye does not know, whose body the eye is, and who controls the eye from within —He is your Self, the Inner Controller, the Immortal.

'He who inhabits the ear, yet is within the ear, whom the ear does not know, whose body the ear is, and who controls the ear from within —He is your Self, the Inner Controller, the Immortal.

'He who inhabits the mind, yet is within the mind, whom the mind does not know, whose body the mind is, and who controls the mind from within—He is your Self, the Inner Controller, the Immortal.

'He who inhabits the skin, yet is within the skin, whom the skin does not know, whose body the skin is, and who controls the skin from within—He is your Self, the Inner Controller, the Immortal.

'He who inhabits the intellect (vijnāna), yet is within the intellect, whom the intellect does not know, whose body the intellect is, and who controls the intellect from within—He is your Self, the Inner Controller, the Immortal.

'He who inhabits the organ of generation, yet is within the organ, whom the organ does not know, whose body the organ is, and who controls the organ from within—He is your Self, the Inner Controller, the Immortal.

'He is never seen, but is the Seer; He is never heard, but is the Hearer; He is never thought of, but is the Thinker; He is never known, but is the Knower. There is no other seer than He, there is no other hearer than He, there is no other thinker than He, there is no other knower than He. He is your Self, the Inner Controller, the Immortal. Everything else but Him is perishable.'

Thereupon Uddālaka, the son of Aruna, held his peace. (III. vii. 16-23)

Then the daughter of Vachaknu said: 'Venerable brāhmins, I shall ask him two questions. If he answers me these, then none of you can defeat him in discussing Brahman.'

[The brāhmins said:] 'Ask, O Gārgi.'[68] (III. viii. 1)

Gārgi said: 'O Yājnavalkya, I [shall ask] you [two questions]: As a man of Kāśi or the King of Videha, scion of a heroic line, might string his unstrung bow, take in his hand two bamboo-tipped arrows highly painful to enemies, and approach [his enemies] closely, even so, O Yājnavalkya, do I confront you with two questions. Answer me these.'

'Ask, O Gārgi.' (III. viii. 2)

She said: 'O Yājnavalkya, what pervades that [Sutra] which is above heaven and below the earth, which is heaven and earth as well as [what is] between them, and which—they say—was, is, and will be?' (III. viii. 3)

He said: 'That, O Gārgi, which is above heaven and below the earth, which is heaven and earth as well as [what is] between them, and which—they say—was, is, and will be, is pervaded by the [unmanifested] ākāśa.' (III. viii. 4)

She said: 'I bow to you, O Yājnavalkya. You have fully answered this question of mine. Now brace yourself for the other.'

'Ask, O Gārgi.' (III. viii. 5)

She said: 'Yājnavalkya, what pervades that [Sutra] which is above heaven and below the earth, which is heaven and earth as well as [what is] between them, and which—they say—was, is, and will be?'

He said: 'That, O Gārgi, which is above heaven and below the earth, which is heaven and earth as well as [what is] between them, and which —they say—was, is, and will be, is pervaded by the [unmanifested] ākāśa.'[69]

'What pervades the ākāśa?' (III. viii. 6-7)

[68] After discussing the nature of the conditioned Brahman (Saguna Brahman), the Upanishad proceeds to describe the Supreme Brahman devoid of attributes.

[69] The question and answer are repeated only to emphasize what has already been stated.

He said: 'That, O Gārgi, the knowers of Brahman call the Imperish-able. It is neither gross nor subtle, neither short nor long, neither red nor moist; It is neither shadow nor darkness, neither air nor ākāśa; It is unattached; It is without taste or smell, without eyes or ears, without tongue or mind; It is non-effulgent, without vital breath or mouth, without measure, and without exterior or interior. It does not eat any-thing, nor is It eaten by anyone.[70] (III. viii. 8)

'Verily, under the mighty rule of this Imperishable, O Gārgi, the sun and moon are held in their respective positions. Under the mighty rule of this Imperishable, O Gārgi, heaven and earth are held in their respective positions. Under the mighty rule of this Imperishable, O Gārgi, moments, muhurtas, days and nights, fortnights, months, seasons, and years are held in their respective positions. Under the mighty rule of this Imperishable, O Gārgi, some rivers flow eastward from the white mountains, others flowing westward continue in that direction, and still others keep to their respective courses. Under the mighty rule of this Imperishable, O Gārgi, men praise those who give, the gods depend upon the sacrificer, and the Manes upon the Darvi offering.[71] (III. viii. 9)

'Whosoever in this world, O Gārgi, without knowing this Imperish-able, offers oblations, performs sacrifices, and practises austerities, even for many thousands of years, finds all such acts but perishable. Whoso-ever, O Gārgi, departs from this world without knowing this Imperish-able is miserable. But he, O Gārgi, who departs from this world after knowing the Imperishable is a knower of Brahman. (III. viii. 10)

'Verily, that Imperishable, O Gārgi, is never seen but is the Seer; It is never heard, but is the Hearer; It is never thought of, but is the Thinker; It is never known, but is the Knower. There is no other seer but This, there is no other hearer but This, there is no other thinker but This, there is no other knower but This. By this imperishable, O Gārgi, is the [unmanifested] ākāśa pervaded.' (III. viii. 11)

Then said Gārgi: 'Venerable brāhmins, you may consider yourselves fortunate if you can get off from him through bowing to him. None of you, I believe, will defeat him in arguments about Brahman.'
Thereupon the daughter of Vachaknu held her peace. (III. viii. 12)

[70] Through this negative description Yājnavalkya implied that Brahman is devoid of all attributes and is one only, without a second.
[71] The Upanishad has indicated Brahman in the preceding verse by the denial of qualifying attributes or characteristic marks. But, anticipating the popular misconception that Brahman might, in that case, be void or non-existent, the Upanishad gives inferential evidence—from the orderliness of creation—to demonstrate Its existence.

Then Vidaghdha, the son of Śakala, asked him: 'How many gods are there, Yājnavalkya?' Yājnavalkya ascertained the number through [the group of mantras known as] the Nivid, and said: 'As many as are mentioned in the Nivid of the Viśve-devas—three hundred and three, and three thousand and three.'

'Very good,' said Śakalya (the son of Śakala), and asked again: 'How many gods are there, Yājnavalkya?'

'Thirty-three.'

'Very good,' said Śakalya, and asked again: 'How many gods are there, Yājnavalkya?'

'Six.'

'Very good,' said the other, and asked again: 'How many gods are there, Yājnavalkya?'

'Three.'

'Very good,' said the other, and asked again: 'How many gods are there, Yājnavalkya?'

'Two.'

'Very good,' said he, and asked again, 'How many gods are there, Yājnavalkya?'

'One and a half.'

'Very good,' said he, and asked again: 'How many gods are there, Yājnavalkya?'

'One.'

'Very good,' said Śakalya, and asked: 'Which are those three hundred and three, and those three thousand and three?'[72] (III. ix. 1)

Yājnavalkya said: 'There are only thirty-three gods. These others are but manifestations of them.'

'Which are these thirty-three?'

'The eight Vasus, the eleven Rudras, and the twelve Ādityas—these are thirty-one. And Indra and Prajāpati make up the thirty-three.' (III. ix. 2)

'Which are the Vasus?' asked Śakalya.

'Fire, the earth, the air, the sky, the sun, heaven, the moon, and the stars—these are the Vasus; for in them all this [universe] is placed (vasavah). Therefore they are called Vasus.' (III. ix. 3)

'Which are the Rudras?' asked Śakalya.

'The ten organs in the human body, with the mind as the eleventh. When they depart from this mortal body, they make [one's relatives]

---

[72] The present chapter is introduced in order to convey the immediacy and directness of Brahman by a reference to the contraction and expansion of the different gods who are ruled by It.

weep. Because they make them weep (rud), therefore they are called Rudras. (III. ix. 4)

'Which are the Ādityas?' asked Śākalya.
'There are twelve months in the year. These are the Ādityas, because they move along carrying (ādadānāh) all this[73] with them; therefore they are called Ādityas.' (III. ix. 5)

'Which is Indra and which is Prajāpati?' asked Śākalya.
'The thunderclap is Indra and the sacrifice is Prajāpati.'
'Which is the thunderclap?'
'The thunderbolt.'
'Which is the sacrifice?'
'The animals.'[74] (III. ix. 6)

'Which are the six [gods]?' asked Śākalya.
'Fire, the earth, the air, the sky, the sun, and heaven; for these six comprise all those.' (III. ix. 7)

'Which are the three gods?' asked Śākalya.
'These three worlds, because all those gods are comprised in these three.'
'Which are the two gods?'
'Matter and the vital breath (prāna).'
'Which are the one and a half?'
'This [air] that blows.' (III. ix. 8)

[Yājnavalkya said:] 'Concerning this some say: "Since the air blows as one substance, how can it be one and a half (adhyardha)?" [The answer is:] It is one and a half because by its presence everything attains surpassing glory (adhyārdhnot).'
'Which is the one God?'
'The vital breath (Hiranyagarbha); it is Brahman which is called That (Tyat).'[75] (III. ix. 9)

[When Śākalya kept silent] Yājnavalkya addressed him thus: 'Śākalya, have these brāhmins made you their instrument [such as tongs] for burning charcoal?' (III. ix. 18)

[73] That is to say, a person's longevity and the results of his works.
[74] The sacrifice is called the animals because it depends on them.
[75] The gods may be regarded as being one as well as many. The infinite number of gods is included in the limited number mentioned in the Nivid; these again are included in the successive smaller numbers—thirty-three and so on—down to the one vital breath. Again, it is this vital breath which expands into all these numbers up to infinity. Thus the vital breath alone is one and infinity; it also includes the intermediate numbers.
Some of the following questions and answers, being of a technical nature, have been omitted.

'Yājnavalkya,' said Śākalya, 'what Brahman do you know, that you have thus flouted these Vedic scholars of Kuru and Panchāla?'[76]

[Yājnavalkya replied:] 'I know the quarters, with their deities and supports.'

[Śākalya said:] 'If you know the quarters, with their deities and supports, what deity are you identified with in the east?'

'With the deity sun.'

'In what does the sun find its support?'

'The eye.'

'In what does the eye find its support?'

'Colours, for one sees colours with the eye.'

'In what do colours find their support?'

'The heart,'[77] [said Yājnavalkya,] 'for one knows colours through the heart. Therefore it is in the heart that colours find their support.'

'Just so, Yājnavalkya.'[78] (III. ix. 19–20)

['Yājnavalkya,' said Śākalya,] 'what deity are you identified with in the south?'

'With the deity Yama (the god of justice).'

'In what does Yama find his support?'

'The sacrifice.'

'In what does the sacrifice find its support?'

'The remuneration of the priests.'

'In what does the remuneration find its support?'

'Faith, for when a man has faith he remunerates the priest. Therefore it is in faith that the remuneration finds its support.'

'In what does faith find its support?'

'The heart (mind),' [said Yājnavalkya,] 'for one knows faith through the heart. Therefore it is in the heart that faith finds its support.'

'Just so, Yājnavalkya.' (III. ix. 21)

['Yājnavalkya,' said Śākalya,] 'what deity are you identified with in the west?'

'With the deity Varuna (the god of rain).'

'In what does Varuna find his support?'

'Water.'

'In what does water find its support?'

'Semen.'

---

[76] Now will be described the quarters, the deities identified with them, and their support; ultimately the diversity of the creation will be unified in the mind.

[77] The word here signifies the mind.

[78] Yājnavalkya had had the experience that his own mind was divided into five forms according to the quarters and was identified with the quarters, and thus with the whole universe as his own self.

'In what does semen find its support?'

'The heart,'[79] [said Yājnavalkya.] 'Therefore they say of a new-born child who resembles [his father] that it seems as if he has sprung from [his father's] heart—that he has been created of [his father's] heart, as it were. Therefore it is in the heart that semen finds its support.'

'Just so, Yājnavalkya.' (III. ix. 21)

['Yājnavalkya,' said Śākalya,] 'what deity are you identified with in the north?'

'With the deity Soma (the moon and the creeper of that name).'

'In what does Soma find its support?'

'The initiatory rite.'[80]

'In what does initiation find its support?'

'Truth. Therefore they say to the one who is initiated: "Speak the truth"; for it is in the truth that initiation finds its support.'

'In what does the truth find its support?'

'The heart,' [said Yājnavalkya,] 'for through the heart one knows the truth; therefore it is in the heart that the truth finds its support.'

'Just so, Yājnavalkya.' (III. ix. 23)

'What deity,' [said Śākalya,] 'are you identified with in the fixed direction (i.e. overhead)?'

'With the deity fire.'

'In what does fire find its support?'

'Speech.'

'In what does speech find its support?'

'The heart.'

'In what does the heart find its support?'[81] (III. ix. 24)

'You ghost,' said Yājnavalkya, 'that you think that the heart should be elsewhere than in ourselves! If it were elsewhere than in ourselves, dogs would eat this body or birds tear it to pieces.'[82] (III. ix. 25)

[79] The semen is the effect of the heart. Lust is a modification of the heart; for the semen issues from the heart of a man under its influence.

[80] The initiated sacrificer purchases the soma creeper and, performing sacrifice with it along with meditation, attains identity with the north, of which the presiding deity is the moon. The moon is named after soma.

[81] Yājnavalkya, through his heart (mind), extending in all directions, had realized all the quarters as his own self; the quarters, with their deities and supports, are part and parcel of him, and he is now identified with name, form, and action. The universe has no existence apart from name, form, and action. All these are modifications of the mind. So Yājnavalkya's mind now embraced the whole universe. But Śākalya asked in what the heart finds its support.

[82] When the heart (mind) is not in the body, the body is dead.

'In what do the body and the heart find their support?' [asked Śākalya.]

'In the prāna.'

'In what does the prāna find its support?'

'In the apāna.'

'In what does the apāna find its support?'

'In the vyāna.'

'In what does the vyāna find its support?'

'In the udāna.'

'In what does the udāna find its support?'

'In the samāna.'

[Here the Upanishad itself states:]

This self is That which has been described as 'Not this, not this'. It is imperceptible, for It is never perceived; undecaying, for It never decays; unattached, for It is never attached; unfettered, for It never feels pain and never suffers injury.

[Yājnavalkya said:] 'These are the eight abodes, the eight organs of vision, the eight deities, and the eight beings.

'Now I ask you about that Person who is to be known only from the Upanishads, who definitely projects those beings and [again] withdraws them into Himself, and who is at the same time transcendental.

'If you cannot clearly explain Him to me, your head shall fall off.'

Śākalya did not know Him; his head fell off; and robbers snatched away his bones, mistaking them for something else.[83] (III. ix. 26)

Then Yājnavalkya said: 'Venerable brāhmins, whosoever among you wishes to question me may now do so, or all of you may. Or whosoever among you desires it, I shall question him, or I shall question all of you.'

But the brāhmins did not dare. (III. ix. 27)

Yājnavalkya interrogated them with the following verses:

1. As is a mighty tree, so indeed is a man: this is true. His hairs are the leaves and his skin is the outer bark.

2. From his skin blood flows and from the bark, sap. Therefore when a man is wounded blood flows, as sap from a tree that is injured.

3. His flesh is its inner bark and his nerves are its innermost layer of bark, which is tough. His bones lie within, as does the wood of the tree. His marrow resembles the pith.

4. A tree, when it is felled, springs again from its root in a new form; from what root, tell me, does a man spring forth after he is cut off by death?

[83] The gist of the story is that one should not be disrespectful to a knower of Brahman. Its purpose is to teach men right conduct towards knowers of Brahman and to extol Self-Knowledge.

5. Do not say: From the semen, for that is produced from the living man. A tree springs from the seed as well; after it is dead it certainly springs again.

6. If a tree is pulled up with its root, it will not spring again. From what root, tell me, does a mortal spring forth after he is cut off by death?

7. [If you think] he is indeed born,[84] [I say: No,] he is born again. Now who should again bring him forth?

[The Upanishad states:] It is Brahman, which is [absolute] Knowledge and Bliss, the ultimate goal of him who offers wealth, and also of him who has realized Brahman and stands firm in It. (III. ix. 28)

---

[84] The naturalist (svabhāva-vādi) observes the fact that a man has been born; he is not interested in finding out where the man has come from. But Yājnavalkya, who believed in rebirth, did not accept the naturalist's position. The doctrine of rebirth is a necessary corollary of the doctrine of the immortality of the soul. That is why Yājnavalkya asked who is the cause of a man's being born again. The Vedic scholars did not know the answer. They did not know Brahman, the ultimate Root of the universe, which is responsible for rebirth and the other phenomena of the relative universe. But Yājnavalkya knew Brahman. Thus he defeated the brāhmins and took away the cows. The story is finished.

OM. JANAKA, EMPEROR of Videha, was seated [to give audience] when Yājnavalkya arrived. The Emperor said to him: 'Yājnavalkya, for what purpose have you come here? With a desire for cattle, or to hear some subtle questions asked?'

'For both, Your Majesty,' said he. (IV. i. 1)

[Yājnavalkya said:] 'Let me hear what anyone among your teachers may have told you.'

'Jitvan, the son of Śilina, told me that the organ of speech[85] is Brahman.'

'As anyone who had [the benefit of being taught by a good] mother, father, and teacher should say, so did the son of Śilina say that the organ of speech is Brahman; for what can be attained by a person who cannot speak? But did he tell you about its abode (body) and support?'

'No, he did not.'

'This Brahman is only one-footed, Your Majesty.'

'Then you tell us, O Yājnavalkya.'

'The [physical] organ of speech is its abode and ākāśa is its support. It should be meditated upon as intelligence.'

'What is intelligence, O Yājnavalkya?'

'It is the organ of speech, Your Majesty,' said Yājnavalkya. 'Through the organ of speech alone, O Emperor, are known the Rig-Veda, the Yajur-Veda, the Sāma-Veda, the Atharvāngirasa, history, ancient lore, the arts, the Upanishads, verses, aphorisms, explanations, commentaries, [the results of] sacrifices, [the result of] offering oblations in the fire, [the result of] giving food and drink, this world, the next world, and all beings.

'The organ of speech, Your Majesty, is the Supreme Brahman. The organ of speech never deserts him who, knowing this, meditates upon it; all beings eagerly approach him; and being a god, he attains the gods.'

'I give you a thousand cows with a bull as large as an elephant,' said Emperor Janaka.

Yājnavalkya replied: 'My father was of the opinion that one should not accept gifts from a disciple without fully instructing him.' (IV. i. 2)

[Yājnavalkya said:] 'Let me hear what anyone among your teachers may have told you.'

---

[85] That is to say, the deity fire. Throughout this and the next six paragraphs the organ refers to its presiding deity, except when it signifies the body, or abode.

'Udanka, the son of Śulba, told me that the vital breath[86] is Brahman.'

'As anyone who had [the benefit of being taught by a good] mother, father, and teacher should say, so did the son of Śulba say that the vital breath is Brahman; for what can be attained by a person who does not live? But did he tell you about its abode and support?'

'No, he did not.'

'This Brahman is only one-footed, Your Majesty.'

'Then you tell us, O Yājnavalkya.'

'The vital breath is its abode and the ākāśa is its support. It should be meditated upon as dear.'

'What is that dearness, O Yājnavalkya?'

'It is the vital breath, Your Majesty,' said Yājnavalkya. 'For the sake of that vital breath (life), O Emperor, one performs sacrifices for him for whom they should not be performed and accepts gifts from him from whom they should not be accepted; nay, for the sake of the vital breath, O Emperor, one may go to a quarter where one runs the risk of losing one's life.

'The vital breath, O Emperor, is the Supreme Brahman. The vital breath never deserts him who, knowing what has just been said, meditates upon it; all beings eagerly approach him; and being a god, he attains the gods.'

'I give you a thousand cows with a bull as large as an elephant,' said Emperor Janaka.

Yājnavalkya replied: 'My father was of the opinion that one should not accept gifts from a disciple without fully instructing him.' (IV. i. 3)

[Yājnavalkya said:] 'Let me hear what anyone among your teachers may have told you.'

'Barku, the son of Vrishna, told me that the eye[87] is Brahman.'

'As anyone who had [the benefit of being taught by a good] mother, father, and teacher should say, so did the son of Vrishna say that the eye is Brahman; for what can be attained by a person who cannot see? But did he tell you about its abode and support?'

'No, he did not.'

'This Brahman is only one-footed, Your Majesty.'

'Then you tell us, O Yājnavalkya.'

'The eye is its abode and the ākāśa is its support. It should be meditated upon as truth.'

'What is truth, O Yājnavalkya?'

---

[86] The Sanskrit word *prāna* in the text here signifies the deity Vāyu, as the organ of speech in the foregoing paragraph meant the deity fire.

[87] The sun is the deity that governs the eye.

'It is the eye, Your Majesty,' said Yājnavalkya. 'Verily, Your Majesty, if one asks a person who has seen with his eyes: "Have you seen?" and he answers: "Yes, I have," then it is true.

'The eye, Your Majesty, is the Supreme Brahman. The eye never deserts him who, knowing what has just been said, meditates upon it; all beings eagerly approach him; and being a god, he attains the gods.'

'I give you a thousand cows with a bull as large as an elephant,' said Emperor Janaka.

Yājnavalkya replied: 'My father was of the opinion that one should not accept gifts from a disciple without fully instructing him.' (IV. i. 4)

[Yājnavalkya said:] 'Let me hear what anyone among your teachers may have told you.'

'Gardabhivipita, a descendant of Bharadvāja, told me that the ear[88] is Brahman.'

'As anyone who had [the benefit of being taught by a good] mother, father, and teacher should say, so did the descendant of Bharadvāja say that the ear is Brahman; for what can be attained by a person who cannot hear? But did he tell you about its abode and support?'

'No, he did not.'

'This Brahman is only one-footed, Your Majesty.'

'Then you tell us, O Yājnavalkya.'

'The ear is its abode and the ākāśa is its support. It should be meditated upon as infinite.'

'What is infinity, O Yājnavalkya?'

'It is the quarters, Your Majesty,' said Yājnavalkya. 'Verily, Your Majesty, to whatever quarter (direction) one may go, one never reaches its end. [Hence] the quarters are infinite. The quarters, O Emperor, are the ear, and the ear, O Emperor, is the Supreme Brahman.

'The ear never deserts him who, knowing this, meditates upon it; all beings eagerly approach him; and being a god, he attains the gods.'

'I give you a thousand cows with a bull as large as an elephant,' said Emperor Janaka.

Yājnavalkya replied: 'My father was of the opinion that one should not accept gifts from a disciple without fully instructing him.' (IV. i. 5)

[Yājnavalkya said:] 'Let me hear what anyone among your teachers may have told you.'

'Satyakāma, the son of Jabālā, told me that the mind[89] is Brahman.'

'As anyone who had [the benefit of being taught by a good] mother, father, and teacher should say, so did the son of Jabālā say that the

[88] The word *ear* here signifies the quarters, or directions.
[89] The moon is the deity that governs the mind.

mind is Brahman; for what can be attained by a person who has no mind? But did he tell you about its abode and support?'

'No, he did not.'

'This Brahman is only one-footed, Your Majesty.'

'Then you tell us, O Yājnavalkya.'

'The mind is its abode and the ākāśa is its support. It should be meditated upon as bliss.'

'What is bliss, O Yājnavalkya?'

'It is the mind, Your Majesty,' said Yājnavalkya. 'Verily, Your Majesty, with the mind a man [desires and] woos a woman; [then] a son resembling him is born of her, and he is the cause of bliss. The mind, O Emperor, is the Supreme Brahman.

'The mind never deserts him who, knowing this, meditates upon it; all beings eagerly approach him; and being a god, he attains the gods.'

'I give you a thousand cows with a bull as large as an elephant,' said Emperor Janaka.

Yājnavalkya replied: 'My father was of the opinion that one should not accept gifts from a disciple without fully instructing him.' (IV. i. 6)

[Yājnavalkya said:] 'Let me hear what anyone among your teachers may have told you.'

'Vidaghdha, the son of Śakala, told me that the heart[90] is Brahman.'

'As anyone who had [the benefit of being taught by a good] mother, father, and teacher should say, so did the son of Śakala say that the heart is Brahman; for what can be attained by a person who is without a heart? But did he tell you about its abode and support?'

'No, he did not.'

'This Brahman is only one-footed, Your Majesty.'

'Then you tell us, O Yājnavalkya.'

'The heart is its abode and the ākāśa is its support. It should be meditated upon as stability.'

'What is stability, O Yājnavalkya?'

'It is the heart,' said Yājnavalkya. 'Verily, Your Majesty, the heart is the abode of all beings, and the heart, Your Majesty, is the support of all beings. The heart, O Emperor, is the Supreme Brahman.

'The heart never deserts him who, knowing this, meditates upon it; all beings eagerly approach him; and being a god, he attains the gods.'

'I give you a thousand cows with a bull as large as an elephant,' said Emperor Janaka.

Yājnavalkya replied: 'My father was of the opinion that one should not accept gifts from a disciple without fully instructing him.' (IV. i. 7)

[90] The controlling deity of the heart is Hiranyagarbha.

Janaka, Emperor of Videha, rose from his lounge, humbly approached Yājnavalkya, and said: 'Salutation to you, O Yājnavalkya. Please instruct me.'

Yājnavalkya said: 'Your Majesty, as one who wishes to go a long distance would procure a chariot or a ship, even so you have fully equipped your mind with so many secret names of Brahman. You are also honoured and wealthy; you have studied the Vedas and heard the Upanishads. But do you know where you will go when you are released from this body?'

'Venerable Sir, I do not know where I shall go.'

'Then I will tell you where you will go.'

'Tell me, venerable Sir.'[91] (IV. ii. 1)

'The person who is in the right eye[92] is named Indha. Though he is Indha, people call him by the indirect name Indra; for the gods are fond of indirect names and hate to be addressed directly. (IV. ii. 2)

'The person who is in the left eye[93] is his wife, Virāj (matter). The ākāśa that lies within the heart is their place of union. Their food is the lump (pinda) of blood in the heart. Their wrap is the net-like structure in the heart. The path on which they move [from sleep to waking] is the nerve that goes upward from the heart; it is like a hair split into a thousand parts. In the body there are nerves called hitā, which are placed in the heart. Through these the essence of our food passes as it moves on. Therefore the subtle body (Taijasa) receives finer food than the gross body (Vaiśvānara). (IV. ii. 3)

'Of the illumined sage[94] [who is identified with Prājna in deep sleep] the east is the eastern vital breath (prāna), the south is the southern

[91] Janaka was a great Vedic scholar and was versed in the theoretical knowledge of the Upanishads. But he was not endowed with Self-Knowledge and therefore could not overcome fear and was far from the realization of the supreme goal of life. Yājnavalkya, in the present section, will instruct Janaka about Brahman through the three states of waking, dreaming, and deep sleep.

[92] The deity who, from the standpoint of the gods, is identified with the sun and who, from the standpoint of the body, is identified with the right eye, is called the Vaiśvānara self (Mā. Up. 9). This self functions in the waking state.

[93] It is Vaiśvānara that becomes Taijasa in the dream state and Prājna in dreamless sleep. The couple, Virāj (matter) and Indra (Vaiśvānara), become united in dreams. Unlike the experiencer and the object of experience in the waking state, the experiencer and the object of experience in a dream are made of the same mind-stuff; they cannot be separated. For the purpose of meditation, Vaiśvānara itself is now described as Taijasa.

[94] The phrase refers to the sage who has realized the Prājna Ātman. In deep sleep, Ātman, limited by the prāna, or vital breath, is called Prājna. The aspirant first realizes his identity with Vaiśvānara, next with Taijasa, and then with Prājna. Finally he becomes one with Turiya, or Pure Consciousness, which both underlies and transcends the three states.

vital breath, the west is the western vital breath, the north is the northern vital breath, the upper direction is the upper vital breath, the direction below is the nether vital breath, and all the directions are all the vital breaths.

'This self is That which has been described as "Not this, not this". It is imperceptible, for It is never perceived; undecaying, for It never decays; unattached, for It is never attached; unfettered, for It never feels pain and never suffers injury.

'Verily, O Janaka, you have attained That which is free from fear,' said Yājnavalkya.

'Venerable Yājnavalkya,' said Emperor Janaka, 'may that fearless Brahman be yours [too], for you have made known to us the fearless Brahman. Salutations to you! Here is the Empire of Videha and also myself at your service.' (IV. ii. 4)

Yājnavalkya called on Janaka, Emperor of Videha. He said to himself: 'I will not say anything.'

But once upon a time Janaka, Emperor of Videha, and Yājnavalkya had had a talk about the Agnihotra sacrifice, and Yājnavalkya had offered him a boon. Janaka had chosen the right to ask him any questions he wished, and Yājnavalkya had granted him the boon.

So it was the Emperor who first questioned him. (IV. iii. 1)

'Yājnavalkya, what serves as light for a man?'[95]

'The light of the sun, O Emperor,' said Yānavalkya, 'for with the sun as light he sits, goes out, works, and returns.'

'Just so, Yājnavalkya.' (IV. iii. 2)

'When the sun has set, Yājnavalkya, what serves as light for a man?'

'The moon serves as his light, for with the moon as light he sits, goes out, works, and returns.'

'Just so, Yājnavalkya.' (IV. iii. 3)

'When the sun has set and the moon has set, Yājnavalkya, what serves as light for a man?'

'Fire serves as his light, for with fire as light he sits, goes out, works, and returns.'

'Just so, Yājnavalkya.' (IV. iii. 4)

'When the sun has set, Yājnavalkya, and the moon has set and the fire has gone out, what serves as light for a man?'

[95] The question seems to imply this: Does a man use a light extraneous to his body, or does some light within this aggregate of parts serve the purpose of a light for him?

'Speech (sound) serves as his light, for with speech as light he sits, goes out, works, and returns. Therefore, Your Majesty, when one cannot see even one's own hand, yet when a sound is uttered, one can go there.'

'Just so, Yājnavalkya.' (IV. iii. 5)

'When the sun has set, Yājnavalkya, and the moon has set and the fire has gone out and speech has stopped, what serves as light for a man?'

'The self, indeed, is his light, for with the self as light he sits, goes out, works, and returns.'[96] (IV. iii. 6)

'Which is the self?'[97]

'This purusha, which is identified with the intellect (vijnānamaya) and is in the midst of the organs, the [self-effulgent] light within the heart (intellect). Assuming the likeness [of the intellect], it wanders between the two worlds; it thinks, as it were,[98] and moves, as it were. Being identified with dreams, it transcends this [waking] world,[99] which represents the forms of death (ignorance and its effects).[100] (IV. iii. 7)

'That person (the individual self), when he is born, that is to say, when he assumes a body, is joined with evils,[101] and when he dies, that is to say, leaves the body, he discards those evils. (IV. iii. 8)

[96] In the waking state a man is helped in his movements by various lights which are outside his body. But what serves as light for a man in dreams and in deep sleep? One cannot see dream objects without light. From deep sleep, again, one awakes with the remembrance that one slept happily and knew nothing; this shows that some kind of light functions in deep sleep too. Therefore Janaka asked about the light which serves a man when he is asleep. Yājnavalkya's answer is that the self (ātman) is the light that serves a man in all the states.

[97] The drift of the question is as follows: Among the intelligent sense-organs, which one is the self?

[98] It is the intellect that does the thinking. The self assumes the likeness of the intellect and appears to think.

[99] That is to say, it transcends the body and organs functioning in the waking state, around which our phenomenal activities are centred. It is only identification with the intellect that gives rise to the delusion that the self moves between the two worlds and performs other activities.

[100] Death has no form of its own; the body and organs created by ignorance are its forms. Hence, in the dream state, the self transcends the body and organs of the waking world, which are its forms and upon which actions and their results in the waking state depend.

[101] Refers to the body and organs, by means of which a man is engaged in all phenomenal activities, good or bad. From the standpoint of the Supreme Self all phenomenal activities are evil.

'And there are only two states for that person: the one here in this world[102] and the other in the next world. The third, the intermediate, is the dream state. When he is in that intermediate state, he surveys both states;[103] the one here in this world and the other in the next world. Now, whatever support he may have for the next world, he provides himself with that and sees both evils (sufferings) and joys.

'And when he dreams, he takes away a little of [the impressions of] this all-embracing world (the waking state), himself makes the body unconscious, and creates [a dream body in its place], revealing his own brightness[104] by his own light—and he dreams. In this state the person becomes self-illumined. (IV. iii. 9)

'There are no [real] chariots in that state, nor animals to be yoked to them, nor roads there, but he creates the chariots, animals, and roads. There are no pleasures in that state, no joys, no rejoicings, but he creates the pleasures, joys, and rejoicings. There are no pools in that state, no reservoirs, no rivers, but he creates the pools, reservoirs, and rivers. He indeed is the agent. (IV. iii. 10)

'Regarding this there are the following verses:
' "The effulgent infinite being (purusha), who travels alone, makes the body insensible in sleep but himself remains awake, and taking with him the luminous particles of the organs,[105] watches those which lie dormant. Again he comes to the waking state. (IV. iii. 11)

' "The effulgent infinite being (purusha), who is immortal and travels alone, guards the unclean nest (body) with the help of the vital breath (prāna) and himself moves out of the nest. That immortal entity wanders wherever he likes. (IV. iii. 12)

' "In the dream world, the luminous one attains higher and lower states and creates many forms—now, as it were, enjoying himself in the company of women, now laughing, now even beholding frightful sights. (IV. iii. 13)

' "Everyone sees his sport but him no one sees." They say: "Do not wake him suddenly." If he does not find the right organ, the body becomes difficult to doctor.

---

[102] The present life.

[103] In dreams he feels both pleasure and pain, consisting of the impressions of experiences of both this life and previous lives.

[104] The word *brightness* (*jyotih*) refers to the sense-objects perceived in dreams. The mind itself is modified into the form of the diverse impressions of sense-objects one sees there.

[105] The phrase 'particles of the organs' refers to the impressions created by external objects and changed into modifications of the mind.

'Others, however, say that the dream state of a man is the same as the waking state, because what he sees while awake, that only he sees when asleep. [This is wrong.] In the dream state the self (purusha) itself becomes the light.'

Janaka said: 'I give you a thousand cows, revered Sir. Please instruct me further about Liberation itself.' (IV. iii. 14)

[Yājnavalkya said:] 'That entity (purusha), after enjoying himself and roaming [in the dream state] and merely witnessing [the results of] good and evil, remains in a state of profound sleep and [then] hastens back in the reverse way to his former condition, the dream state. He remains unaffected by whatever he sees in that [dream] state, for this infinite being is unattached.'

[Janaka said:] 'Just so, Yājnavalkya. I give you, Sir, a thousand cows. Please instruct me further about Liberation itself.' (IV. iii. 15)

[Yājnavalkya said:] 'That entity (purusha), after enjoying himself and roaming in the dream state and merely witnessing [the results of] good and evil, hastens back in the reverse way to his former condition, the waking state. He remains unaffected by whatever he sees in that state, for this infinite being is unattached.'

[Janaka said:] 'Just so, Yājnavalkya. I give you, Sir, a thousand cows. Please instruct me further about Liberation itself.' (IV. iii. 16)

[Yājnavalkya said:] 'That entity (purusha), after enjoying himself and roaming in the waking state and merely witnessing [the results of] good and evil, hastens back in the reverse way to its former condition, the dream state [or that of dreamless sleep]. (IV. iii. 17)

'As a large fish swims alternately to both banks [of a river]—the east and the west—so does the infinite being move to both these states: dreaming and waking. (IV. iii. 18)

'As a hawk or a falcon roaming in the sky becomes tired, folds its wings, and makes for its nest, so does this infinite entity (purusha) hasten for this state, where, falling asleep, he cherishes no more desires and dreams no more dreams. (IV. iii. 19)

'There are in his body nerves (nadis) called hitā, which are as fine as a hair divided into a thousand parts and are filled with white, blue, brown, green, and red [fluids]. [They are the seat of the subtle body, which is the storehouse of impressions.] Now, when he feels as if he were being killed or overpowered, or being chased by an elephant, or falling into a pit, [in short,] when he fancies at that time, through ignorance, whatever frightful thing he has experienced in the waking state, [that is the dream state]. So also, when he thinks he is a god, as it were, or a king, as it were, or thinks: "This [universe] is myself and I am all," that is his highest state. (IV. iii. 20)

'That[106] indeed is his form—free from desires, free from evils, free from fear, As a man fully embraced by his beloved wife knows nothing that is without, nothing that is within, so does this infinite being (the self), when fully embraced by the Supreme Self, know nothing that is without, nothing that is within.

'That indeed is his form, in which all his desires are fulfilled, in which all desires become the self, and which is free from desires and devoid of grief. (IV. iii. 21)

'In this state a father is no more a father, a mother is no more a mother, the worlds are no more the worlds, the gods are no more the gods, the Vedas are no more the Vedas. In this state a thief is no more a thief, the killer of a noble brāhmin is no more a killer, a chandāla is no more a chandāla, a paulkasa is no more a paulkasa, a monk is no more a monk, an ascetic is no more an ascetic.

'This form [of his] is untouched by good deeds and untouched by evil deeds, for he is then beyond all the woes of his heart. (IV. iii. 22)

'And when [it appears that] in deep sleep it does not see, yet it is seeing though it does not see; for there is no cessation of the vision of the seer, because the seer is imperishable. There is then, however, no second thing separate from the seer that it could see.[107] (IV. iii. 23)

'And when [it appears that] in deep sleep it does not smell, yet it is smelling though it does not smell; for there is no cessation of the smelling of the smeller, because the smeller is imperishable. There is then, however, no second thing separate from the smeller that it could smell. (IV. iii. 24)

'And when [it appears that] in deep sleep it does not taste, yet it is tasting though it does not taste; for there is no cessation of the tasting of the taster, because the taster is imperishable. There is then, however, no second thing separate from the taster that it could taste. (IV. iii. 25)

'And when [it appears that] in deep sleep it does not speak, yet it is speaking though it does not speak; for there is no cessation of the speak-

---

[106] That is to say, the identity with all experienced in deep sleep.

[107] The organs, the minds, and the forms, which cause specific experiences during the states of waking and dreaming, become unified with the self in deep sleep. Therefore one does not, at that time, have any knowledge of particular objects. But the imperishable consciousness of the self is present in all the states.

ing of the speaker, because the speaker is imperishable. There is then, however, no second thing separate from the speaker that it could speak about. (IV. iii. 26)

'And when [it appears that] in deep sleep it does not hear, yet it is hearing though it does not hear; for there is no cessation of the hearing of the hearer, because the hearer is imperishable. There is then, however, no second thing separate from the hearer that it could hear. (IV. iii. 27)

'And when [it appears that] in deep sleep it does not think, yet it is thinking though it does not think; for there is no cessation of the thinking of the thinker, because the thinker is imperishable. There is then, however, no second thing separate from the thinker that it could think of. (IV. iii. 28)

'And when [it appears that] in deep sleep it does not touch, yet it is touching though it does not touch; for there is no cessation of the touching of the toucher, because the toucher is imperishable. There is then, however, no second thing separate from the toucher that it could touch. (IV. iii. 29)

'And when [it appears that] in deep sleep it does not know, yet it is knowing though it does not know; for there is no cessation of the knowing of the knower, because the knower is imperishable. There is then, however, no second thing separate from the knower that it could know. (IV. iii. 30)

'When [in the waking and dream states] there is, as it were, another, then one can see the other, then one can smell the other, then one can speak to the other, then one can hear the other, then one can think of the other, then one can touch the other, then one can know the other. (IV. iii. 31)

'In deep sleep it becomes [transparent] like water, the witness, one and without a second. This is the World of Brahman, Your Majesty. This is its supreme attainment, this is its supreme glory, this is its highest world, this is its supreme bliss. On a particle of this bliss other creatures live.'
Thus did Yājnavalkya teach Janaka. (IV. iii. 32)

'If a person is perfect of body and is prosperous, lord of others, and most lavishly supplied with all human enjoyments, he represents the highest blessing among men. This human bliss multiplied a hundred times makes one measure of the bliss of the Manes who have won their own world. The bliss of these Manes who have won their world, multiplied a hundred times, makes one measure of bliss in the world of the gandharvas. The bliss of the gandharvas, multiplied a hundred times, makes one measure of the bliss of the gods by action (those who attain godhood through sacrificial rites). The bliss of the gods by action, multiplied a hundred times, makes one measure of the bliss of the gods by birth, as also of one who is versed in the Vedas, sinless, and free from desire. The bliss of the gods by birth, multiplied a hundred times, makes one measure of bliss in the World of Prajāpati (Virāj), as also of one who is versed in the Vedas, sinless, and free from desire. The bliss in the World of Prajāpati, multiplied a hundred times, makes one measure of bliss in the World of Brahmā (Hiranyagarbha), as also of one who is versed in the Vedas, sinless, and free from desire. This, indeed, is the supreme bliss. This is the state of Brahman, O Emperor,' said Yājnavalkya.

Janaka said: 'I give you a thousand cows, venerable Sir. Please instruct me further about Liberation itself.'

At this Yājnavalkya was afraid that the intelligent emperor was driving him to give the solution [of all his questions]. (IV. iii. 33)

[Yājnavalkya said:] 'That entity (the self), after enjoying himself and roaming in the dream state and merely witnessing [the results of] merits and demerits, hastens back in the reverse way to its former condition, the waking state. (IV. iii. 34)

'Just as a heavily loaded cart moves along, creaking, even so the self identified with the body, being presided over by the Self which is all consciousness (the Supreme Self), moves along, groaning, when breathing becomes difficult [at the approach of death].[108] (IV. iii. 35)

'When this [body] grows thin—becomes emaciated through old age or disease—then, as a mango or a fig or a fruit of the peepul tree becomes detached from its stalk, so does this infinite being (the self),[109] completely detaching himself from the parts of the body, again move on, in the same way that he came, to another body for the remanifestation of his vital breath (prāna). (IV. iii. 36)

'Just as, when a king comes, the ugras appointed to deal with crimes, the sutas, and the leaders of the village await him with food and drink and lodgings ready, saying: "Here he comes, here he comes," even so,

[108] Now the rebirth of the soul will be described. An example is given to show that just as the self wanders from the dream to the waking state, so it passes from the present body to the next body.

[109] The self identified with the subtle body.

for the person who knows [about the fruits of his own work], there wait all the elements, saying: "Here comes Brahman, here he comes."[110] (IV. iii. 37)

'Just as, when the king wishes to depart, the ugras appointed to deal with crimes, the sutas, and the leaders of the village gather around him, even so do all the organs gather around the self, at the time of death, when it struggles for breath. (IV. iii. 38)

'Now, when that self becomes weak and unconscious, as it were,[111] the organs gather around it. Having wholly seized these particles of light,[112] the self comes to the heart. When the presiding deity of the eye turns back from all sides, the dying man fails to notice colour. (IV. iv. 1)

'[The eye] becomes united [with the subtle body]; then people say: "He does not see." [The nose] becomes united [with the subtle body]; then they say: "He does not smell." [The tongue] becomes united [with the subtle body]; then they say: "He does not taste." [The vocal organ] becomes united [with the subtle body]; then they say: "He does not speak." [The ear] becomes united [with the subtle body]; then they say: "He does not hear." [The mind] becomes united [with the subtle body]; then they say: "He does not think." [The skin] becomes united [with the subtle body]; then they say: "He does not touch." [The intellect] becomes united [with the subtle body]; then they say: "He does not know."

'The upper end of the heart lights up,[113] and by that light the self departs, either through the eye or through the head or through any other part (aperture) of the body.[114]

'And when the self departs, the vital breath follows, and when the vital breath departs, all the organs follow.

---

[110] When a person leaves his present body, how does he reincarnate? Where does he find the materials for his future body? In answer it is said that there is the whole universe to help him realize the fruit of his past action. It awaits him with all the material ingredients for his future body and also for the enjoyment of the results of his past work. From these ingredients he chooses what will be helpful for his next embodiment.

[111] It is really the body that becomes weak and unconscious at the time of death.

[112] The phrase 'particles of light' is used with reference to the organs, such as the eye, because, like light, they reveal colour, etc.

[113] At the time of death the light of the self, when the organs are united in the heart, reveals the impressions of the kind of future body which will be suitable for the experience of the results of the self's past actions. The phrase 'lights up' refers to the knowledge of the impressions, which latter are effects of past actions and not inherent in the self.

[114] The way of exit is determined by past action. The self, departing through the eye, goes to the sun; departing through the head, to Hiranyagarbha; and so on.

'Then the self becomes endowed with specific consciousness[115] and passes on to the body to be attained by that consciousness.

'Knowledge, work, and past experience[116] follow the self. (IV. iv. 2)

'And just as a leech moving on a blade of grass reaches its end, takes hold of another, and draws itself together towards it, so does the self, after throwing off this body, that is to say, after making it unconscious, take hold of another support and draw itself together towards it.[117] (IV. iv. 3)

'And just as a goldsmith takes a small quantity of gold and fashions [out of it] another—a newer and better—form, so does the self, after throwing off this body, that is to say, after making it unconscious, fashion another—a newer and better—form, suited to the Manes, or the gandharvas, or the gods, or Virāj, or Hiranyagarbha, or other beings. (IV. iv. 4)

'That self is indeed Brahman; it is also identified with the intellect, the mind, and the vital breath, with the eyes and ears, with earth, water, air, and ākāśa, with fire and with what is other than fire, with desire and with absence of desire, with anger and with absence of anger, with righteousness and unrighteousness, with all—it is identified, as is well known, with this (i.e. what is perceived) and with that (i.e. what is inferred). According as it acts and according as it behaves, so it becomes: by doing good it becomes good, and by doing evil it becomes evil. It becomes virtuous through virtuous action, and evil through evil action.

'Others, however, say that the self is identified with desire alone. As is its desire, so is its resolution; and as is its resolution, so is its deed; and whatever deed it does, that it reaps. (IV. iv. 5)

[115] That is to say, the specific consciousness which determines the next body to be assumed by the self. This consciousness is determined by one's past actions.

[116] 'Without these impressions no action can be done; for the organs are not skilful in unaccustomed work. But when the organs are prompted to work by impressions of past experience, they can attain skill even without experience in this life. It is frequently observed that some are clever in certain kinds of work, such as painting, from their very birth, even without practice in the present life, while others are unskilful even in some very easy task. Similarly, in the enjoyment of sense-objects some are observed to be skilful and some dull. All this is due to the revival or non-revival of past experience. Without past experience we cannot understand how anyone can proceed to accomplish any work or to enjoy the fruit of past actions. One should therefore be endowed with good knowledge, good work, and good experience, so that one may obtain a desirable body and desirable enjoyments. This is the purport of the whole passage.' (Śankarāchārya.)

[117] In the new body, the organs, under the control of the person's past karma, become active and are co-ordinated. The physical body also is formed. When the organs have been arranged, the presiding deities come to the body to help the organs. This is the process of formation of the new body.

'Regarding this there is the following verse:

' "Because of attachment, the [transmigrating] self, together with its work, attains that result to which its subtle body or mind clings. Having exhausted [in the other world] the results of whatever work it did in this life, it returns from that world to this world for [fresh] work."

'Thus does the man who desires [transmigrate]. But as to the man who does not desire—who is without desire, who is freed from desire, whose desire is satisfied, whose only object of desire is the Self—his organs do not depart. Being Brahman, he merges in Brahman. (IV. iv. 6)

'Regarding this there is the following verse:

' "When all the desires that dwell in his heart are got rid of, then does the mortal [man] become immortal and attain Brahman in this very body."[118]

'Just as the slough of a snake lies, dead and cast away, on an ant-hill, even so lies this body. Then the self becomes disembodied and immortal Spirit, the Supreme Self (Prāna), Brahman, the Light.'

Janaka, Emperor of Videha, said: 'I give you, venerable Sir, a thousand cows.' (IV. iv. 7)

'Regarding this there are the following verses:

' "The subtle, ancient path stretching far away has been touched (reached) by me; nay, I have realized it myself. By this path the wise, the knowers of Brahman, move on to the celestial sphere (Liberation) after the fall of this body, having been freed [even while living]." (IV. iv. 8)

' "Some speak of it as white, [others as] blue, grey, green, or red.[119] This path is realized by a knower of Brahman and is trod by whoever knows Brahman, has done good deeds, and is identified with the Supreme Light." (IV. iv. 9)

' "Into blinding darkness enter those who worship ignorance; into a greater darkness than that, as it were, enter those who are devoted to knowledge."[120] (IV. iv. 10)

[118] It is not necessary to go to some other plane of existence in order to obtain Liberation. Therefore the organs of a man who has attained Brahman do not depart; they merge in their cause, the Self.

[119] These colours denote the finite experience of the seekers. But the path itself is Knowledge and free from any colour.

[120] The ceremonial portion of the Vedas, dealing with various injunctions and prohibitions. The passage refers to those who deny the primacy of the Upanishads, which alone show the way to Liberation. This and the following verse occur also in the *Iśa Upanishad*.

' "Cheerless indeed are those worlds covered with blinding darkness. To them after death go those people who are ignorant and unwise." (IV. iv. 11)

' "If a man knows the Self as *I am this*, then desiring what and for whose sake will he suffer in the wake of the body?" (IV. iv. 12)

' "Whoever has realized and intimately known the Self, which has entered this perilous and perplexing place (the body), is the maker of the universe;[121] for he is the maker of all. [All] is his Self, and he, again, is indeed the Self of all." (IV. iv. 13)

' "Dwelling in this very body, we have somehow realized Brahman; otherwise we should have remained ignorant and great destruction would have overtaken us. Those who know Brahman become immortal, while others only suffer misery." (IV. iv. 14)

' "When a person following [the instructions of a teacher] directly beholds the effulgent Self, the Lord of all that has been and will be, he no longer wishes to hide himself from It." [122] (IV. iv. 15)

' "That under which the year with its days rolls on—upon that immortal Light of all lights the gods meditate as longevity."[123] (IV. iv. 16)

' "That in which the five groups of five[124] and the ākāśa rest, that very Ātman I regard as the Immortal Brahman. Knowing that Brahman, I am immortal." (IV. iv. 17)

' "They who know the Vital Breath (Prāna) of the vital breath (prāna), the Eye of the eye, the Ear of the ear, the Mind of the mind, have realized the ancient, primordial Brahman.' (IV. iv. 18)

' "Through the mind[125] alone is Brahman to be realized. There is in It no diversity. He goes from death to death who sees in It, as it were, diversity." (IV. iv. 19)

[121] That is to say, completely blessed.

[122] That is to say, from the Lord. He who sees diversity wishes to hide himself from the Lord. Or the passage may mean that when he directly realizes the Lord as identical with his own self, he no longer finds fault with anyone, for he sees all as his self.

[123] Things other than the Self perish. The gods meditate upon the Self through Its attribute of longevity and thus are long-lived.

[124] Namely, the celestial minstrels, the Manes, the gods, the demons, and the rākshasas (monsters); or the four castes and the untouchables as the fifth; or the vital breath, eye, ear, food (or light), and mind.

[125] Purified by the knowledge of the Supreme Truth, following the instructions of a teacher versed in the scriptures.

"Unknowable and constant, It should be realized in one form[126] only. The Self is free from taint, beyond the ākāśa, birthless, infinite, and unchanging." (IV. iv. 20)

' "The intelligent seeker of Brahman, learning about the Self alone, should practise wisdom (prajñā). Let him not think of too many words, for that is exhausting to the organ of speech." (IV. iv. 21)

'That great, unborn Self, which is identified with the intellect (vijñānamaya) and which dwells in the midst of the organs, lies in the ākāśa within the heart. It is the controller of all, the lord of all, the ruler of all. It does not become greater through good deeds or smaller through evil deeds. It is the lord of all, the ruler of all beings, the protector of all beings. It is the dam that serves as the boundary to keep the different worlds apart. The brāhmins seek to realize It through the study of the Vedas, through sacrifices, through gifts, and through austerity which does not lead to annihilation.[127] Knowing It alone one becomes a sage (muni). Wishing for this World (i.e. the Self) alone, monks renounce their homes.

'The knowers of Brahman of olden times, it is said, did not wish for offspring [because they thought]: "What shall we do with offspring—we who have attained this Self, this World?" They gave up, it is said, their desire for sons, for wealth, and for the worlds, and led the life of [religious] mendicants. That which is the desire for sons is the desire for wealth, and that which is the desire for wealth is the desire for the worlds; for both these, indeed, are but desires.

' "This Self is That which has been described as *Not this, not this*. It is imperceptible, for It is not perceived; undecaying, for It never decays; unattached, for It is never attached; unfettered, for It never feels pain and never suffers injury.

' "Him [who knows this] these two thoughts do not overcome: *For this I did an evil deed*, and *For this I did a good deed*. He overcomes both. Things done or not done do not afflict him." (IV. iv. 22)

'This has been expressed by the following rik verse:
' "This is the eternal glory of Brahman: It neither increases nor decreases through work. [Therefore] one should know the nature of That alone. Knowing It one is not touched by evil action."
'Therefore he who knows It as such becomes self-controlled, calm, withdrawn into himself, patient, and collected; he sees the Self in his

---

[126] That is to say, as homogeneous Pure Intelligence.

[127] The spiritual seeker should enjoy helpful sense-objects, being free from attachment and aversion. Indiscriminate austerity—starving oneself, for example —leads to death and not to Self-Knowledge.

own self (body); he sees all as the Self. Evil does not overcome him, but he overcomes all evil. Evil does not afflict him, but he consumes all evil. He becomes sinless, taintless, free from doubts, and a true Brāhmana (knower of Brahman). This is the World of Brahman, O Emperor, and you have attained It.' Thus said Yājnavalkya.

Janaka said: 'Venerable Sir, I give you the empire of Videha and myself, too, with it, to wait upon you.' (IV. iv. 23)

That great, unborn Self is the eater of food[128] and the giver of wealth.[129] He who knows this obtains wealth.[130] (IV. iv. 24)

That great, unborn Self is undecaying, immortal, undying, fearless; It is Brahman (infinite). Brahman is indeed fearless. He who knows It as such becomes the fearless Brahman. (IV. iv. 25)

[128] The Self dwells in all beings and eats all the food that they eat.
[129] Giver of the fruit of actions.
[130] A eulogy of the Knowledge of Brahman.

V

OM. INFINITE IS That,[131] infinite is this.[132] From the Infinite [Brahman] proceeds the infinite. [After the realization of the Great Identity or after the cosmic dissolution,] when the infinity of the infinite [universe] merges [in the Infinite Brahman], there remains the Infinite [Brahman] alone.

Om is the Ākāśa Brahman[133]—the primeval ākāśa.[134] [It is] the ākāśa containing air, says the son of Kauravāyani. It (Om) is the Veda—thus the knowers of Brahman know; [for] through it one knows what is to be known.[135] (V. i. 1)

Prajāpati had three kinds of offspring: gods, men, and demons (asuras). They lived with Prajāpati, practising the vows of brahmachārins. After finishing their term, the gods said to him: 'Please instruct us, Sir.' To them he uttered the syllable da[136] [and asked]: 'Have you understood?' They replied: 'We have. You said to us, "Control[137] yourselves (dāmyata)." ' He said: 'Yes, you have understood.' (V. ii. 1)

Then the men said to him: 'Please instruct us, Sir.' To them he uttered the same syllable da[138] [and asked]: 'Have you understood?' They replied: 'We have. You said to us, "Give (datta)." ' He said: 'Yes, you have understood.' (V. ii. 2)

Then the demons said to him: 'Please instruct us, Sir.' To them he uttered the same syllable da[139] [and asked]: 'Have you understood?'

---

[131] The Supreme Brahman.

[132] The conditioned Brahman, or the visible universe.

[133] The word *Brahman*, without any qualifying term, may mean any vast object. The word *Ākāśa* makes it specific.

[134] Lest the word ākāśa should be taken to mean the material ākāśa, it is described as the primeval ākāśa, that is to say, the Supreme Self. The primeval ākāśa cannot be meditated upon without an external help; therefore the seeker is asked to contemplate it through the symbol *Om*, with faith and devotion.

[135] This verse, which forms also the invocation of the *Brihadāranyaka Upanishad*, has been translated here in a slightly different way, without, however, changing the general meaning.

[136] This is the first syllable of the word *dāmyata*, which signifies self-control.

[137] The gods, in spite of possessing many virtues, are naturally unruly.

[138] The Sanskrit word *datta* begins with the syllable *da*. Men are naturally avaricious; so they are asked to distribute their wealth to the best of their power.

[139] The Sanskrit word *dayadhvam* also begins with the syllable *da*. The demons are naturally cruel and given to injuring others.

They replied: 'We have. You said to us: "Be compassionate (daya-dhvam)." ' He said: 'Yes, you have understood.'

That very thing is repeated [even today] by the heavenly voice, in the form of thunder, as 'Da,' 'Da,' 'Da,' which means: 'Control your-selves,' 'Give,' and 'Have compassion.' Therefore one should learn these three: self-control, giving, and mercy.[140] (V. ii. 3)

Prajāpati is this—the heart (intellect). It (the heart) is Brahman. It is all. Hridayam (the heart) consists of three syllables. One syllable is *hri*;[141] and to him who knows this, his own people and others bring [presents].[142] One syllable is *da*; and to him who knows this, his own people and others give [their powers]. One syllable is *yam*; and he who knows this goes to heaven. (V. iii. 1)

That [intellect Brahman] was verily this—Satya alone.[143] And who-soever knows this great, glorious first-born one as the Satya Brahman conquers these worlds. And his [enemy] is thus conquered and becomes non-existent—yes, whosoever knows this great, glorious first-born one as the Satya Brahman; for Satya indeed is that Brahman. (V. iv. 1)

In the beginning this universe was water alone. That water produced Satya.[144] Satya is Brahman. Brahman produced Prajāpati, and Prajā-pati the gods. Those gods meditate on Satya. This [name] *Satya* con-sists of three syllables. *Sa* is one syllable, *ti* is one syllable, and *ya* is one syllable. The first and last syllables are the truth. In the middle is untruth. This untruth is enclosed on both sides by truth; thus truth preponderates. Untruth does not hurt him who knows this. (V. v. 1)

[140] Gods and demons (asuras) may be found among men. Those human beings who are wanting in self-control, but otherwise endowed with many good qualities, are the gods; those who are particularly greedy are men; while those who are cruel and given to injuring others are the demons.

[141] The meaning of the word is 'to bring', 'to gather'.

[142] The organs are parts of the intellect and are designated as 'his own people', and the objects, such as sound etc., which are not so related, are designated as 'others'. The organs and the objects, through the performance of their respective functions, bring offerings to the intellect, which, in its turn, passes them to the self.

[143] That is to say, Satya Brahman, or the Brahman that is both sat and tyat, both in the gross and the subtle elements. Brahman as the five elements has been described in I. vi. 3. See also V. v. 1.

[144] The word means 'the true' and here connotes the manifested universe, whose symbol is Hiranyagarbha. In the preceding verse, the word *Satya* was analysed as meaning sat and tyat. Here it is analysed in a different way. These analyses are intended to assist meditation.

Now, that which is Satya is the sun—the being who dwells in yonder orb and the being who is in the right eye. These two rest on each other. The former (the being in the sun) rests on the latter (the being in the right eye) through his rays, and the latter rests on the former through his organs.[145] When the individual self is about to leave the body, he sees the solar orb clearly (i.e. without rays).[146] Those rays no longer come to him. (V. v. 2)

Of this being who is in the solar orb, the syllable *Bhuh* is the head, for there is one head and there is this one syllable; the word *Bhuvah* is the arms, for there are two arms and there are these two syllables; the word *Svah* is the legs, for there are two legs and there are these two syllables. His secret name is Ahar.[147] He who knows this destroys evil and leaves it behind. (V. v. 3)

Of this being who is in the right eye, the syllable *Bhuh* is the head, for there is one head and there is this one syllable; the word *Bhuvah* is the arms, for there are two arms and there are these two syllables; the word *Svah* is the legs, for there are two legs and there are these two syllables. His secret name is Aham.[148] He who knows this destroys evil and leaves it behind. (V. v. 4)

This being identified with the mind and resplendent by nature [is realized by yogis] within the heart as [of the size of] a grain of rice or barley. He is the lord of all, the ruler of all, and governs all this—whatever there is. (V. vi. 1)

They say that lightning is Brahman. It is called lightning (vidyut) because it scatters (vidānāt) darkness. Whosoever knows this—that lightning is Brahman—scatters the evils [that are ranged against him]; for lightning is indeed Brahman. (V. vii. 1)

When a man departs from this world, he reaches the air. The air opens there for him as wide as the hole of a chariot wheel. Through this [opening] he ascends and reaches the sun. The sun opens there for him

[145] The organs reveal the being in the sun.

[146] The solar being, who is the presiding deity of the eye, withdraws his rays and the sun appears to the dying man shorn of its rays and clear, like the moon. This may be taken as a portent of death.

[147] The word is derived from the root *han* or *hā*, meaning to kill or shun.

[148] The word means 'I', that is to say, the inner self, and is derived from the root *han* or *hā*. See the note on the preceding verse.

as wide as the hole of a lambara.[149] By this [opening] he ascends and reaches the moon. The moon opens there for him as wide as the hole of a drum. By this [opening] he ascends and reaches a World free from grief and cold. There he dwells for endless years. (V. x. 1)

The supreme austerity is indeed that a man suffers when he is ill.[150] He who knows this wins the highest world.

The supreme austerity is indeed that a man, after death, is carried to the forest.[151] He who knows this wins the highest world.

The supreme austerity is indeed that a man, after death, is laid on the fire.[152] He who knows this wins the highest world.[153] (V. xi. 1)

The words *Bhumi* (*earth*), *Antariksha* (*sky*), and *Dyaus* (*heaven*) form eight syllables, and the first foot of the Gāyatri[154] consists of eight syllables. So the three worlds constitute the first foot of the Gāyatri. Whosoever knows this about the [first] foot of the Gāyatri wins all that is in the three worlds. (V. xiv. 1)

Richah, Yajumshi, and *Sāmāni*[155] form eight syllables, and the second foot of the Gāyatri consists of eight syllables. So these [three] Vedas constitute the second foot of the Gāyatri. Whosoever thus knows the second foot of the Gāyatri wins as much as that treasury of knowledge, the three Vedas, has to confer. (V. xiv. 2)

Prāna, apāna, and *vyāna* form eight syllables, and the third foot of the Gāyatri consists of eight syllables. So these [three] forms of the vital breath constitute the third foot of the Gāyatri. Whosoever knows this about the third foot of the Gāyatri wins all the living beings that are in the universe.

[149] A kind of musical instrument like a tabor.

[150] A sick person, while he is suffering pain, should think he is performing a penance; he should not condemn the disease or be dejected over it. This ungrudging endurance of suffering wipes out evils.

[151] By the priests for the funeral ceremony. Retirement to the forest from home is a form of austerity.

[152] For cremation.

[153] The acceptance of the threefold suffering as a form of penance destroys past sin and produces the same result as one gains from the practice of austerity.

[154] The same as Sāvitri. It is the most sacred verse of the Vedas and reads as follows: *Tat saviturvarenyam, bhargo devasya dhimahi, dhiyo yo nah prachodayāt*—'We meditate on the adorable light of the radiant sun. May he stimulate our intellect.' (*Ri.* III. lxii. 10.) There is also a metre called Gāyatri which has three feet of eight syllables each. It will be seen that the Gāyatri verse is composed in this metre. (The syllable *ya* in the word *varenya* should be divided to make up the eighth syllable.)

[155] These three words are the plural forms of the names of the three Vedas.

Now, its turiya, [apparently] visible (darśata), and supramundane (parorajā) foot is this—the sun that glows yonder. That which is fourth is called turiya. He (the being in the solar orb) is [apparently] visible (darśata), because he is seen, as it were, [by the yogis]. He is supramundane (parorajā), because he shines alone on the whole universe as its overlord. He who thus knows the fourth foot of the Gāyatri shines with splendour and glory. (V. xiv. 3)

That Gāyatri rests on that fourth, [apparently] visible, supramundane foot. And that, again, rests on truth. The eye is truth, for the eye is indeed truth. Therefore, even today, if two persons come disputing, one saying: 'I saw it,' and another: 'I heard of it,' we should trust the one who says: 'I saw it.'

That truth rests on strength. The vital breath (prāna) is strength. Hence truth rests on the vital breath. Therefore they say that strength is more powerful than truth.

Thus the Gāyatri is based on the vital breath within the body. That Gāyatri protected the gayas. The organs are the gayas; therefore the Gāyatri protected (tatrē) the organs. Because it protected the organs, it is called the Gāyatri. The Sāvitri [verse],[156] which the teacher communicates to the pupil, is no other than this. It saves the organs of the pupil to whom it is imparted by the teacher. (V. xiv. 4)

Some impart [to the pupil] the Sāvitri which is in the Anushtubh metre,[157] saying: '[The goddess of] speech is Anushtubh; [so] we shall impart it to him.'

But one should not do that. One should impart only that Sāvitri which is Gāyatri. Verily, if one who knows this accepts too much as a gift,[158] as it were, it is not enough for even one foot of the Gāyatri. (V. xiv. 5)

If he (the knower of the Gāyatri) accepts [as a gift] the three worlds full of wealth, he will be receiving [the fruit of knowing] only the first

[156] The hymn to the sun which the teacher teaches the pupil when the latter is brought to him at the age of eight. The teacher makes the pupil repeat first a quarter of the verse, then a half, and finally the whole, till he knows the whole of the Sāvitri. In this manner the pupil is really taught that the prāna, or vital breath, is the World Soul.

[157] The Sāvitri verse composed in the Anushtubh metre is as follows: *Tat savitur vrinimahe vayam devasya bhojanam. Śreshtham sarvadhātamam turam bhagasya dhimahi.*—'We supplicate the best food of the radiant sun, which pervades all things. We meditate without delay on the sun.' (*Ṛi.* V. lxxxii. 1; also quoted in *Chh. Up.* V. ii. 7.) The sun is the presiding deity of this hymn.

[158] The receiving of gifts is generally condemned by the scriptures. But the knower of the Gāyatri is identified with the whole universe; therefore there is no such thing as too much of a gift for him.

foot of the Gāyatri. If he accepts [as a gift] as much as this treasury of knowledge, the Vedas, [has to confer,] he will be receiving [the fruit of knowing] only the second foot of the Gāyatri. And if he accepts [as a gift] as much as [is covered by] all living creatures in the world, he will be receiving [the fruit of knowing] only the third foot of the Gāyatri. While [the fruit of knowing] its fourth, [apparently] visible, supramundane foot—yonder sun that glows—is not to be counterbalanced by any gift received.

Indeed, how could anyone receive so much as a gift? (V. xiv. 6)

The salutation to the Gāyatri:

'O Gāyatri, thou art one-footed,[159] two-footed,[160] three-footed,[161] and four-footed.[162] And thou art without any feet,[163] for thou art unattainable. Salutation to thee, fourth foot, [apparently] visible and supramundane! May the enemy never attain his object!'

[Should the knower of the Gāyatri] bear hatred towards anyone, [he should] either [use this mantra]: 'May his desired object never flourish!' —in which case that object of the person against whom he thus salutes the Gāyatri never flourishes—or [he may say]: 'May I attain that [cherished object] of his!' (V. xiv. 7)

On this subject Janaka, Emperor of Videha, said to Budila, the son of Aśvatarāśva: 'Well, how is it that you, who called yourself a knower of the Gāyatri, have come to be an elephant and are carrying me?'

He replied: 'Because, Your Majesty, I did not know its mouth.'[164]

Janaka said: 'Fire is its mouth. If people put a large quantity of fuel into the fire, it is all burnt up. Similarly, a man who knows this, even if he commits a great many sins, consumes them all and becomes pure, clean, and free from decay and death.' (V. xiv. 8)

---

[159] Refers to the three worlds.
[160] Refers to the three Vedas.
[161] Refers to the three forms of the prāna, or vital breath.
[162] Refers to the sun.
[163] This refers to the supreme and unconditioned form of the Gāyatri, described as 'Not this, not this'.
[164] The knowledge of the Gāyatri, being deficient in one part, had been fruitless.

VI

OM. HE WHO knows what is the oldest and greatest becomes the oldest and greatest among his kinsmen. The vital breath (prāna) is indeed the oldest[165] and greatest. He who knows this becomes the oldest and greatest among his kinsmen and also among those of whom he wishes to be so. (VI. i. 1)

He who knows what is the most excellent (vasishtha) becomes the most excellent among his kinsmen. The organ of speech is indeed the vasishtha. He who knows this becomes the most excellent among his kinsmen and also among those of whom he wishes to be so. (VI. i. 2)

He who knows what has [the attribute of] steadiness (pratishthā) lives steadily in rough as well as smooth places and times. The eye indeed is endowed with steadiness, for with the help of the eye one remains steady in rough as well as smooth places and times. He who knows this lives steadily in rough as well as smooth places and times. (VI. i. 3)

He who knows prosperity (sampad) attains whatever object he desires. The ear indeed is prosperity, for when the ear is intact all the Vedas are acquired. He who knows this attains whatever object he desires. (VI. i. 4)

He who knows the abode (āyatana) becomes the abode of his kinsmen and also of [other] people. The mind indeed is the abode. He who knows this becomes the abode of his kinsmen as well as of [other] people. (VI. i. 5)

He who knows [what has the attribute of] procreation (prajāti) is enriched with children and animals. Semen[166] verily has this attribute. He who knows this is enriched with children and animals. (VI. i. 6)

These organs, disputing about who was superior among them, went to Prajāpati and asked: 'Which one among us is the most excellent (vasishtha)?' He said: 'That one among you is the most excellent by whose departure this body is considered to suffer most.' (VI. i. 7)

The organ of speech departed. After being absent for a whole year it came back and said: 'How have you been able to live without me?'

---

[165] The vital breath in the embryo begins to function earlier than the eye and the other organs. Hence it is said to be the oldest.
[166] Refers to the organ of generation.

The other organs said: 'We lived just as dumb people live, without speaking through the tongue, but living through the vital breath, seeing through the eye, hearing through the ear, knowing through the mind, and procreating through the organ of generation.' Then the organ of speech entered [the body]. (VI. i. 8)

The eye departed. After being absent for a whole year it came back and said: 'How have you been able to live without me?' The other organs said: 'We lived just as blind people live, without seeing through the eye, but living through the vital breath, speaking through the organ of speech, hearing through the ear, knowing through the mind, and procreating through the organ of generation.' Then the eye entered [the body]. (VI. i. 9)

The ear went out. After being absent for a whole year it came back and said: 'How have you been able to live without me?' The other organs said: 'We lived just as deaf people live, without hearing through the ear, but living through the vital breath, speaking through the organ of speech, seeing through the eye, knowing through the mind, and procreating through the organ of generation.' Then the ear entered [the body]. (VI. i. 10)

The mind went out. After being absent for a whole year it came back and said: 'How have you been able to live without me?' The other organs said: 'We lived just as idiots live, without knowing through the mind, but living through the vital breath, speaking through the organ of speech, seeing through the eye, hearing through the ear, and procreating through the organ of generation.' Then the mind entered [the body]. (VI. i. 11)

Then the organ of generation went out. After being absent for a whole year it came back and said: 'How have you been able to live without me?' The other organs said: 'We lived just as impotent people live, without procreating children through the organ of generation, but living through the vital breath, speaking through the organ of speech, seeing through the eye, hearing through the ear, and knowing through the mind.' Then the organ of generation entered [the body]. (VI. i. 12)

Then as the vital breath was about to depart, it uprooted the organs [from their places] just as a great, noble horse of the Sindhu country tears up the pegs to which his feet are tied. They said: 'Venerable Sir, please do not go out. We shall not be able to live without you.'
    'If I am such, then give me an offering.'
    'So be it.' (VI. i. 13)

The organ of speech said: 'That attribute of being most excellent which I possess is yours.'

The eye said: 'That attribute of steadiness which I possess is yours.'

The ear said: 'That attribute of prosperity which I possess is yours.'

The mind said: 'That attribute of being an abode which I possess is yours.'

The organ of generation said: 'That attribute of procreation which I possess is yours.'

Then the vital breath said: 'If I am such, then what will be my food and what will be my dress?'

They replied: 'Whatever food there is—including that of dogs, worms, insects, and moths—will be your food, and water will be your dress.'

He who knows the food of the vital breath to be such never happens to eat anything or accept anything that is not food. Wise men who are versed in the Vedas therefore take a sip of water just before and after eating; they think that thereby they remove the nakedness of the vital breath. (VI. i. 14)

Śvetaketu, the grandson of Aruna, came to the assembly of the Panchālas. He approached Pravāhana, the son of Jivala, who was being waited upon by his courtiers. As soon as the king saw him, he said: 'Is it you, boy?' He replied: 'Yes, Sir.'

Then the king asked: 'Have you been taught by your father?' 'Yes,' he replied. (VI. ii. 1)

The king said: 'Do you know how people, after departing [from this life], proceed on different paths?' 'No,' he replied.

'Do you know how they return to this world?' 'No,' he replied.

'Do you know why the other world is never filled up [even though] so many people go there again and again?' 'No,' he replied.

'Do you know after how many offerings of oblations the water (the liquid oblation) becomes endowed with a human voice,[167] rises up, and speaks?' 'No,' he replied.

'Do you know the means of access to the path leading to the gods or to that leading to the Manes, that is to say, through what deeds men attain the path leading to the gods or that leading to the Manes? We have heard the following words of the Mantra: "I have heard of the two paths for men, one leading to the Manes and the other to the gods. Going along them they (departed souls) are united [with their destination]. They (the paths) lie between the father (heaven) and the mother (earth)." '

Śvetaketu said: 'I do not know even one of these.' (VI. ii. 2)

---

[167] This happens when the offering takes a human form. Or the passage may mean 'under the name of a man'.

Then the king invited him to stay. But the boy, disregarding the invitation, hurried away. He went to his father and said: 'Did you not tell me before that you had fully instructed me?'

'What then, my intelligent child?'

'That fellow of a kshatriya asked me five questions, and I did not know one of them.'

'What were they?'

'These,' said Śvetaketu, and he recited them. (VI. ii. 3)

The father said: 'My child, believe me, whatever I myself knew, I told you. But come, let us go there and live as religious students (brahmachārins).' 'You may go, Sir,' the son replied.

Then Gautama went to where King Pravāhana, the son of Jivala, was giving audience. The king offered him a seat, ordered water for him, and made him the reverential offering. Then he said: 'Revered Gautama, we will give you a boon.' (VI. ii. 4)

Gautama said: 'You have promised me this boon. Now please tell me what you spoke about to my boy.' (VI. ii. 5)

The king said: 'Ah, those are divine boons, Gautama. Please ask a human boon.' (VI. ii. 6)

Gautama said: 'You know well that I have gold, cows, horses, maid-servants, retinue, and apparel. Please do not be ungenerous towards me in regard to that gift which is plentiful, infinite, and inexhaustible.'

The king said: 'Then, verily, O Gautama, you should ask it in the prescribed way.'

Gautama replied: 'I approach you as a disciple.'

The ancients[168] used to approach a teacher through mere declaration.[169] So Gautama lived [with the king] by merely announcing that he was a student. (VI. ii. 7)

The king said: 'Please do not be offended with us even as your paternal grandfather was not [offended with ours]. Before now this knowledge never rested with a brāhmin. But I shall teach it to you, for who can refuse you when you speak like this? (VI. ii. 8)

'Yonder world[170] is the [sacrificial] fire, the sun is its fuel, the rays its smoke, the day its flame, the four quarters its cinders, and the inter-

[168] Refers to the brāhmins who sought instruction from the kshatriyas and vaiśyas, or the kshatriyas who sought instruction from the vaiśyas.

[169] That is to say, not actually rendering any menial service, such as touching the teacher's feet.

[170] Heaven. We are enjoined to look upon heaven, which is not fire, as fire. The same is so with man, woman, etc., in the verses which follow. The points of resemblance are given.

mediate quarters its sparks. In this fire the gods offer faith as libation. Out of that offering King Moon is born.[171] (VI. ii. 9)

'Parjanya (the god of rain),[172] O Gautama, is the fire, the year is its fuel, the clouds its smoke, lightning its flame, the thunderbolt its cinders, the rumbling its sparks. In this fire the gods offer King Moon as libation. Out of that offering rain is produced.[173] (VI. ii. 10)

'This world,[174] O Gautama, is the fire, the earth is its fuel, fire its smoke, the night its flame, the moon its cinders, the stars its sparks. In this fire the gods offer rain as libation. Out of that offering food is produced. (VI. ii. 11)

'Man, O Gautama, is the fire, the open mouth is its fuel, the vital breath its smoke, speech its flame, the eye its cinders, and the ear its sparks. In this fire the gods offer food as libation. Out of that offering semen is produced. (VI. ii 12)

'Women, O Gautama, is the fire, her sexual organ is the fuel, the hairs the smoke, the vulva the flame, sexual intercourse the cinders, enjoyment the sparks. In this fire the gods offer semen as libation. Out of this offering a man[175] is born. He lives as long as he is to live. Then, when he dies—(VI. ii. 13)

---

[171] The fourth question is being dealt with first. The solution of the other questions depends upon the answer to this question. Milk and other liquids are offered in the Agnihotra and similar sacrifices; they ascend, in a subtle form, together with the sacrificer, along the Way of the Manes, first to the sky and then to heaven. The liquids that are offered in the sacrifice, as they rise up, become subtle and are called 'faith'. These subtle liquids, when offered as libations in heaven by the gods, produce for the sacrificer an aqueous body which enables him to live in the World of the Moon. Though this body contains other materials, it is mainly aqueous.

[172] The second receptacle of the oblations during the return trip of the soul for rebirth.

[173] Aruni asked King Pravāhana about the path followed by the soul after death and also how it reincarnates in a human body. The king answered him through the symbol of a sacrifice in order to give a spiritual interpretation of life and the universe. This is called the doctrine of the Five Fires, hitherto known only to the kshatriya kings.

[174] This is the third fire. The word *world* means the abode where all created beings are born and experience the results of their past work, and which consists of action, its accessories, and its results.

[175] Water (the liquid offering), designated as 'faith', is successively offered in the sacrificial fire of heaven, the rain-god, the world, man, and woman. Out of these offerings are produced, in increasingly gross forms, the moon, rain, food, semen, and the fifth, called man. Thus the fifth oblation (that is to say, water transformed into semen) offered in the fire of woman, assumes a human form and speaks with a human voice.

'They carry him to be offered in the fire. The fire becomes his fire, the fuel his fuel, the smoke his smoke, the flame his flame, the cinders his cinders, and the sparks his sparks. In this fire the gods offer the man as libation. Out of this offering the man emerges in radiant splendour. (VI. ii. 14)

'Those [even among] householders who know this, as described, and those too who, living in the forest, meditate with faith upon the Satya Brahman (Hiranyagarbha), reach [the deity identified with] flame, from him [the deity of] the day, from him [the deity of] the fortnight in which the moon waxes, from him [the deities of the] six months during which the sun travels northward, from them [the deity identified with] the world of the gods (devaloka), from him the sun, from the sun [the deity of] lightning. [Then] a being created from the mind [of Hiranyagarbha] comes and leads them to the worlds of Brahmā. In those worlds of Brahmā they become exalted and live for many years. They no more return to this world.[176] (VI. ii. 15)

'But those[177] who conquer the worlds through sacrifices, charity, and austerity reach [the deity of] smoke, from smoke, [the deity of] the night, from night [the deity of] the fortnight in which the moon wanes, from the decreasing half of the moon [the deities of] the six months during which the sun travels southward, from these months [the deity of] the world of the Manes, and from the world of the Manes, the moon. Reaching the moon they become food.[178] There the gods enjoy them, just as [here] the priests drink the shining soma juice—saying [as it were]: 'Flourish, dwindle.'[179] And when their past work is exhausted they reach this very ākāśa, from the ākāśa they reach the air, from the air rain, from rain the earth. Reaching the earth they become food.[180] Then they are again offered in the fire of man,[181] and thence in the fire of woman.[182]

---

[176] This is the answer to the first question.
[177] Refers to those householders who do not know the meditation on the Five Fires but are mere ritualists.
[178] That is to say, they become like servants of the gods.
[179] By these words the text indicates that they frequently fill up the cups and empty them. Likewise, the gods enjoy the ritualists who have got new bodies in the moon and have become the materials of their luxury. They reward these ritualists according to their past work by giving them frequent intervals of rest. Their services are utilized by the gods. The intervals of rest are like the filling up of the cups.
[180] That is to say, they enter with the rain into barley, rice, and other edible cereals.
[181] When an adult man eats the food out of which his semen is produced. The soul of the ritualist enters the semen.
[182] At the time of the sexual act.

Out of the fire of woman they are born [and perform rites] with a view to going to other worlds. Thus do they rotate.

'Those, however, who do not know these two ways become insects and moths, and those creatures which often bite (i.e. mosquitoes and gnats).'[183] (VI. ii. 16)

The earth is verily the essence of all these beings, water is the essence of the earth, herbs of water, flowers of herbs, fruits of flowers, man of fruits, and semen is the essence of man.[184] (VI. iv. 1)

Prajāpati said to Himself: 'Well, let Me make a firm basis for it (semen).' So He created woman. Having created her, He placed her below and worshipped her.[185] Therefore one should worship a woman, placing her below. He (Prajāpati) extended His organ that projects and with it impregnated her. (VI. iv. 2)

Her lap is the [sacrificial] altar, her hair the [sacrificial] grass, her skin [within the organ] the lighted fire; the two labia of the vulva are the two stones of the soma-press.

He who, knowing this, practises sexual intercourse wins as great a world as is won through the Vājapeya sacrifice; he acquires for himself [the fruit of] the good deeds of the woman. But he who, without knowing this, practises sexual intercourse turns over to the woman his own good deeds.[186] (VI. iv. 3)

[In praise of the wife who will bear him a son:] She (his wife) has put on the soiled clothes [of impurity]; she is, verily, loveliness among women. Therefore when she has removed the clothes of impurity and appears beautiful, he should approach her and speak to her. (VI. iv. 6)

If a man wishes that a son with a fair complexion should be born to him, that he should study one Veda, and that he should attain a full term of life, then they (husband and wife) should have rice cooked in milk and eat it with clarified butter. Thus they should be able to beget such a son. (VI. iv. 14)

[183] This verse answers the second and third questions.

[184] Now are described the methods by which one can obtain the right kind of son, who will win the higher world both for himself and for his father. The birth of such a son depends upon the performance of the sexual act according to certain religious rites.

[185] That is to say, performed the sexual act, which is to be regarded as a sacrifice.

[186] The similarity of different parts of the woman's body to the corresponding factors of the Vājapeya sacrifice is pointed out.

If a man wishes that a son with a tawny or brown complexion should be born to him, that he should study two Vedas, and that he should attain a full term of life, then they should have rice cooked in curds and eat it with clarified butter. Thus they should be able to beget such a son. (VI. iv. 15)

If a man wishes that a son with a dark complexion and red eyes should be born to him, that he should study three Vedas, and that he should attain a full term of life, then they should have rice cooked in water and eat it with clarified butter. Thus they should be able to beget such a son. (VI. iv. 16)

If a man wishes that a daughter should be born to him who will be a scholar and attain a full term of life, then they should have rice cooked with sesamum and eat it with clarified butter. Thus they should be able to beget such a daughter. (VI. iv. 17)

If a man wishes that a son should be born to him who will be a famous scholar, frequenting assemblies and speaking delightful words, a student of all the Vedas, and an enjoyer of the full term of life, he should have rice cooked with the meat of a young bull or of one more advanced in years, and he and his wife should eat it with clarified butter. Then they should be able to beget such a son. (VI. iv. 18)

Then he embraces her, repeating the following mantra:
'I am the vital breath and you are speech. You are speech and I am the vital breath. I am Sāman and you are Rig; I am heaven and you are earth. Come, let us strive together so that we may have a male child.' (VI. iv. 20)

When she is about to deliver the child, he sprinkles her with water, repeating the following mantra:
'As the wind agitates a pond on every side, even so let your foetus stir and come out along with the chorion. Indra (prāna) made a path [when the seed entered the womb]. O Indra, follow that path and come out with the foetus and the covering, and cause also the after-birth to come forth with the babe.' (VI. iv. 23)

When [the son] is born, he should light a fire, take the child on his lap, put a mixture of curds and clarified butter in a bell-metal cup, and offer oblations in the fire repeatedly, uttering the mantra:
'May I increase [as the son] in my own home and support a thousand people! May [the Goddess of Fortune] never depart, with children and cattle, from his line! Svāhā! The vital breath that is in me, I mentally offer to you. Svāhā! If I have done anything too much or too little in

this ceremony, may the all-knowing and highly beneficent fire make it just right and proper for me. Svāhā!' (VI. iv. 24)

Then, putting [his mouth] to the child's right ear, he should say thrice: 'Speech! Speech!'[187] Next he should mix together curds, honey, and clarified butter and feed the child with a golden stick which is not placed inside [the mouth], saying [these mantras]:
'I put the earth (Bhuh) into you; I put the sky (Bhuvah) into you; I put heaven (Svah) into you. The whole of earth, sky, and heaven I put into you.' (VI. iv. 25)

Then he (the father) gives him (the son) a name: 'You are the Veda (knowledge).' That is his secret name. (VI. iv. 26)

Then he presents him to the mother to give him her breast, uttering the mantra:
'O Sarasvati, that breast of thine which is fruitful, the sustainer of all, full of milk, the bestower of wealth, and generous, and by which thou nourishest all who are worthy—transfer that [breast] here [to my wife, for my child] to suck.' (VI. iv. 27)

Then he addresses the mother [of the child] thus:
'You are the adorable Arundhati, the wife of Vasishtha, and with me, who am a man, as your partner you have brought forth a male child. Be the mother of many male children, for you have given us a son.'
And people say to the son who is born as the child of a brāhmin endowed with this particular knowledge:
'You have surpassed your father and you have surpassed your grandfather. Oh, truly you have reached the extreme limit of attainment through your splendour, fame, and brāhminical power.'[188] (VI. iv. 28)

---

[187] Wishing that the Vedas may enter into him.
[188] A noble son born of noble parents in a noble manner is extolled by the Vedic seers.

THE PEACE CHANT

OM. THAT IS full; this is full. This fullness has been projected from that fullness. When this fullness merges in that fullness, all that remains is fullness.

Om. Peace! Peace! Peace!

TAITTIRIYA UPANISHAD

INTRODUCTION

THE *TAITTIRIYA UPANISHAD*, a section of the Krishna or Black Yajur-Veda, forms the seventh, eighth, and ninth parts of the *Taittiriya Āranyaka*, which itself is a section of the *Taittiriya Brāhmana*. The division of the Yajur-Veda into the White and Black recensions has been explained in the General Introduction.

Though comparatively short, the *Taittiriya Upanishad* is one of the important Upanishads and is recited in many parts of India, even today, with proper accent and intonation. It is regarded as a source-book of the Vedānta philosophy. The topics discussed in it are arranged methodically, and the commentary written by Śankarāchārya enhances its value.

Śankarāchārya has divided the *Taittiriya Upanishad* into three parts, called vallis. The first part, dealing with pronunciation, consists of twelve chapters, of which the first and last contain prayers to the deities for the removing of obstacles to spiritual wisdom. The second part, consisting of nine chapters, discusses the Knowledge of Brahman, which alone destroys ignorance, the root of the phenomenal life; this is done through the explanation of the five sheaths which hide the Self, as a scabbard hides a sword. The third part, consisting of ten chapters, begins with a dialogue between Varuna and his son Bhrigu, which teaches Brahman as the cause of the creation, continuance, and dissolution of the universe.

INVOCATION[1]

HARIH OM.

May Mitra be propitious unto us! May Varuna be propitious unto us! May Aryamān be propitious unto us! May Indra and Brihaspati be propitious unto us! May Vishnu, of wide strides, be propitious unto us!

Salutation to Brahman! Salutation to thee, O Vāyu! Thou indeed art the visible Brahman. Thee indeed I shall proclaim as the visible Brahman. Thee indeed, O Vāyu, I shall proclaim as the right (ritam). Thee indeed I shall proclaim as the true (satyam).

May It protect me! May It protect the teacher! May It protect me! May It protect the teacher! OM. Peace! Peace! Peace!

---

[1] This invocation forms the first verse of the first chapter of Part One of the *Taittiriya Upanishad*.

I

OM. WE WILL expound[2] śikshā, or the science of pronunciation.[3] [It deals with] sound,[4] pitch,[5] quantity,[6] force,[7] modulation,[8] and combination.[9] Thus is explained the lesson on pronunciation. (I. ii. 1)

May glory come to both of us (teacher and pupil) together! May the light of Brahman shine alike through both of us!

Now[10] we will explain the Upanishad (i.e. the upāsanā, or meditation) on the Samhitā (combinations) under five heads: with regard to the worlds, the heavenly lights, knowledge, progeny, and the ātman (body). People call these the great Samhitās.

First, with regard to the worlds: The earth is the first form (i.e. sound) [of the word *Samhitā*], heaven is the last form, the ākāśa[11] is the union, and the air is the medium. Thus with regard to the worlds. (I. iii. 1)

Next, with regard to the heavenly lights: Fire is the first form, the sun is the second form, water is the union, and lightning is the medium. Thus with regard to the heavenly lights. (I. iii. 2)

[2] The knowledge of the meaning of the text is, no doubt, the most important element in the Vedic studies. But one must also learn how to recite the text correctly. Hence a chapter is devoted to the science of pronunciation.

[3] Śikshā is the first of the six Vedāngas, or auxiliaries of the Vedas. The other five are: chhandas, or the science of prosody; vyākarana or the science of grammar; nirukta, or the science of etymology; jyotish, or the science of astronomy; and kalpa, or the science of rituals.

[4] That is to say, of the letters, such as *a*.

[5] Various pitches are used in the recital of the Vedic mantras. There are three main classifications: high pitch (udātta), low pitch (anudātta), and medium pitch (svarit).

[6] Quantity, or mātrā, is of three kinds. A short vowel consists of one mātrā; a long vowel, of two mātrās; a prolonged vowel, of three mātrās. The last is used when calling a person standing far away, or when singing or weeping.

[7] Stress or intensity of effort.

[8] Pronunciation of each sound with a medium tone, that is to say, neither too loud nor too soft.

[9] Conjunction of several sounds or letters.

[10] After the pupil has practised the recitation of the sounds, rhythms, etc., of the text as laid down in the preceding section, he is given instruction as to how to meditate on the combination of the words. On account of his long habit of recitation, his mind might have become fixed on the mere letters of the text. Now through meditation he will understand its symbolic significance, which will gradually make his mind pure and one-pointed, enabling him in the end to grasp the subtle meaning of the Vedas.

[11] The words in the text, namely, *earth*, *heaven*, and *ākāśa*, refer to their respective governing deities.

Next, with regard to knowledge: The teacher is the first form, the pupil is the second form, knowledge is the union, and the [Vedic] recitation is the medium. Thus with regard to knowledge. (I. iii. 3)

Next, with regard to progeny: The mother is the first form, the father is the second form, the progeny is the union, and procreation is the medium. Thus with regard to the progeny. (I. iii. 4)

Next, with regard to the ātman (body): The lower jaw is the first form, the upper jaw is the second form, speech is the union, and the tongue is the medium. Thus with regard to the ātman. (I. iii. 5)

These are the great Samhitās. He who meditates on these Samhitās, as here explained, becomes united with progeny, cattle, the light of Brahman, food, and the heavenly world.[12] (I. iii. 6)

May he (Om) who is the bull (i.e. the foremost) of the Vedic hymns, who assumes all forms,[13] who has sprung from the immortal hymns of the Vedas—may that Indra (the Lord) cheer me with wisdom (medhā). O God, may I be the possessor of immortality!

May my body be competent [to acquire Self-Knowledge]; may my tongue be exceedingly sweet; may I hear abundantly with my ears. Thou (Om) art the sheath of Brahman, concealed by [worldly] intelligence. Guard for me what I have learnt.[14] (I. iv. 1)

Om. Next bring me, without delay, fortune accompanied by wool and cattle—fortune which always provides me with clothes and cattle, food and drink. Increase them when they have been acquired, and preserve them long when increased. Svāhā!

May brahmachārins come to me from all directions [for the acquiring of knowledge]! Svāhā!

May brahmachārins come to me variously! Svāhā!

May brahmachārins come to me [according to the scriptural injunctions]! Svāhā!

---

[12] A material result is attained by those whose meditation is not free from worldly motives. But those who are free from such motives obtain, through this meditation, purity of heart, which in the end helps them to realize Brahman.

[13] Om pervades all words.

[14] A man who does not possess retentiveness of mind cannot acquire the Knowledge of Brahman. Nor can he who, owing to sickness or some other cause, lacks physical vigour, nor he who suffers from want of food and clothing, devote himself to the study of the scriptures and acquire the Knowledge of Brahman. The present section of the Upanishad shows the way to remove all such obstacles.

May brahmachārins practise self-control! Svāhā!
May brahmachārins enjoy peace! Svāhā![15] (I. iv. 2)

May I become famous among men! Svāhā!
May I become richer than the rich! Svāhā![16]
O gracious Lord, may I enter into Thee! Svāhā!
May Thou, O gracious Lord, enter into me! Svāhā!
O Lord, I am cleansing [my sins] in that Self of Thine, which is like [a river of] a thousand branches. Svāhā!
O Preserver, as waters flow downward, as the months merge in the year, so may brahmachārins come to me from all directions! Svāhā!
Thou art a refuge. To me do Thou shine forth. Accept me unto Thyself completely. (I. iv. 3)

Bhuh, Bhuvah, Suvah—these are, verily, the three utterances (vyāhritis). Besides these there is a fourth, called Mahah, which became known to the son of Mahāchamasa. That [Mahah] is Brahman, that is the Self. The other gods are its limbs.

Bhuh is, verily, this world; Bhuvah, the mid-region; Suvah, the world yonder; Mahah, the sun. Through the sun, indeed, do all the worlds become great (mahiyantē).

Bhuh is, verily, fire; Bhuvah, the air; Suvah, the sun; Mahah, the moon. By the moon, indeed, do all the heavenly lights become great.

Bhuh is, verily, the Rik-verses; Bhuvah, the Sāman; Suvah, the Yajus; Mahah, Brahman (i.e. Om). By Brahman, indeed, do all the Vedas become great.

Bhuh is, verily, the prāna (the upward breath); Bhuvah, the apāna (the downward breath); Suvah, the vyāna (the diffused breath); Mahah, food. By food, indeed, do all the breaths become great.

They, these four (vyāhritis], become fourfold. Four and four are the vyāhritis. He who knows these knows Brahman. All the gods bring offerings to him.[17] (I. v. 1)

There is a space (ākāśa) within the heart; in its lies the Person (Purusha) consisting of mind (manomaya),[18] immortal and luminous.

[15] The seeker of wealth should offer oblations with this mantra.
[16] A spiritual aspirant seeks wealth in order to perform the sacrificial rites by means of which the accumulated sins of the past are destroyed. Wisdom shines forth after the destruction of sin.
[17] The fifth chapter teaches of Brahman through meditation on the subordinate divinities, of which the three vyāhritis Bhuh, Bhuvah, and Suvah are the symbols.
[18] The incorporeal Brahman consists of consciousness (vijñāna). Or He is called manomaya because He can be realized by the purified mind alone. Mind, or manas, is His most characteristic feature.

The Sushumnā passes through the piece of flesh which hangs down like a nipple (i.e. the uvula) between the two palates and ends where the skull splits and the roots of the hair lie apart. That Sushumnā is the path for the realization of Indra (i.e. the Lord, or Saguna Brahman). The soul of the aspirant, passing through the Sushumnā, rests in fire, represented by the vyāhriti Bhuh;[19] he rests in the air, represented by the vyāhriti Bhuvah. (I. vi. 1)

He (i.e. the illumined soul) rests in the sun, represented by the vyāhriti Suvah; he rests in Brahman, represented by the vyāhriti Mahah.

He attains self-rule. He attains the lordship of the mind; he attains the lordship of speech; he attains the lordship of sight; he attains the lordship of hearing; he attains the lordship of intelligence (vijnāna). Furthermore, he becomes this—he becomes Brahman, whose body is space (ākāśa), whose nature is true, who delights in life (prāna) and rejoices in the mind, who abounds in peace, who is immortal.

Thus do thou, O Prāchinayogya, contemplate. (I. vi. 2)

Earth, the mid-region, heaven, the [four main] quarters, and the intermediate quarters [constitute the fivefold world]. Agni (fire), Vāyu (air), Āditya (sun), Chandramā (moon), and the Nakshatras (stars) [constitute the five divinities]. Water, herbs, trees, space (ākāśa), and the body (ātmā) [constitute the five elements]. So much with reference to material objects.

Now with reference to the body: The prāna, vyāna, apāna, udāna, and samāna [constitute the five prānas]; the eye, the ear, the mind, speech, and touch [constitute the five sense-organs]; the skin, flesh, muscle, bone, and marrow [constitute the five ingredients of the physical body].

Having thus ordained [the contemplation of the pānkta, the fivefold], a rishi said: 'Whatever exists is fivefold (pānkta).' Through the [inner] fivefold one becomes united with the [outer] fivefold material object.[20] (I. vii. 1)

---

[19] The illumined soul, after coming out of the body, becomes established in fire—represented by the vyāhriti Bhuh—which is, as it were, a limb of Brahman. That is to say, he pervades the whole world. Similarly, he is established in the air, which is another limb of Brahman.

[20] This verse teaches the contemplation of Brahman through the symbol of the pānktas, or sets of five objects. The universe consisting of a set of five objects is a pānkta. Brahman manifested as the universe is a pānkta. There is a Vedic metre called pankti, consisting of five feet, or pādas, of eight syllables each. Furthermore, the sacrifice consisting of five factors, namely, the sacrificer, his wife, his son, contemplation, and the materials used in the sacrifice, is a pānkta. Thus the contemplation recommended in this chapter is a form of sacrifice which brings

Om is Brahman. Om is all this. This syllable *Om* is used to indicate compliance. When they (i.e. the priests) are told: 'Om, recite,' they recite. Uttering Om, they sing the Sāman chants. With 'Om, Som,' they recite the prayers. Uttering Om, the adhvaryu priest gives the response. Uttering Om, the Brahmā [priest] gives assent. Uttering Om, [a qualified priest] gives permission for the offering in the Agnihotra sacrifice. When a Vedic teacher wishes to obtain Brahman he utters Om; thus desiring Brahman, he verily obtains Brahman.[21] (I. viii. 1)

[The disciplines are] rightness[22] and also the learning and teaching [of the Vedas];[23] truth and also the learning and teaching [of the Vedas]; austerity and also the learning and teaching [of the Vedas]; self-control and also the learning and teaching [of the Vedas]; tranquillity and also the learning and teaching [of the Vedas]; [the kindling of sacrificial] fires and also the learning and teaching [of the Vedas]; [the performance of] the Agnihotra sacrifice and also the learning and teaching [of the Vedas]; [hospitality to] guests and also the learning and teaching [of the Vedas]; [the performance of] social duties and also the learning and teaching [of the Vedas]; procreation and also the learning and teaching [of the Vedas]; propagation [of the race][24] and also the learning and teaching [of the Vedas].

[Differing views on the subject:] Truth alone, according to Satyavachas of the line of Rathitara, should be practised; austerity alone, according to Taponitya the son of Puruśishti; according to Nāka the son of Mudgalya, the learning and teaching [of the Vedas] alone, for that is austerity. (I. ix. 1)

about the result of identity with Brahman. The argument is based on the common feature of five. The sets of five described in the first paragraph of the text refer to external objects. The sets of five described in the second paragraph refer to internal objects, that is to say, to those in the body. The former should be meditated on as identical with the latter. The two together constitute the whole universe, which is a manifestation of Brahman. A certain Vedic rishi laid down this form of meditation and taught it to his disciples.

[21] Om as the symbol of Brahman is meant for superior students. In this meditation the mind of the worshipper is free from all gross upādhis of Brahman, such as the earth and the mind. He simply repeats the word *Om* and meditates on Brahman, which it denotes. Om can be used as the symbol of both the higher and the lower Brahman.

[22] The word *ritam* in the text here denotes the truth as determined by the scriptures, usage, and one's discriminative faculty.

[23] The Vedic knowledge can be acquired by reading the text of the Vedas; but that text is retained in one's memory only through daily recitation and teaching. While engaged in various activities, social or personal, the aspirant must not neglect the study and teaching of the Vedas.

[24] The race should be preserved through grandchildren. The implication is that one's son should be married.

I am the mover of the tree [of the universe].[25] My fame rises high, like a mountain peak. My root is the Supremely Pure [Brahman]. I am the unstained essence of the Self, like the [nectar of] immortality that resides in the sun. I am the brightest treasure. I am the shining wisdom. I am immortal and undecaying.

Thus did Triśanku proclaim after the attainment of the Knowledge [of the Self].[26] (I. x. 1)

Having taught the Vedas, the teacher thus instructs the pupil:

Speak the truth. Practise dharma.[27] Do not neglect the study [of the Vedas]. Having brought to the teacher the gift desired by him, [enter the householder's life and see that] the line of progeny is not cut off. Do not swerve from the truth. Do not swerve from dharma. Do not neglect [personal] welfare.[28] Do not neglect prosperity. Do not neglect the study and teaching of the Vedas.[29] (I. xi. 1)

Do not neglect your duties to the gods and the Manes. Treat your mother as God. Treat your father as God. Treat your teacher as God. Treat your guest as God. Whatever deeds are faultless, these are to be performed—not others. Whatever good works have been performed by us, those should be performed by you—not others. (I. xi. 2)

Those brāhmins who are superior to us—you should comfort them by giving them seats.

Whatever is to be given should be given with faith, not without faith —according to one's plenty, with modesty, with fear, with sympathy. (I. xi. 3)

Now, if there arises in your mind any doubt concerning any act, or any doubt concerning conduct, you should conduct yourself in such

[25] The universe is compared to a tree on account of its perishable nature. As a tree is cut down with an axe, so is the phenomenal universe destroyed with the sword of detachment. The word *mover* implies the inner guide (antaryāmin).

[26] The mantra is meant for daily recitation by the seeker of Self-Knowledge. It is conducive to purity and progress, and finally leads to the Knowledge of Brahman.

[27] Prescribed duties, especially ritualistic worship as laid down in the scriptures.

[28] Refers to action which is conducive to self-preservation. Longevity and good health are emphasized.

[29] At the teacher's house the student obtains the theoretical knowledge of the Vedas. He has not yet attained oneness with Brahman. Prior to this attainment he must fulfil his human aspirations; this is possible only through the proper performance of his duties. Their performance purifies the heart and ultimately leads to the Highest Good. Once Self-Knowledge is attained, human aspirations reach their fulfilment. Thereafter one is free from all worldly duties.

matters as brāhmins would conduct themselves—brāhmins who are competent to judge, who [of their own accord] are devoted [to good deeds] and are not urged [to their performance] by others, and who are not too severe, but are lovers of dharma.

Now, with regard to persons spoken against, you should conduct yourself in such a way as brāhmins would conduct themselves—brāhmins who are competent to judge, who [of their own accord] are devoted [to good deeds] and are not urged [to their performance] by others, and who are not too severe, but are lovers of dharma.

This is the rule. This is the teaching. This is the secret wisdom of the Vedas. This is the command [of God].

This you should observe. This alone should be observed. (I. xi. 4)

II

OM. HE WHO knows Brahman attains the Supreme.

On the above, the following mantra (Rig) is recorded:

'He who knows Brahman which is Reality, Knowledge, and Infinity, hidden in the cave of the heart and in the highest ākāśa—he, being one with the omniscient Brahman, enjoys simultaneously all desires.'

From that Ātman (Brahman) was born ākāśa; from ākāśa, air; from air, fire; from fire, water; from water, earth; from earth, herbs; from herbs, food;[30] from food, man.

He, that man, verily consists of the essence of food. This indeed is his head, this [right arm] is his right wing, this [left arm] is his left wing, this, [trunk] is his body (ātman), this support [below the navel] is his tail.[31] On the above, there is recorded the following mantra: (II. i. 3)

'From food, verily, are produced all creatures—whatsoever dwell on earth. By food[32] alone, furthermore, do they live, and to food, in the end, do they return; for food alone is the eldest of all beings, and therefore it is called the panacea for all.

'They who worship food as Brahman obtain all food. Food alone is the eldest of all beings, and therefore it is called the panacea for all. From food all creatures are born: by food, when born, they grow. Because it is eaten (adyatē) by beings and because it eats (atti) beings, therefore it is called food (anna).'

Verily, different from this,[33] which consists of the essence of food, but within it, is another self,[34] which consists of the vital breath (prāna). By this the former is filled. This too has the shape of a man. Like the human shape of the former (the sheath of food) is the human shape of the latter

[30] That is to say, semen, which is a transformation of food.

[31] In this particular verse, the physical man is pictured as a bird, which resembles a sacrificial fire. This fire—arranged in the form of a hawk, a heron, or some other bird—has a head, two wings, a trunk, and a tail. The *Taittiriya Upanishad* describes all the different sheaths in a like manner.

[32] Here the word *food* is used in the more general sense of matter.

[33] The first part of the text describes the annamayakośa, or gross physical sheath, the physical man which consists of food. The use of the word *sheath* (*kośa*) is apposite because the kośa resembles a scabbard which holds within it a sword. Four other sheaths will be described, one after another, in order to point out the innermost Self, or Ātman, which is identical with Brahman and is beyond the body, the vital breath, the mind, the intellect, and bliss. The five sheaths, though not Ātman, are described as such, in a figurative sense, from the relative standpoint. They appear to be conscious, like Ātman, because of their close proximity to Ātman, as iron filings near a magnet appear to be active.

[34] The prānamayakośa, or sheath of the prāna.

(the sheath of the vital breath). Prāna (the upward breath), indeed, is its head; vyāna (the diffused breath) is its right wing; apāna (the downward breath) is its left wing; ākāśa (samāna) is its trunk; the earth is its tail, its support.[35]

On the above there is also the following mantra: (II. ii. 1–2)

'The gods breathe after[36] prāna, so also do men and cattle; for the prāna is the life of creatures.[37] Therefore it is called the life of all (sarvāyusham). Those who worship the prāna as Brahman obtain a full life;[38] for the prāna is the life of creatures. Therefore it is called the life of all.' (II. iii. 1)

This [sheath of the prāna] is the embodied soul of the former (the sheath of food).[39] Verily, different from this [sheath], which consists of the essence of the prāna, but within it, is another self, which consists of the mind (manomayakośa). By this the former is filled. This too has the shape of a man. Like the human shape of the former is the human shape of the latter. The Yajur-Veda is its head, the Rig-Veda is its right wing, the Sāma-Veda is its left wing, the teaching (ādeśa) is its trunk, the hymns of Atharvā and Angirās are its tail, its support.

On the above there is also the following mantra: (II. iii. 2)

'He who knows the Bliss of Brahman,[40] whence all words together with the mind turn away,[41] unable to reach it—he never fears.' (II. iv. 1)

This [sheath of the mind] is the embodied soul of the former (the sheath of the prāna).

[35] That is to say, the deity which controls the earth. But for the support of this deity, the body would go upwards by the action of the udāna or drop of its own weight.

[36] The meaning of the passage is that the gods breathe or become active after being energized by the prāna, or air.

[37] The passage indicates that even the animals possess life and a soul. They too are endowed with five sheaths.

[38] According to the Vedic tradition, the full life of a man extends to one hundred years.

[39] That is to say, the sheath of food is the body of the sheath of the prāna. The latter dwells in the former. When one meditates on the sheath of the prāna as the self, one is freed from the idea that the physical body is the self.

[40] Refers to the sheath of the mind (manomayakośa), and not to the Supreme Brahman. The Upanishad asks the student to contemplate Brahman as limited by the upādhi, or conditioning adjunct, of the mind. The mind is, in essence, one with the Cosmic Mind, or Hiranyagarbha.

[41] The true nature of the mind cannot be known either by words or by the mind itself. The mind which seeks to know the mind is only a mental state (vritti). Hence the mind remains unknown to the mind.

Verily, different from this [sheath], which consists of the essence of the mind, but within it, is another self, which consists of intellect (vijñāna). By this the former is filled. This too has the shape of a man. Like the human shape of the former is the human shape of the latter. Faith (śraddhā) is its head, what is right is its right wing, what is truth is its left wing, absorption (yoga) is its trunk, Mahat (Hiranyagarbha) is its tail, its support.

On the above there is also the following mantra: (II. iv. 2)

'The intellect accomplishes the sacrifice; it also accomplishes all actions. All the gods worship the intellect, who is the eldest, as Brahman (i.e. Hiranyagarbha).

'If a man knows the intellect as Brahman, and if he does not swerve from it, he leaves behind in the body all evils[42] and attains all his desires.' (II. v. 1)

This [sheath of the intellect] is the embodied soul of the former (the sheath of the mind).

Verily, different from this [sheath], which consists of the essence of the intellect, but within it, is another self, which consists of bliss (ānanda). By this the former is filled. This too has the shape of a man. Like the human shape of the former is the human shape of the latter. Joy (priyam) is its head, delight (moda) is its right wing, great delight (pramoda) is its left wing, bliss is its trunk, Brahman is its tail, its support.[43]

On the above there is also the following mantra: (II. v. 2)

'If a person knows Brahman as non-existent, he himself becomes non-existent. If he knows Brahman as existent, then [knowers of Brahman] know him as existent.'

This [sheath of bliss] is the embodied soul of the former (the sheath of the intellect).

Thereupon the following questions of the pupil:[44] Does anyone who

[42] Evils arise from the identification of the Self with the body. By realizing one's identity with Hiranyagarbha, one ceases to identify oneself with the body and therefore leaves behind all evils associated with the body.

[43] Verses II. i. 3 to II. v. 2 describe the five sheaths which constitute the embodied creature. They are the sheaths of food or matter, the prāna or vital breath, the mind, the intellect, and bliss—arranged in telescopic manner, one inside another. The outer derives its reality from the inner. Brahman is the innermost reality; It is untouched by any of the sheaths, but is the unrelated ground of all. The physical sheath cannot function without being energized by the sheath of the prāna, or vital breath; the mind directs the prāna, and the intellect controls the mind; the intellect is dependent upon bliss.

[44] After the pupil has heard the exposition of Brahman from the teacher, he raises the following doubts: Since Brahman is the Self of both the enlightened

knows not [Brahman] attain that World after departing this life? Or
does he who knows [Brahman] attain that World after departing this
life?

[The answer:] He (the Supreme Soul) desired: 'May I be many, may
I be born. He performed austerities.[45] Having performed austerities, He
created all this—whatever there is.[46] Having created all this, He entered
into it. Having entered into it, He became both the manifest and the
unmanifest, both the defined and the undefined, both the supported and
the unsupported, both the intelligent and the non-intelligent, both the
real and the unreal. The Satya (the True) became all this: whatever
there is. Therefore [the wise] call It (Brahman) Satya (the True).
On the above there is also the following mantra: (II. vi. 1)

'In the beginning all this (i.e. the manifested universe) was non-
existent.[47] From it was born what exists. That (i.e. Brahman described
as non-existent) created Itself by Itself; therefore It is called the Self-
made (Sukritam).'[48]

That which is Self-made is flavour (rasa, or essence);[49] for truly, on
obtaining the flavour one becomes blissful.

Who could direct the prana and the apana [to perform their functions]
if this Bliss (Brahman) did not exist in the akasa [of the heart]? Brahman verily exists because It alone bestows bliss.

When a man finds fearless support in That which is invisible, incorporeal, indefinable, and supportless, he has then obtained fearlessness.

If he makes the slightest differentiation in It, there is fear for him.
That [Brahman] becomes [the cause of] fear for the knower [of differen-
tiation] who does not reflect.

On the above there is also the following mantra: (II. vii. 1)

'From fear of It (Brahman) the wind blows; from fear of It the sun
rises; from fear of It Agni and Indra, and Death, the fifth, run.'

and the unenlightened, being the same in all, do the unenlightened attain to the
World of Brahman after death, or do they not? Do the enlightened attain to the
World of Brahman after death, or do they not? Brahman is present in everything.
If the enlightened attain to Brahman, then the unenlightened, too, should attain
It; if the latter cannot realize Brahman, then the former, too, cannot realize It.

[45] The word *tapas* in the text here means the intense thought of Brahman
concerning the creation.

[46] After intense thinking, Brahman projected the universe determined by the
past karma and desires of the sentient beings of the previous cycle. The nature of
the new creation is determined by these desires and actions.

[47] That is to say, the unmanifested Brahman, as distinguished from the universe
of manifested names and forms.

[48] Brahman is both the material and the efficient cause of the universe.

[49] On account of the flavour of Brahman, the physical universe, which in itself
is without flavour, makes all joyous.

Now this is an inquiry regarding the Bliss [of Brahman].

Suppose there is a young man—a noble young man—versed [in the Vedas], the best of rulers, firm in body, and strong; and suppose the whole world, full of wealth, is his: that is one measure of human bliss.

This human bliss, multiplied one hundred times, is one measure of the bliss of the human gandharvas, as also of a man versed in the Vedas and free from desires.

This bliss of the human gandharvas, multiplied one hundred times, is one measure of the bliss of the celestial gandharvas, as also of a man versed in the Vedas and free from desires.

This bliss of the celestial gandharvas, multiplied one hundred times, is one measure of the bliss of the Manes, who dwell in the long-enduring world, as also of a man versed in the Vedas and free from desires.

The bliss of the Manes who dwell in the long-enduring world, multiplied one hundred times, is one measure of the bliss of the gods born in the Ājāna heaven, as also of a man versed in the Vedas and free from desires.

The bliss of the gods born in the Ājāna heaven, multiplied one hundred times, is one measure of the bliss of the sacrificial gods who have attained to divinity by means of [Vedic] sacrifices, as also of a man versed in the Vedas and free from desires.

The bliss of the sacrificial gods, multiplied one hundred times is one measure of the bliss of the [thirty-three] gods, as also of a man versed in the Vedas and free from desires.

The bliss of the [thirty-three] gods, multiplied one hundred times, is one measure of the bliss of Indra, as also of a man versed in the Vedas and free from desires.

The bliss of Indra, multiplied one hundred times, is one measure of the bliss of Brihaspati, as also of a man versed in the Vedas and free from desires.

The bliss of Brihaspati, multiplied one hundred times, is one measure of the bliss of Prajāpati, as also of a man versed in the Vedas and free from desires.

The bliss of Prajāpati, multiplied one hundred times, is one measure of the bliss of Brahmā, as also of a man versed in the Vedas and free from desires.

He who is here in man and he who is in yonder sun[50]—both are one.[51]

[50] Refers to Saguna Brahman, who, according to the Vedas, dwells in the sun and is the embodiment of the bliss directly experienced by the illumined sage versed in the Vedas and free from desires. The sun represents the highest perfection in the phenomenal world.

[51] They are one in the sense that the ākāśa inside a pot is the same as the ākāśa without. When we ignore the limiting adjunct (upādhi) created by avidyā, we find that the bliss which is realized in man is identical with the bliss which is realized in the sun.

He who knows this [as described above], after dying to (i.e. withdrawing from) this world, attains the self which consists of food, attains the self which consists of the vital breath, attains the self which consists of the mind, attains the self which consists of intellect, attains the self which consists of bliss.[52]

On the above there is also the following mantra: (II. viii. 1)

'He who knows the Bliss of Brahman, whence words together with the mind turn away, unable to reach It—he is not afraid of anything whatsoever.'

He does not distress himself[53] with the thought: Why did I not do what is good? Why did I do what is evil? Whosoever knows this regards both these (i.e. good and evil) as Ātman [and thus strengthens It]; indeed he cherishes both these as Ātman.[54]

Such, indeed, is the Upanishad (i.e. the secret Knowledge of Brahman). (II. ix. 1)

---

[52] He does not see any difference between his own physical body and that of Virāt, which is the aggregate of all physical bodies. He loses attachment to his individual self and attains to that Being in whom the physical universe takes its rise, has its being, and in the end attains dissolution. He realizes, likewise, that the self consisting of food is none other than the self consisting of the vital breath, and rises above the former by identifying himself with the latter. Thus, passing to higher and higher selves, he gives up attachment to the lower ones, until he finally attains the fearless Brahman, which is beyond the visible and the invisible.

[53] That is to say, at the approach of death.

[54] When avidyā is destroyed, both good and evil, like all other phenomenal categories, merge in Ātman. Thus the knower of Ātman strips good and evil of their phenomenal nature and realizes them as Ātman. This realization makes good and evil powerless. Furthermore, it reveals their identity with Ātman and thus strengthens Ātman.

III

HARIH OM. BHRIGU, the son of Varuna, approached his father Varuna and said: 'Venerable Sir, teach me about Brahman.'

To him, the son, he said this: 'Food, the vital breath, the eye, the ear, the mind, speech.'[55]

To him he said further: 'That from which these beings are born, That by which, when born, they live, That into which [at the time of dissolution] they enter, they merge—seek to know That. That is Brahman.'

He performed austerities (tapah). Having performed austerities[56]— (III. i. 1)

He realized that food[57] is Brahman; for from food, verily, are these beings born; by food, when born, do they live; into food [at the time of dissolution] do they enter, do they merge.

Having realized this, he approached his father again and said: 'Venerable Sir, teach me Brahman.'

To him, the son, he said this: 'Seek to know Brahman by means of austerities.[58] For austerities are [the means of knowing] Brahman.'

He practised austerities. Having practised austerities— (III. ii. 1)

He realized that the prāna (vital breath) is Brahman; for from the prāna, verily, are these beings born; by the prāna, when born, do they live; into the prāna [at the time of dissolution] do they enter, do they merge.

Having realized this, he approached his father again and said: 'Venerable Sir, teach me Brahman.'[59]

To him, the son, he said this: 'Seek to know Brahman by means of austerities. For austerities are [the means of knowing] Brahman.'

He practised austerities. Having practised austerities— (III. iii. 1)

[55] These are the gateways or instruments for the realization of Brahman. The word *food* here means the body.

[56] The implication is that Bhrigu withdrew his mind from all outer objects and concentrated it on what his father taught. Thus he passed through a kind of spiritual travail.

[57] The word means body or matter. In this verse it especially denotes Virāt, the aggregate of all material bodies.

[58] The reiteration of the word *austerities* is intended to impress the student with the fact that concentration of the mind, together with other disciplines, is the most efficient means by which to attain knowledge.

[59] The prāna, or vital breath, is non-intelligent and therefore cannot be Brahman.

He realized that the mind is Brahman; for from the mind, verily, are these beings born; by the mind, when born, do they live; into the mind [at the time of dissolution] do they enter, do they merge.

Having realized this, he approached his father again and said: 'Venerable Sir, teach me Brahman.'[60]

To him, the son, he said this: 'Seek to know Brahman by means of austerities; for austerities are [the means of knowing] Brahman.'

He practised austerities. Having practised austerities— (III. iv. 1)

He realized that the intellect (vijñāna) is Brahman; for from the intellect, verily, are these beings born; by the intellect, when born, do they live; into the intellect [at the time of dissolution] do they enter, do they merge.

Having realized this, he approached his father again and said: 'Venerable Sir, teach me Brahman.'[61]

To him, the son, he said this: 'Seek to know Brahman by means of austerities; for austerities are [the means of knowing] Brahman.'

He practised austerities. Having practised austerities— (III. v. 1)

He realized that bliss (ānanda) is Brahman; for from bliss, verily, are these beings born; by bliss, when born, do they live; into bliss [at the time of dissolution] do they enter, do they merge.

This is the wisdom taught by Varuna and learnt by Bhrigu. It is established in the supreme ākāśa [in the heart]. He who knows this is established in the Bliss of Brahman. He becomes a possessor of food and an eater of food. He becomes great in offspring and cattle and in spiritual radiance, and great in fame. (III. vi. 1)

Let him (the knower of Brahman) never condemn food; that is the vow.

The prāna is, verily, food; the body is the eater of food. The body rests on the prāna; the prāna rests on the body. Thus food rests on food.

He who knows this resting of food on food is established; he becomes a possessor of food and an eater of food. He becomes great in offspring and cattle, and in spiritual radiance, and great in fame.[62] (III. vii. 1)

[60] The mind creates doubt. Further, it is an organ or instrument, like the eye, ear, etc. Therefore it cannot be Brahman.

[61] Such sensations as pain and pleasure are experienced by the intellect or the intelligent agent; hence the intellect cannot be Brahman. Furthermore, the intellectual life is associated with seeking.

[62] This verse shows the interdependence of food and life. The phenomenal world reveals the existence of an enjoyer (subject) and an enjoyed (object); but this distinction does not exist in Ātman.

Let him (the knower of Brahman) never abandon food; that is the vow.

Water is, verily, food; fire is the eater.[63] Fire rests on water,[64] and water rests on fire.[65] Thus food rests on food.

He who knows this resting of food on food is established; he becomes a possessor of food and an eater of food. He becomes great in offspring and cattle and in spiritual radiance, and great in fame. (III. viii. 1)

Let him (the knower of Brahman) make food plentiful; that is the vow.

The earth is, verily, food; the ākāśa is the eater. The ākāśa rests on the earth, and the earth rests on the ākāśa. Thus food rests on food.

He who knows this resting of food on food is established; he becomes a possessor of food and an eater of food. He becomes great in offspring and cattle, and in spiritual radiance, and great in fame. (III. ix. 1)

Let him not deny lodgings to anyone: this is the vow. Therefore he should procure much food by any means whatsoever. [To guests] he should say: 'The food has been prepared for you.'

If this food is given first, food comes to the giver first.[66] If this food is given in the middle, food comes to the giver in the middle. If this food is given last, food comes to the giver last. (III. x. 1)

He who knows this [obtains the fruit mentioned above].

[One should meditate on Brahman] as preservation in speech, as acquisition and preservation in the prāna (upward breath) and the apāna (downward breath), as action in the hands, as movement (walking) in the feet, as evacuation in the anus. These are the meditations on Brahman through human actions.

Next [follows the meditation on Brahman] through the gods: [One should meditate on Brahman] as satisfaction in rain, as power in lightning. (III. x. 2)

As fame in cattle, as light in the stars, as procreation, immortality, and joy in the organ of generation, and as everything in the ākāśa.

---

[63] The water that one drinks is digested by the fire in the stomach.

[64] For example, lightning is present in a rain-cloud.

[65] For example, one perspires when the body is heated.

[66] The word *mukhatah* in the text connotes either youth or great respect. The gist of the passage is that in whatever manner or at whatever period of life a person gives food, he reaps the reward in the same manner or at the same period of life. If he gives food in youth and with great respect, he will get ample food, served in the best manner, during youth.

Let him contemplate [Brahman] as the support, and he will be supported; let him contemplate [Brahman] as greatness, and he will become great; let him contemplate [Brahman] as the mind, and he will be endowed with mind. (III. x. 3)

Let him contemplate Brahman as adoration, and all desires will fall down before him in adoration. Let him contemplate Brahman as the Supreme Lord, and he will be endowed with supremacy. Let him contemplate Brahman (i.e. the ākāśa) as the destructive agent [of Brahman],[67] and his enemies who hate him and also those who do not hate him will perish.

This he who is in this man, and that he who is in yonder sun, both are one. (III. x. 4)

He who knows this [as described above], after dying to (i.e. withdrawing from) this world, attains the self which consists of food, attains the self which consists of the vital breath, attains the self which consists of the mind, attains the self which consists of the intellect, attains the self which consists of bliss. Then he goes up and down these worlds, eating the food he desires, assuming the forms he likes. He sits, singing the chant of the non-duality of Brahman: 'Ah! Ah! Ah!'[68]

'I am food, I am food, I am food! I am the eater of food, I am the eater of food, I am the eater of food![69] I am the uniter, I am the uniter, I am the uniter!

'I am the first-born of the true, prior to the gods, and the navel of

[67] Rain, lightning, the moon, the sun, and fire are said to be dissolved in vāyu (*Chh. Up.* IV. iii. 1–2); therefore vāyu is their destructive agent. Vāyu, being the effect of the ākāśa, is one with the ākāśa. Therefore the ākāśa is the destructive agent.

[68] An expression of extreme wonder. The cause of this wonder is that though the seer is the non-dual Ātman, yet he himself is the food and the eater, that is to say, that he is both the object and the subject. The knower of Brahman becomes the All. Thus he enjoys all objects of pleasure at one and the same time. By realizing one and the same Ātman in man and the sun, he dissociates all inferiority and superiority from Ātman. He transcends, one by one, the sheaths of food, the prāna, etc., created by avidyā, and becomes one with Brahman, which has been described as Reality, Knowledge, and Infinity. Having realized this oneness, he eats what food he likes and assumes what form he desires. He is no longer limited by the scriptural injunctions regarding food, drink, or conduct of life. Or the meaning of the text may be that, being convinced of his oneness with all, from Brahmā to the blade of grass, he finds satisfaction in the thought that any movement of any creature whatsoever is his own movement. Furthermore, he sits, singing from the Sāma-Veda the oneness (sama) of Brahman.

[69] The illumined seer proclaims his oneness with the universe of subject and object.

Immortality. He who gives me away, he alone preserves me.[70] He who eats food—I, as food, eat him.

'I [as the Supreme Lord] overpower the whole world. I am radiant as the sun.'

Whosoever knows this [attains Liberation]. Such, indeed, is the Upanishad. (III. x. 6)

[70] Whosoever gives food to the seeker of food preserves it without losing it. Another meaning of the passage is that the teacher who gives instruction regarding Brahman to his disciples preserves the instruction.

THE PEACE CHANT

OM. MAY BRAHMAN protect us both! May Brahman bestow upon us both the fruit of Knowledge! May we both
obtain the energy to acquire Knowledge! May what we both
study reveal the Truth! May we cherish no ill-feeling toward
each other.
   Om. Peace! Peace! Peace!

CHHĀNDOGYA UPANISHAD

INTRODUCTION

THE SĀMA-VEDA includes among its treasures the *Chhāndogya Brāhmana*, consisting of ten parts; of these, the last eight constitute the *Chhāndogya Upanishad*. In turn, the Upanishad itself may be broadly divided into two sections. The first, consisting of five parts, deals with upāsanā, or ritualistic worship with emphasis on meditation. The second section, of three parts, discusses certain fundamental doctrines of the Vedānta philosophy, namely, the Vedāntic dictum 'Tattvamasi', or 'That thou art'; the doctrine of Bhumā, or Infinity; and the doctrine of Ātman.

The *Brihadāranyaka* and the *Chhāndogya*, regarded as the oldest of the Upanishads, occupy a superior position among the Upanishads known to us. Discussing profound philosophical truths through numerous anecdotes, they form the basis of the later development of the Vedānta philosophy. Śankarāchārya, in establishing the philosophy of non-dualism, derived support from such statements of the *Chhāndogya Upanishad* as: 'One only without a second' (VI. xiv. 1), 'From It the universe comes forth, into It the universe merges, and in It the universe breathes. Therefore a man should meditate on Brahman with a calm mind' (III. xiv. 1), and 'That is the Self. That thou art' (VI. viii. 7). If a serious student carefully reads the *Chhāndogya Upanishad* with the help of Śankarāchārya's commentary, he will come to know all the major topics of the Upanishads and will be directed toward the philosophy of the inscrutable Brahman.

Both the *Chhāndogya Upanishad* and the *Brihadāranyaka Upanishad* devote a considerable part of their texts to the subject of upāsanā, or ritualistic worship associated with meditation. A few words are necessary to show the relationship of such worship to the Knowledge of Brahman.

The ultimate goal of the Upanishads is to show the way to Liberation through Jnāna, or the unitive Knowledge of Brahman, in which all distinctions between the doer, the result of action, and the instrument of action, and also between the embodied self, the universe, and Ultimate Reality, are completely effaced. This attainment requires stern disciplines on the part of the aspirant. He therefore prepares himself through two preliminary disciplines known as karma and upāsanā. Karma comprises ritualistic worship with a view to enjoying happiness on earth and, after death, in the heavenly worlds. This is coveted by average persons who are still attached to physical pleasures. But since these pleasures come to an end when the momentum given to them by the cause is exhausted, reflective persons before long become dissatisfied with them. For them the Upanishads prescribe upāsanā.

Upāsanā has been defined variously by different Hindu philosophers. According to Sadānanda it is a mental activity related to Saguna Brahman. Vidyāranya states that it consists of an uninterrupted meditation by the mind on an object of worship learnt from a teacher whose words the aspirant accepts with unquestioning faith. Śankarāchārya, in his introduction to the *Chhāndogya Upanishad*, says with reference to upāsanā that its purpose is 'to procure a support for the mind approved by the teachings of the scriptures, and make the uniform states of the mind flow towards it in such a way that they will not be interrupted by any idea foreign to them.' This support, or the object of meditation, can be Saguna Brahman, or any other deity approved by the scriptures; or a material symbol. Further, upāsanā can be associated with a sacrifice, or the accessories of a sacrifice, or such symbols as Om, the sun, the akāśā, or the mind. In upāsanā the idea of Brahman or a deity is superimposed upon the symbol as representative of the idea.

The general result of upāsanā is that it endows the mind of the worshipper with calmness, devotion, introspection, and concentration. It gradually loosens attachment to physical objects. The highest direct and tangible result of upāsanā is the attainment of Brahmaloka; but if it is performed without any motive, the result is purification of the mind, which creates the mood for the final practice of Jnāna, or the Knowledge of Brahman.

When the mind of the aspirant has become purified, by stages, through the performance of rituals and upāsanā, he finds it easy to cultivate the four virtues requisite for the attainment of Jnāna. These include discrimination between the Real and the unreal; renunciation of the unreal, control of the sense-organs and the mind, withdrawal from the world, forbearance, concentration, and faith in the words of the teacher and the scriptures; and lastly, the cherishing of an unwavering desire for Liberation. As a result, the seeker realizes Brahman as tangibly as a fruit lying on the palm of his hand, gets rid of doubt, misgiving, fear, and attachment to the unreal world, and experiences peace, immortality, and bliss. Thus the different parts of the Upanishad describing ritual, upāsanā, and Jnāna hang together. Rituals and upāsanā play an important part in the attaining of the highest goal of life.

INVOCATION

OM. MAY THE different limbs of my body, my tongue, prāna, eyes, ears, and my strength, and also all the other sense-organs, be nourished! All, indeed, is Brahman, as is declared in the Upanishads. May I never deny Brahman! May Brahman never deny me! May there never be denial on the part of Brahman! May there never be denial on my part! May all the virtues described in the Upanishads belong to me, who am devoted to Ātman! Yea, may they all belong to me!

Om. Peace! Peace! Peace!

I

THE SYLLABLE *OM*, called the Udgitha,[1] should be meditated upon;
for people sing the Udgitha, beginning with Om.
Now follows the [detailed] explanation [of the syllable]:[2] (I. i. 1)

The essence of [all] these beings is the earth; the essence of the earth
is water; the essence of water is plants; the essence of plants is a person;[3]
the essence of a person is speech; the essence of speech is the Rig-Veda;
the essence of the Rig-Veda is the Sāma-Veda;[4] the essence of the
Sāma-Veda is the Udgitha [which is Om].[5] (I. i. 2)

That Udgitha (Om) is the best of all essences, the supreme, deserving
the highest place, the eighth.[6] (I. i. 3)

This syllable *Om* is used to give assent, for wherever one assents to
something, one says Om (yes). Now, what is assent is gratification.[7]
He who knows this and meditates on the syllable *Om*, the Udgitha,
becomes, indeed, a gratifier of desires. (I. i. 8)

By means of this [syllable] the threefold knowledge[8] proceeds. When
the [adhvaryu] priest gives an order [in a sacrifice], he says Om. When
the [hotri] priest recites [the hymn], he says Om. When the [udgātri]
priest sings [the Sāman], he says Om. All this is done for the glory of the

[1] A hymn of the Sāma-Veda. A part of the ritualistic worship laid down in the
Sāma-Veda, this hymn is sung at the time of a sacrifice. Om, again, is a part of the
Udgitha hymn.

[2] People accustomed to action, through long practice, cannot give it up all at
once and meditate with a steady mind. Therefore the Upanishad first describes
meditation as an auxiliary to ritualistic work, and not independent of such work.

[3] Because a person is produced from the seminal fluid, which is the essence of
plants.

[4] Most of the hymns of the Sāma-Veda are taken from the Rig-Veda.

[5]'Earth is the support of all beings; water pervades the earth; plants arise from
water; man lives by plants; speech is the best part of man; the Rig-Veda the best
part of speech; the Sāma-Veda the best extract from the Rik; the Udgitha, or the
syllable *Om*, the crown of the Sāma-Veda.' (*Max Müller*.)

[6] It is the eighth or last in the series of essences described in verse 2.

[7] If someone seeks wealth from a rich person, the latter gives his assent by
saying Om. Assent is gratification because it is the source of the latter. A person
who is fully gratified acquiesces in the gift. Thus the passage means that Om is
endowed with the virtue of gratification.

[8] That is to say, the sacrifices prescribed in the three Vedas, namely, the Rig-
Veda, the Sāma-Veda, and the Yajur-Veda. The reference is to the Soma-sacrifice.

Imperishable [Ātman] by the greatness of that syllable and by its essence.[9] (I. i. 9)

[It may be contended] that he who knows this [true meaning of the syllable *Om*] and he who does not, perform the same sacrifice [and therefore must reap the same fruit]. But [this is not so]. [The results of] knowledge and ignorance are different. Work that is done with knowledge, faith, and the Upanishad (i.e. meditation on the deities) produces the more powerful fruit.
This is, verily, the [detailed] explanation of the syllable *Om*. (I. i. 10)

When the gods and the demons,[10] both offspring of Prajāpati,[11] fought with each other, the gods took hold of the Udgitha,[12] thinking that with this they would vanquish the demons.[13] (I. ii. 1)

They (i.e. the gods) meditated on the Udgitha (Om) as the prāna, which functions through the nose. But the demons pierced it (i.e. the prāna) with evil.[14] Therefore with it (i.e. the breath) one smells both

[9] 'These are allusions to sacrificial technicalities, all intended to show the importance of the syllable *Om*, partly as a mere word used at the sacrifices, partly as the mysterious name of the Highest Self. As every priest at the Soma-sacrifice, in which three classes of priests are always engaged, has to begin his part of the ceremonial with Om, therefore the whole sacrifice is said to be dependent on the syllable *Om*, and to be for the glory of that syllable, as an emblem of the Highest Self, a knowledge of whom is the indirect result of all sacrifices. The greatness of Om is explained by the vital breaths of the priest, the sacrificer, and his wife; its essence by rice, corn, etc., which constitute the oblations. Why breath and food are due to the syllable *Om* is explained by the sacrifice, which is dependent upon that syllable, ascending to the sun, the sun sending rain, rain producing food, and food producing breath and life.' (*Max Müller.*)
[10] The gods stand for such functions of the sense-organs as are illumined by the scriptural precepts. The demons, or asuras, as opposed to the gods, stand for such functions of the sense-organs as take delight in all sensuous activities; they are of the nature of darkness.
[11] The word usually refers to a virtuous person who, as a result of extremely meritorious action performed in the preceding cycle, has attained in the present cycle the exalted position of Prajāpati, or the Lord of creation. In the present verse the word signifies man in general, entitled to perform ritualistic work and pursue knowledge.
[12] The word refers to the Jyotishtoma and other Soma-sacrifices, which are performed by the udgātri priest with the Udgitha hymns.
[13] The text refers to the perpetual fight going on inside every man between his good and evil desires, the one trying to subdue the other. This fight is described through a story, with a view to explaining the nature of righteousness and unrighteousness, and emphasizing the purity of the prāna, or vital breath. A similar story is given in *Br. Up.* I. iii.
[14] A form of attachment which has its root in the demons, that is to say, in unrighteous desires. The nose thought that it smelt only what is good, and became vain about it. This robbed it of its power of discrimination and made it a victim of evil.

what is pleasant-smelling and what is foul-smelling. For the breath is pierced by evil. (I. ii. 2)

Then they meditated on the Udgitha as speech. But the demons pierced it with evil. Therefore one speaks both truth and falsehood. For speech is pierced by evil. (I. ii. 3)

Then they meditated on the Udgitha as the eye. But the demons pierced it with evil. Therefore one sees both what is sightly and what is unsightly. For the eye is pierced by evil. (I. ii. 4)

Then they meditated on the Udgitha as the ear. But the demons pierced it with evil. Therefore one hears both what is worth hearing and what is not worth hearing. For the ear is pierced by evil. (I. ii. 5)

Then they meditated on the Udgitha as the mind. But the demons pierced it with evil. Therefore one thinks both proper and improper thoughts. For the mind is pierced by evil. (I. ii. 6)

Then they meditated on the Udgitha as the principal (mukhya) prāna.[15] But as a clod of earth hitting a stone is scattered, even so the demons were destroyed when they hit it. (I. ii. 7)

As a clod of earth is scattered when hitting a stone, thus will he be scattered who wishes evil to one who knows this or who injures him; for he is a solid stone. (I. ii. 8)

With this (i.e. the principal vital breath) one does not discern what is pleasant-smelling and what is foul-smelling; for it is unsmitten by evil. Whatever a person eats or drinks with it (the principal vital breath) supports the other prānas.[16] That is why they depart when, at the time of death, it no longer supports them [by eating and drinking]. It opens the mouth at the time of death [as if the dying man wished to eat]. (I. ii. 9)

The syllable *Om*, called the Udgitha, should be meditated upon; for people sing the Udgitha, beginning with Om.

Now follows the [detailed] explanation [for this syllable]. (I. iv. 1)

[15] The prāna that sustains life is free from attachment and therefore is not subdued by evil. Compare *Br. Up.* I. iii. 7.

[16] The nose, ear, and other organs are selfish because they gather objects for their own sake; but the principal vital breath supports the organs by what it eats and drinks. Being the unselfish supporter of others, it is pure.

The gods, afraid of death, entered upon the threefold knowledge.[17] They covered themselves with the metrical hymns.[18] Because they covered (chhand) themselves with the hymns, the hymns are called chhandas. (I. iv. 2)

As a fisherman might observe a fish in [shallow] water, so death observed the gods in the Rik, the Yajus, and the Sāman.[19] They, too, came to know this, rose from the Rik, the Yajus, and the Sāman,[20] and entered the Svara (Om) alone.[21] (I. iv. 3)

When a man has mastered the Rig-Veda he loudly utters Om; he does the same when he has mastered the Sāma-Veda and the Yajur Veda. The Svara is the syllable [Om]; it is immortal and fearless. The gods, by entering it, became immortal and fearless. (I. iv. 4)

He who, knowing this, sings the praise of the syllable [Om] enters this same syllable, called the Svara, which is immortal and fearless. Having entered it, he becomes immortal as the gods are immortal. (I. iv. 5)

Now, verily, that which is the Udgitha is the Pranava; that which is the Pranava is the Udgitha.[22] Yonder sun is the Udgitha. It is the Pranava, because it moves along uttering Om. (I. v. 1)

Kaushitaki [in olden times] said to his son: 'I sang the praise of the sun [regarding it as one with its rays]; therefore you are my only [son]. Meditate [on the rays and the sun as different from each another], and you will have many sons.
So much with reference to the gods. (I. v. 2)

Now with reference to the body:
One should meditate on the Udgitha as the principal prāna, for it (i.e. the prāna) moves [in the body] uttering Om. (I. v. 3)

[17] That is to say, engaged in the performance of the sacrifices prescribed in the Rig-Veda, the Sāma-Veda, and the Yajur-Veda.
[18] They thought that through their performance of the Vedic sacrifices they would be freed from death.
[19] Because work and its result are transitory, the gods, after reaping the fruit of the sacrifices, would come under the sway of death.
[20] They gave up the performance of sacrifices because they realized that the sacrifices would not liberate them from death.
[21] The gods meditated on Om.
[22] The syllable Om is called the Pranava in the Rig-Veda, and the Udgitha in the Sāma-Veda.

Kaushitaki [in olden times] said to his son: 'I sang the praise [of the principal prāna alone]; therefore you are my only [son]. Meditate on the Udgitha as the manifold prāna, and you will have many sons.'[23] (I. v. 4)

Now, verily, that which is the Udgitha is the Pranava; that which is the Pranava is the Udgitha. He (i.e. the udgātri priest) who knows this, rectifies from the seat of the hotri priest any mistake committed by him (the udgātri priest), yea he rectifies it. (I. v. 5)

There were three men versed in the Udgitha: Śilaka the son of Śalāvat, Chaikitāyana of the line of Dalbhya, and Pravāhana the son of Jivala. They said: 'We are indeed versed in the Udgitha. Let us have a discussion of the Udgitha.' (I. viii. 1)

'Let it be so,' they said and sat down. Then Pravāhana the son of Jivala said: 'Revered Sirs, you speak first, and I shall listen to what the two brāhmins have to say.' (I. viii. 2)

Then Śilaka the son of Śalāvat said to Chaikitāyana of the line of Dalbhya: 'Well, may I question you?'
'Do ask,' he said. (I. viii. 3)

'What is the support of the Sāman?'[24] 'Tone (svara),' he replied.
'What is the support of tone?'
'The prāna (vital breath),' he replied.
'What is the support of the prāna?'
'Food,' he replied.
'What is the support of food?'
'Water,' he replied.
'What is the support of water?'
'Yonder world (heaven),' he replied.
'What is the support of yonder world?'
'Let no one carry the Sāman beyond the heavenly world. We place the Sāman in the heavenly world, for the Sāman is praised as heaven.' (I. viii. 4–5)

Then Śilaka the son of Śalāvat said to Chaikitāyana of the line of Dalbhya: 'O Dālbhya, your Sāman is not firmly established. If at this

[23] The sun may be regarded as one, if dissociated from its rays. Likewise, the vital breath may be regarded as one, if dissociated from the sense-organs. The result of such meditation is one son only. But one can meditate on the sun together with its rays, as also on the vital breath together with the sense-organs. The result of such meditation is many sons.
[24] The word here means the Udgitha, or Om.

time anyone [who knew the support of the Sāman] were to say: "Your head shall fall off," surely your head would fall off.' (I. viii. 6)

'Well then, revered Sir, let me learn it from you,' said Chaikitāyana.
'Learn it,' replied Śilaka.
'What is the support of that world?'
'This world,'[25] he replied.
'What is the support of this world?'
'Let no one carry the Sāman beyond this world, which is its support. We place the Sāman in this world as its support, for the Sāman is praised as the support (i.e. this world).' (I. viii. 7)

Then said Pravāhana the son of Jivala: 'O son of Śalāvat, your Sāman (i.e. this earth) has an end. If at this time anyone [who knew the support of the Sāman] were to say: "Your head shall fall off," surely your head would fall off.'
'Well then, let me learn this from you, revered Sir,' said Śilaka.
'Learn it,' said Pravāhana. (I. viii. 8)

'What is the support of this world?' asked Śilaka.
'The ākāśa,'[26] said Pravāhana. 'For all these beings are created from the ākāśa and return to the ākāśa. The ākāśa is greater than these; therefore the ākāśa is the supreme support.' (I. ix. 1)

This is the Udgitha (Om), the most excellent; this is endless.
He who, knowing this, meditates on the Udgitha obtains the most excellent [life] and wins the most excellent worlds. (I. ix. 2)

Atidhanvan the son of Śunaka, having taught this [Udgitha] to Udaraśāndilya, said: 'As long as any of your descendants know this Udgitha, their life shall be the most excellent in this world, and likewise in the other world.'
He who thus knows the Udgitha and meditates on it—his life shall be the most excellent in this world, and likewise in the other world, yea, in the other world. (I. ix. 3–4)

When the crops of the Kurus were destroyed by thunderstorms, Ushasti the son of Chakra, with his child-wife, lived in a deplorable condition in the village of a man who owned an elephant. (I. x. 1)

He (Ushasti) begged food from the owner of the elephant, who was eating some wretched beans. He (the owner of the elephant) said: 'I have nothing but what is set before me.' (I. x. 2)

---

[25] The earth supports heaven by means of sacrifices, offerings, etc.
[26] It is a symbol of the Supreme Self.

Ushasti said: 'Give me these.'

He gave the beans and said: 'Here is some water [left over from my drinking].'

Ushasti said: 'If I drink this, I will then be drinking what has been left by another.' (I. x. 3)

The owner of the elephant said: 'Were not those beans also left over [and therefore unclean]?'

Ushasti replied: 'I should not have lived if I had not eaten them; but I can get water wherever I like.' (I. x. 4)

Having himself eaten, Ushasti gave his wife what was left. But she, having eaten before, took them (i.e. the beans) and put them away. (I. x. 5)

Next morning, on awaking, he said: 'Alas, if I could get even a little to eat, I might earn some money. The king over here is going to perform a sacrifice; he would choose me for all the priestly offices.' (I. x. 6)

His wife said to him: 'Here, my husband, are the beans.' After eating them, he went to the sacrifice that was about to be performed. (I. x. 7)

He saw there the assembled udgātri priests and sat near them in the place where they would sing the hymns. He said to the prastotri priest: (I. x. 8)

'O prastotri priest, if without knowing the deity that belongs to the Prastāva, you sing the Prastāva, your head will fall off.' (I. x. 9)

In the same manner he addressed the udgātri priest: 'O udgātri priest, if without knowing the deity that belongs to the Udgitha, you sing the Udgitha, your head will fall off.'

In the same manner he addressed the pratihārtri priest: 'O pratihārtri priest, if without knowing the deity that belongs to the Pratihāra, you sing the Pratihāra, your head will fall off.'

They all stopped [performing their duties] and sat in silence. (I. x. 10–11)

Then the sacrificer said to him (Ushasti): 'I should like to know who you are, revered Sir.'

'I am Ushasti the son of Chakra,' he replied. (I. xi. 1)

He (the sacrificer) said: 'Revered Sir, I looked for you to perform all these priestly offices, but not finding you, Sir, I have chosen others.' (I. xi. 2)

'But now, Sir, please take up all the priestly offices.'

'So be it,' said Ushasti, 'but let these [priests], with my permission, sing the hymns of praise. You will, however, give me as much wealth as you give them.'

'So be it,' said the sacrificer. (I. xi. 3)

Thereupon the prastotri priest approached him and said: 'Sir, you said to me: "O prastotri priest, if without knowing the deity that belongs to the Prastāva, you sing the Prastāva, your head will fall off." Which is that deity?' (I. xi. 4)

Ushasti said: 'The prāna [is that deity]. For all these beings merge in the prāna alone,[27] and from the prāna alone do they rise.[28] This is the deity which belongs to the Prastāva. If without knowing him you had chanted the Prastāva after having been cursed by me, your head would have fallen off.' (I. xi. 5)

Then the udgātri priest approached him and said: 'Sir, you said to me: "O udgātri priest, if without knowing the deity that belongs to the Udgitha, you sing the Udgitha, your head will fall off." Which is that deity?' (I. xi. 6)

Ushasti said: 'The sun [is that deity]. For all these beings praise the sun which is high up. This is the deity which belongs to the Udgitha. If without knowing him you had chanted the Udgitha after having been cursed by me, your head would have fallen off.' (I. xi. 7)

Then the pratihārtri priest approached him and said: 'Sir, you said to me: "O pratihārtri priest, if without knowing the deity that belongs to the Pratihāra, you sing the Pratihāra, your head will fall off." Which is that deity?' (I. xi. 8)

Ushasti said: 'Food [is that deity]. For all these beings take food and live. This is the deity that belongs to the Pratihāra. If without knowing him you had chanted the Pratihāra, after having been cursed by me, your head would have fallen off.'[29] (I. xi. 9)

[27] At the time of cosmic dissolution.

[28] At the beginning of a cycle.

[29] There are certain etymological similarities between the names of the portions of the Sāma-Veda ceremonial and of the deities with which they are associated. Thus similarities are found between the words *Prastāva* and *prāna* because both begin with *pra*. Āditya is assigned to the Udgitha because the sun is high up (ut) and the word *Udgitha* also begins with *ut*. Anna (food) is assigned to the Pratihāra because food is taken (*pratihriyatē*). The tenth and eleventh chapters teach that one should meditate on the Prastāva, the Udgitha, and the Pratihāra hymns of the Sāma-Veda as the prāna, the sun, and food. The result of such meditations is the attainment of identity with those deities.

II

THERE ARE THREE divisions of dharma: Sacrifice, study, and charity form the first. Austerity is the second. Dwelling in the house of the teacher as a brahmachārin, always[30] mortifying the body in the house of the teacher, is the third. All those [who practise these dharmas] attain the worlds of the virtuous. But one who is established in Brahman obtains Immortality.[31] (II. xxiii. 1)

Prajāpati brooded on the worlds. From them, thus brooded upon, there was revealed [in His heart] the threefold knowledge.[32] He brooded on it, and from it, thus brooded upon, there issued forth these syllables: *Bhuh, Bhuvah,* and *Svah.* (II. xxiii. 2)

He brooded on them (the three syllables), and from them, thus brooded upon, there issued forth Om. As all leaves are held together by a midrib, so is all speech held together by Om (Brahman). Om is all this, yea, Om is all this. (II. xxiii. 3)

---

[30] Till death. There are two classes of brahmachārins: One, called the upa-kurvāna, leaves the teacher's house after the completion of his study and becomes a householder. The other, called the naisthika, dwells in the teacher's house till death. The latter is entitled, after death, to the worlds of the virtuous.

[31] This sentence refers to the sannyāsin, who belongs to the fourth stage. He obtains absolute Immortality and not the relative one.

[32] That is to say, the three Vedas (the Sāma-Veda, Rig-Veda, and Yajur-Veda).

III

YONDER SUN[33] IS, verily, the honey of the gods. Heaven is the cross-beam.[34] The mid-region is the hive.[35] The [particles of] water-vapour [drawn by the sun through its rays] are the eggs.[36] (III. i. 1)

The eastern rays of the sun[37] are the eastern honey-cells. The Rik-verses are the bees. [The ritual laid down in] the Rig-Veda is the flower.[38] The water [of the sacrificial libations][39] is the nectar [of the flower].

These Riks heated the Rig-Veda. From it, thus heated, issued forth —as its essence—fame, radiance [of the body], [vigour of] the senses, virility, and the food that is eaten.[40] (III. i. 2–3)

That [essence] flowed forth and went towards the sun, and that forms what is called the red colour [of the rising sun]. (III. i. 4)

The southern rays of the sun are the southern honey-cells. The Yajus-verses are the bees. [The ritual laid down in] the Yajur-Veda is the flower. The water [of the sacrificial libation] is the nectar [of the flower]. (III. ii. 1)

These Yajus-verses heated the Yajur-Veda. From it, thus heated, issued forth—as its essence—fame, radiance [of the body], [vigour of] the senses, virility, and the food that is eaten. (III. ii. 2)

[33] The sacrificial rites attain fruition in the sun, which gives enjoyment to various creatures according to the merit of their action. The worship of the sun will now be described. This, through successive steps, leads to the Highest Good.
[34] Heaven is compared to the cross-beam from which the hive containing the honey-bees hangs.
[35] The mid-region is the hive because it hangs, as it were, from the beam of heaven; also because it is the support of the honey in the shape of the sun.
[36] Water-vapours are drawn from the earth by the sun's rays. They remain in the rays, which are in the mid-region, that is to say, in the hive. Thus these vapours are compared to the eggs which remain in the cells of the honeycomb.
[37] Refers to the red rays seen at the time of the sunrise.
[38] 'Just as bees produce honey by extracting the nectar from flowers, so do the Riks make their honey (i.e. the result of action) by extracting the nectar from the rituals prescribed in the Rig-Veda.' (*Śaṅkarāchārya*.)
[39] The water stands for the soma-juice, butter, milk, etc., which are poured into the sacrificial fire. These, being cooked there, become the nectar because, it is said, they lead to immortality through purification of the mind.
[40] The bees heat the nectar of flowers, as it were, and turn it into honey; like-wise the soma-juice, milk, etc., are heated in the sacrificial fire and become trans-formed into the fruit of the sacrifices, called apurva and also amrita. The former name suggests that the fruit of the sacrifices is still in an invisible form, and the latter suggests that these sacrifices gradually purify the mind and lead it to the Highest Good.

That [essence] flowed forth and went towards the sun. That forms what is called the white colour of the sun. (III. ii. 3)

The western rays of the sun are the western honey-cells. The Sāman-verses are the bees. The Sāma-Veda is the flower. The water is the nectar. (III. iii. 1)

The Sāmans heated the Sāma-Veda. From it, thus heated, issued forth—as its essence—fame, radiance, [vigour of] the senses, virility, and the food that is eaten. (III. iii. 2)

That flowed forth and went towards the sun. That forms what is called the dark colour of the sun.

The northern rays of the sun are the northern honey-cells. The [verses of the] Atharvāngirasa[41] are the bees. The Itihāsa-purāna[42] is the flower. The water is the nectar. (III. iv. 1)

These very hymns of the Atharvāngirasa heated the Itihāsa-purāna. From it, thus heated, issued forth—as its essence—fame, radiance, [vigour of] the senses, virility, and the food that is eaten. (III. iv. 2)

That flowed forth and went towards the sun. That forms what is called the extremely dark colour of the sun. (III. iv. 3)

Now, the upward rays of the sun are the honey-cells above. The secret teachings[43] [of the Upanishads] are the bees. Brahman (Om) is the flower. The water[44] is the nectar. (III. v. 1)

These secret teachings [as the bees] heated Brahman (Om). From It, thus heated, issued forth—as Its essence—fame, radiance, [vigour of] the senses, virility, and the food that is eaten. (III. v. 2)

That flowed forth and went towards the sun. That forms what appears to stir in the centre of the sun. (III. v. 3)

These [different colours in the sun] are the essences of the essences; for the Vedas are the essences and these [colours] are, again, their essences.

[41] The Atharva-Veda.

[42] The books of mythology and ancient lore, which are part of the Vedic literature. Some of them were repeated during the nocturnal rites of the Aśvamedha sacrifice in order to keep the priests from falling asleep. These myths and ancient lore are first mentioned in the Brāhmana section of the Vedas. Later they were embodied in the *Mahābhārata* and the Purānas.

[43] Teachings such as mentioned in II. xxiv. 4. These also include the various meditations employed in the sacrifice.

[44] That is to say, the juice or essence extracted from the meditation on Om.

These are the nectars of the nectars; for the Vedas are the nectars (i.e. immortal), and of them these [colours in the sun] are the nectars. (III. v. 4)

On the first of these nectars the Vasus[45] live, with Agni (fire) at their head. Truly, the gods do not eat or drink. They are satisfied by merely looking at the nectar. (III. vi. 1)

They retire into that [red] colour and rise up from that colour. (III. vi. 2)

He who thus knows this nectar becomes one of the Vasus, with Agni (fire) at their head; he is satisfied by merely looking at the nectar. He retires into that [red] colour and again rises up from that colour.[46] (III. vi. 3)

As long as the sun rises in the east and sets in the west, so long does he, like the Vasus, enjoy rulership and sovereignty. (III. vi. 4)

On the second of these nectars the Rudras live, with Indra at their head. Truly, the gods do not eat or drink. They are satisfied by merely looking at the nectar. (III. vii. 1)

They retire into that [white] colour and rise up from that colour. (III. vii. 2)

He who thus knows this nectar becomes one of the Rudras, with Indra at their head; he is satisfied by merely looking at the nectar. He retires into that [white] colour and again rises up from that colour. (III. vii. 3)

As long as the sun rises in the east and sets in the west, twice as long does it rise in the south and set in the north, and just so long does he, like the Rudras, enjoy rulership and sovereignty. (III. vii. 4)

On the third of these nectars the Ādityas live, with Varuna at their head. Truly, the gods do not eat or drink. They are satisfied by merely looking at the nectar. (III. viii. 1)

---

[45] The presiding deities of the morning.

[46] Whoever knows that the bees in the shape of Riks produce honey from the flower in the shape of the sacrificial actions laid down in the Rig-Veda, that the nectar lies in the red colour of the rising sun which will be enjoyed by the Vasus, that the knower of all this becomes one with the Vasus with Agni as their head, and that the Vasus become satisfied by merely looking at the nectar, rising when the occasion for enjoyment arises and retiring when the opportunity lapses— whoever knows all this enjoys all this, like the Vasus.

They retire into that [dark] colour and rise up from that colour. (III. viii. 2)

He who thus knows this nectar becomes one of the Ādityas, with Varuna at their head; he is satisfied by merely looking at the nectar. He returns into that [dark] colour and again rises from that colour. (III. viii. 3)

As long as the sun rises in the south and sets in the north, twice as long does it rise in the west and set in the east, and just so long does he, like the Ādityas, enjoy rulership and sovereignty. (III. viii. 4)

On the fourth of these nectars the Maruts live, with Soma at their head. Truly, the gods do not eat or drink. They are satisfied by merely looking at the nectar. (III. ix. 1)

They retire into that [extremely dark colour] and rise up from that colour. (III. ix. 2)

He who thus knows this nectar becomes one of the Maruts, with Soma at their head; he is satisfied by merely looking at the nectar. He retires into that [extremely dark] colour and again rises from that colour. (III. ix. 3)

As long as the sun rises in the west and sets in the east, twice as long does it rise in the north and set in the south: and just so long does he, like the Maruts, enjoy rulership and sovereignty. (III. ix. 4)

On the fifth of these nectars the Sādhyas live, with Brahmā at their head. Truly, the gods do not eat or drink. They are satisfied by merely looking at the nectar. (III. x. 1)

They retire into that form and rise up from that form. (III. x. 2)

He who thus knows this nectar becomes one of the Sādhyas, with Brahmā at their head; he is satisfied by merely looking at the nectar. He retires into that form and again rises from that form. (III. x. 3)

As long as the sun rises in the north and sets in the south, twice as long does it rise above and set below, and just so long does he, like the Sādhyas, enjoy rulership and sovereignty.[47] (III. x. 4)

[47] For the explanation of III. vi. 1 to III. x. 4, see the notes in the regular edition.

Now, after having risen thence upwards, it (i.e. the sun) rises and sets no more.[48] It remains alone in the centre. And on this there is the following verse: (III. xi. 1)

'There (i.e. in Brahmaloka) the sun neither rises nor sets at any time. O ye gods, if this is true, may I never fall from Brahman!' (III. xi. 2)

Verily, for him who thus knows this Brahma-Upanishad, the sun does not rise or set. For him it is day for ever.[49] (III. xi. 3)

This doctrine Brahmā told to Prajāpati, Prajāpati to Manu, Manu to his offspring. And to Uddālaka Āruni this doctrine of Brahman was narrated by his father. (III. xi. 4)

A father may therefore tell that doctrine of Brahman to his eldest son or to a worthy disciple. (III. xi. 5)

It must not be told to anyone else, even if he should offer one the whole sea-girt earth, full of treasure; for this [doctrine] is worth more than that, yea, it is worth more. (III. xi. 6)

The Gāyatri[50] is everything, whatever here exists. Speech is verily the Gāyatri, for speech sings forth (gāya-ti) and protects (trāya-tē) everything, whatever here exists.[51] (III. xii. 1)

That Gāyatri is also the earth; for everything that exists here rests on this earth and does not go beyond. (III. xii. 2)

---

[48] The sun, through its rising and setting, helps the creatures to experience the effects of their past actions. When these experiences are over, it gathers the creatures within itself. Then it rises within itself, because there are no creatures for whose sake it should rise. Neither rising nor setting, it remains alone.

[49] The meaning is that the knower becomes one with Brahmā, not conditioned by time as marked by the rising and setting of the sun.

[50] The name of one of the metres of the Vedas. The Gāyatri metre has four feet, with six letters in each foot. All other metres have more than twenty-four letters. Containing the minimum of letters, the Gāyatri metre is present in all other metres; therefore it is the foremost among metres. The word *Gāyatri* also denotes a certain hymn written in the Gāyatri metre, which is regarded as the most sacred hymn in the Vedas. It is an effective symbol of Brahman for the purpose of meditation.

[51] Speech sings forth an object, that is to say, gives it a name. It also protects others from fear by pointing out the name of the object and exhorting them to give up fear. Speech is able to perform these two functions because it is one with the Gāyatri.

In man, that Gāyatri is also the body; for the prānas[52] exist in this body and do not go beyond. (III. xii. 3)

That body, in man, is again the heart within a man; for the prānas exist in it and do not go beyond. (III. xii. 4)

That Gāyatri has four feet and is sixfold.[53] The same is also declared by a Rik-verse:[54] (III. xii. 5)

'Such is its greatness (i.e. of Brahman as known through the symbol of the Gāyatri). Greater than it is the Person (Brahman). One of Its feet covers all beings; the immortal three feet are in heaven[55] (i.e. in Itself).' (III. xii. 6)

The Brahman which has been thus described is the same as the [physical] ākāśa outside a person. The ākāśa which is outside a person is the same as that which is inside a person. The ākāśa which is inside a person is the ākāśa within the heart. The ākāśa which is within the heart is omnipresent and unchanging. He who knows this obtains full and unchanging prosperity.[56] (III. xii. 7–9)

Of that heart there are five doors[57] controlled by the devas. That which is the eastern door is the prāna[58]—that is the eye, that is Āditya (the sun).[59] One should meditate on that as brightness and the source of food.[60] He who knows this becomes bright and an eater of food. (III. xiii. 1)

[52] The word means both the five vital breaths and the sense-organs, and also the bhutas, or elements.

[53] The Gāyatri is identified with all creatures, and with speech, earth, body, heart, and the prānas. It is therefore called sixfold.

[54] See Rig-Veda X. xc. 3.

[55] The word *immortal* here means immutable. That three of Its feet are in heaven denotes that the Pure Brahman is greater than the Gāyatri.

[56] The ākāśa is, in reality, one. It is described as threefold on account of the threefold experiences associated with it. During the waking state we see the ākāśa outside us and experience therein pleasure and pain, though the measure of the pain is greater than that of the pleasure. In the dream state we feel pleasure and pain in the ākāśa within the body, but the pleasure exceeds the pain. In dreamless sleep we gather our experience in the ākāśa of the heart. It is an experience of pleasure alone, without pain. Thus the ākāśa within the heart is the best of all the forms of ākāśa, and one should concentrate on it.

[57] Through these doors one reaches the Supreme Self, which resides in the heart.

[58] The vital breath which moves through the nose and the mouth.

[59] The eye cannot function without the prāna. The sun, the governing deity of the eye, has its abode in the eye. Therefore the sun, the prāna, and the eye are not different from one another.

[60] From the sun comes rain, and from rain, food. Therefore the sun is the source of food.

That which is the southern gate is the vyāna—that is the ear, that is Chandramā (the moon). One should meditate on that as prosperity and fame. He who knows this becomes prosperous and famous. (III. xiii. 2)

That which is the western gate is the apāna—that is speech, that is Agni (fire). One should meditate on that as the radiance of Brahman and the source of food. He who knows this becomes radiant and an eater of food. (III. xiii. 3)

That which is the northern gate is the samāna—that is the mind, that is Parjanya (the rain-god). One should meditate on that as fame and beauty. He who knows this becomes famous and beautiful. (III. xiii. 4)

That which is the upper gate is the udāna—that is Vāyu, that is the ākāśa. One should meditate on that as strength and greatness. He who knows this becomes strong and great. (III. xiii. 5)

These are the five servants of Brahman, the door-keepers of the world of heaven. He who thus knows these five servants of Brahman, the door-keepers of the world of heaven—in his family, a hero is born. He who thus knows the five servants of Brahman, the door-keepers of the world of heaven, himself attains the world of heaven. (III. xiii. 6)

Now, the light which shines above this heaven, above all the worlds, above everything, in the highest worlds not excelled by any other worlds, that is the same light which is within man. There is this visible proof [of this light]: when we thus perceive by touch the warmth in the body. And of it we have this audible proof: when we thus hear, by covering the ears, what is like the rumbling of a carriage, or the bellowing of an ox, or the sound of a blazing fire. One should worship [as Brahman] that [inner] light which is seen and heard. He who knows this becomes conspicuous and celebrated, yea, he becomes celebrated.[61] (III. xiii. 7–8)

All this is Brahman. From It the universe comes forth, into It the universe merges, and in It the universe breathes.[62] Therefore a man should meditate on Brahman with a calm mind.

[61] 'The presence of Brahman in the heart of man is not to rest on the testimony of revelation alone, but is here to be established by the evidence of the senses. Childish as the argument may seem to us, it shows at all events how intently the old brāhmins thought on the problem of the evidence of the invisible.' (*Max Müller.*)

[62] The passage emphasizes that the universe, at all periods of time, remains one with Brahman. It can never exist apart from Brahman. The universe is Brahman Itself, and consequently Brahman is one and without a second.

Now, verily, a man consists of will. As he wills in this world, so does he become when he has departed hence. Let him [with this knowledge in mind] form his will. (III. xiv. 1)

He who consists of the mind, whose body is subtle, whose form is light, whose thoughts are true, whose nature is like the ākāśa, whose creation is this universe, who cherishes all [righteous] desires, who contains all [pleasant] odours, who is endowed with all tastes, who embraces all this, who never speaks, and who is without longing—

He is my Self within the heart, smaller than a grain of rice, smaller than a grain of barley, smaller than a mustard seed, smaller than a grain of millet; He is my Self within the heart, greater than the earth, greater than the mid-region, greater than heaven, greater than all these worlds. (III. xiv. 2–3)

He whose creation is this universe, who cherishes all desires, who contains all odours, who is endowed with all tastes, who embraces all this, who never speaks, and who is without longing—He is my Self within the heart, He is that Brahman. When I shall have departed hence I shall certainly reach Him: one who has this faith and has no doubt [will certainly attain to that Godhead]. Thus said Śāndilya, yea, thus he said. (III. xiv. 4)

A person, indeed, is a sacrifice. His [first] twenty-four years constitute the morning libation. The Gāyatri [metre] has twenty-four syllables, and the morning libation is offered with Gāyatri hymns. The Vasus are connected with that part of the sacrifice. The prānas[63] are the Vasus; for, verily, they make everything abide (vāsayanti) in this body.[64] (III. xvi. 1)

If anything ails him during that period, he should recite [the following mantra]: 'O ye prānas, ye Vasus, unite this morning libation with the midday libation. May I, who am a sacrifice, not disappear[65] in the midst of the prānas, who are the Vasus.' Thus he rises from his illness and becomes free of it. (III. xvi. 2)

His next forty-four years constitute the midday libation. The Tristubh [metre] has forty-four syllables, and the midday libation is offered with Tristubh hymns. The Rudras[66] are connected with that part of the

[63] That is to say, the sense-organs.

[64] The Upanishad lays down in the present chapter the meditation whereby one can prolong one's own life. It is only when a man lives long that he enjoys the company of his sons and other earthly pleasures.

[65] That is to say, not die.

[66] The word *Rudras* is derived from the root *rud*, which means *to cry*. Rudra means one who cries or makes others cry. It is generally during middle age that a man becomes cruel. He himself suffers pain and inflicts it upon others.

sacrifice. The prānas are the Rudras; for, verily, they make everything weep (rodayanti).[67] (III. xvi. 3)

If anything ails him during that [second] period, he should recite [the following mantra]: 'O ye prānas, ye Rudras, unite this midday libation with the third libation. May I, who am a sacrifice, not disappear in the midst of the prānas, who are the Rudras.' Thus he rises from his illness and becomes free of it. (III. xvi. 4)

His next forty-eight years constitute the third oblation. The Jagati [metre] has forty-eight syllables, and the third oblation is offered with Jagati hymns. The Ādityas are connected with that part of the sacrifice. The prānas are the Ādityas; for, verily, they take up (ādadate) everything. (III. xvi. 5)

If anything ails him during that [third] period, he should recite [the following mantra]: 'O ye prānas, ye Ādityas, extend this my third libation to the full age. May I, who am a sacrifice, not disappear in the midst of the prānas, who are the Ādityas.' Thus he rises from his illness and becomes free of it. (III. xvi. 6)

Mahidāsa, the son of Itarā, knew this and said [addressing a disease]: 'O you [disease]! Why do you afflict me? I shall not die of this [affliction].' He lived a hundred and sixteen years. He, too, who knows this lives on to a hundred and sixteen years. (III. xvi. 7)

When a man hungers, thirsts, and abstains from pleasures—these are his initiatory rites.[68] (III. xvii. 1)

---

[67] The day when the Soma-sacrifice is performed is divided into three periods, namely, morning, midday, and evening, and three libations are offered during the three periods. According to the *Aitareya Brāhmana*, the Vasus and Agni (fire) are the controlling deities of the morning libation, the Rudras and Indra of the midday libation, and the Viśve-devas and Ādityas (suns) of the evening libation. In ancient times, Prajāpati divided the libations and the metres for the gods. He assigned the morning libation and the Gāyatri metre to the Vasus and Agni, the midday libation and the Tristubh metre to the Rudras and Indra, and the evening libation and the Jagati metre to the Viśve-devas and the Ādityas.

[68] The initiatory rites in the Soma-sacrifice require several acts of penance on the part of the sacrificer. He should practise self-control, use a hard deer-skin for his seat, live on a diminishing quantity of milk, and confine himself to a particular spot between sunrise and sunset. Thus the initiatory rites are painful. One should look upon the afflictions of life as initiatory rites. The experience of pain is common to both.

When he eats, drinks, and enjoys pleasures, he then participates in the Upasadas.[69] (III. xvii. 2)

When a man laughs, eats, and enjoys sexual intercourse—these are the Stuta[70] and Śastra.[71] (III. xvii. 3)

Austerity, almsgiving, uprightness, non-violence, and truthfulness—these are the gifts (dakshinā) for the priests.[72] (III. xvii. 4)

[Because the life of a man is a sacrifice] therefore they say that his mother will give birth (soshyati) to him, or his mother has given birth (asoshtā) to him.[73] [The same words are used in the Soma-sacrifice and mean: 'He will pour out the soma-juice' and 'He has poured out the soma-juice.'] This is his birth.[74] His death is the Avabhritha.[75] (III. xvii. 5)

Ghora, of the line of Angirasa, communicated this [teaching] to Krishna,[76] the son of Devaki—and it quenched Krishna's thirst [for any other knowledge]—and said: 'When a man approaches death he should take refuge in these three [thoughts]: "Thou art indestructible (akshata)," "Thou art unchanging (aprachyuta)," and "Thou art the subtle prāna." '
On this subject there are two Rik-verses: (III. xvii. 6)

'They (i.e. the knowers of Brahman) see everywhere the Supreme Light, which shines in Brahman, which is all-pervading like the light of day, and which belongs to the primeval Seed.

[69] A ceremony which constitutes a part of the Soma-sacrifice. The sacrificer, in this ceremony, drinks milk, but before the initiatory rites the sacrificer must fast. Thus the former is a happier man. One is asked to look upon eating, drinking, etc., as the Upasadas. The whole of life is to be regarded as a sacrifice.
[70] A class of mantras recited in the sacrifice.
[71] A Śastra is a hymn of the Rig-Veda sung with a proper melody and thus turned into a Sāman. Laughter, etc., are accompanied by sounds. The hymns and recitations are also full of sounds. This is the similarity.
[72] The similarity between austerity, etc., and the gifts for the priests is this: the former enhance the righteousness of a man, and the latter make a religious act fruitful.
[73] The words soshyati and asosthā are both derived from the root su, which means both to give birth and to extract the soma-juice.
[74] The extraction of the soma-juice, in the Soma-sacrifice, and the birth of a person have similarities because of their association with the same root su.
[75] After the completion of the Soma-sacrifice the sacrificer and his wife take a bath called the Avabhritha. Then he changes his clothes. Similar ceremonies are performed after death. The corpse is given a bath and dressed in new clothes. On account of this similarity, also, the life of a man is regarded as a sacrifice.
[76] He is quite different from the famous Krishna of the Mahābhārata.

'Perceiving the higher light[77] [in the sun]—which is above the darkness [of ignorance]—as the higher light in the heart, [perceiving] the Supreme Light which is higher than all lights, we have reached the Highest Light, the Sun, the most luminous among the gods, yea, we have reached the Highest Light, the Sun, the most luminous among the gods.' (III. xvii. 7)

One should meditate on the mind as Brahman—this is said with reference to the body. One should meditate on the ākāśa as Brahman—this is said with reference to the gods. Thus both—the meditation with reference to the body and the meditation with reference to the gods—are being taught. (III. xviii. 1)

That Brahman has four feet (quarters): speech is one foot, the prāna (the nose) is one foot, the eye is one foot, the ear is one foot—this is said with reference to the body. Now with reference to the gods: Agni (fire) is one foot. Vāyu (air) is one foot, Āditya (the sun) is one foot, and the quarters (diśāh) are one foot. This is the twofold meditation with reference to the body and with reference to the gods. (III. xviii. 2)

Speech is, indeed, a fourth foot (quarter) of Brahman [of which the mind is a symbol].[78] It shines and warms with the light of fire.[79] He who knows this shines and warms with fame, with renown, and with the radiance of Brahman. (III. xviii. 3)

Prāna (the nose) is, indeed, a fourth foot of Brahman. It shines and warms with the light of the air.[80] He who knows this shines and warms with fame, with renown, and with the radiance of Brahman. (III. xviii. 4)

The eye, indeed, is a fourth foot of Brahman. It shines and warms with the light of the sun.[81] He who knows this shines and warms with fame, with renown, and with the radiance of Brahman. (III. xviii. 5)

The ear, indeed, is a fourth foot of Brahman. It shines and warms with the light of the quarters.[82] With fame, with renown, and with the

[77] That is to say, Saguna Brahman.

[78] As an animal goes out, with the help of its legs, in search of food, so the mind seeks, with the help of the organ of speech, to express its thought. That is to say, speech is to be regarded as a foot of the Mind-Brahman. The same applies to the other senses.

[79] The organ of speech obtains its energy from such heat-giving substances as oil, butter, etc.

[80] The air stimulates the organ of smell.

[81] The sun stimulates the eye and reveals the objects seen by the eye.

[82] The quarters stimulate the ear and reveal sound.

radiance of Brahman he shines and warms who knows this, yea, who knows this. (III. xviii. 6)

The sun is Brahman: this is the teaching. An explanation thereof follows:

In the beginning this [universe] was non-existent.[83] It became existent.[84] It grew.[85] It turned into an egg. The egg lay for the period of a year. Then it broke open. Of the two halves of the egg-shell, one half was of silver, the other of gold.[86] (III. xix. 1)

That which was of silver became the earth; that which was of gold, heaven. What was the thick membrane [of the white] became the mountains; the thin membrane [of the yolk], the mist and the clouds. The veins became the rivers; the fluid in the bladder, the ocean. (III. xix. 2)

And what was born of it was yonder Āditya, the sun. When it was born shouts of 'Hurrah!' arose, together with all beings and all objects of desire. Therefore at its rise and its every return shouts of 'Hurrah!' together with all beings and all objects of desire arise. (III. xix. 3)

He who, knowing this, meditates on the sun as Brahman—pleasant sounds will quickly approach him and continue to delight him, yea, will continue to delight him. (III. xix. 4)

[83] Before the creation the universe was not differentiated into name and form; it was as if non-existent. From the relative standpoint, the existence and non-existence of an object seem to depend upon the sun. In the absence of the sun, when everything is pitch dark, nothing is seen to exist. When the sun shines, all objects are seen to exist. It is said in common parlance that in the absence of the king, the capital appears to be non-existent. Thus the purpose of the text is to eulogize the sun and not to describe the existence or non-existence of the universe. The sun is to be regarded as Brahman.

[84] What had been dormant and inert before, became slightly active and mobile.

[85] It showed a slight manifestation of name and form, like the sprouting of a seed. It became further materialized.

[86] The whole verse is a eulogy of the sun, which is to be regarded as a symbol of Brahman.

IV

THERE ONCE LIVED [a king named] Jānaśruti, who was a great-grandson of Janaśruta. He bestowed his gifts with respect, gave away liberally, and cooked much food [for the hungry]. He built rest-houses everywhere with the thought that people everywhere would eat his food. (IV. i. 1)

One night some flamingos[87] were flying along. One flamingo said to another: 'Hey! Ho! Short-sighted, Short-sighted! The radiance of Jānaśruti, the great-grandson of Janaśruta, has spread to the sky. Do not touch it, lest it should burn you.' (IV. i. 2)

The other replied: 'Say, who is this person about whom you have spoken as though he were like Raikva, the man with the cart?' 'What sort of person is this Raikva, the man with the cart?' (IV. i. 3)

[The short-sighted flamingo replied]: 'As [in a game of dice], when the krita[88] is won, the lower ones also are won, so whatever merits people acquire all accrue to that Raikva.[89] As Raikva I describe him, too, who knows what Raikva knows.' (IV. i. 4)

Jānaśruti the great-grandson of Janaśruta overheard this [conversation]. Immediately after getting out of bed, he said to his attendant: 'Friend, did you speak of me as though I were Raikva, the man with the cart?'[90]
'What sort of person is Raikva, the man with the cart?'
'As [in a game of dice], when the krita is won, the lower ones also are

---

[87] According to Śankarāchārya, certain sages or gods, being pleased with the generosity of the king and having assumed the form of flamingos, were flying over the palace and had come within sight of him.

[88] A game of dice is played with four dice. They are marked with one, two, three, and four spots and are called, respectively, kali, dvāpara, tretā, and krita. The krita represents the highest number. When a person succeeds in throwing it, he wins the other three dice, also. The higher number includes the lower.

[89] Because Raikva was the most virtuous of all. The results of the good deeds performed by him included the results of the good deeds of other living beings.

[90] The king, lying on the terrace of his palace, overheard the conversation of the flamingos, deprecating him and praising Raikva, another learned person. Brooding over this, he passed the remaining portion of the night and in the morning was aroused by the eulogistic chants of his bards. He felt that the eulogistic chants sung by the bards were proper only for Raikva, and not for him. Or the passage may mean: 'Friend, please tell Raikva, with the cart, that I want to call on him.'

won, so whatever merits people acquire all accrue to that Raikva. As Raikva I describe him, too, who knows what Raikva knows.'[91] (IV. i. 5–6)

The attendant searched for him and returned without finding him. Then the king said to him: 'Listen, where a knower of Brahman is to be searched for, look for him there.' (IV. i. 7)

[After proper search] the attendant came upon a person who, lying underneath his cart, was scratching an itch. [Humbly] he took his seat near him and said: 'Revered Sir, are you Raikva, the man with the cart?'

'Oh yes, I am he,' he answered.

Then the attendant returned, saying to himself: 'I have found him out.' (IV. i. 8)

Then Jānaśruti the great-grandson of Janaśruta took with him six hundred cows, a necklace, and a chariot with mules, and went to Raikva and said:

'Raikva, here are six hundred cows, a necklace, and a chariot with mules. Pray, revered Sir, teach me the deity whom you worship.' (IV. ii. 1–2)

To him the other said: 'Ah, may the necklace and the chariot remain with you, O Śudra,[92] along with the cows.'

Thereupon Jānaśruti the great-grandson of Janaśruta took with him a thousand cows, a chariot with mules, a necklace, and his own daughter, too, and went to Raikva. (IV. ii. 3)

Jānaśruti said to him: 'Raikva, here are a thousand cows, a necklace, a chariot with mules, this wife, and this village where you shall dwell. Revered Sir, teach me.' (IV. ii. 4)

Then considering her (the princess) as the door for imparting knowledge, Raikva said: 'O Śudra! You brought these [cows and other

[91] The king repeated the words of the flamingo.

[92] According to Śankarāchārya, the king did not belong to the śudra caste. 'The old teachers have explained this point thus: By addressing him as "Śudra", the sage Raikva shows that he already knows what is passing in the king's mind. The word śudra means: "one who is melting (dravati) with sorrow at hearing of the greatness of Raikva as spoken of by the flamingoes." Or it may be that the king is addressed as "Śudra" because he comes for instruction with an offering of riches, like a śudra, without serving him, like a religious student, with salutations and attendance, as befits a person belonging to a higher caste; the word does not mean that the king is a śudra by caste. Others, however, have explained that Raikva addressed him thus because he was enraged at his offering so little; it is said that wealth is to be accepted when a sufficient amount is offered.' (Śankarāchārya.)

presents; this is good]. But you will make me speak now only through this means (i.e. the princess).'

These are the villages named Raikvaparna, in the country of Mahā-vrishas, where Raikva lived.

Now Raikva said to the king: (IV. ii. 5)

'Verily, vāyu[93] is the swallower (samvarga). For when fire goes out it is indeed swallowed by the air.[94] When the sun sets it is swallowed by the air. When the moon sets it is swallowed by the air. (IV. iii. 1)

'When water dries up it is swallowed by the air. For indeed the air absorbs them all. So much with reference to the gods. (IV. iii. 2)

'Now with reference to the body: Verily, the prāna is the swallower. When a man sleeps, speech goes into the prāna, sight goes into the prāna, hearing goes into the prāna, and the mind goes into the prāna. For indeed the prāna absorbs them all. (IV. iii. 3)

'These are the two swallowers: the air among the gods, the prāna among the senses.' (IV. iii. 4)

Once Śaunaka of the line of Kapi, and Abhipratārin the son of Kakshasena, were being waited upon at their meal, when a brahma-chārin begged food of them. They did not give him anything. (IV. iii. 5)

He said: 'One God, Prajāpati, swallowed the four great ones.[95] He is the Guardian of the world. O descendant of Kapi, O Abhipratārin, mortals do not see Him though he abides in manifold forms. Verily, this food has not been given to Him to whom it belongs.'[96] (IV. iii. 6)

Śaunaka of the line of Kapi, pondering on those words, went to the brahmachārin [and said]: 'He is the self of the gods, the creator of all beings, with unbroken teeth,[97] the eater, the truly wise one. They speak of His magnificence as great, because without being eaten, He eats even what is not [common] food. O brahmachārin, we meditate upon this [Brahman].'
Then he said [to the attendants]: 'Give him food.' (IV. iii. 7)

---

[93] The word *vāyu* here means the external air. Vāyu is a symbol of Prajāpati.
[94] The air makes these cosmic divinities one with itself.
[95] As vāyu, Prajāpati swallowed fire, the sun, the moon, and water; and as the prāna, He swallowed speech, sight, hearing, and the mind.
[96] The brahmachārin knew his identity with Prajāpati, who, as the prāna, is the real eater. Therefore to deny him food was to deny it to Prajāpati.
[97] That is to say, though He swallows everything, yet He never grows weary.

They gave [food] to him. Now these five (i.e. the eater vāyu, and fire, the sun, the moon, and water, which are its food) and those five (i.e. the eater prāna, and the organs of speech, the eye, the ear, and the mind, which are its food) make ten. These together constitute the krita (the highest throw in a game of dice).[98] [On account of this similarity of ten,] these ten are the food in the [ten] quarters,[99] and further, they are Virāt, the eater of food, by which all this becomes seen. All this he sees, and the eater of food he becomes, who knows this, yea, who knows this. (IV. iii. 8)

Once upon a time, Satyakāma the son of Jabālā addressed his mother and said: '[Revered] Mother, I wish to become a brahmachārin. Of what ancestry am I?' (IV. iv. 1)

She said to him: 'I do not know, my child, of what ancestry you are. In my youth I was preoccupied with many [household] duties and with attending [on guests] when I conceived you.[100] I do not know of what ancestry you are. I am Jabālā by name, and you are Satyakāma. So you may speak of yourself as Satyakāma Jābāla (the son of Jabālā). (IV. iv. 2)

He [came to] Gautama the son of Haridrumata and said: 'Revered Sir, I wish to live with you as a brahmachārin. May I approach you, Sir [as a pupil]?' (IV. iv. 3)

Gautama said to him: 'Of what ancestry are you, dear friend?'
Satyakāma said: 'I do not know, Sir, of what family I am. I asked my mother about it, and she replied: "In my youth I was preoccupied with many [household] duties and with attending [on guests] when I conceived you. I do not know of what ancestry you are. I am Jabālā by name, and you are Satyakāma." I am therefore, Sir, Satyakāma Jābāla.' (IV. iv. 4)

---

[98] The krita throw comprises ten: kali (1)+dvāpara (2)+treta (3)+krita (4): (See IV. i. 4.) It is because the krita represents the highest number that it includes the others. Therefore it is the eater and the others are its food. Thus the krita and its food make ten. Again, vāyu and its food make five, and the prāna and its food make five. Thus the total is ten, which includes both the eater and the food. On account of this similarity, the krita and its food are non-different from vāyu and its food, and also from prāna and its food, because they too make ten.

[99] There are ten quarters: east, west, north, south, the four subsidiary quarters, and the upper and lower quarters.

[100] When a young woman, she had been extremely busy with various household duties. It was than that she had conceived Satyakāma, and at that time her husband had died. Hence she had not had an opportunity to find out her husband's ancestry. According to some modern writers, Satyakāma did not have a legitimate father.

Gautama said: 'None but a [true] brāhmin would thus speak out.[101] Fetch the fuel, dear friend; I shall initiate you. You have not departed from truth.'

He initiated Satyakāma. Having separated out four hundred lean and weak cows [from his herd], he said: 'Dear friend, go with these.' Driving them away [towards the forest], Satyakāma said: 'I shall not return until they become a thousand.' He lived a number of years [in the forest].

When the cows had become a thousand— (IV. iv. 5)

The bull [of the herd], addressing him, said: 'Satyakāma!' 'Revered Sir!' Satyakāma replied.[102] The bull said: 'Dear friend, we have become a thousand, take us to the teacher's house. (IV. v. 1)

'I will declare to you one foot of Brahman.' 'Declare it, Revered Sir.' The bull said to him: 'The east is one quarter, the west is one quarter, the south is one quarter, the north is one quarter. This, dear friend, is one foot of Brahman, consisting of four quarters, and this foot is called Prakāśavat (shining). (IV. v. 2)

'He who knows this and meditates on the foot of Brahman consisting of four quarters as shining, becomes shining on this earth. He conquers shining worlds—he who knows this and meditates on the foot of Brahman consisting of four quarters as shining.' (IV. v. 3)

[The bull further said:] 'Agni (fire) will declare to you another foot of Brahman.'

Satyakāma then, when it was the morrow, drove the cows [in the direction of the teacher's house]. And when they came together toward evening, he lighted a fire, penned the cows, laid fuel [on the fire], and sat down behind the fire, facing the east. (IV. vi. 1)

Agni (fire) addressing him, said: 'Satyakāma!' 'Revered Sir!' Satyakāma replied. (IV. vi. 2)

'Dear friend, I will declare to you one foot of Brahman.' 'Declare it, revered Sir.' Agni said to him: 'The earth is one quarter, the sky is one quarter,

---

[101] That is to say, would make such a straightforward answer in spite of the possibility of his being misunderstood as being a person of illegitimate birth.

[102] Satyakāma found out that the deity Air (Vāyu) controlling the quarters, pleased with his faith and austerity, was speaking to him through the bull. He therefore addressed him with respect.

heaven is one quarter, the ocean is one quarter. This, dear friend, is one foot of Brahman, consisting of four quarters, and this foot is called Anantavat (endless). (IV. vi. 3)

'He who knows this and meditates on the foot of Brahman consisting of four quarters as endless, becomes endless on this earth. He conquers endless worlds—he who knows this and meditates on the foot of Brahman consisting of four quarters as endless.' (IV. vi. 4)

[Agni further said:] 'A hamsa (swan)[103] will declare to you another foot.'
Satyakāma then, when it was the morrow, drove the cows [in the direction of the teacher's house]. And when they came together toward evening, he lighted a fire, penned the cows, laid fuel [on the fire], and sat down behind the fire, facing the east. (IV. vii. 1)

Then a swan flew to him and said: 'Satyakāma!'
'Revered Sir!' Satyakāma replied. (IV. vii. 2)

'Dear friend, I will declare to you one foot of Brahman.'
'Declare it, revered Sir.'
The swan said to him: 'Fire is one quarter, the sun is one quarter, the moon is one quarter, lightning is one quarter. This, dear friend, is one foot of Brahman, consisting of four quarters, and this foot is called Jyotishmat (luminous). (IV. vii. 3)

'He who knows this and meditates on the foot of Brahman consisting of four quarters as luminous, becomes luminous on this earth. He conquers luminous worlds—he who knows this and meditates on the foot of Brahman consisting of four quarters as luminous.' (IV. vii. 4)

[The swan further said:] 'A madgu (diver-bird)[104] will declare to you another foot.'
Satyakāma then, when it was the morrow, drove the cows [in the direction of the teacher's house]. And when they came together toward evening, he lighted a fire, penned the cows, laid fuel [on the fire], and sat down behind the fire, facing the east. (IV. viii. 1)

Then a diver-bird flew to him and said: 'Satyakāma!'
'Revered Sir!' Satyakāma replied. (IV. viii. 2)

[103] Here the word *hamsa* signifies the deity sun, because both are white and both fly in the sky.
[104] A kind of water-bird. Being intimately related to water, it signifies here the prāna, which cannot dwell in the body without water.

'Dear friend, I will declare to you one foot of Brahman.'

'Declare it, revered Sir.'

The diver-bird said to him: 'The prāna is one quarter, the eye is one quarter, the ear is one quarter, the mind is one quarter. This, dear friend, is one foot of Brahman, consisting of four quarters, and this foot is called Āyatanavat (having support). (IV. viii. 3)

'He who knows this and meditates on the foot of Brahman consisting of four quarters as Āyatanavat, possesses a support (i.e. home) on this earth. He conquers the worlds which offer a home—he who knows this and meditates on the foot of Brahman consisting of four quarters as Āyatanavat.' (IV. viii. 4)

Satyakāma reached the teacher's house. The teacher said to him: 'Satyakāma!'

'Revered Sir!' Satyakāma replied. (IV. ix. 1)

The teacher said: 'Dear friend, you shine like one who knows Brahman. Who has taught you?'

'Others than men,' he replied. 'But I wish, revered Sir, that you alone should teach me. (IV. ix. 2)

'For I have heard from persons like your good self that only knowledge which is learnt from a teacher (āchārya) leads to the highest good.'

Then he (Gautama) taught him the same knowledge. Nothing whatsoever was left out, yea, nothing whatsoever was left out. (IV. ix. 3)

Upakosala the son of Kamala dwelt as a brahmachārin (religious student) with Satyakāma the son of Jabālā. He tended his [teacher's] fires for twelve years. Satyakāma allowed his other pupiis to return to their homes [after they had finished their Vedic studies] but did not allow Upakosala to depart. (IV. x. 1)

Then his wife said to him: 'This brahmachārin, practising austerities, has intelligently tended your fires. Give him instruction lest the fires should blame you.' The teacher, however, went away on a journey without teaching him. (IV. x. 2)

The brahmachārin out of [mental] grief began to fast. Then the teacher's wife said to him: 'Brahmachārin, why do you not eat?' He said: 'There are in a man [like me] many desires directed to various objects. I am full of sorrows. I will not eat.' (IV. x. 3)

Thereupon the fires said among themselves: 'This brahmachārin, practising austerities, has intelligently tended us. Come, let us teach him.'

They said to him: 'The prāna is Brahman, ka (joy) is Brahman, kha (the ākāśa) is Brahman.' (IV. x. 4)

He said: 'I understand that the prāna is Brahman,[105] but I do not understand "joy" (ka) and "the ākāśa" ' (kha).'[106]
They said: 'What is joy (ka) is the ākāśa (kha), what is the ākāśa (kha) is joy (ka).'[107]
They taught him the prāna (i.e. Brahman) and the ākāśa related to it. (IV. x. 5)

Next the Gārhapatya (Household) Fire taught him: 'The earth, fire, food, and the sun [are my forms]. The person that is seen in the sun—I am he, I am he indeed. (IV. xi. 1)

'He who, knowing this, meditates [on the fire] frees himself from sinful actions, obtains the World [of the Gārhapatya Fire], reaches his full age, and lives brightly. His descendants do not perish. We support him in this world and in the other who, knowing this, meditates [on the fire].' (IV. xi. 2)

Then the Anvāhārya (Southern) Fire taught him: 'Water, the quarters, the stars, and the moon [are my forms]. The person that is seen in the moon—I am he, I am he indeed. (IV. xii. 1)

'He who, knowing this, meditates [on the fire] frees himself from sinful actions, obtains the World [of the Anvāhārya Fire], reaches his full age, and lives brightly. His descendants do not perish. We support him in this world and in the other who, knowing this, meditates [on the fire].' (IV. xii. 2)

Then the Āhavaniya (Eastern) Fire taught him: 'The prāna, the ākāśa, heaven, and lightning [are my forms]. The person that is seen in lightning—I am he, I am he indeed. (IV. xiii. 1)

[105] A man's life depends upon the prāna. From this universal experience one can assume that the prāna is Brahman.

[106] Joy (ka) generally signifies the transitory pleasures derived from the contact of the senses with physical objects. Ākāśa generally signifies an element material and non-intelligent in nature. It is difficult to understand how they can be Brahman.

[107] Joy (ka), qualified by the all-pervading ākāśa (kha), becomes free from the taint of physical pleasures. Likewise the ākāśa (kha), qualified by joy (ka), becomes free from the taint of the physical ākāśa. Thus, through mutual qualification, joy and the ākāśa signify Ākāśa, or the Causal Brahman, which is endowed with imperishable joy. The meaning of the text is that what is said to represent Brahman is the joy residing in the ākāśa of the heart and the ākāśa which is the support of joy. Between the ākāśa and joy there is the mutual relationship of qualifier and qualified.

'He who, knowing this, meditates [on the fire] frees himself from sinful actions, obtains the World [of the Āhavaniya Fire], reaches his full age, and lives brightly. His descendants do not perish. We support him in this world and in the other who, knowing this, meditates [on the fire].' (IV. xiii. 2)

Then they (i.e. all the fires) said: 'Upakośala, dear friend, thus we have taught you the knowledge of ourselves and the knowledge of the Self. But the teacher will teach you the way.'
The teacher returned and said to him: 'Upakośala!' (IV. xiv. 1)

He replied: 'Revered Sir!'
'Dear friend, your face shines like that of one who knows Brahman. Who has taught you?'
'Who should teach me, Sir?'
Here he conceals [the fact], as it were.
And he said [pointing to the fires]: 'For this reason they are of this form now, though they were of a different form before.'[108]
'Dear friend, what did they teach you?'
'This,' Upakośala replied [and repeated some of what the fires had told him].
The teacher said: 'They told you, dear friend, only about the worlds, but I shall tell you [about Brahman]. As water does not cling to the lotus leaf, so no evil clings to one who knows this.'
Upakośala said to him: 'Revered Sir, please tell me.' (IV. xiv. 2-3)

He said: 'The person that is seen in the eye[109]—that is the Self. This is the immortal, the fearless; this is Brahman. That is why, if one drops melted butter or water in the eye, it flows away on both sides.'[110] (IV. xv. 1)

'The seers call him Samyadvāma,[111] for all blessings (vāma) go towards him (samyanti). All blessings go towards him who knows this. (IV. xv. 2)

---

[108] The fires, pleased with Upakośala's service, had given him instruction. But now, seeing the teacher, they began to quiver, as it were. They were not as they had been before. Pointing out this fact, Upakośala hinted that the fires had given him instruction.

[109] Brahman is described as the Seer of seeing by those who have withdrawn their minds from the external world and practise continence, calmness, and discrimination between the real and the unreal.

[110] As water does not cling to the lotus leaf. If such is the greatness of the place where Brahman dwells, the Dweller Himself must be immensely great. He is not affected by actions, good or evil.

[111] This word, as also the other two mentioned in the two following verses, are secret names of Brahman.

'He is also Vāmani, for he carries to living beings (nayati) all blessings (vāma). He who knows this carries all blessings. (IV. xv. 3)

'He is also called Bhāmani, for he shines (bhāti) in all the worlds. He who knows this shines in all the worlds.' (IV. xv. 4)

'Now, whether or not they perform the cremation obsequies for such a person, he goes to light, from light to day, from day to the bright half of the moon, from the bright half of the moon to the six months during which the sun goes to the north, from [those] months to the year, from the year to the sun, from the sun to the moon, from the moon to lightning. There a person who is not a human being[112] meets him and leads him to Brahman.[113] This is the Path of the Gods (Devayāna), the path leading to Brahman. Those who travel by it do not return to the whirl of humanity, yea, they do not return.' (IV. xv. 5)

Prajāpati brooded over the worlds; from them, thus brooded over, he squeezed the essences: agni (fire) from the earth, vāyu (air) from the mid-regions, and āditya (the sun) from heaven. (IV. xvii. 1)

He brooded over these three deities; from them, thus brooded over, he squeezed the essences. The Rik-verses from fire, the Yajus-verses from the air, and the Sāman-verses from the sun.[114] (IV. xvii. 2)

He brooded over the threefold knowledge (i.e. the three Vedas); from them, thus brooded over, he squeezed the essences: Bhuh from the Rik-verses, Bhuvah from the Yajus-verses, and Svah from the Sāman-verses.[115] (IV. xvii. 3)

---

[112] He comes from Brahmaloka.
[113] That is to say, to Brahmaloka. The attainment of the Pure Brahman is not meant. The knower of the Pure Brahman realizes the oneness of existence while living on earth and does not go anywhere.
[114] Prajāpati, through intense thinking, obtained the knowledge of the three Vedas.
[115] Bhuh, Bhuvah, and Svah are called the three vyāhritis. They are the essences of the three Vedas, from which they have been extracted, of the worlds, and of the gods.

V

Om. He who knows what is the oldest and greatest becomes himself the oldest and greatest. The prāna, indeed, is the oldest[116] and greatest. (V. i. 1)

He who knows what is the most excellent (vasishtha) becomes the most excellent among his kinsmen. The organ of speech, indeed, is the most excellent.[117] (V. i. 2)

He who knows what has [the attributes of] firmness (pratishthā) becomes firm in this world and the next. The eye, indeed, is endowed with firmness.[118] (V. i. 3)

He who knows prosperity (sampad), his wishes are fulfilled—both divine and human wishes. The ear, indeed, is prosperity.[119] (V. i. 4)

He who knows the abode (āyatana) becomes the abode of his kinsmen. The mind, indeed, is the abode.[120] (V. i. 5)

The prānas (sense-organs) disputed among themselves about who was the best [among them], [each] saying: 'I am better,' 'I am better.' (V. i. 6)

They went to Prajāpati, their progenitor, and said: 'O revered Sir, who is the best among us?'
He said to them: 'He by whose departure the body looks worse than the worst is the best among you.' (V. i. 7)

The organ of speech departed. After being away for a whole year, it came back and said: 'How have you been able to live without me?' The other organs replied: 'We lived just as dumb people live, without

---

[116] The prāna is said to be the oldest among the sense-organs because, while the child is in the womb, the prāna functions first and then the other sense-organs begin to function.

[117] The eloquent person becomes rich, defeats his opponents, and lives in splendour. The result is determined by the nature of the object of meditation.

[118] It is with the help of the eye that one remains firm in rough as well as in smooth places. He who knows this lives firmly in rough and smooth times, in both this world and the next.

[119] With the help of the ears the Vedas are heard, and then their meaning is understood. One versed in the Vedas performs sacrifices by which he obtains all desirable objects.

[120] The mind is the abode or support of the impressions of the objects gathered by the sense-organs.

speaking, but breathing with the prāna (nose), seeing with the eye, hearing with the ear, and thinking with the mind.' Then the organ of speech entered [the body]. (V. i. 8)

The eye departed. After being away for a whole year, it came back and said: 'How have you been able to live without me?' The other organs replied: 'We lived just as blind people live, without seeing, but breathing with the prāna, speaking with the tongue, hearing with the ear, and thinking with the mind.' Then the eye entered [the body]. (V. i. 9)

The ear went out. After being away for a whole year, it came back and said: 'How have you been able to live without me?' The other organs replied: 'We lived just as deaf people live, without hearing, but breathing with the prāna, speaking with the tongue, seeing with the eye, and thinking with the mind.' Then the ear entered [the body]. (V. i. 10)

The mind went out. After being away for a whole year, it came back and said: 'How have you been able to live without me?' The other organs replied: 'We lived just like children whose minds are not yet formed, without thinking with the mind, but breathing with the prāna, speaking with the tongue, seeing with the eye, and hearing with the ear.' Then the mind entered [the body]. (V. i. 11)

Then as the vital breath was about to depart, he uprooted the organs [from their places] just as a noble horse tears up the pegs to which its feet are tied. They came to him and said: 'Revered Sir, be thou our lord; thou art the best among us. Do not depart from us.' (V. i. 12)

Then the organ of speech said to him: 'That attribute of being most excellent which I possess is thine.'
Then the eye said: 'That attribute of firmness which I possess is thine.' (V. i. 13)

Then the ear said: 'That attribute of prosperity which I possess is thine.'
Then the mind said: 'That attribute of being the abode which I possess is thine.' (V. i. 14)

And people do not call them (i.e. the sense-organs) the organs of speech, the eyes, the ears, or the mind, but the prānas. The prāna alone is all these. (V. i. 15)

The prāna said: 'What will be my food?'
They answered: 'Whatever food there is—including that of dogs and birds.'[121]

---

[121] Whatever food is eaten by living beings belongs to the prāna; that is to say, it is eaten by the prāna alone.

[The Upanishad says:] All that [is eaten] is the food of the ana. Ana is his (i.e. the prāna's) direct name. For one who knows this, there exists nothing which is not food.[122] (V. ii. 1)

He said: 'What will be my dress?'
They answered: 'Water.' Therefore when people eat they cover him (the prāna), both before and after eating, with water.[123] Thus the prāna obtains clothing and is no longer naked. (V. ii. 2)

Satyakāma the son of Jabālā explained this [doctrine of the prāna] to Gośruti, the son of Vyāghrapada, and said: 'If one should tell this to a dry stump, branches would grow and leaves spring forth.' (V. ii. 3)

Śvetaketu the grandson of Aruna came to the assembly of the Panchālas. Pravāhana[124] the son of Jibala said to him: 'Boy, has your father instructed you?'[125]
'Yes, revered Sir,' he replied. (V. iii. 1)

[The king said:] 'Do you know to what place men go after departing from here?'
'No, revered Sir.'
'Do you know how they return again?'
'No, revered Sir.'
'Do you know where the paths leading to the gods and leading to the Manes separate?'
'No, revered Sir.' (V. iii. 2)

'Do you know why yonder world[126] is not filled up?'[127]
'No, revered Sir.'
'Do you know how water, in the fifth oblation, comes to be called man?'
'No, revered Sir.' (V. iii. 3)

---

[122] A person who knows himself to be the prāna, residing in all beings, and the eater of all foods—for such a person there is nothing that is not eatable; everything becomes his food.

[123] People take a sip of water both before and after a meal. This is to be symbolically regarded as the wearing-cloth and wrap for the prāna.

[124] The king of the Panchālas.

[125] Through this story the various ways of rebirth are described in order to create, in the mind of the aspirant, dispassion for all objects, ranging from a blade of grass to Hiranyagarbha. Only when he has cultivated dispassion is he qualified for the Knowledge of Brahman, which bestows Liberation.

[126] The World of the Moon.

[127] In spite of the fact that many people go there.

'Then why did you say that you had been instructed? How could he
who did not know these things say that he had been instructed?'

Then Śvetaketu went back to his father with a sorrowful mind and
said to him: 'Revered Sir, you told me that you had instructed me,
though you had not instructed me. (V. iii. 4)

'That fellow of a kshatriya asked me five questions, and I could not
answer one of them.'

The father said: 'As you have stated these [questions] to me, [let me
assure you that] I do not know even one of them. If I had known them,
why should I not have told them to you?' (V. iii. 5)

Then Gautama went to the king's place. When he arrived the king
showed him proper respect. Next morning, when the king came to the
assembly, Gautama, too, came there.

The king said to him: 'Gautama, Sir, ask of me a boon relating to
human wealth.'

He replied: 'May human wealth remain with you. Tell me that
speech which you addressed to my boy.'

The king became sad.[128] (V. iii. 6)

The king commanded him: 'Stay with me for a long time.'

Then he said to him: 'As to what you have told me, O Gautama, this
knowledge did not reach any brāhmin before you. Thus it was to the
kshatriya alone, among all the people, that the teaching [of this knowl-
edge] belonged.'

Then he began [to teach him]: (V. iii. 7)

'Yonder world[129] is the [sacrificial] fire, O Gautama, the sun the fuel,
the rays the smoke, daytime the flame, the moon the embers, and the
stars the sparks.[130] (V. iv. 1)

'In this fire the gods offer faith[131] as libation. Out of that offering
King Moon is born.' (V. iv. 2)

---

[128] The knowledge which Gautama sought was confined to the kshatriyas. The
brāhmins were ignorant of it. He was unwilling to part with this secret knowledge.

[129] Heaven. The sacrificer is asked to look upon heaven, which is not fire, as
fire. This is so with man, woman, etc., in the verses that follow. There are certain
points of resemblance upon which the meditation is based.

[130] The fifth question (V. iii. 3.) is taken up first for facility of understanding.

[131] The liquid libation that is offered with faith in the Agnihotra and other
sacrifices assumes a subtle form called apurva, which is denoted here by the word
faith (śraddhā). This apurva leads the sacrificer to various worlds (*Br. Su.* III. i.
5–6). The libations, as described in this section, assume more and more subtle
forms, of which faith is the most important part. The sacrificer, endowed with
faith, performs the sacrifice with the offering of liquid libations and as a result
rises up to heaven and is born, in the World of the Moon, as the moon.

'Parjanya (the god of rain), O Gautama, is the fire, the air the fuel, the cloud the smoke, lightning the flame, the thunderbolt the embers, and thunderings the sparks.[132] (V. v. 1)

'In this fire the gods offer King Moon as libation. Out of that offering rain is born.' (V. v. 2)

'The earth, O Gautama, is the fire, the year the fuel, the ākāśa the smoke, the night the flame, the quarters the embers, and the intermediate quarters the sparks. (V. vi. 1)

'In this fire the gods offer rain as libation. Out of that offering food is born.' (V. vi. 2)

'Man, O Gautama, is the fire, speech is the fuel, the prāna the smoke, the tongue the flame, the eye the embers, and the ear the sparks. (V. vii. 1)

'In this fire the gods offer food as libation. Out of that offering semen is produced.' (V. vii. 2)

'Woman, O Gautama, is the fire, her sexual organ is the fuel, what invites is the smoke, the vulva is the flame, what is done inside is the embers, the pleasures are the sparks. (V. viii. 1)

'In this fire the gods offer semen as libation. Out of that offering the foetus is formed.'[133] (V. viii. 2)

'Thus in the fifth libation water comes to be called man.[134] The foetus enclosed in the membrane, having lain inside for ten or nine months, or more or less, is born. (V. ix. 1)

'Having been born, he lives whatever the length of his life may be.[135]

132 On account of the similarities described in the text, Parjanya should be meditated upon as the fire of the Agnihotra sacrifice.
133 Water—that is to say, the liquid offering—designated as 'faith', is successively offered in the sacrificial fires of heaven, the rain-god, the earth, man, and woman. Out of these offerings are produced, in increasingly gross forms, the moon, rain, food, semen, and the fifth, called man. Thus the fifth oblation—that is to say, water transformed into semen—offered in the fire of woman, assumes a human form and speaks with a human voice.
134 Here is given the answer to the last question (V. iii. 3.) and is introduced the answer to the first question.
135 As long as his prārabdha karma, the past action which has determined his present longevity, lasts.

When he is dead, they carry him to the fire [of the funeral pyre] whence he came, whence he arose.'[136] (V. ix. 2)

'Those who know this[137] and those who, dwelling in the forest, practise faith and austerities go to light, from light to day, from day to the bright half of the moon, from the bright half of the moon to the six months during which the sun goes to the north, from [those] months to the year, from the year to the sun, from the sun to the moon, from the moon to lightning. There a person who is not a human being meets him and leads him to Brahman. This is the Path of the Gods (Devayāna). (V. x. 1–2)

'But those who, living in the village, perform sacrifices, undertake works of public utility, and give alms go to smoke, from smoke to night, from night to the dark half of the moon, from the dark half of the moon to the six months during which the sun goes to the south. But they do not reach the year.[138] (V. x. 3)

'From [those] months they go to the World of the Manes, from the World of the Manes to the ākāśa, from the ākāśa to the moon. This is King Soma. They are the food of the gods.[139] Them the gods eat. (V. x. 4)

'Having dwelt there [in the lunar world] till their [good] works are consumed, they return again the same way they came.[140] They [first] reach the ākāśa, and from the ākāśa the air. Having become air, they become smoke; having become smoke, they become mist;
'Having become mist, they become cloud; having become cloud, they fall as rain-water. Then they are born as rice and barley, herbs and trees, sesamum and beans. Thence the exit is most difficult; for whoever

[136] It is, in essence, the same fire from which he has been produced in due course through the various forms of libation, namely, faith, the moon, rain, food, and semen. The fire of the funeral pyre has been previously seen as the sun, the rain-god, the earth, man, and woman.
[137] The answer to the first question is now given.
[138] The way of the Gods and the Way of the Fathers separate from the funeral fire. (This is a part answer to the third question in V. ii. 2.) The followers of the Northern Path go from the northern solstice to the year and finally reach Brahmaloka. But the others, who follow the Southern Path, go to the southern solstice. Without going through the year, they ultimately reach the World of the Moon (Chandraloka).
[139] They become the food, that is to say, the objects of enjoyment of the gods, as men, women, and cattle are enjoyed by a king. The gods enjoy them as the master enjoys his servants. The servants, too, have their share of enjoyments. Thus the householders also experience pleasures in the lunar world.
[140] This is the answer to the second question (V. iii. 2).

[capable of begetting children] eats that food and injects semen, they become like unto him.[141] (V. x. 5–6)

'Those whose conduct here [on earth] has been good will quickly attain some good birth—birth as a brāhmin, birth as a kshatriya, or birth as a vaiśya. But those whose conduct here has been evil will quickly attain some evil birth—birth as a dog, birth as a pig, or birth as a chandāla. (V. x. 7)

'[Those who do not practise meditation or perform rituals] do not follow either of these ways. They become those insignificant creatures[142] which are continually revolving and about which it may be said: "Live and die." This is the third place.

'Therefore that world never becomes full.[143] Let a man despise this course. To this end there is the following verse: (V. x. 8)

' "A man who steals the gold [of a brāhmin], he (i.e. a brāhmin) who drinks liquor, he who dishonours his teacher's bed, and he who kills a brāhmin—these four fall, as also a fifth who associates with them." (V. x. 9)

'But he who knows these Five Fires is not stained by sin even though associating with them. He becomes pure and clean, and obtains the world of the blessed—he who knows this, yea, he who knows this.' (V. x. 10)

Prāchinaśāla the son of Upamanyu, Satyayajna the son of Pulusha, Indradyumna the grandson of Bhallavi, Jana the son of Śarkarāksha,

---

[141] When the food containing the soul is eaten by a person capable of procreation, the soul enters that person and goes into his semen. Then the semen is poured into the womb at the right time, and the latent soul becomes the foetus and lies in the mother's womb in the shape of the father. Different kinds of future are indicated for departed souls. There is the Devayāna, or Way of the Gods, which is followed by the ascetics, brahmachārins, vānaprasthins, and those who are versed in the doctrine of the Five Fires. Those who go by this path ultimately reach Brahmaloka. The performers of the Agnihotra and other sacrifices, and the philanthropists, follow the Pitriyāna, or Way of the Manes, and reach the lunar world (Chandraloka), where they experience the results of their action. The residuum of their action brings them back to earth. There are some who engage in sinful actions and as a result are born immediately after death as cereals, etc., and, having experienced the fruit of their action, are born again as human beings. Then there are the extremely wicked and also the knowers of Brahman. The former are born as insects; the latter go beyond birth and death and attain Liberation.

[142] Like flies and mosquitoes.

[143] It is because of the fact that those who proceed by the Southern Path return again to earth, and those who are neither ritualists nor philanthropists cannot go to the World of the Moon, that that world is not filled.

and Buḍila the son of Aśvatarāśva—great householders and great
scriptural scholars—came together and discussed the question:
'What is our self and what is Brahman?'[144] (V. xi. 1)

They solved the problem [with the words]: 'Revered Sirs, Uddālaka
the son of Aruna knows, at present, about the Vaiśvānara Self. Let us
go to him.'
They went to him. (V. xi. 2)

He (Uddālaka) concluded: 'These great householders and great
scriptural scholars will question me. [Perhaps] I shall not be able to tell
them everything. Therefore I shall direct them to another teacher.'
(V. xi. 3)

He said to them: 'Revered Sirs, King Aśvapati the son of Kekaya
knows, at present, about the Vaiśvānara Self. Let us all go to him.'
They went to him. (V. xi. 4)

When they arrived, the king ordered that proper respect should be
paid to each of them. The next morning, after leaving bed, he said to
them:
'In my kingdom there is no thief, no miser, no wine-bibber, no man
without a sacrificial fire, no ignorant person, no adulterer, much less
adulteress.

'Revered Sirs, I am going to perform a sacrifice. I shall give to you as
much wealth as I give to each priest. Please, revered Sirs, stay here.'
They said: 'If a person comes to another with a purpose, he should
tell the other only about that. At present, you know about the Vaiśvānara Self. Please tell us about Him.'
He said to them: 'I shall give you a reply tomorrow morning.' Next
morning they approached him with fuel in their hands. Without having
performed any initiatory rites,[145] the king said to them: (V. xi. 5-7)

'O Son of Upamanyu, whom do you meditate on as the Self?'
'Heaven only, venerable King,' he replied.
'The Self you meditate on,' said the king, 'is the Vaiśvānara Self
called the Good Light (Sutejas). Therefore one sees in your family the
Suta libation as also the Prasuta libation and the Āsuta libation, and
you eat food and see what is pleasing. Whoever thus meditates on the
Vaiśvānara Self eats food, sees what is pleasing, and has in his family
the glory of Brahman. That, however, is only the head of the Self.

---

[144] The question is related to the Universal Self called Vaiśvānara.
[145] A good teacher does not require of capable students any initiatory rites.
They do not have to stay at his house for a stipulated length of time rendering
him personal service or practising austerities.

Surely your head would have fallen off if you had not come to me.'[146]
(V. xii. 1–2)

Then he said to Satyayajna the son of Pulusha: 'O Prāchinayogya,
whom do you meditate on as the Self?'

'The sun only, venerable King,' he replied.

'The Self you meditate on,' said the king, 'is the Vaiśvānara Self
called the Universal Form (Viśvarupa). Therefore, one sees in your
family much and manifold wealth—there are ready the chariot with
mules, female servants, and gold necklaces—and you eat food and see
what is pleasing. Whoever thus meditates on the Vaiśvānara Self eats
food, sees what is pleasing, and has in his family the glory of Brahman.
That, however, is only the eye of the Self. Surely you would have
become blind if you had not come to me.' (V. xiii. 1–2)

Then he said to Indradyumna the grandson of Bhallavi: 'O Vaiyāghrapadya, whom do you meditate on as the Self?'

'The vāyu only, venerable King,' he replied.

'The Self you meditate on,' said the king, 'is the Vaiśvānara Self of
varied courses (Prithagvartmā). Therefore gifts come to you in various
ways, rows of chariots follow you in various ways, and you eat food and
see what is pleasing. Whoever thus meditates on the Vaiśvānara Self
eats food, sees what is pleasing, and has in his family the glory of
Brahman. That, however, is only the prāna of the Self. Surely your
prāna would have left you if you had not come to me.' (V. xiv. 1–2)

Then he said to Jana the son of Śarkarāksha: 'Whom do you meditate on as the Self?'

'The ākāśa only, venerable King,' he replied.

'The Self you meditate on,' said the king, 'is the Vaiśvānara Self
called Bahula (full). Therefore you are full of offspring and wealth, and
you eat food and see what is pleasing. Whoever thus meditates on the
Vaiśvānara Self eats food, sees what is pleasing, and has in his family
the glory of Brahman. That, however, is only the trunk of the Self.
Surely your trunk would have been destroyed if you had not come to
me.' (V. xv. 1–2)

Then he said to Budila the son of Aśvatarāśva: 'O Vaiyāghrapadya,
whom do you meditate on as the Self?'

'Water only, venerable King,' he replied.

'The Self you meditate on,' said the king, 'is the Vaiśvānara Self
called Rayi (wealth). Therefore you are wealthy and flourishing, and

[146] Evidently he meditated on the head as the complete Vaiśvānara, that is to
say, on a part as the whole. His head would have fallen off in a discussion, on
account of his cherishing this wrong view.

you eat food and see what is pleasing. Whoever thus meditates on the Vaiśvānara Self eats food, sees what is pleasing, and has in his family the glory of Brahman. That, however, is only the bladder of the Self. Surely your bladder would have burst if you had not come to me.' (V. xvi. 1–2)

Then he said to Uddālaka the son of Aruna: 'O Gautama, whom do you meditate on as the Self?'
'The earth only, venerable King,' he replied.
'The Self you meditate on,' said the king, 'is the Vaiśvānara Self called Pratishthā (the support). Therefore you are supported by off-spring and cattle, and you eat food and see what is pleasing. Whoever thus meditates on the Vaiśvānara Self eats food, sees what is pleasing, and has in his family the glory of Brahman. That, however, is only the feet of the Self. Surely your feet would have withered away if you had not come to me.' (V. xvii. 1–2)

Then he (the king) said to them all: 'You [being endowed with limited knowledge] eat your food, knowing that Vaiśvānara Self as if He were many. But he who worships the Vaiśvānara Self as the measure of the span [from earth to heaven] and as identical with the self, eats food in all worlds, in all beings, and in all selves. (V. xviii. 1)

'Of this Vaiśvānara Self the head is Sutejas (the Good Light), the eye Viśvarupa (the Universal Form), the prāna Prithagvartmā (of various courses), the trunk Bahula (full), the bladder Rayi (wealth), the feet Prithivi (the earth), the chest the Vedi (altar), the hair the [kuśa] grass [on the altar], the heart the Gārhapatya Fire, the mind the Anvahārya Fire, and the mouth the Āhavaniya Fire.' (V. xviii. 2)

Therefore the food that comes first should be offered as an oblation. The first oblation that he (i.e. the eater) offers, he should offer, saying: 'Svāhā to the prāna!' Then the prāna is satisfied.[147] (V. xix. 1)

The prāna being satisfied, the eye is satisfied. The eye being satisfied, the sun is satisfied. The sun being satisfied, heaven is satisfied. Heaven being satisfied, whatever is under heaven and under the sun is satisfied. They being satisfied, he (i.e. the eater or sacrificer) is satisfied with off-spring, cattle, food, brightness [of the body], and the light of Brahman. (V. xix. 2)

[147] The object now is to show that to him who knows the Vaiśvānara Self, the act of feeding himself is like feeding Vaiśvānara, and that feeding Vaiśvānara is the true Agnihotra.

The second oblation that he offers, he should offer, saying: 'Svāhā to the vyāna!' Then the vyāna is satisfied. (V. xx. 1)

The vyāna being satisfied, the ear is satisfied. The ear being satisfied, the moon is satisfied. The moon being satisfied, the quarters are satisfied. The quarters being satisfied, whatever is under the quarters and under the moon is satisfied. They being satisfied, the eater is satisfied with off-spring, cattle, food, brightness [of the body], and the light of Brahman. (V. xx. 2)

The third oblation that he offers, he should offer, saying: 'Svāhā to the apāna!' Then the apāna is satisfied. (V. xxi. 1)

The apāna being satisfied, speech (i.e. the tongue) is satisfied. Speech being satisfied, fire is satisfied. Fire being satisfied, the earth is satisfied. The earth being satisfied, what is under the earth and under fire is satisfied. They being satisfied, the eater is satisfied with offspring, cattle, food, brightness [of the body], and the light of Brahman. (V. xxi. 2)

The fourth oblation that he offers, he should offer, saying: 'Svāhā to the samāna!' Then the samāna is satisfied. (V. xxii. 1)

The samāna being satisfied, the mind is satisfied. The mind being satisfied, the rain-god is satisfied. The rain-god being satisfied, the lightning is satisfied. The lightning being satisfied, what is under the lightning and under the rain-god is satisfied. They being satisfied, the eater is satisfied with offspring, cattle, food, brightness [of the body], and the light of Brahman. (V. xxii. 2)

The fifth oblation that he offers, he should offer, saying: 'Svāhā to the udāna!' Then the udāna is satisfied. (V. xxiii. 1)

The udāna being satisfied, the skin is satisfied. The skin being satisfied, the air is satisfied. The air being satisfied, the ākāśa is satisfied. The ākāśa being satisfied, what is under the air and under the ākāśa is satisfied. They being satisfied, the eater is satisfied with offspring, cattle, food, brightness [of the body], and the light of Brahman. (V. xxiii. 2)

If, without knowing this [knowledge of the Vaiśvānara Self], one offers an Agnihotra oblation, it is like an oblation offered in dead ashes after removing the live coals.[148] (V. xxiv. 1)

---

[148] The purpose of this verse is to extol the performance of the Agnihotra sacrifice by a person who is endowed with the knowledge of the Vaiśvānara Self.

But if, knowing this, one offers an Agnihotra oblation, it is like an oblation offered in all the worlds, in all beings, and in all ātmans.[149] (V. xxiv. 2)

Even as the soft fibres of the ishikā reed, when thrown into fire, are burnt, so also are burnt all the sins of one who, knowing this, offers an Agnihotra oblation. (V. xxiv. 3)

Therefore even if a man who knows this gives what is left of his food to a chandāla, he verily offers it to his Vaiśvānara Self. On this there is the following verse:[150] (V. xxiv. 4)

'As here on earth hungry children gather around their mother, so do all beings gather around the Agnihotra sacrifice, yea around the Agnihotra sacrifice.'[151] (V. xxiv. 5)

[149] The food of all beings becomes his food. He eats through all. (Compare V. xviii. 1.)

[150] He who has realized that the same Self dwells in all is released from scriptural restrictions. He rises above all the laws regarding caste and untouchability.

[151] All beings expectantly wait to see when the knower of the Agnihotra sacrifice will eat his food. Because such a knower has realized his self to be the Self dwelling in all, by eating food himself he really feeds all. Through his eating the whole universe is satisfied.

VI

OM. THERE ONCE lived Śvetaketu the grandson of Aruna. To him his father[152] said: 'Śvetaketu, lead the life of a brahmachārin; for there is none belonging to our family, my dear, who, not having studied the Vedas, is a brāhmin only by birth.' (VI. i. 1)

Śvetaketu went to his teacher's house when he was twelve years old and studied the Vedas till he was twenty-four. Then he returned to his father, serious, considering himself well read, and arrogant.

His father said to him: 'Śvetaketu, since you are now so serious, think yourself well read, and are so arrogant, have you, my dear, ever asked for that instruction by which one hears what cannot be heard, by which one perceives what cannot be perceived, by which one knows what cannot be known?'

Śvetaketu asked: 'What is that instruction, venerable Sir?' (VI. i. 2–3)

'Just as, my dear, by one clod of clay all that is made of clay is known,[153] the modification[154] being only a name, arising from speech,[155] while the truth is that all is clay;

'Just as, my dear, by one nugget of gold all that is made of gold is known, the modification being only a name, arising from speech, while the truth is that all is gold;

'And just as, my dear, by one pair of nail-scissors all that is made of iron is known, the modification being only a name, arising from speech, while the truth is that all is iron—even so, my dear, is that instruction.' (VI. i. 4–6)

'Surely those venerable men did not know that. For if they had known it, why should they not have told it to me? [Therefore] do you, venerable Sir, tell me about it.'

'So be it, my dear,' said the father. (VI. i. 7)

[Āruni said:] 'In the beginning,[156] my dear, this [universe] was Being

---

[152] The son of Aruna; he was called Āruni Uddālaka.
[153] Because the effect is non-different from the cause.
[154] The Sanskrit word *vikāra* in the text means difference, variety, development, manifestation.
[155] That is to say, based upon mere words. The modification is not real; the only reality is the clay.
[156] That is to say, prior to the manifestation of names and forms. Before the creation no object could be cognized as 'this', differentiated from other objects by a name and a form. All that existed was Pure Being. At the present moment, also, the universe is Pure Being, but it is differentiated by names and forms.

(Sat) alone, one only without a second. Some[157] say that in the beginning this was non-being (asat) alone, one only without a second; and from that non-being, being was born. (VI. ii. 1)

'But how, indeed, could it be thus, my dear? How could being be born from non-being? No, my dear, it was Being alone that existed in the beginning, one only without a second. (VI. ii. 2)

'It (Being, or Brahman) thought:[158] "May I be many; may I grow forth." It created fire.[159] That fire thought: "May I be many; may I grow forth." It created water. That is why, whenever a person is hot and perspires, water is produced from fire (heat) alone. (VI. ii. 3)

'That water thought: "May I be many; may I grow forth." It created food (i.e. earth). That is why, whenever it rains anywhere, abundant food is produced. From water alone is edible food produced.[160] (VI. ii. 4)

'Of all these [living] beings, there are only three origins: those born from an egg, those born from a living being, and those born from a sprout. (VI. iii. 1)

'That Deity[161] thought: "Let Me now enter into those three deities[162] by means of this living self[163] and let Me then develop names and forms."[164] (VI. iii. 2)

'That Deity having thought: "Let Me make each of these three tri-

[157] Refers to the nihilists, who affirm a total non-existence.

[158] This verb suggests that Sat, or Being, is a conscious entity, and not unconscious, and that the universe is a thought of the Creator. According to the Sāmkhya philosophy, the cause of the universe is non-intelligent pradhāna, or matter.

[159] The *Taittiriya Upanishad* (II. i. 3.) says that from Ātman was produced ākāśa, from ākāśa air, and from air fire. In reality there is no contradiction between the two statements. The purpose of the present text is not to show the order of creation, but to emphasize that all things are produced from Being alone. Or the present text assumes that prior to the creation of fire, ākāśa and air were created.

[160] The three elements fire, water, and earth will presently be described as devatās (gods or divinities).

[161] Sat, or Being, which had produced fire, water, and earth (VI. ii. 3-4.).

[162] Namely, fire, water, and earth.

[163] The living self is only a shadow or reflection, as it were, of the Supreme Self, like the reflection of the sun in water or a mirror. The reflection of the Self in the buddhi is called the jiva. It is the jiva that experiences pleasure and pain.

[164] Name and form constitute individuality and create the idea of separation from Pure Consciousness.

partite," entered into these three deities by means of the living self and developed names and forms.[165] (VI. iii. 3)

'It made each of these tripartite; and how these three deities became, each of them, tripartite, that learn from me now, my dear. (VI. iii. 4)

'The red colour of [gross] fire is the colour of [the original] fire; the white colour of [gross] fire is the colour of [the original] water; the black colour of [gross] fire is the colour of [the original] earth. Thus vanishes from fire what is commonly called fire, the modification being only a name, arising from speech, while the three colours (forms) alone are true.[166] (VI. iv. 1)

'The red colour of the sun is the colour of fire, the white [the colour] of water, the black [the colour] of earth. Thus vanishes from the sun what is commonly called the sun, the modification being only a name, arising from speech, while the three colours alone are true. (VI. iv. 2)

'The red colour of the moon is the colour of fire, the white [the colour] of water, the black [the colour] of earth. Thus vanishes from the moon what is commonly called the moon, the modification being only a name, arising from speech, while the three colours alone are true. (VI. iv. 3)

'The red colour of lightning is the colour of fire, the white [the colour] of water, the black [the colour] of earth. Thus vanishes from lightning what is commonly called lightning, the modification being only a name, arising from speech, while the three colours alone are true.[167] (VI. iv. 4)

'It was just through this knowledge that the great householders and great Vedic scholars of olden times declared: "No one can now mention to us anything which we have not heard, thought of, or known." They knew all from these [three forms]. (VI. iv. 5)

[165] Pure Being made each of the three deities, or elements, the principal ingredient, and joined with it the other two as secondary ingredients. The process is as follows: It took half of the original fire and added to it one fourth of water and one fourth of earth, and thus created gross fire. The same process applies to the creation of gross water and gross earth.

[166] The three colours, or forms, constitute the visible fire. When these three colours are explained as belonging to the original fire, water, and earth, fire as it is commonly known disappears, and also the word *fire*. For fire has no existence apart from a word and the idea denoted by that word. Therefore what the ignorant designate by the word *fire* is false, the only truth being the three colours.

[167] All things being only modifications of Pure Being, the knowledge of Pure Being makes all things known. Hence it has been rightly said that by the knowledge of One, all things become known.

'Whatever appeared red they knew to be the colour of fire; whatever appeared white they knew to be the colour of water; whatever appeared black they knew to be the colour of earth.

'Whatever appeared to be unknown they knew to be the combination of these three deities (i.e. colours). Now learn from me, my dear, how these three deities, when they reach man, become each of them, tripartite. (VI. iv. 6–7)

'Food when eaten becomes threefold. What is coarsest in it becomes faeces, what is medium becomes flesh, and what is subtlest becomes mind. (VI. v. 1)

'Water when drunk becomes threefold. What is coarsest in it becomes urine, what is medium becomes blood, and what is subtlest becomes prāna. (VI. v. 2)

'Fire[168] when eaten becomes threefold. What is coarsest in it becomes bone, what is medium becomes marrow, and what is subtlest becomes speech. (VI. v. 3)

'The mind, my dear, consists of food, the prāna of water, and speech of heat.'
[The son said:] 'Please, venerable Sir, instruct me further.'
[The father said:] 'So be it, my dear. (VI. v. 4)

'That, my dear, which is the subtlest part of curds rises, when they are churned, and becomes butter. (VI. vi. 1)

'In the same manner, my dear, that which is the subtlest part of the food that is eaten rises and becomes mind. (VI. vi. 2)

'The subtlest part of the water that is drunk rises and becomes prāna. (VI. vi. 3)

'The subtlest part of the fire that is eaten rises and becomes speech. (VI. vi. 4)

'Thus, my dear, the mind consists of food, the prāna consists of water, and speech consists of fire.'
[The son said:] 'Please, venerable Sir, instruct me further.'
[The father said:] 'So be it, my dear. (VI. vi. 5)

[168] That is to say, oil, butter, and other fatty substances which generate heat in the body.

'A person, my dear, consists of sixteen parts.[169] Do not eat [any food] for fifteen days, but drink as much water as you like. Since the prāna consists of water, it will not be cut off if you drink water.' (VI. vii. 1)

Śvetaketu did not eat [any food] for fifteen days. Then he came to his father and said: 'What, Sir, shall I recite?'
His father said: 'The Rik, Yajus, and Sāman verses.'
He replied: 'They do not occur to me, Sir.' (VI. vii. 2)

His father said to him: 'Just as, my dear, of a great blazing fire a single coal the size of a firefly may be left, which would not burn much more than that, even so, my dear, of your sixteen parts only one part is left; and therefore with that one part you do not remember the Vedas. Now go and eat and you will understand me.' (VI. vii. 3)

Śvetaketu ate and approached his father. Then whatever his father asked him, he showed that he knew it. (VI. vii. 4)

Then his father said to him: 'Just as, my dear, of a great lighted fire a single coal the size of a firefly, if left, may be made to blaze up again by adding grass to it, and will thus burn much more,
'Even so, my dear, of your sixteen parts only one part was left, and that, when strengthened by food, blazed up. With it you now remember the Vedas. Therefore, my dear, the mind consists of food, the prāna consists of water, and speech consists of fire.'
After that he understood what his father said, yea, he understood it. (VI. vii. 5–6)

Uddālaka the son of Aruna said to his son Śvetaketu: 'Learn from me, my dear, the true nature of sleep. When a person has entered into deep sleep, as it is called, then, my dear, he becomes united with Pure Being (Sat),[170] he has gone to his own [Self]. That is why they say he is in deep sleep (svapiti); it is because he has gone (apita) to his own (svam). (VI. viii. 1)

'Just as a bird tied by a string [to the hand of the bird-catcher] first flies in every direction, and [then] finding no rest anywhere, settles down at the place where it is bound, so also the mind (i.e. the individual soul reflected in the mind), my dear, after flying in every direction and find-

---

[169] The subtlest part of the food adds to the strength of the mind, and this strength of the mind is divided into sixteen parts.
[170] He transcends his human form, brought about by contact with the buddhi. The self reverts to its own pristine nature of Pure Being.

ing no rest anywhere, settles down in the prāna (i.e. Pure Being);[171] for the mind (the individual soul) is fastened to the prāna (Pure Being). (VI. viii. 2)

'Learn from me, my dear, what hunger and thirst are. When a man is hungry, as they say, it is water that has led (i.e. carried away) what was eaten. Therefore, just as they speak of a leader of cows, a leader of horses, a leader of men, so do they speak of water as the leader [of food]. So, my dear, know this offshoot (i.e. the body) to have sprung forth [from a cause], for it cannot be without a root. (VI. viii. 3)

'And where could its root be except in food (earth)? And in the same way, my dear, as food, too, is an offshoot, seek for water as its root. And as water, too, my dear, is an offshoot, seek for fire as its root. And as fire, too, my dear, is an offshoot, seek for Being (Sat) as its root. Yes, all these creatures, my dear, have their root in Being, they dwell in Being, they [finally] rest in Being. (VI. viii. 4)

'When a man is said to be thirsty, it is fire that has led (i.e. carried away) what was drunk by him. Therefore as they speak of a leader of cows, a leader of horses, a leader of men, so do they speak of fire as the leader [of water]. So, my dear, know this offshoot (the body) to have sprung forth [from a cause], for it cannot be without a root. (VI. viii. 5)

'And where could its root be except in water? And in the same way, my dear, as water is an offshoot, seek for fire as its root. And as fire, too, my dear, is an offshoot, seek for Being as its root. Yes, my dear, all these creatures have their root in Being, they dwell in Being, they [finally] rest in Being.

'And how these three deities (fire, water, and earth), on reaching a human being, become each of them tripartite has already been said (VI. iv. 7). When a person departs hence, his speech merges in his mind, his mind in his prāna, his prāna in heat (fire), and the heat in the Highest Being. (VI. viii. 6)

'Now, that which is the subtle essence—in it all that exists has its self. That is the True. That is the Self. That thou art, Śvetaketu.'
'Please, venerable Sir, give me further instruction,' said the son.
'So be it, my dear,' the father replied. (VI. viii. 7)

---

[171] The human soul limited by the mind moves about during the waking and dream states, experiencing the pleasure and pain which result from desires and actions, which again are results of ignorance. It does not, however, obtain real peace from these experiences and at last settles down, in deep sleep, in Pure Being.

'As bees, my dear, make honey by collecting the juices of trees located at different places, and reduce them to one form,

'And as these juices have no discrimination [so as to be able to say]: "I am the juice of this tree," or "I am the juice of that tree"—even so, indeed, my dear, all these creatures, though they reach Pure Being,[172] do not know that they have reached Pure Being. (VI. ix. 1–2)

'Whatever these creatures are, here in this world—a tiger, a lion, a wolf, a boar, a worm, a fly, a gnat, or a mosquito—that they become again. (VI. ix. 3)

'Now, that which is the subtle essence—in it all that exists has its self. That is the True. That is the Self. That thou art, Śvetaketu.'
'Please, venerable Sir, give me further instruction,' said the son.
'So be it, my dear,' the father replied. (VI. ix. 4)

[The father said:] 'These rivers, my dear, flow—the eastern towards the east, and the western towards the west. They arise from the sea and flow into the sea. Just as these rivers, while they are in the sea, do not know: "I am this river" or "I am that river,"
'Even so, my dear, all these creatures, even though they have come from Pure Being, do not know that they have come from Pure Being. Whatever these creatures are, here in this world—a tiger, a lion, a wolf, a boar, a worm, a fly, a gnat, or a mosquito—that they become again. (VI. x. 1–2)

'Now, that which is the subtle essence—in it all that exists has its self. That is the True. That is the Self. That thou art, Śvetaketu.'
'Please, venerable Sir, give me further instruction,' said the son.
'So be it, my dear,' the father replied. (VI. x. 3)

[The father said:] 'If, my dear, someone were to strike at the root of this large tree here, it would bleed but live. If he were to strike at the middle, it would bleed but live. If he were to strike at the top, it would bleed but live. Pervaded by the living self, that tree stands firm, drinking in again and again its nourishment and rejoicing. (VI. xi. 1)

'But if the life (i.e. living self) leaves one of its branches, that branch withers; if it leaves a second, that branch withers; if it leaves a third, that branch withers. If it leaves the whole tree, the whole tree withers. (VI. xi. 2)

[172] That is to say, during deep sleep or at death.

'In exactly the same manner, my dear,' said he, 'Know this: This body dies, bereft of the living self; but the living self dies not.

'Now, that which is the subtle essence—in it all that exists has its self. That is the True. That is the Self. That thou art, Śvetaketu.'

'Please, venerable Sir, give me further instruction,' said the son.

'So be it, my dear,' the father replied. (VI. xi. 3)

[The father said:] 'Bring me a fruit of that nyāgrodha (banyan) tree.'

'Here it is, venerable Sir.'

'Break it.'

'It is broken, venerable Sir.'

'What do you see there?'

'These seeds, exceedingly small, venerable Sir.'

'Break one of these, my son.'

'It is broken, venerable Sir.'

'What do you see there?'

'Nothing at all, venerable Sir.' (VI. xii. 1)

The father said: 'That subtle essence, my dear, which you do not perceive there—from that very essence this great nyāgrodha arises.[173] Believe me, my dear. (VI. xii. 2)

'Now, that which is the subtle essence—in it all that exists has its self. That is the True. That is the Self. That thou art, Śvetaketu.'

'Please, venerable Sir, give me further instruction,' said the son.

'So be it, my dear,' the father replied. (VI. xii. 3)

[The father said:] 'Place this salt in water and then come to me in the morning.'

The son did as he was told.

The father said to him: 'My son, bring me the salt which you placed in the water last night.'

Looking for it, the son did not find it, for it was completely dissolved. (VI. xiii. 1)

The father said: 'My son, take a sip of water from the surface. How is it?'

'It is salt'

'Take a sip from the middle. How is it?'

'It is salt.'

'Take a sip from the bottom. How is it?'

'It is salt.'

'Throw it away and come to me.'

[173] The gross universe with all its names and forms proceeds from the subtle essence, or Pure Being.

The son did as he was told, saying: 'The salt was there all the time.' Then the father said: 'Here also, my dear, in this body, verily, you do not perceive Sat (Being); but It is indeed there.' (VI. xiii. 2)

'Now, that which is the subtle essence—in it all that exists has its self. That is the True. That is the Self. That thou art, Śvetaketu.' 'Please, venerable Sir, give me further instruction,' said the son. 'So be it, my dear,' the father replied. (VI. xiii. 3)

[The father said:] 'Just as someone, my dear, might lead a person, with his eyes covered, away from [the country of] the Gandhāras, and leave him in a place where there were no human beings; and just as that person would turn toward the east, or the north, or the south, or the west, shouting: "I have been brought here with my eyes covered, I have been left here with my eyes covered!" (VI. xiv. 1)

'And as thereupon someone might loosen the covering and say to him: "Gandhāra is in that direction; go that way"; and as thereupon, having been informed and being capable of judgement, he would, by asking his way from one village to another, arrive at last at Gandhāra— in exactly the same manner does a man who has found a teacher to instruct him obtain the true knowledge. For him there is delay only so long as he is not liberated [from the body];[174] then he reaches perfection. (VI. xiv. 2)

'Now, that which is the subtle essence—in it all that exists has its self. That is the True. That is the Self. That thou art, Śvetaketu.' 'Please, venerable Sir, give me further instruction,' said the son. 'So be it, my dear,' the father replied. (VI. xiv. 3)

[The father said:] 'Around a [dying] person afflicted [with illness], my dear, his relatives gather and ask: "Do you know me? Do you know me?" He knows them as long as his speech is not merged in his mind, his mind in his prāna (breath), his prāna in heat (fire), and the heat in the Highest Deity. (VI. xv. 1)

'But when his speech is merged in his mind, his mind in his prāna, his prāna in heat, and the heat in the Highest Deity, then he does not know them.[175] (VI. xv. 2)

174 Even a man who has attained perfection cannot avoid the fruit of the prārabdha action. Only after yielding its fruit is this action consumed; after death the man becomes completely free.

175 The manner of dying of the ignorant and the illumined person is the same. The former is born again as a phenomenal being—an animal, a man, or a god—as determined by his past action. The latter realizes at once his true Self and never returns to the world. He does not go to any sphere, solar or other, in order to attain Liberation.

'Now, that which is the subtle essence—in it all that exists has its self. That is the True. That is the Self. That thou art, Śvetaketu.'

'Please, venerable Sir, give me further instruction,' said the son.

'So be it, my dear,' the father replied. (VI. xv. 3)

[The father said:] 'My dear, they (i.e. the police) bring a man whom they have seized by the hand, and say: "He has taken something, he has committed a theft." [When he denies it, they say:] "Heat the axe for him." If he has committed the theft [but denies it], then he makes himself a liar. Being false-minded, he covers himself with falsehood, grasps the heated axe, and is burnt. Then he is killed. (VI. xvi. 1)

'But if he did not commit the theft, then he makes himself what he really is. Being true-minded, he covers himself with truth, grasps the heated axe, and is not burnt. He is released. (VI. xvi. 2)

'As that [truthful] man is not burnt [so also one who has known Sat is not born again]. Thus in That (Sat) all that exists has its self. That is the True. That is the Self. That thou art, Śvetaketu.'

Then he understood that Sat [from his father], yea, he understood it. (VI. xvi. 3)

VII

OM. NĀRADA APPROACHED Sanatkumāra [as a pupil] and said:
'Venerable Sir, please teach me.'
Sanatkumāra said to him: 'Please tell me what you already know.
Then I shall tell you what is beyond.' (VII. i. 1)

Nārada said: 'Venerable Sir, I know the Rig-Veda, the Yajur-Veda,
the Sāma-Veda, the Atharva-Veda as the fourth [Veda], the epics
(Purānas) and ancient lore (Itihāsa) as the fifth, the Veda of the Vedas
(i.e. grammar), the rules of the sacrifices by which the Manes are gratified, the science of numbers, the science of portents, the science of time,
logic, ethics, etymology, Brahma-vidyā (i.e. the science of pronunciation, ceremonials, prosody, etc.), the science of elemental spirits, the
science of weapons, astronomy, the science of serpents, and the fine
arts.[176] All this I know, venerable Sir. (VII. i. 2)

'But, venerable Sir, with all this I know words[177] only; I do not know
the Self. I have heard from men like you that he who knows the Self
overcomes sorrow. I am one afflicted with sorrow. Do you, venerable
Sir, help me to cross over to the other side of sorrow.'
Sanatkumāra said to him: 'Whatever you have read is only a name.[178]
(VII. i. 3)

'Verily, a name is the Rig-Veda; [so also] are the Yajur-Veda, the
Sāma-Veda, the Atharva-Veda as the fourth [Veda], the epics and the
ancient lore as the fifth, the Veda of the Vedas, the rules of the sacrifices
by which the Manes are gratified, the science of numbers, the science of
portents, the science of time, logic, ethics, etymology, Brahma-vidyā,
the science of elemental spirits, the science of weapons, astronomy, the
science of serpents, and the fine arts.
'Meditate on the name.[179] (VII. i. 4)

[176] The art of making perfumes, dancing, singing, playing on musical instruments, etc.
[177] That is to say, the outer meaning. It also signifies rituals.
[178] A name is a mere word or sound. Through words one cannot know the nature
of the Self. This is known only from a qualified teacher. The real Self, which is
beyond everything, cannot be denoted by words. Nārada, through his study, knew
only the modifications, and not the Ātman, which is beyond modification.
[179] Regarding the name as Brahman. It is like worshipping an image, regarding
it as Vishnu Himself.

'He who meditates on a name as Brahman can, of his own free will, reach as far as the name reaches—he who meditates on a name as Brahman.'

Nārada said: 'Venerable Sir, is there anything greater than a name?'

'Of course there is something greater than a name.'

'Please tell that to me, venerable Sir.' (VII. i. 5)

[Sanatkumāra said:] 'Speech is, verily, greater than a name.[180] Speech makes one understand the Rig-Veda, the Yajur-Veda, the Sāma-Veda, the Atharva-Veda as the fourth, the epics and the ancient lore as the fifth, the Veda of the Vedas, the rules of sacrifices by which the Manes are gratified, the science of numbers, the science of portents, the science of time, logic, ethics, etymology, Brahma-vidyā, the science of elemental spirits, the science of weapons, astronomy, the science of serpents, and the fine arts, as well as heaven, earth, air, ākāśa, water, fire, gods, men, cattle, birds, herbs, trees, animals, together with worms, flies, and ants, and also righteousness and unrighteousness, the true and the false, the good and the bad, the pleasant and the unpleasant.

'Verily, if there were no speech, neither righteousness nor unrighteousness would be known, neither the true nor the false, neither the pleasant nor the unpleasant.

'Speech, verily, makes us know all this. Meditate upon speech. (VII. ii. 1)

'He who meditates on speech as Brahman can, of his own free will, reach as far as speech reaches—he who meditates on speech as Brahman.'

Nārada said: 'Venerable Sir, is there anything greater than speech?'

'Of course there is something greater than speech.'

'Please tell that to me, venerable Sir.' (VII. ii. 2)

[Sanatkumāra said:] 'The mind is, verily, greater than speech. Just as the closed fist holds two āmalakas, or two plums, or two aksha fruits, so does the mind hold speech and name. For when a man thinks in his mind that he would read the sacred hymns, then he reads them. When he thinks in his mind that he would perform actions, then he performs them. When he thinks in his mind that he would have sons and cattle, then he desires them. When he thinks in his mind that he would have this world and the other, then he desires them. Mind, indeed, is the self; mind is the world; mind is Brahman.

'Meditate on the mind. (VII. iii. 1)

---

[180] Speech denotes the organ of speech, which gives expression to the letters, which, in turn, constitute a name.

'He who meditates on mind as Brahman can, of his own free will, reach as far as mind reaches—he who meditates on mind as Brahman.' Nārada said: 'Venerable Sir, is there anything greater than mind?' 'Of course there is something greater than mind.' 'Please tell that to me, venerable Sir.' (VII. iii. 2)

[Sanatkumāra said:] 'Will (samkalpa)[181] is, verily, greater than mind. For when a man wills, then he thinks in his mind, then he utters speech, and then he employs speech in [the recital of] a name. The sacred hymns are included in a name, and all sacrifices are included in the sacred hymns. (VII. iv. 1)

'Will, indeed, is the goal of all these [beginning with mind and ending in sacrifice]; from will they arise and in will they all abide. Heaven and earth willed,[182] air and ākāśa willed, water and fire willed. Through the will [of heaven and earth, etc.] the rain wills; through the will of the rain, food wills; through the will of food, the prānas will; through the will of the prānas, the sacred hymns will; through the will of the sacred hymns, the sacrifices will; through the will of the sacrifices, the world wills; through the will of the world, everything wills. Such is will. Meditate on will. (VII. iv. 2)

'He who meditates on will as Brahman can, of his own free will, reach as far as will reaches—he who meditates on will as Brahman.' Nārada said: 'Venerable Sir, is there anything greater than will?' 'Of course there is something greater than will.' 'Please tell that to me, venerable Sir.' (VII. iv. 3)

[Sanatkumāra said:] 'Consideration '(chitta)[183] is, verily, greater than will. For when a man considers, then he wills, then he thinks in his mind, then he utters speech, then he engages speech in [the recitation of] a name. The sacred hymns are included in a name, and all sacrifices are included in the sacred hymns. (VII. v. 1)

'Consideration is, indeed, the goal of all these [beginning with mind and ending in sacrifice]; from consideration they arise and in considera-

181 The Sanskrit word *samkalpa* in the text denotes the activity of the inner organ by which one discriminates between what ought to be done and what ought not to be done. Will implies conception, determination, and desire. When a person has determined what is to be done, then the desire to do it follows.
182 They appear motionless because they willed, as it were, to be so.
183 That faculty of the inner organ by which one can understand present events and also the past and the future. First the chitta realizes the true import of a situation, then the samkalpa (will) decides whether to react to it affirmatively or negatively, and finally the mind cherishes the appropriate desire.

tion they all abide. Therefore if a person is without consideration, even though he possesses much knowledge, people say of him that he is nothing, and whatever he knows [is useless]; for if he were [really] learned, he would not be so inconsiderate. But if a person is considerate, though he knows but little, to him people are eager to listen. Consideration, indeed, is the goal of all these; consideration is the self; consideration is the support. Meditate on consideration. (VII. v. 2)

'He who meditates on consideration as Brahman, he, being permanent, firm, and undistressed, obtains the worlds which are permanent, firm, and undistressed; he can, of his own free will, reach as far as consideration reaches—he who meditates on consideration as Brahman.'

Nārada said: 'Venerable Sir, is there anything greater than consideration?'

'Of course there is something greater than consideration.'

'Please tell that to me, venerable Sir.' (VII. v. 3)

[Sanatkumāra said:] 'Meditation (dhyāna) is, verily, greater than consideration. Earth meditates, as it were.[184] The mid-region meditates, as it were. Heaven meditates, as it were. The waters meditate, as it were. The mountains meditate, as it were. The gods meditate, as it were. Men meditate, as it were. Therefore he who, among men, attains greatness here on earth seems to have obtained a share of meditation. Thus while small people are quarrelsome, abusive, and slandering, great men appear to have obtained a share of meditation. Meditate on meditation. (VII. vi. 1)

'He who meditates on meditation as Brahman can, of his own free will, reach as far as meditation reaches—he who meditates on meditation as Brahman.'

Nārada said: 'Venerable Sir, is there anything greater than meditation?'

'Of course there is something greater than meditation.'

'Please tell that to me, venerable Sir.' (VII. vi. 2)

[Sanatkumāra said:] 'Understanding[185] is, verily, greater than meditation. Understanding makes one understand the Rig-Veda, the Yajur-Veda, the Sāma-Veda, the Atharva-Veda as the fourth, the epics and the ancient lore as the fifth, the Veda of the Vedas, the rules of sacrifices by which the Manes are gratified, the science of numbers, the science of portents, the science of time, logic, ethics, etymology, Brahma-vidyā,

---

[184] A yogi practising meditation is steady and firm. Thus from the fact that the earth is steady and firm, it appears that it is meditating.
[185] The knowledge of the meaning of the scriptures.

the science of elemental spirits, the science of weapons, astronomy, the science of serpents, and the fine arts; heaven, earth, air, ākāśa, water, fire, gods, men, cattle, birds, herbs, trees; animals, together with worms, flies and ants; and also righteousness and unrighteousness, the true and the false, the good and the bad, the pleasant and the unpleasant, food and taste, this world and yonder [world]. Meditate on understanding. (VII. vii. 1)

'He who meditates on understanding as Brahman attains the worlds of understanding and knowledge and can, of his own free will, reach as far as understanding reaches—he who meditates on understanding as Brahman.'

Nārada said: 'Venerable Sir, is there anything greater than understanding?'

'Of course there is something greater than understanding.'

'Please tell that to me, venerable Sir.' (VII. vii. 2)

[Sanatkumāra said:] 'Strength[186] is, verily, greater than understanding. One strong man causes a hundred men of understanding to tremble. When a man is strong he can rise. If he rises he can attend [on the teachers]. If he attends on them he can become their intimate companion [as a pupil]. If he is their intimate companion he can watch [their conduct], listen [to their instruction], reflect [on what he hears], become convinced [of what he reflects on], act, and enjoy the result [of action]. By strength the earth stands firm, by strength the mid-region, by strength heaven, by strength the mountains, by strength the gods and men, by strength cattle and birds, herbs and trees, and animals together with worms, flies, and ants, by strength the world stands firm. Meditate upon strength. (VII. viii. 1)

'He who meditates on strength as Brahman can, of his own free will, reach as far as strength reaches—he who meditates on strength as Brahman.'

Nārada said: 'Venerable Sir, is there anything greater than strength?'

'Of course there is something greater than strength.'

'Please tell that to me, venerable Sir.' (VII. viii. 2)

[Sanatkumāra said:] 'Food is, verily, greater than strength. Therefore if a man abstains from food for ten days, even though he might live, yet he would not be able to see, hear, reflect, become convinced, act, and enjoy the result. But when he obtains food, he is able to see, hear, reflect, become convinced, act, and enjoy the result. (VII. ix. 1)

[186] The power of the mind produced from food.

'He who meditates on food as Brahman obtains the world rich in food and drink; he can, of his own free will, reach as far as food reaches— he who meditates on food as Brahman.'

Nārada said: 'Venerable Sir, is there anything greater than food?'

'Of course there is something greater than food.'

'Please tell that to me, venerable Sir.' (VII. ix. 2)

[Sanatkumāra said:] 'Water is, verily, greater than food. Therefore if there is not sufficient rain, then living creatures are afflicted with the thought that there will be less food. But if there is sufficient rain, then living creatures rejoice in the thought that there will be much food. It is water that assumes the form of this earth, this mid-region, this heaven, these mountains, these gods and men, cattle and birds, herbs and trees, and animals, together with worms, flies, and ants. Water indeed is all these forms. Meditate on water. (VII. x. 1)

'He who meditates on water as Brahman obtains all his desires and becomes satisfied; he can, of his own free will, reach as far as water reaches—he who meditates on water as Brahman.'

Nārada said: 'Venerable Sir, is there anything greater than water?'

'Of course there is something greater than water.'

'Please tell that to me, venerable Sir.' (VII. x. 2)

[Sanatkumāra said:] 'Fire is, verily, greater than water. For, having seized the air, it warms the ākāśa. Then people say: "It is hot, it burns; it will rain." Thus does fire first manifest itself and then create water. Furthermore, thunderclaps roll with lightning upward and across the sky. Then people say: "There is lightning, there is thunder; it will rain." Here also does fire first manifest itself and then create water. Meditate on fire. (VII. xi. 1)

'He who meditates on fire as Brahman becomes radiant himself and obtains radiant worlds, full of light and free from darkness; he can, of his own free will, reach as far as fire reaches—he who meditates on fire as Brahman.'

Nārada said: 'Venerable Sir, is there anything greater than fire?'

'Of course there is something greater than fire.'

'Please tell that to me, venerable Sir.' (VII. xi. 2)

[Sanatkumāra said:] 'The ākāśa is, verily, greater than fire. For in the ākāśa exist both the sun and the moon, lightning, stars, and fire. It is through the ākāśa that a person calls [another]; it is through the ākāśa that the other hears; it is through the ākāśa that the person hears back. In the ākāśa we rejoice [when we are together], and in the ākāśa we rejoice not [when we are separated]. In the ākāśa everything is born, and towardthe ākāśa all things grow. Meditate upon the ākāśa. (VII. xii. 1)

'He who meditates on the ākāśa as Brahman obtains the worlds extending far and wide, luminous, free from pain, and spacious; he can, of his own free will, reach as far as the ākāśa reaches—he who meditates on the ākāśa as Brahman.'
Nārada said: 'Venerable Sir, is there anything greater than the ākāśa?'
'Of course there is something greater than the ākāśa.'
'Please tell that to me, venerable Sir.' (VII. xii. 2)

[Sanatkumāra said:] 'Memory is, verily, greater than the ākāśa. Therefore even when many people assemble, if they had no memory they would not hear anyone at all, they would not think, they would not understand. But surely, if they had memory, they would hear, think, and understand. Through memory one knows one's sons, through memory one's cattle. Meditate on memory. (VII. xiii. 1)

'He who meditates on memory as Brahman can, of his own free will, reach as far as memory reaches—he who meditates on memory as Brahman.'
Nārada said: 'Venerable Sir, is there anything greater than memory?'
'Of course there is something greater than memory.'
'Please tell that to me, venerable Sir.' (VII. xiii. 2)

[Sanatkumāra said:] 'Hope is, verily, greater than memory. Kindled by hope, [a person endowed with] memory reads the sacred hymns, performs sacrifices, desires sons and cattle, desires this world and the other. Meditate on hope. (VII. xiv. 1)

'He who meditates on hope as Brahman—all his desires are fulfilled through hope, his prayers are not in vain; he can, of his own free will, reach as far as hope reaches—he who meditates on hope as Brahman.'
Nārada said: 'Venerable Sir, is there anything greater than hope?'
'Of course there is something greater than hope.'
'Please tell that to me, venerable Sir.' (VII. xiv. 2)

[Sanatkumāra said:] 'The prāna[187] is, verily, greater than hope. As the spokes of a wheel are fastened to the nave, so are all these [beginning

---

[187] The prāna is the self of all, and includes action, the agent, and the result of action. It manifests itself in three principal forms: Hiranyagarbha, the external air, and the principal vital breath in a living creature.

with the name and ending with hope] fastened to the prāna. The prāna moves by the prāna. The prāna gives the prāna to the prāna.[188] The prāna is the father, the prāna is the mother, the prāna is the brother, the prāna is the sister, the prāna is the teacher, the prāna is the brāhmin. (VII. xv. 1)

'If one says something unbecoming to a father, mother, brother, sister, teacher, or brāhmin, then people say: "Shame on you! Verily, you are a slayer of your father, a slayer of your mother, a slayer of your brother, a slayer of your sister, a slayer of your teacher, a slayer of a brāhmin." (VII. xv. 2)

'But if, when the prāna has departed from them, one shoves them together with a poker and burns every bit of them, no one would say: "You are a slayer of your father, a slayer of your mother, a slayer of your brother, a slayer of your sister, a slayer of your teacher, a slayer of a brāhmin." (VII. xv. 3)

'The prāna, verily, is all this. He (i.e. the knower of the prāna) who sees this, reflects on this, is convinced of this, becomes an ativādi (superior speaker). If people say to such a man: "You are an ativādi," he may say: "Yes, I am an ativādi"; he need not deny it.' (VII. xv. 4)

[Sanatkumāra said:] 'But in reality he is an ativādi who has become an ativādi by the knowledge of the True.'
[Nārada said:] 'May I, venerable Sir, become an ativādi by the knowledge of the True.'
'But one should desire to know the True.'
'Venerable Sir, I desire to know the True.' (VII. xvi. 1)

[Sanatkumāra said:] 'When one understands the True, only then does one declare the True. One who does not understand the True does not declare It. Only one who understands It declares the True. One must desire to understand this understanding.'
'Venerable Sir, I desire to understand.' (VII. xvii. 1)

[Sanatkumāra said:] 'When one reflects, only then does one understand. One who does not reflect does not understand. Only one who reflects understands. One must desire to understand this reflection.'
'Venerable Sir, I desire to understand reflection.' (VII. xviii. 1)

---

[188] That is to say, all the different forms of agents, means, and results exist in the prāna, there being nothing apart from the Prāna.

[Sanatkumāra said:] 'When one has faith, only then does one reflect. One who does not have faith does not reflect. Only one who has faith reflects. One must desire to understand faith.'
'Venerable Sir, I desire to understand faith.' (VII. xix. 1)

[Sanatkumāra said:] 'When one is single-minded [in one's devotion to the teacher], only then does one have faith. One who does not have single-mindedness does not have faith. Only one who has single-mindedness has faith. One must desire to understand single-mindedness.'
'Venerable Sir, I desire to understand single-mindedness.' (VII. xx. 1)

[Sanatkumāra said:] 'When one performs one's duties (i.e. practises concentration), only then does one have single-mindedness. One who does not perform his duties does not have single-mindedness. Only one who performs his duties has single-mindedness. One must desire to understand the performance of duties.'
'Venerable Sir, I desire to understand the performance of duties.' (VII. xxi. 1)

[Sanatkumāra said:] 'When one obtains bliss, only then does one perform one's duties. One who does not obtain bliss does not perform his duties. Only one who obtains bliss performs his duties. One must desire to understand bliss.'
'Venerable Sir, I desire to understand bliss.' (VII. xxii. 1)

[Sanatkumāra said:] 'The Infinite is bliss. There is no bliss in anything finite. Only the Infinite is bliss. One must desire to understand the Infinite.'
'Venerable Sir, I desire to understand the Infinite.' (VII. xxiii. 1)

[Sanatkumāra said:] 'Where one sees nothing else, hears nothing else, understands nothing else—that is the Infinite. Where one sees something else, hears something else, understands something else—that is the finite. The Infinite is immortal, the finite mortal.'
'Venerable Sir, in what does the Infinite find Its support?'
'In Its own greatness—or not even in greatness. (VII. xxiv. 1)

'Here on earth people describe cows and horses, elephants and gold, slaves and wives, fields and houses, as "greatness". I do not mean this,' he said, 'for in such cases one thing finds its support in another. But what I say is: (VII. xxiv. 2)

'That Infinite, indeed, is below. It is above. It is behind. It is before. It is to the south. It is to the north. The Infinite, indeed, is all this.[189]

'Next follows the instruction about the Infinite with reference to "I": I, indeed, am below. I am above. I am behind. I am before. I am to the south. I am to the north. I am, indeed, all this.[190] (VII. xxv. 1)

'Next follows the instruction about the Infinite with reference to the Self: The Self, indeed, is below. It is above. It is behind. It is before. It is to the south. It is to the north. The Self, indeed, is all this.

'Verily, he who sees this, reflects on this, and understands this delights in the Self, sports with the Self, rejoices in the Self, revels in the Self. [Even while living in the body] he becomes a self-ruler. He wields unlimited freedom in all the worlds.

'But those who think differently from this have others for their rulers; they live in perishable worlds. They have no freedom in all the worlds. (VII. xxv. 2)

'For him who sees this, reflects on this, and understands this, the prāna springs from the Self, hope springs from the Self, memory springs from the Self, the ākāśa springs from the Self, fire springs from the Self, water springs from the Self, appearance and disappearance spring from the Self, food springs from the Self, strength springs from the Self, understanding springs from the Self, meditation springs from the Self, consideration springs from the Self, will springs from the Self, mind springs from the Self, speech springs from the Self, the name springs from the Self, the sacred hymns spring from the Self, the sacrifices spring from the Self—ay, all this springs from the Self. (VII. xxvi. 1)

'On this there is the following verse:
' "The knower of Truth does not see death or disease or sorrow. The knower of Truth sees everything and obtains everything everywhere."
'He (the knower) is one [before the creation], becomes three,[191] becomes five, becomes seven, becomes nine; then again he is called eleven, one hundred and ten, and one thousand and twenty.[192]
'[Now is described the discipline for inner purification by which Self-

[189] Now is explained why the Infinite does not rest upon anything. It is because there is nothing apart from the Infinite on which It could rest. The Infinite Itself is everything. Therefore It does not rest upon anything.
[190] The purpose of the text is to show the oneness of the Infinite and the jiva.
[191] That is to say, fire, water, and earth.
[192] The various numbers are intended to show the endless variety of forms the Self assumes after the creation. Again, at the time of dissolution, the Self returns to Its pristine unity.

Knowledge is attained:] When the food[193] is pure, the mind becomes pure. When the mind is pure the memory becomes firm. When the memory is firm all ties are loosened.'[194]

The venerable Sanatkumāra showed Nārada, after his blemishes had been wiped out, the other side of darkness. They call Sanatkumāra Skanda,[195] yea, Skanda they call him.

[193] The word *āhāra* in the text means anything that is taken in (āhriyatē) by the senses, that is to say, sounds, sights, smells, etc.

[194] Ties created by ignorance, which have accumulated through numerous births and which reside in the heart.

[195] The dictionary meaning of this word is 'wise man'. It is also a name of Kārtika, a son of the Divine Mother Durga. Śankara has not explained its meaning.

VIII

OM. THERE IS in this city of Brahman[196] an abode, the small lotus [of the heart];[197] within it is a small ākāśa.[198] Now what exists within that small ākāśa, that is to be sought after, that is what one should desire to understand. (VIII. i. 1)

If they (the pupils) should say to him (the teacher): 'Now, with regard to the abode, the small lotus, in this city of Brahman, and the small ākāśa within it—what is there in it that is to be sought after and what is there that one should desire to understand?'

Then he should say: 'As far as, verily, this [great] ākāśa extends, so far extends the ākāśa within the heart.[199] Both heaven and earth are contained within it, both fire and air, both sun and moon, both lightning and stars; and whatever belongs to him (i.e. the embodied creature) in this world, and whatever does not, all that is contained within it (i.e. the ākāśa in the heart).' (VIII. i. 2-3)

If they should say: 'If everything that exists—all beings and all desires—is contained in this city of Brahman, then what is left of it when old age overcomes it or when it perishes?' (VIII. i. 4)

Then he should say: 'With the old age of the body, That (i.e. Brahman, described as the ākāśa in the heart) does not age; with the death of the body, That does not die. That Brahman [and not the body] is the real city of Brahman. In it all desires are contained. It is the Self— free from sin, free from old age, free from death, free from grief, free from hunger, free from thirst; Its desires come true, Its thoughts come true. Just as, here on earth, people follow as they are commanded [by a leader] and depend upon whatever objects they desire, be it a country or a piece of land [so also those who are ignorant of the Self depend upon other objects and experience the result of their good and evil deeds]. (VIII. i. 5)

[196] That is to say, the body, which is a dwelling-place of Brahman. The body is compared to a royal city. As a royal city is protected by many officers of the king, so is the body protected by the various sense-organs, the mind, etc. They work for the benefit of the soul.

[197] The heart is compared to the royal palace. Its shape is like that of a lotus bud. Though Brahman pervades the entire body, yet Its presence is especially felt in the heart.

[198] The word *ākāśa* (*space*) denotes Brahman, because the latter is, like the ākāśa, incorporeal, subtle, and all-pervading.

[199] The individual is a replica of the universe. Whatever exists in the world also exists in the individual body.

'And just as, here on earth, whatever is earned through work perishes, so does the next world, won by virtuous deeds, perish. Those who depart hence without having realized the Self and these true desires[200]—for them there is no freedom in all the worlds. But those who depart hence after having realized the Self and these true desires—for them there is freedom in all the worlds. (VIII. i. 6)

'If he desires the world of the Manes, by his mere thought the Manes come to him. Having obtained the world of the Manes he is happy. (VIII. ii. 1)

'And if he desires the world of the mothers, by his mere thought the mothers come to him. Having obtained the world of the mothers, he is happy. (VIII. ii. 2)

'And if he desires the world of the brothers, by his mere thought the brothers come to him. Having obtained the world of the brothers, he is happy. (VIII. ii. 3)

'And if he desires the world of the sisters, by his mere thought the sisters come to him. Having obtained the world of the sisters, he is happy. (VIII. ii. 4)

'And if he desires the world of the friends, by his mere thought the friends come to him. Having obtained the world of the friends, he is happy. (VIII. ii. 5)

'And if he desires the world of perfumes and garlands, by his mere thought perfumes and garlands come to him. Having obtained the world of perfumes and garlands, he is happy. (VIII. ii. 6)

'And if he desires the world of food and drink, by his mere thought food and drink come to him. Having obtained the world of food and drink, he is happy. (VIII. ii. 7)

'And if he desires the world of song and music, by his mere thought song and music come to him. Having obtained the world of song and music, he is happy. (VIII. ii. 8)

'And if he desires the world of women, by his mere thought women come to him. Having obtained the world of women, he is happy. (VIII. ii. 9)

'Whatever country he longs for, whatever objects he desires, by his mere thought all these come to him. Having obtained them, he is happy. (VIII. ii. 10)

[200] They are produced from true thoughts and reside in the Self.

'These true desires are covered by what is false.[201] Though they exist always, yet they have a covering which is false. Thus, whosoever belonging to the embodied creature has departed from this life, him he cannot see in this world with his eyes.[202] (VIII. iii. 1)

'Those of his fellows who belong to him here, and those who are dead, and whatever else there is which he wishes for and does not obtain—he finds all that by going in there (i.e. into his own Self). For there, indeed, lie those true desires of his, covered by what is false.

'As people who do not know the spot where a treasure of gold has been hidden somewhere in the earth, walk over it again and again without finding it, so all these creatures day after day go into the World of Brahman[203] and yet do not find it, because they are carried away by untruth. (VIII. iii. 2)

'That Self abides in the heart. The etymological explanation of *heart* (hridayam) is this: This one (ayam) is in the heart (hridi); therefore It is called the heart. He who knows this goes every day [in deep sleep] to Heaven (i.e. Brahman, dwelling in the heart). (V III. iii. 3)

'Now, this serene being, after rising from this [physical] body[204] and attaining the Highest Light, reaches his own [true] form. This is the Self.' Thus he (i.e. the teacher, questioned by his pupils) spoke. [Continuing, he said:] 'This is the immortal, the fearless. This is Brahman. And of this Brahman the name is Satyam, the True.' (VIII. iii. 4)

This name *Satyam* consists of three syllables: *Sat, ti* and *yam*. That which is *Sat* signifies the Immortal; and that which is *ti* is the mortal; and *yam* binds[205] them both. Because this syllable binds both, therefore it is called *yam*. He who knows this goes every day [in deep sleep] to Heaven (i.e. Brahman, dwelling in the heart).[206] (VIII. iii. 5)

The Self is a dam, a [separating] boundary, for keeping these worlds

---

[201] That is to say, longing for the external objects of the senses, and capricious conduct to satisfy this longing.

[202] He exists all the time in the Self. But we search for him in the outside world and therefore cannot see him.

[203] That is to say, during deep sleep.

[204] After renouncing all attachment to the body.

[205] That is to say, controls.

[206] If the very letters constituting the word *Satyam*, which is a name of Brahman, have such rich significance, how much more rich is Brahman, which bears that name! This is a eulogy of Brahman, which should be the object of meditation.

apart.[207] This dam is not passed by day and night, by old age, death, and grief, or by good and evil deeds. All evils turn back from It, for the World of Brahman is free from all evil. (VIII. iv. 1)

Therefore, having reached this dam, he who is blind ceases to be blind, he who is miserable ceases to be miserable, he who is afflicted [with disease] ceases to be afflicted. Therefore, having reached this dam, the night becomes day; for the World of Brahman is lighted once for all. (VIII. iv. 2)

That World of Brahman belongs to those who realize It by means of continence (brahmacharya)—for them there is freedom in all the worlds. (VIII. iv. 3)

Now, what people call yajna (sacrifice), that is really continence. For he who knows [Brahman] obtains that World [of Brahman, which others obtain through sacrifice,] by means of continence.

What people call ishta (worship), that is really continence. For having desired (ishtvā) the Knowledge of the Self, by means of continence one realizes the Self. (VIII. v. 1)

Now, what people call the Satrāyana [sacrifice], that is really continence. For by means of continence one obtains from the True (Sat) the safety (trāna) of the self.

What people call [the vow of] silence (mauna), that is really continence. For after knowing the Self [from the scriptures] one meditates (manutē) on It. (VIII. v. 2)

Now, what people call [the vow of] fasting (anāśakāyana), that is really continence. For that Self does not perish (na naśyati) which one realizes by means of continence.

What people call the life of a hermit (aranyāyana), that is really continence. There are in the World of Brahman, in the third heaven from here (i.e. from earth), two seas, Ara and Nya by name, and also there is the lake called Airammadiya.[208] Furthermore, there are the Aśvattha tree, which showers soma-juice, and the city of Brahman (i.e. Hiranyagarbha), called Aparājita,[209] and the golden hall built by Brahman (Hiranyagarbha) Himself. (VIII. v. 3)

---

[207] The Lord, or the Self, has created this variegated universe according to the law of cause and effect, and ordered it according to the rules of caste and the stages of life. After the creation He keeps all things in their right places; otherwise there would be a great confusion, followed by destruction.

[208] Filled with a gruel which makes one exhilarated or intoxicated.

[209] Which is not won by anyone besides a brahmachārin.

The World of Brahman belongs to those who obtain by means of continence the seas Ara and Nya in the World of Brahman. For them there is freedom in all the worlds.[210] (VIII. v. 4)

Now, those arteries of the heart are filled with the essences of brown, white, blue, yellow, and red liquid substances.[211] Verily, the sun yonder is brown, it is white, it is blue, it is yellow, it is red. (VIII. vi. 1)

As a long highway runs between two villages, this one and that yonder, so do the rays of the sun go to both worlds, this one and that yonder.[212] They start from yonder sun and enter into these arteries; they start from these arteries and enter into yonder sun. (VIII. vi. 2)

When a man is asleep, with the senses withdrawn, and serene, and sees no dream, then he has entered into these arteries.[213] Then no evil touches him, for he has obtained the light [of the sun]. (VIII. vi. 3)

And when he becomes weak, then those sitting around him say: 'Do you know me? Do you know me?' As long as he has not departed from this body, he knows them. (VIII. vi. 4)

[210] The purpose of this section (VIII. iv. 1 to VIII. v. 4) is to extol brahmacharya, or continence, without which the Knowledge of Brahman is not attained. This is shown by pointing out the similarities between certain words, a method often followed by the rishis in the Upanishads. Thus continence is said to be identical with yajna, or sacrifice, because the words yo jnāta (he who knows, VII. v. 1) have a certain similarity to the word yajna. Ishtvā, a kind of worship, is compared to eshanā, desire; satrāyana to Sat, the True, and trāyana, protection; mauna, silence, to manana, meditation; anāsakāyana, fasting, to nas, to perish; and aranyāyana, the hermit's life, to Ara and Nya.

'All the fulfilled desires, as enumerated in chapters two to five, whether the finding again of our fathers and mothers, or entering the Brahmaloka, with its lakes and palaces, must be taken, not as material, but as mental only. On that account, however, they are, by no means, considered as false or unreal—as little as dreams are. [After all, the creation itself is the result of the thinking of the Sat.] Dreams are false and unreal, relatively only, i.e. relatively to what we see, when we awake, but not in themselves. Whatever we see in waking, also, has been shown to be false, because it consists of forms and names only; yet these names and forms have a true element in them, viz. the Sat. Before we know that Sat, all the objects we see in waking seem true; as dreams seem true in dreaming. But when once we awake from our waking by true knowledge, we see that nothing is true but the Sat. When we imagine we see a serpent, and then discover that it is a rope, the serpent disappears as false, but what was true in it, remains true.' (Max Müller).

[211] These substances are formed when the food is assimilated. The different colours are due to contact with the sun's rays.

[212] Refers to the solar orb and the body.

[213] That is to say, he has entered into the ākāśa of the heart by way of these arteries; for there is no cessation of dream perception unless one reaches Pure Being, which dwells in the heart.

When he departs from the body [if he is a mere ritualist and ignorant of Brahman] he then goes upwards by these rays [towards the worlds which he has gained by his meritorious work]. Or [if he is a knower of the doctrines of the ākāśa in the lotus of the heart, as described in VIII. i. 1] he then meditates on Om [and thus secures entrance into Brahmaloka]. Or [if he is ignorant he attains lower bodies]. The knower attains the solar orb as quickly as one directs one's mind from one object to another. This indeed is the door [to the World of Brahman] for those who know; for the ignorant it is closed. (VIII. vi. 5)

On this there is the following verse:
'There are one hundred and one arteries of the heart, one of which pierces the crown of the head. Going upwards by it, a man [at death] attains immortality. Other arteries, going in different directions, only serve as channels for his departing from the body, yea, only serve as channels for his departing from the body.' (VIII. vi. 6)

Prajāpati said: 'The Self which is free from sin, free from old age, free from death, free from grief, free from hunger, free from thirst, whose desires come true, and whose thoughts come true—That it is which should be searched out, That it is which one should desire to understand. He who has known this Self [from the scriptures and a teacher] and understood It obtains all the worlds and all desires. (VIII. vii. 1)

The devas (gods) and asuras (demons) both heard these words, and said: 'Well, let us search out this Self by searching out which one obtains all the worlds and all desires.'
Indra, among the gods, went forth, and Virochana, among the demons. Without communicating with each other, the two came into the presence of Prajāpati, fuel in hand. (VIII. vii. 2)

They dwelt there for thirty-two years, practising brahmacharya. Then Prajāpati said to them: 'For what purpose have you both been living here?'
They said: 'A saying of yours is being repeated [by learned people]: "The Self which is free from sin, free from old age, free from death, free from grief, free from hunger, free from thirst, whose desires come true, and whose thoughts come true—That it is which should be searched out, That it is which one should desire to understand. He who has known this Self and understood It obtains all the worlds and all desires." Now, we both have dwelt here because we desire that Self.' (VIII. vii. 3)

Prajāpati said to them: 'The person that is seen in the eye[214]—that is the Self.' He further said: 'This is immortal, fearless. This is Brahman.'

They asked: 'Venerable Sir, he who is perceived in the water and he who is perceived in a mirror—which of these is he?'

Prajāpati replied: 'The same one, indeed, is perceived in all these.' (VIII. vii. 4)

[Prajāpati said:] 'Look at yourself in a pan of water, and then what you do not understand of the Self, come and tell me.'

They cast their glance in a pan of water. Then Prajāpati said to them: 'What do you see?'

They said: 'Venerable Sir, we see the entire self even to the very hairs and nails, a veritable picture.' (VIII. viii. 1)

Prajāpati said to them: 'After you have well adorned yourselves [with ornaments], put on your best clothes, and cleansed yourselves, look into the pan of water.'

After having adorned themselves well, put on their best clothes, and cleansed themselves, they looked into the pan of water.

'What do you see?' asked Prajāpati. (VIII. viii. 2)

They said: 'Just as we ourselves are well adorned, well dressed, and clean, so, venerable Sir, are these two [reflections] well adorned, well dressed, and clean.'

Prajāpati said: 'This is the Self, this is immortal, fearless. This is Brahman.'

They both went away satisfied in heart. (VIII. viii. 3)

Prajāpati saw them [going] and said: 'They are both going away without having known and without having realized the Self. And whoever of these, whether gods or demons, follow this doctrine shall perish.'

Virochana, satisfied in heart, went to the demons and preached this doctrine (Upanishad) to them: 'The self (i.e. body) alone is to be worshipped here on earth, the self (i.e. body) alone is to be served. It is only by worshipping the self here and by serving the self that one gains both worlds—this and the next.' (VIII. viii. 4)

Therefore even today they say of one who does not practise charity, who has no faith, and who does not perform sacrifices: 'He is verily a demon'; for such is the doctrine of the demons. The demons deck the

---

[214] Prajāpati referred to the Supreme Self that is experienced by pure-souled yogis in meditation, with their eyes closed, as the Seer of seeing, that is to say, as Pure Spirit. The two disciples evidently understood, by Prajāpati's words, the figure that is imaged in the eye. They therefore asked if the reflection seen in the mirror or water was not the Self. Here the disciples confused the true Self with the body.

bodies of the dead with garlands and perfume, with raiment, and with ornaments, for they think that thus they will win the world beyond. (VIII. viii. 5)

But Indra, even before he had reached the gods, saw this difficulty: 'As this [reflection in the water] is well adorned when the body is well adorned, well dressed when the body is well dressed, clean when the body is clean, so this [reflection in the water] will be blind if the body is blind, one-eyed if the body is one-eyed, crippled if the body is crippled, and will perish if the body perishes.[215] (VIII. ix. 1)

'I do not see any good in this [doctrine].' He returned with fuel in hand.

To him Prajāpati said: 'Well, Indra, you went away with Virochana, satisfied in heart; now for what purpose have you come back?'

He (Indra) said: 'Venerable Sir, as this [reflection in the water] is well adorned when the body is well adorned, well dressed when the body is well dressed, clean when the body is clean, so this [reflection in the water] will be blind if the body is blind, one-eyed if the body is one-eyed, crippled if the body is crippled, and will perish if the body perishes. Therefore I do not see any good in this [doctrine].' (VIII. ix. 2)

'So it is Indra,' replied Prajāpati. 'I shall explain the Self to you further. Live with me another thirty-two years.'[216]

He lived with Prajāpati another thirty-two years. Then Prajāpati said to Indra: (VIII. ix. 3)

'He who moves about, exalted, in dreams—this is the Self, this is immortal, fearless. This is Brahman.'

Then Indra went away satisfied in heart. But even before he had reached the gods, he saw this difficulty: 'Although this [dream self] is not blind even if the body is blind, nor do its eyes and nose run when the eyes and nose of the body run; although this self is not affected by the defects of the body,

'Nor killed when it (the body) is killed, nor one-eyed when it is one-eyed—yet they kill it (the dream self), as it were; they chase it, as it were. It becomes conscious of pain, as it were; it weeps, as it were. I do not see any good in this [doctrine].' (VIII. x. 1–2)

---

[215] Indra wondered how, if the reflection cast by the body in water or in a mirror was the Self, it could be immutable, since it changes with the changes in the body.

[216] Prajāpati wanted Indra to cultivate more inner purity, so that he could understand the meaning of the instruction; for the Knowledge of the Self is indeed extremely subtle.

He returned with fuel in hand. To him Prajāpati said: 'Well, Indra, you went away satisfied in heart; now for what purpose have you come back?'

He (Indra) said: 'Venerable Sir, although this [dream self] is not blind even if the body is blind, nor do its eyes and nose run when the eyes and nose of the body run; although this self is not affected by the defects of the body,

'Nor killed when it (the body) is killed, nor one-eyed when it is one-eyed—yet they kill it (the dream self), as it were; they chase it, as it were. It becomes conscious of pain, as it were; it weeps, as it were. I do not see any good in this.'

'So it is, Indra,' replied Prajāpati. 'I shall explain the Self further to you. Live with me another thirty-two years.'

He lived with Prajāpati another thirty-two years. Then Prajāpati said to Indra: (VIII. x. 3–4)

'When a man is asleep, with senses withdrawn, and serene, and sees no dream—that is the Self. This is immortal, fearless. This is Brahman.'

Then Indra went away satisfied in heart. But even before he had reached the gods, he saw this difficulty: 'In truth it (i.e. the self in dreamless sleep) does not know itself as "I am it", nor these [other] creatures. It has therefore reached [in dreamless sleep] utter annihilation, as it were.[217] I do not see any good in this.' (VIII. xi. 1)

He returned with fuel in hand. To him Prajāpati said: 'Well, Indra, you went away satisfied in heart; now for what purpose have you come back?'

He (Indra) said: 'Venerable Sir, in truth it (i.e. the self in dreamless sleep) does not know itself as "I am it", nor these [other] creatures. It has therefore reached utter annihilation, as it were. I do not see any good in this.' (VIII. xi. 2)

'So it is, Indra,' replied Prajāpati. 'I shall explain the Self further to you, and nothing else. Live with me another five years.'

Indra lived with Prajāpati another five years. This made in all one hundred and one years. Therefore people say that Indra lived with Prajāpati as a brahmachārin one hundred and one years.

Then Prajāpati said to him: (VIII. xi. 3)

'O Indra, this body is mortal, always held by death. It is the abode of the Self, which is immortal and incorporeal. The embodied self is the

---

[217] As there were no objects to be experienced in dreamless sleep, Indra felt that there was no subject, either, to experience them.

victim of pleasure and pain. So long as one is identified with the body, there is no cessation of pleasure and pain. But neither pleasure nor pain touches one who is not identified with the body. (VIII. xii. 1)

'The wind is without body; the cloud, lightning, and thunder are without body. Now, as these, arising from yonder ākāśa[218] and reaching the highest light,[219] appear in their own forms,[220]

'So does this serene Being, arising from this body and reaching the Highest Light, appear in His own form.[221] [In that state] He is the Highest Person. There He moves about, laughing, playing, rejoicing— be it with women, chariots, or relatives, never thinking of the body into which He was born.[222]

'As an animal is attached to a cart, so is the prāna (i.e. the conscious self) attached to the body. (VIII. xii. 2–3)

'When the person in the eye resides [in the body], he resides where [the organ of] sight has entered into the ākāśa (i.e. the pupil of the eye); the eye is the instrument of seeing. He who is aware of the thought: "Let me smell this", he is the Self; the nose is the instrument of smelling. He who is aware of the thought: "Let me speak", he is the Self; the tongue is the instrument of speaking. He who is aware of the thought: "Let me hear", he is the Self; the ear is the instrument of hearing. (VIII. xii. 4)

'He who is aware of the thought: "Let me think this", he is the Self; the mind is his divine eye. He, the Self, sees all these desires in the World of Brahman through the divine eye, the mind, and rejoices. (VIII. xii. 5)

[218] The wind, cloud, etc., before they are seen in their visible forms during the rainy season, remain merged in the ākāśa as the Self remains merged in the body.

[219] The heat of the summer sun.

[220] The wind takes the form of the strong east wind etc., the cloud of a hill or an elephant etc., lightning of tortuous luminous lines, and thunder of thundering and the thunderbolt. Before the summer they remained invisible; now, coming in contact with the intense heat of the sun, they appear in their respective forms.

[221] The embodied soul, who in essence is non-different from the serene being, remains merged in the body during the state of ignorance, as the wind, cloud, etc., remain merged in the ākāśa. In that state he regards himself as born or dead, happy or miserable, etc. Then, being instructed by a teacher about his true nature, he rises from the body, as the wind, cloud, etc., rise from the ākāśa, reaches the Highest Light (i.e. the Knowledge of the Self), and recognizes his true nature, that is to say, relinquishes the notion that the body is the Self.

[222] The laughing, rejoicing, etc., are all mental, created by the mere will of the Self. The Self enjoys these pleasures as an inward spectator only, without identifying Himself with either pleasure or pain. He sees them with His divine eye. He perceives in all things His Self only. What from the relative standpoint are called objects, are to Him Brahman only.

'The gods meditate on that Self. Therefore all worlds belong to them, and all desires. He who knows that Self and understands It obtains all worlds and all desires.' Thus said Prajāpati, yea, thus said Prajāpati. (VIII. xii. 6)

'From the dark[223] I come[224] to the variegated;[225] from the variegated I come to the dark.[226] Shaking off evil as a horse shakes [dust] from its hair, freeing myself from the body as the moon frees itself from the mouth of Rāhu, I fulfil all ends and obtain the uncreated World of Brahman.'[227] (VIII. xiii. 1)

That which is called the ākāśa[228] is the revealer of names and forms. That within which these names and forms exist is, verily, Brahman. That is the Immortal; that is the Self.

[Now is stated a mantra:] 'I come to the assembly, the palace of Prajāpati.[229] I am the glory of the brāhmins, the glory of the kings, the glory of the vaiśyas. I wish to obtain that glory. I am the glory of glories. May I never go to the red and toothless, all-devouring, slippery place, yea, may I never go to it.'[230] (VIII. xiv. 1)

Brahmā told this [knowledge of the Self] to Prajāpati (Kaśyapa),[231] Prajāpati to Manu,[232] Manu to mankind. He who has studied the Vedas at the house of a teacher, according to the prescribed rules, during the time left after the performance of his duties to the teacher; he who, after leaving the teacher's house, has settled down into a householder's

---

[223] Denotes a deep colour and is used here to indicate Brahman as dwelling in the heart, on account of Its incomprehensibility.

[224] That is to say, either now through the mind, or after the falling of the body.

[225] That is to say, Brahmaloka, or the World of Brahman, where one finds many desires. The meaning of the passage is this: 'May I, through meditation on the inscrutable Brahman who dwells in the heart, attain the World of Brahman, where the diverse desires of a man are fulfilled.'

[226] That is to say, coming from Brahmaloka, I have entered the heart as Brahman for the purpose of manifesting names and forms. The meaning of the first sentence is this: 'As I have come to the heart from Brahmaloka, may I enter Brahmaloka from the heart.'

[227] The text is in the form of a mantra to be used for meditation and repetition.

[228] A name of Brahman.

[229] The word refers to Brahmā, endowed with four faces, who is the personification of the Cosmic Mind.

[230] The seeker prays that he may never be born again. The repetition is meant to show the extremely repugnant character of going to the womb through the female organ.

[231] That is to say, the Supreme Lord, through Brahmā, or Hiranyagabha, imparted the knowledge of the Self to Kasyapa.

[232] The son of Kaśyapa.

life and continued the study of the Vedas in a sacred spot and made others (i.e. his sons and disciples) virtuous; he who has withdrawn all the sense-organs into the Self;[233] he who has not given pain to any creature except as approved by the scriptures—he who conducts himself thus, all through his life, reaches the World of Brahman after death, and does not return, yea, does not return. (VIII. xv. 1)

[233] The monastic life is here indicated.

THE PEACE CHANT

OM. MAY THE different limbs of my body, my tongue, prāna, eyes, ears, and my strength, and also all the other sense-organs be nourished! All, indeed, is Brahman, as is declared in the Upanishads. May I never deny Brahman! May Brahman never deny me! May there never be denial on my part! May all the virtues described in the Upanishads belong to me, who am devoted to Ātman! Yea, may they all belong to me!

   Om. Peace! Peace! Peace!

GLOSSARY

āchārya: 'knowing or teaching the āchāra, or rules'; spiritual guide or teacher (especially one who invests the student with the sacrificial thread and instructs him in the Vedas, in the law of sacrifice and in religious mysteries); the title *āchārya* is affixed to the names of learned men.

adhvaryu (priest): any officiating priest in a Vedic sacrifice; (plural) the adherents of the Yajur-Veda; *priests of a particular class (as distinguished from the hotri, udgātri, and Brahmā)*, who had to measure the ground of the sacrifice, build the altar, prepare the sacrificial vessels, fetch wood and water, and bring the animal and immolate it (while engaged in these duties, they had to repeat the hymns of the Yajur-Veda).

Aditi: the devourer or experiencer; death; *name of Hiranyagarbha (Ka. Up.* II. i. 7) because, as the World Soul, He is the experiencer of sound, taste, and the other objects of the relative world; free, boundless; name of one of the most ancient Vedic goddesses, often mentioned in the Rig-Veda as the daughter of Daksha and wife of Kaśyapa, mother of the Ādityas and of the gods.

Āditya: belonging to or coming from Aditi; the name of seven deities of the heavenly sphere (the chief being Varuna, others being Mitra, Aryaman, Bhaga, Daksha, Anśa; that of the seventh is probably Surya or Sāvitri); *sometimes applied to a group of eight or twelve deities*; name of a god in general, especially of Surya (Sun); name of Vishnu in His incarnation as the Dwarf, or Vāmana (as son of Kaśyapa and Aditi).

Advaita: *non-duality*; the name of a school of Vedānta philosophy teaching the ultimate oneness of Brahman, embodied souls (jivas), and the universe (jagat), and the unreality of the last two apart from Brahman. (The chief and classic exponents of the Advaita philosophy are Gauḍapāda and Śankarāchārya; according to Advaita Vedānta, the purpose of the three canonical books of Hinduism, viz. the Upanishads, the Bhagavad Gītā, and the *Brahma Sutras*, is to establish the non-duality of ultimate reality.)

agni: *fire*; (with capital *a*) *the god of fire*; the sacrificial fire (of three kinds: Gārhapatya, Āhavaniya, and Dakshina); the fire in the stomach by which food is digested. (The two principal names by which the god of fire was known among the Vedic seers were Agni, because of his being the first among the gods to receive the offering at the sacrifice, and Jātavedā, because of his being nearly omniscient. *See Ke. Up.* III. 4.)

Agnihotra (sacrifice): a *Vedic sacrifice in which oblations (chiefly of clarified butter, milk, and curds) were offered to Agni, the god of fire.*

(Two kinds of Agnihotra are mentioned: the Nitya Agnihotra, to be performed daily, and the Kāmya Agnihotra, which is optional and to be performed on special occasions.)

Āhavaniya Fire: consecrated fire taken from the householders' perpetual fire called Gārhapatya and kindled for receiving oblations to the gods; the eastern of the three fires burning at a sacrifice. *See also* Gārhapatya Fire.

Ājāna: name of a heavenly world, also called the Devaloka or dwelling-place of the gods, which lies just above the Plane of the Manes. (Souls attain to this heaven as a reward for the performance of the social duties prescribed by the Smriti.)

ajnāna: same as avidyā and māyā; *nescience, ignorance*; a kind of metaphysical ignorance on account of which Brahman, or non-dual reality, appears as the material universe and embodied creatures. (The cause of this appearance remains inscrutable to the finite mind, which itself is a product of ajnāna. Ajnāna consists of the three gunas, namely, sattva or the principle of light, rajas or the principle of activity, and tamas or the principle of inertia, which are present in all phenomenal objects. Ajnāna can be destroyed only through the Knowledge of Brahman, when the phenomenal being attains to Liberation.)

ākāśa: often translated as ether, sky, space, or atmosphere; a subtle material substance which pervades the universe and is the vehicle of sound; the first of the five material elements to be evolved from Brahman, by the power of māyā, at the time of creation, the other four being vāyu (air), agni (fire), ap (water), and prithivi (earth). (The ākāśa, or space, inside the heart is often used as a symbol of Brahman because both are incorporeal and subtle.)

Ānanda: happiness; one of the three attributes of Ātman or Brahman in the Vedānta philosophy, the two others being Sat, or Existence, and Chit, or Consciousness.

antahkarana: the 'internal organ', which consists of manas or mind, buddhi or intellect, chitta or mind-stuff, and ahamkāra or egoity.

Anvāhārya Fire: the fire on the right, also called the Dakshina or Southern Fire, chiefly intended for offering oblations to the Manes. *See also* Gārhapatya Fire.

apāna: one of the five manifestations of the vital breath (prāna); it moves downward and out at the anus, ejecting unassimilated food. *See also* prāna.

Āranyaka: forest; forest-born, or relating to a forest; *name of a part of the Vedas included in the Brāhmana section, so called because it was either composed in a forest (aranya) or studied there,* describing upāsanā, meditations or symbolic worship, which can be used by a householder who has retired into the forest to spend the third stage of his life, as substitutes for actual sacrifice, the material accessories for which cannot be obtained in a forest. (The Upanishads, with rare exceptions, form the concluding part of the Āranyaka.)

Aryaman: *name of the deity identified with the eye and the solar orb*; name of an Āditya who is commonly invoked together with Mitra and Varuna; he is regarded as the chief of the Manes.

āśrama: the hermitage or abode of a holy man leading a life of retirement in the forest; any of the stages in the life of a brāhmin (according to some, of the members of the three upper castes), of which there are four: during the first, he is a brahmachārin, or student of the Vedas; during the second, he is a grihastha, or householder; during the third, he is a vānaprasthin, dwelling in the forest; during the fourth, he is a sannyāsin, or monk. Each āśrama has its prescribed duties and responsibilities.

asura: a spirit, good spirit; supreme spirit (said of Varuna); an evil spirit, opponent of the gods. (These asuras are often regarded as the children of Diti by Kaśyapa, and as such they are demons of the first order in perpetual hostility with the gods, and must not be confused with rākshasas, or monsters, who disturb sacrifices. *Iśa Upanishad* 3 speaks of the asuras as those who delight in material enjoyments and are devoid of Self-Knowledge; they may even live in the higher worlds, where they enjoy the fruit of their meritorious deeds performed on earth.)

Āsuta: a kind of libation of soma-juice in the Soma-sacrifice.

Aśvamedha: *see* Horse-sacrifice.

aśvattha: the well-known fig tree of India, whose branches go downward, strike root, and form new stems, one tree thus growing into a kind of forest; a symbol of the universe, with its root in Brahman and its branches (which include heaven, earth, hell, and all other spheres of relative existence inhabited by embodied or disembodied souls) extending downward.

Aśvins: 'the two charioteers'; name of two divinities (who appear in the sky before dawn in a golden chariot drawn by horses or birds; they bring treasures to men and avert misfortune and sickness, and are considered as the physicians of heaven).

Atharvan: *the hymns of the Atharva-Veda*; name of the priest who is said to have been the first to institute the worship of fire and offer Soma and prayers; (he is represented variously as a Prajāpati, as Brahmā's eldest son, as the first learner and earliest teacher of the Brahma-Vidyā or Knowledge of Brahman, as the author of the Atharva-Veda, as identical with Angiras, as the father of Agni, etc.)

Atharvāngirasa: (plural) *the hymns of the Atharva-Veda*; connected with the sacerdotal class called Atharvāngiras, descendants of Atharva and Angiras.

Atharva-Veda: *the name of the fourth Veda* (excluded from the Vedas proper by certain scholars), revealed to Atharvan and containing texts known as chhandas. (This Veda deals mainly with magic formulas, spells, and incantations, intended to counteract disease and calamities; it also discusses kingly duties and contains lofty spiritual truths; (the highly metaphysical *Māndukya Upanishad* belongs to the Atharva-Veda).

Ātman: (variously derived from *an*, to breathe; *at*, to move; *va*, to blow); *the self or soul*; essence, nature, peculiarity; (with capital *a*) the Supreme Soul or Brahman, (with small *a*) the individual soul (both are essentially identical, according to Non-dualistic Vedānta); the unchanging spirit in the universe and the individual creature; the experiencer (called Viśva or Vaisvānara) of the gross world during the waking state, the experiencer (called Taijasa) of the subtle or mental world during the dream state, and the experiencer (called Prājna) of the causal world during dreamless sleep; also called Turiya as the witness of the experiences of the three states.

avidyā: ignorance; in Vedānta philosophy, a kind of metaphysical ignorance which conceals the true nature of the non-dual Brahman through its concealing power (āvarana-śakti) and projects the universe of multiplicity through its projecting power (vikshepa-śakti); especially used with reference to Ātman, which in association with it appears as the individual embodied creature. *See also* ajnāna and māyā.

Aum: *see* Om.

Bādarāyana: *see* Vyāsa.

Bhagavad Gita: a sacred book of the Hindus (comprising eighteen chapters, from the twenty-fifth through the forty-second, of the section on Bhishma in the Hindu epic *Mahābhārata*); one of the three principal canonical books of the Vedānta philosophy (the other two being the Upanishads and the *Brahma Sutras*).

Bhagavān: an epithet of God signifying His six supernatural powers, namely, total majesty, righteousness, glory, affluence, knowledge, and renunciation; an epithet of such divinities as Vishnu, Śiva, Krishna, and Buddha; used as a term of respect while addressing a holy man.

bhakti: love of God, especially in His personal aspect; a religious discipline emphasizing attachment to God, and also devotion, trust, homage, worship, piety, and faith; regarded by dualistic philosophers as the sole means of salvation.

Bhrigu: name of a celebrated sage mentioned in both the Mantra and the Brāhmana section of the Vedas.

Bhuh: the earth (the first of the seven upper worlds, namely, Bhuh or Bhur, Bhuvah or Bhuvar, Svah or Svar, Mahah or Mahar, Janah or Janar, Tapah or Tapar, and Satya; the first three, called the great vyāhritis or mystical syllables, are pronounced after Om, by every brāhmin at the commencement of his daily devotions).

Bhuvah: one of the three great vyāhritis (utterances or declarations or mystical syllables) representing the earth. *See* Bhuh.

Brahmā: the Creator God; the first person of the Hindu Triad (the other two being Vishnu and Śiva); an epithet of Saguna Brahman (other epithets being Virāt, Hiranyagarbha, Sutrātmā, Prāna); mentioned in the Rig-Veda as the first-born when Brahman becomes conditioned by māyā; the first manifestation of the Impersonal Absolute endowed with the consciousness of individuality. (Brahmā identifies Himself with the totality of individuals. He is the presiding deity of Brahmaloka.)

Brahmā (priest): one of the four principal priests in a Vedic sacrifice (the others being the hotri, adhvaryu, and udgātri). The Brahmā priest, the most learned of the four, was required to know the three Vedas, supervise the sacrifice, and set right mistakes committed by the other priests.

brahmachārin: an unmarried student studying the Vedas and practising chastity; a young unmarried brāhmin who is a student of the Vedas (under a preceptor) and who practises chastity, self-control, and other spiritual disciplines; one belonging to the first āśrama or stage of life. *See also* āśrama.

brahmacharya: continence, chastity; the first of the four stages of life of a Hindu, when he studies the Vedas under a qualified preceptor and practises various spiritual disciplines. *See also* āśrama and brahmachārin.

Brahmaloka: the Plane or Heaven of Brahmā; the highest or most exalted plane in the creation, where Brahmā dwells. (Extremely pious souls go there after death, live in communion with God, and attain final liberation, that is to say, oneness with Brahman, at the end of the cycle; but those who go to Brahmaloka as a result of practising life-long brahmacharya or the performance of one hundred Horse-sacrifices come back to the earth.)

Brahman: (literally, growth, expansion, evolution, from the root *brih*) the non-dual, self-existent, impersonal Spirit, or the divine essence and source from which all created things emanate, by which they are preserved, and to which they return; the Absolute (not generally an object of worship but rather of meditation and knowledge). When associated with māyā, Brahman is called Saguna Brahman (Brahman with attributes), who is called the Creator, Preserver, and Destroyer of the universe.

Brāhmana: a portion of the Vedas, as distinct from the Mantra and Upanishad. (The Brāhmanas contain rules for the employment of the mantras, or hymns, at various sacrifices, with detailed explanations of their origin and meaning and numerous old legends; they are said by Sāyanāchārya to contain two parts: vidhi, or rules or directions for rites, and arthavāda, or explanatory remarks. Each Veda has its own Brāhmana. That of the Rig-Veda is preserved in two works, viz. the *Aitareya* and the *Kaushitaki*. The White Yajur-Veda has the *Śatapatha Brāhmana*; the Black Yajur-Veda has the *Taittiriya Brāhmana*; the Sāma-Veda has eight Brāhmanas, the best known of which are the *Praudha* and the *Shadvinśa*; the Atharva-Veda has one Brāhmana, called the *Gopatha*.)

Brahma Sutras: an authoritative treatise on the Vedānta philosophy dealing with the Knowledge of Brahman. (It is ascribed to Vyāsa and known by various names, such as *Bādarāyana Sutras*, *Vedānta Sutras*, *Vyāsa Sutras*, and *Śāriraka Sutras*. Śankarāchārya's commentary on this book, along with his commentaries on the Upanishads and the Bhagavad Gitā, is considered the most authoritative interpretation of Non-dualistic Vedānta. Other Vedāntists, such as the qualified non-dualists and the dualists, have also written commentaries on the *Brahma Sutras*.)

Brahmavidyā: the Knowledge of Brahman.

brāhmin: a member of the priestly caste; the highest caste in Hindu society.

Brihaspati: *the deity identified with speech and intellect*; name of a deity in whom piety and religion are personified (he is the chief offerer of prayers and sacrifices, and is represented as the priest of the gods, with whom he intercedes for men; in later times he becomes the god of wisdom and eloquence, to whom various works are ascribed).

buddhi: intellect; the discriminative faculty by which doubts raised by the mind are resolved; (in Vedānta) one of the four inner organs, the others being manas (mind or the doubting organ), chitta (the mind-stuff or storehouse of past impressions), and ahamkāra (ego or I-consciousness); the soul reflected in or conditioned by the buddhi is called the jiva; (in Sāmkhya) the second of the twenty-five categories.

chandāla: an outcaste in Hindu society; an offspring of a śudra father and a brāhmin mother.

Chandraloka: the Plane or World of the Moon, reached by the Southern Path (Pitriyāna), which is characterized by such unpleasant stages as smoke, night, the dark fortnight of the moon, and the winter months. (Householders who perform their daily obligatory duties and religious rites with a view to enjoying their results go, after death, to Chandraloka and afterwards return to the earth.)

chhandas: *sacred hymns of the Atharva-Veda* (as distinguished from those of the three other Vedas); the incantation hymn; the Vedas; the name of one of the Vedāngas, or auxiliaries to the Vedas; the name of a metre.

Chit: consciousness or knowledge. *See also* Sachchidānanda.

cosmology: name of the science dealing with the evolution of the universe. (The different systems of Hindu philosophy have different cosmologies, but all postulate a spiritual substance as the First Principle.)

cycle: a world period representing the duration of the universe between its states of manifestation and non-manifestation. After the dissolution of the universe (that is to say, of names and forms), the created beings, with the impressions of their past actions, return to the state of non-manifestation and remain merged in prakriti, or māyā. In the next cycle, initiated by the will of God, they become manifest again. The universe is without beginning or end, but is repeated in cycles. The patterns of names and forms are the same in every cycle. 'The Lord creates the sun and the moon in each cycle as they existed in a previous cycle.' (*Rig-Veda*.)

Dakshina Fire: the same as Anvāhārya Fire.

Darvi offering: a class of independent offerings which neither have subsidiary parts nor are subsidiary to any other sacrifice; oblations made with a ladle.

Death: the god of death personified as Yama; the dissolution of the physical body.

Devaloka: the World of the Gods; any one of the three or seven or twenty-one higher worlds.

deva(s): shining ones; gods (such as the god of fire, the god of wind, the god of water, etc.); sense-organs (*Iś. Up.* 4).

devatās: deities.

Devayāna: the way leading to the gods, also called the Northern Path (characterized by various luminous stages, such as flame, day, the bright fortnight of the moon, the bright half of the year when the sun travels northward, the sun, and lightning). Those who follow this path and reach Brahmaloka generally do not return to the earth.

dharma: duty, right, justice, virtue, religion; law or justice personified; (in Buddhism) the Law.

dikshā: initiation in general; consecration for a religious ceremony in which, among other things, the initiate wears a cord of munjā grass.

Dualism: a system of Hindu philosophy which asserts the reality of two principles, namely, the Supreme Being and the individual soul.

dvija: twice-born; a man of any one of the three castes of Hindu society; a brāhmin (reborn through investiture with the sacred thread); a bird or any oviparous animal (appearing first as an egg); a tooth (in growing twice).

Ekarshi Fire: name of a sacrifice described in the Atharva-Veda, through the performance of which one acquires concentration and mental purity.

Fathers, Way of the: the Southern Path, by which souls attain the Plane of the Moon. *See also* Chandraloka.

Five Fires: the symbolic names for the Plane of the Moon, rain-clouds, the earth, man, and woman, as described in *Chh. Up.* V. 4–8 in connexion with the soul's rebirth. (After the body is cremated, the soul ascends to the Plane of the Moon, where it enjoys the reward for its meritorious work done on earth. Next it falls into the rain-clouds. Then it falls as rain-water and is absorbed by cereals or other plants. Then it enters a man with his food and is transformed into semen. Lastly it enters a woman when the semen is injected into her womb. These are the successive stages, called the Five Fires, through which a soul passes before it is born again as a human being.)

Gāndhāra: a city in Afghanistan, its modern name being Kāndāhāra.

gandharva: member of a class of demigods. (A gandharva's habitation is the sky, or mid-region, and the heavenly waters. It is his special duty to guard the soma, which the gods obtained through his intervention. The gandharva is supposed to be a physician because the soma is the best medicine. He knows and makes known the secrets of heaven and divine truths generally. He is the parent of the first pair of human beings, as mentioned in *Ri.* X. x. 4, and has a peculiar mystical power over women, and for this reason is invoked in marriage ceremonies: *see Ath.* XIV. ii. 35–36. In the epic poetry, the gandharvas are the celestial musicians or heavenly singers.)

gandharvas (celestial): the musicians of heaven who have existed from the very beginning of creation.

gandharvas (human): a special kind of creatures who have the power of making themselves invisible at will, who have subtle bodies and senses, and who are expert in dancing and music. They possess the power of resisting heat and cold and the other pairs of opposites, and can command all material pleasures.

Gārhapatya Fire: the Householder's Fire, received from a householder's father and handed down to his descendents, in which oblations are offered to the gods. (One of the sacred fires, from which the two other sacrificial fires are lighted, it is never allowed to go out. The Āhavaniya Fire, in which the principal oblations to the gods are offered, is lighted from this fire and is placed to the east of the sacrificial altar, whereas the Gārhapatya Fire is placed to the west and the Anvāhārya or Dakshina Fire to the south).

gārhasthya: the second of the four āśramas (stages) of life, when a man marries and becomes a householder. *See also* āśrama.

Gaudapāda: the teacher of Govindapāda, who was in turn the teacher of Śankarāchārya; the famous author of the *Kārikā*, a commentary on the *Māndukya Upanishad*, one of the earliest systematic philosophical expositions of Advaita Vedānta.

gayā(s): the vital breaths (used only for the etymology of the word *Gāyatri*).

Gāyatri: *name of a very sacred verse of the Vedas repeated by every brāhmin at his morning and evening devotions*; also called Sāvitri from being addressed to the sun as the generator of life; personified as a goddess, the wife of Brahmā and the mother of the three Vedas; often mentioned in connexion with the amrita (nectar of immortality), both constituting, as it were, the essence of the sacred hymns in general; a song, a hymn; a hymn composed in the Gāyatri metre of twenty-four syllables (variously arranged, but generally as a triplet of eight syllables each); in a personified form regarded as the mother of the three upper classes in Hindu society. The Gāyatri mantra is as follows: 'Tat saviturvarenyam/bhargo devasya dhimahi/dhiyo yo nah prachodayāt.' ('We meditate on the adorable light of the radiant sun. May He stimulate our intellect.')

Gitā: same as Bhagavad Gitā.

gods: *see* devas.

gods (thirty-three): consisting of the eight Vasus, the eleven Rudras, the twelve Ādityas, Indra, and Prajāpati, who live on the oblations offered in the sacrificial rites.

gods (sacrificial): deities who have attained their celestial status through the performance of Vedic rituals. (They do not possess the Knowledge of Brahman.)

Gods, Way of the: *see* Devayāna.

guna(s): quality, peculiarity, attribute, or property; (in the Sāmkhya philosophy) *the name of the three ingredients or constituents of prakriti* (nature, or matter): the three gunas are sattva (having the property of goodness or virtue), rajas (having the property of passion), and tamas (having the property of darkness or ignorance), and they are present in varying proportions in all entities which are products of matter; (in the Nyāya philosophy) the twenty-four gunas which form the characteristics of all created things; (in Vedānta) the attribute of each of the five elements, namely, ākāśa, air, fire, water, and earth: ākāśa has sound for its attribute; air has tangibility and sound; fire has colour, tangibility, and sound; water has flavour, colour, tangibility, and sound; earth has all the preceding attributes with the addition of its own peculiar one, namely, odour.

guru: the spiritual teacher; a spiritual parent or preceptor from whom a youth receives the initiatory mantra or prayer, who instructs him in the scriptures, and who conducts the necessary ceremonies in connexion with his investiture with a sacred thread (the ceremony itself is performed by an āchārya, or priest.)

hamsa: *see* swan.

Hara: (literally) the destroyer (of ignorance); an epithet of Śiva or Rudra, the manifestation of Brahman in Its destructive aspect; the Supreme Lord (*Śvet. Up.* I. 10).

Hari: an epithet of the Lord, who takes away or destroys (hri) man's sin.

Hiranyagarbha: a name of Brahmā, the first manifestation of Brahman. (The word means, literally, 'Golden Egg'. This egg was formed from the seed deposited in the primordial waters by the self-existent Brahman on the eve of creation. The seed took the form of a golden egg, out of which Brahman was born as Brahmā, the Creator God.)

homa: sacrificial fire.

Horse-sacrifice: a celebrated ritualistic ceremony whose antiquity reaches back to the Vedic period. In later times the efficacy of this sacrifice was considered so high that a person performing one hundred of them was entitled to go to Brahmaloka or to displace Indra, the king of heaven, from his domain. Kings, in performing the Horse-sacrifice, spent enormous sums in gifts to brāhmins.

hotri (priest): an offerer of oblations in a Vedic sacrifice; especially a priest who at a sacrifice invokes the gods or recites the hymns of the Rig-Veda; one of the four classes of priests officiating at a sacrifice. *See also* Brahmā (priest).

Indra: *the deity identified with strength*; the god of the atmosphere and sky; the god of rain, who in the Vedic mythology rules over the deities of the mid-region and fights against and conquers, with his thunderbolt (vajra), the demons or forces of darkness. (His deeds are most useful to mankind, and Indra is therefore addressed in prayers and hymns more than any other deity; in later mythology, he is subordinated to the Triad of Brahmā, Vishnu, and Śiva, but remains the chief of deities in the popular mind.)

Iśāna: a ruler or master; the king of the luminous celestial orbs; *one of the older names of Śiva*; also a name of Vishnu.

Iśvara: *name of Saguna Brahman as the Lord of the entire universe*; Śiva; master, lord, king, husband.

jagat: the universe.

Jataveda: *one of the two epithets of the god of fire*, given on account of his being nearly omniscient; the possessor of whatever is born or created; he who is the knower of, or is known by, all created beings. *See also* Agni.

jiva: living being; the individual soul, as distinguished from the Universal Soul; a reflection of Brahman in the buddhi, or intellect. (According to non-dualistic Vedānta, Brahman, on account of māyā, appears as the jiva, which in essence, is one with It.)

jivanmukta: one who, even while living in the body, is liberated from ignorance and its effects, such as the notions of birth and death, pain and pleasure, and sickness and grief. *See also* jivanmukti.

jivanmukti: liberation from avidyā, or ignorance, while living in the body. (There is another kind of liberation, called videhamukti, which is attained only after the discarding of the body.)

jivātmā: a living or individual soul (as distinguished from the Paramātmā, or Supreme Soul).

jnāna: knowledge; (in Vedānta, with capital *j*) the Knowledge of Brahman, derived through meditation on the Supreme Spirit; (in Sāmkhya) knowledge about anything, cognizance.

Jnānakānda: a portion of the Vedas, comprising the Upanishads, which deals with the Knowledge of Brahman (as distinguished from the Karmakānda, which deals with rituals for the propitiation of the deities).

jnāni: a person illumined with the Knowledge of Reality; a follower of the path of jnāna.

karma: action; duty; social service; a religious act or rite (such as sacrifice performed for a future recompense) as opposed to Jnāna, or the Knowledge of Reality.

Karmakānda: the part of the Vedas dealing with rituals and sacrifices, which produces, for the agent, rewards on earth or in heaven.

Kāśi: name of one of the holy places in India, identified with modern Benares.

kośa: sheath; (in Vedānta) a term for the five sheaths, arranged one inside another, which constitute the various bodily frames enveloping the soul. (They are as follows: the annamayakośa or sheath of food, forming the sthula-śarira or gross frame; the prānamayakośa or sheath of the vital breath, the manomayakośa or sheath of the mind, and the vijnānamayakośa or the sheath of intellect—these three forming the sukshma śarira or subtle frame; and the ānandamayakośa or sheath of bliss, forming the kārana-śarira or causal frame.)

Kratus: name of a sacrifice (such as the Aśvamedha) which requires a sacrificial post for the slaughter of the animal.

kshatriya: member of the military or reigning order, which constitutes the second caste in Hindu society.

loka: *see* worlds.

Madhvāchārya: one of the chief interpreters of the dualistic system of Hindu philosophy, born in South India (AD 1199–1276).

Madra: name of a country in the northwest of India.

Maghavān: name of Indra (especially on account of his distributing gifts.)

Mahābhārata: a great Hindu epic, about 215,000 lines in length, describing the acts and contests of the sons of the two brothers, Dhritarāshtra and Pāndu, descendants of Bharata, who were of the lunar line of kings, reigning in the neighbourhood of Hastināpura (modern Delhi). (The epic, attributed to Vyāsa, consists of eighteen books, with a supplement called the *Hari-vamśa*.)

manas: the mind; the inner organ which consists of 'desire, deliberation, doubt, faith, want of faith, patience, impatience, shame, intelligence, and fear' (*Br. Up.* I. v. 3); the inner organ, which shapes into ideas the impressions carried by the sense-organs; (often applied to) one of four inner organs, which is the cause of doubt and volition, the other three organs being the buddhi (intellect), chitta (mind-stuff), and ahamkāra (I-consciousness).

Manes: ancestors, dead and deified, who accept offerings from their descendants. (They inhabit a higher world, which they have attained as a result of performing certain meritorious ceremonies while on earth, for the satisfaction of the souls of their own ancestors, and live a much longer life than that of ordinary mortals on earth.)

mantra: a Vedic hymn or a sacrificial formula; (with capital *m*) another name of the Samhitā part of the Vedas (containing the texts called Rik, Yajur, and Sāman) as opposed to the Brāhmana and the Upanishad; a sacred formula addressed to any individual deity; a mystical verse or a magical formula (often personified); incantation, charm, spell (especially as employed in modern times by the Śāktas to acquire superhuman powers.)

Marichi: a particle of light; a ray of light (of the sun or the moon); the name of one of the Prajāpatis or Lords of creation; mirage.

Marut(s): the gods in general; described in the Vedas as the sons of Rudra and Priśni, or the children of heaven or of ocean; reckoned in the Rig-Veda to be three times sixty in number; (in the later literature) designated as children of Diti, either seven or seven times seven in number; the god of wind and the regent of the northwest quarter of the sky; wind, air, breath.

Mātariśvā: (in the Vedas) name of the god of air, meaning etymologically 'he who travels in space'; name of the god of fire or of a divine being closely connected with him, who brought down the hidden fire to Bhrigu, and who is identified by Sāyanāchārya with Vāyu, the god of wind; the World Soul, or Sutrātmā, a manifestation of Saguna Brahman (*Iś. Up.* 4).

māyā: illusion; unreality; (in the Vedānta philosophy) a power inherent in Brahman and non-existent without It (in association with māyā, the attributeless Brahman appears to be endowed with the attributes of creation, preservation, and destruction; māyā is the material cause of the universe); (in Sāmkhya) identified with prakriti, and, as in Vedānta, the source of the visible creation; (with the Śaivas) one of the four snares which entangle the soul; (with the Vaishnavas) one of the nine Śaktis or powers of Vishnu; wisdom; extraordinary or supernatural powers. *See also* avidyā and ajnāna.

Mitra: *name of the deity identified with prāna and the day*; the deity controlling the sun; name of an Āditya (generally invoked with Varuna, and often associated with Aryamān; described in the Rig-Veda as calling men to activity, sustaining earth and sky, and beholding all creatures with unblinking eyes).

moksha: liberation; release from worldly existence or rebirth through the Knowledge of Brahman (non-dualism) or of the Personal God (dualism).

muhurta: a moment or any short space of time; a particular division of time (the thirtieth part of a day or a period of forty-eight minutes).

Nārada: known in the Purānas as a devarshi, or divine sage.

Nirguna Brahman: Brahman, or the Absolute, devoid of qualifying characteristics or indicative marks; Brahman in its aspect of pure and undifferentiated consciousness; also called the Para (Supreme) Brahman.

Nivid: a group of verses in the Rig-Veda giving the number of gods, recited in the eulogistic hymn to the Viśve-devas; name of particular sentences or short formulas inserted in a liturgy, and containing epithets or short invocations of the gods.

non-dualism: *see* Advaita.

nyāgrodha: the banyan or Indian fig tree, from the branches of which fibres descend to the earth, take root, and form new stems.

Om: also written Aum; *a symbol of both Saguna Brahman, or the Creator God, and Nirguna Brahman, or the attributeless Absolute; a word of solemn affirmation, sometimes translated by 'yes', 'verily', 'So be it'*; placed at the beginning of most Hindu spiritual treatises; uttered as a sacred exclamation at the beginning and end of a recital of the Vedas or at the beginning of a prayer; the symbol of the Gāyatri mantra, the essence of the Vedas. The three letters *A*, *U*, and *M* are symbols of creation, preservation, and destruction; of Brahmā the Creator, Vishnu the Preserver, and Śiva the Destroyer; of the three states of waking, dreaming, and dreamless sleep. The undifferentiated sound *m-m-m* which follows the utterance of the three letters is the symbol of Turiya, or transcendental consciousness. The word *Om* is held in high respect by the Buddhists and Jainas as well as by the Hindus.)

organs: according to Hinduism there are three sets of organs: the five organs of perception (eyes, ears, nose, tongue, and skin); the five organs of action (larynx, hands, feet, anus, and the organ of generation); and the four inner organs (manas or mind, buddhi or intellect, ahamkāra or I-consciousness, and chitta or mind-stuff). (The organs are physical in nature and function when controlled by a devatā, or deity, who is a manifestation of Brahman, or Pure Consciousness.)

orthodox: (in Hinduism) an orthodox philosophy must acknowledge the Vedas as its ultimate authority. (Buddhism and Jainism, which repudiate this authority, are regarded as heterodox.)

pāda: a quarter of a coin; about one third of an ounce.

paramahamsa: a sannyāsin or monk of the highest order.

Parjanya: a rain-cloud; the god of rain; name of one of the twelve Ādityas.

Patanjali: the author of the *Yoga Sutras*, a treatise on the Yoga system of Hindu philosophy, which deals principally with concentration and its methods, control of the mind, the separation of the soul from the body, and other similar matters; the author of the celebrated Sanskrit grammar, the *Mahābhāshya*.

paulkasa: son of a śudra father and a kshatriya mother.

Pitriloka: name of the world or plane where the Pitris (*see below*) dwell; same as Chandraloka. *See also* Chandraloka.

Pitris: deceased father, grandfather, and great-grandfather.

Pitriyāna: the way (the Southern Path) leading to the Pitriloka.

Pradhāna: (in Sāmkhya) the primary or unevolved matter, the source of the visible universe.

Prajāpati: the highest manifestation of Brahman, also known by such names as Hiranyagarbha, Virāj, Sutrātmā, and Prāna; Lord of creation (as a result of extremely meritorious action performed in the preceding cycle, a virtuous person attains in the present cycle the exalted position of Prajāpati, or Lord of creation); a divinity presiding over procreation; protector of life; a supreme god among the Vedic deities.

Prājna: the jivātmā, or individual soul, functioning in deep sleep. (The jivātmā functioning in the waking state is called Viśva or Vaiśvānara, and functioning in the dream state, Taijasa. Prājna, the knower *par excellence*, is the witness of the general consciousness, whereas Viśva and Taijasa experience the knowledge of particulars in the waking and dream states. Viśva, Taijasa, and Prājna are not three different souls, but three names by which Turiya, or Pure Consciousness, is known while functioning in the three states of waking, dreaming, and deep sleep.)

prakriti: (in Sāmkhya) name of the primordial matter prior to the evolution of names and forms, when the three gunas (sattva, rajas, and tamas, which are the ingredients of prakriti) remain in a state of equilibrium; (in Vedānta philosophy) māyā, as distinct from Brahman; original or natural form or condition of anything; nature, character, constitution.

prāna: breath; breath of life; sense-organ; an epithet of Saguna Brahman. (The prāna, according to Vedānta, is a manifestation, in the individual body, of the cosmic energy, also called prāna, which pervades all animate and inanimate objects. In the individual body it functions in five different ways and is given five different names: [1] prāna, the vital energy that controls breathing; [2] apāna, the vital energy that moves downward and out at the anus, and ejects unassimilated food; [3] vyāna, the vital energy that pervades the entire body; [4] samāna, the vital energy that carries nutrition to all parts of the body; [5] udāna, the vital energy by which the contents of the stomach are ejected through mouth, and the soul is conducted from the body at the time of death.)

Pranava: the syllable *Om* is called the Pranava in the Rig-Veda, and the Udgitha in the Sāma-Veda.

prārabdha: commenced, begun; (in Hindu philosophy) name of one of the three kinds of action, the other two being the sanchita and the āgāmi. (The prārabdha action, performed in a previous life, begins to bear fruit at the beginning of the present life, which endures as long as the impetus given to it by the prārabdha action lasts. The sanchita action, performed in a previous life and remaining stored up, will bear fruit in a future life. The āgāmi action, which is being performed in this life, will produce its result in a future life. According to Vedānta, the Knowledge of Brahman, like a fire, reduces to ashes all the three kinds of action. But even an illumined person reaps, as long as he lives, the fruit of his prārabdha action, though he remains undisturbed by it.)

Prastāva: a hymn of the Sāma-Veda.

prastotā: the prastotri priest, the singer of the Prastāva.

Prasuta: a kind of libation of soma juice in the Soma-sacrifice.

Pratihāra: a hymn of the Sāma-Veda.

pratihartā: the pratihārtri priest, the singer of the Pratihāra.

psychology: the science of the soul, which treats of the sense-organs, the prānas, the three bodies (gross, subtle, and causal), the three states (waking, dreaming, and deep sleep), eschatalogy, and similar subjects.

Purānas: books of Hindu mythology; name of a class of sacred works attributed to Vyāsa. (The chief Purānas are eighteen in number, grouped in three divisions: [1] Rājasa, exalting Brahmā: the *Brahmā Purāna, Brahmānda P., Brahmavaivarta P., Mārkandeya P., Bhavishya P., Vāmana P.*; [2] Sāttvika, exalting Vishnu: the *Vishnu P., Bhāgavata P., Nāradiya P., Garuda P., Padma P., Varāha P.*; [3] Tāmasa, exalting Śiva: the *Śiva P., Linga P., Skanda P., Agni P.* or in place of it *Vāyu P., Matsya P., Kurma P.*

purusha: man; a human being; (with capital *p*) *the Supreme Being*, the Soul of the universe; (in Vedānta) the all-pervading Absolute, also the Spirit that dwells in the body; (in Sāmkhya philosophy) the conscious but passive principle by whose mere presence prakriti evolves the diversified universe.

Pushan: the nourisher; he who nourishes through work; an epithet of the śudra caste (*Br. Up.* I. iv. 13).

Qualified Non-dualism: a system of Hindu philosophy whose chief exponent was Rāmānuja (AD 1017–1137), according to which ultimate reality, though non-dual, admits the distinctions of God, living beings, and nature.

Rāhu: a demon in Hindu mythology who swallows the sun and the moon and thus causes the solar and lunar eclipses.

Rājanya: princely; a man of regal or military caste; ancient name of the second or kshatriya caste; name of Agni, or Fire.

rajas: impurity, dust, the darkening quality of passion; (in Sāmkhya) the second of the three gunas. *See also* guna.

Rājasuya: a great sacrifice performed at the coronation of a king.

Rākshasa: *a demon in general*; (according to some) the Rākshasas are of three classes: one being of a semi-divine and benevolent nature and ranking with Yākshas etc., a second being relentless enemies of the gods, and a third being nocturnal demons, imps, fiends, and goblins, which go about at night, haunting cemeteries, disturbing sacrifices, and even devouring human beings.

Rāmānuja: shortened form of Rāmānujāchārya.

Rāmānujāchārya: the principal interpreter of the Qualified Non-dualistic system of Hindu philosophy (AD 1017–1137); often called Rāmānuja for short.

Rig-Veda: one of the four Vedas, consisting of chants set to fixed melodies. (According to Hindu tradition, the division of the Vedas was made by Vyāsa at the command of Brahmā. The arranged collection of the hymns of the Rig-Veda is called the Rig-Veda Samhitā; it contains 1,017 hymns, arranged in eight ashtakas or ten mandalas.) See also Vedas.

Rik: a verse of the Rig-Veda (as distinguished from a Yajus or a Sāman).

rishi: a singer of sacred hymns; *an inspired poet or sage*; any person who, alone or with others, invokes deities in rhythmical speech or song of a sacred character; *the authors, or rather seers, of the Vedic texts.* (Such an expression as 'The rishi says' is equivalent to 'So it stands in the sacred text.')

Rudra: crying, roaring, howling; terrible (when applied to certain deities such as Aśvins, Agni, Mitra, and Varuna); *the destroyer of the universe* (*Pr. Up.* II. 9); *Brahman, the destroyer of ignorance* (*Śvet. Up.* III. 3); (in the Purānas) called Śiva, the personification of Brahman in Its destructive aspect; a group of twelve deities (*Br. Up.* I. iv. 12); name of the god of tempests and father and ruler of the Maruts; (in the Vedas) closely associated with Indra, and still more with Agni, the god of fire, which, as a destroying agent, rages and crackles like the roaring storm, also with Kāla, or Time, the all-consumer with whom he is afterwards identified; sometimes used as an epithet of Śiva (benevolent or auspicious) and supposed to possess the power of healing from his chasing away vapours and purifying the atmosphere; (in later mythology) often identified with Śiva, while a new class of beings (described as eleven, or thirty-nine in number), took the place of the original Rudras or Maruts, and came to be called Rudras.

Śabda-Brahman: the Word-Brahman; the Vedas, regarded as the revealed Sound or Word identified with the Supreme Brahman. (The primary meaning of the Vedas is Knowledge, and the secondary reference is to the words in which that Knowledge is embodied; hence the Vedas too are known as the Śabda-Brahman.)

Sachchidānanda: a compound consisting of three words: Sat (Existence, Reality), Chit (Consciousness), and Ānanda (Bliss); a term for the Pure Brahman, of which Existence, Consciousness, and Bliss are the very stuff. (In Dualism, Sat, Chit, and Ānanda are attributes of God.)

sādhyas: *a class of celestial beings*, whose world is said, in the *Śa. Br.*, to be above the sphere of the gods. (According to Yaska, their dwelling-place is the Bhuvar-loka or the mid-region between the earth and the sun. In later books they are described as created after the gods, with a nature exquisitely refined; in the Purānas their number is variously described as twelve or seventeen.)

Saguna Brahman: Brahman with attributes. (According to Non-dualism, the attributeless Brahman, when desirous to create the universe, becomes endowed, through māyā, with the attributes of creation, preservation, and destruction. It is to be noted that the attributeless Brahman and Brahman with attributes are not, essentially, two different beings, because māyā, which makes the apparent difference, inheres in Brahman and has no existence of its own. The Personal God worshipped in different religions is an aspect of Saguna Brahman.)

Śakti: power; *the active principle in creation and immanent in it*; the creative power of Brahman and as such inseparable from It; the energy or active power of a deity personified as his wife and worshipped by his devotees. (The Śakti of Indra is Indrāni, of Brahmā is Brahmāni.)

samādhi: trance; intense application of the mind to an object; deep meditation on a particular object in which the meditator loses his identity in the object meditated upon; the eighth and last stage in the spiritual discipline taught in Patanjali's yoga system; (in Buddhism) the fourth and last stage of dhyāna, or intense abstract meditation.

Sāman: name of a particular Vedic text intended to be chanted at the Soma-sacrifice.

samāna: a modification of the vital breath (prāna) which carries to all parts of the body the nutrition of the food digested in the stomach. *See also* prāna.

Sāma-Veda: the Veda of chants; name of one of the principal Vedas, consisting mostly of stanzas taken from the Rig-Veda, and chanted by the udgātri priest at the Soma-sacrifice. (The Samhitā of the Sāma-Veda consists of two parts; the first, called Archika, contains 585 verses, and the second, called Uttarārchika, 1,225 verses; the Sāma-Veda is said to have special reference to the Pitris, or deceased ancestors, whereas the Rig-Veda has the gods for its objects, and the Yajur-Veda men. The Sāma-Veda includes eight Brāhmanas.)

Samhitā: 'put together' (from *sam*, 'together' and *hita*, 'put'); *name of the Mantra part of the Vedas*; (in *Tai. Up.* I. iii. 1) a conjunction of two letters or words (formed out of the pādas, or separate words, by proper phonetic changes).

Sāmkhya: one of the six orthodox systems of philosophy, ascribed to Kapila. (Sāmkhya admits a plurality of purushas, or selves, and one undifferentiated prakriti, or matter. The latter, by the mere presence of the purusha, undergoes evolution in which the purusha becomes entangled. The purpose of this evolution is the ultimate emancipation of the purusha. Prakriti and a number of other categories constitute the twenty-four cosmic principles, or tattvas, which form the evolutionary series of the Sāmkhya philosophy. The five other orthodox systems of Hindu philosophy are as follows: the Purva-mimāmsā of Jaimini, Uttara-mimāmsā of Bādarāyana Vyāsa, Vaiśeshika of Kanāda, Yoga of Patanjali, and Nyāya of Gautama.)

samsāra: the round of worldly life; succession of births.

Samvarga: devouring, consumption.

Samyadvāma: a secret name of Brahman: 'uniting all that is pleasant or dear.'

Sanatkumāra: described in the Purānas as an eternal child, five years old, with virtue as his father and non-violence as his mother.

Śankara: shortened form of Śankarāchārya (see Śankarāchārya); an epithet of Śiva.

Śankarāchārya: one of the greatest Non-dualistic philosophers of India (AD 788–820), born in Kālādi in South India. (Besides writing commentaries on the eleven principal Upanishads, the Brahma Sutras, and the Bhagavad Gitā, he wrote several Advaita treatises, such as Vivekachudāmani and Ātmabodha, and composed many hymns in praise of Hindu deities. Śankarāchārya reformed the monastic order of India and established four monasteries at the four cardinal points of the country for the study and practice of Vedānta.)

sannyāsa: renunciation of the world; the fourth stage of life. See also āśrama.

sannyāsin: a renouncer; an ascetic who renounces all earthly concerns and devotes himself to meditation and scriptural study; one belonging to the fourth stage of life. See also āśrama.

Sat: Reality.

sattva: existence; true nature; the quality of purity and goodness (regarded in the Sāmkhya philosophy as the highest of the three gunas, because it renders a person truthful, honest, and wise). See also guna(s).

Satya Brahman: the manifested universe whose symbol is Hiranya-garbha (Br. Up. V. iv; V. v. 1). The word Satya means true, and Brahman, vast.

Sāvitri: see Sun.

Self: the unchanging entity (Ātman) in a changing body (in this sense the Self is one with Brahman); (with small s) the individual self (atman) identified with the body senses, mind, and prāna.

sheath: *see* kośa.

Śiva: auspicious, benevolent; *name of the destructive aspect of the Deity, the third god of the Hindu Triad, or Trimurti,* the other two being Brahmā and Vishnu (these three deities, through unceasing creation, preservation, and destruction, ensure the continuance of the cosmic process); Rudra, the Vedic deity of destruction, in later times called Śiva, the Auspicious One; (in the Purānas) identified by His devotees with the Supreme God as Destroyer; sometimes called Kāla, and identified with time. (Śiva is generally worshipped in India today through the phallic symbol, or linga.)

Smriti: 'what is remembered'; the whole body of sacred tradition, of human origin, as distinguished from Śruti, or what is directly heard by or revealed to the rishis. (In its wider acceptation, Smriti includes the following: the six Vedāngas; the Sutras, both Śrauta and Grihya; the law books of Manu, Yājnavalkya, and others; the Itihāsas, including the *Mahābhārata* and *Rāmāyana*; and the Nitiśāstras. It also includes the whole body of the codes of law handed down by tradition.)

soma: the juice of the soma plant and also the plant itself; sometimes described in the Vedas as having been brought from the sky by a falcon and guarded by gandharvas. (The soma plant was collected by the Vedic priests by moonlight from certain mountains. The stalks were then pressed between stones by the priests, sprinkled with water and purified in a strainer. Afterwards the strained material was mixed with clarified butter, flour, etc., and made to ferment. The fermented liquid was offered in libations to the gods and drunk by the priests, both of whom enjoyed its exhilarating effect. Soma is personified as one of the most important Vedic gods, to whose praise all the 114 hymns of the ninth book, besides six hymns of some other books of the Rig-Veda, and the whole of Sāma-Veda, are dedicated. Soma is often identified with the god of the moon, being called rājan (king), and appears among the eight Vasus and eight Lokapālas (or protectors of the quarters.)

Soma-sacrifice: a great triennial sacrifice at which soma juice was drunk.

Sphota: bursting; (in philosophy) sound (conceived as eternal, indivisible, and creative); the eternal and imperceptible element of sounds and words and the real vehicle of ideas, which bursts or flashes on the mind when a sound is uttered.

Śruti: 'what is heard or revealed'; the sacred Vedic knowledge transmitted orally by brāhmins from generation to generation; *the Vedas* (i.e. the sacred eternal words or sounds revealed to certain sages called rishis, and so differing from Smriti.)

subtle body: formed of the five subtle elements (namely, ākāśa, air, fire,

water, and earth in their subtle and rudimentary form) and consisting of seventeen parts, namely, the five organs of perception,
the five organs of action, the five prānas, the mind, and the intellect. At the time of death, the soul, accompanied by the subtle
body, leaves the gross body for rebirth.

śudra: a man of the fourth or lowest of the four original castes or classes,
whose only duty, according to Manu, is to serve the three upper
castes. (In the Vedas, the śudra caste is said to have sprung from
the feet of the Purusha or Universal Soul.)

Sun: the sun deity; (in the Vedas) sometimes identified with the sun
itself, at other times distinguished from it, being conceived and
personified as the divine influence vivifying the sun. (According to
Sāyanāchārya, the sun, before rising, is called Sāvitri, and after
rising till it sets, Surya. Many hymns of the Vedas are addressed
to Sāvitri, who is visualized as endowed with golden head, golden
arms, golden hair, etc.)

Surya: see Sun.

Sushumnā: an important naḍi, or artery, in the body, lying between
the naḍis Iḍā and Pingalā, and supposed to be the path through
which the soul of a yogi leaves the body at the time of death.

suta: son of a kshatriya father and a brāhmin mother; (with capital s)
a kind of libation of soma juice in the Soma-sacrifice (the two other
kinds being called Prasuta and Āsuta.)

sutra: thread; the sacred thread or cord worn by members of the three
upper castes in Hindu society; that which, like a thread, runs
through and holds things together; a short sentence or aphoristic
statement; (with capital s) any work or manual consisting of a
collection of such statements hanging together as if on a thread
(books of sutras form manuals of teaching in rituals, philosophy,
grammar, etc.; each system of Hindu philosophy has its regular
text-book of aphorisms, called a Sutra, written by its supposed
founder); (with capital s) an epithet of Saguna Brahman conceived
as a thread that holds together the universe and all creatures; the same
as Hiranyagarbha, Prāna, Sutrātmā, and Vāyu.

Sutrātmā: the 'Thread Soul', the Soul on which the diversified universe
is strung, like objects on a thread. See also Saguna Brahman and
Sutra.

Suvah: the same as Svah.

Svah: heaven; the heaven of Indra and the temporary abode of virtuous people after their death; the sky; the space above the sun or
between the sun and the pole-star; the third of the three vyāhritis,
or mystic words, pronounced by brāhmins in their daily prayers.

Svāhā: an exclamation used in making oblations to the gods; an oblation
offered to Agni, Indra, etc.

swan (hamsa): an aquatic bird; a mythical bird described in the Rig-Veda as able to separate soma from a mixture of soma and water, and in later literature, milk from a mixture of milk and water; the soul or spirit (on account of its resembling the white colour of a swan or the migratory nature of a goose); (with capital s) an epithet of the Universal Soul or Supreme Spirit, identified with Virāj, Nārāyana, Śiva, and the Sun.

Taijasa: see Prājna.

tamas: darkness; mental darkness, ignorance, error; (in Sāmkhya philosophy) one of the three ingredients (gunas) of prakriti and all created objects (the cause of heaviness, ignorance, illusion, dullness, and solidity). See also gunas.

Tantra: a class of religious and philosophical treatises, abounding in mystical formulas, in which ultimate reality is conceived of as Śiva-Śakti, or the Absolute and Its Power, eternally united with each other. Tantra deals mainly with five topics, namely, the creation, the destruction of the universe, the worship of the deities, the attainment of all desires (especially of superhuman powers), and the modes of union with ultimate reality through meditation.

tapas: 'consuming by heat'; religious austerity.

teacher: religious preceptor. See also guru.

Turiya: 'the Fourth'; an epithet of Ātman as Pure Consciousness. See also Prājna.

twice-born: refers to a brāhmin, whose first birth takes place when he comes out of his mother's womb, and whose second birth when he enters upon the spiritual life after being invested with the sacred thread by his teacher. See also dvija.

udāna: the upward breathing; one of the five modifications of the vital breath in the human body (which resides in the throat and rises upwards). See also prāna.

udgātri (priest): one of the chief priests in a Vedic sacrifice (viz., the one who chants the Sāma-Veda).

Udgitha: chanting of the Sāma-Veda; a hymn of the Sāma-Veda sung at the time of the sacrifice. See also Pranava.

ugra(s): violent, terrible; name of a mixed class born of kshatriya father and śudra mother. (According to Manu, an ugra is of cruel and rude conduct, and chiefly employed as the catcher and killer of snakes.)

Umā: name of the daughter of Haimavat (King Himālaya), consort of Śiva, also called Pārvati and Durgā; Śakti, or the active principle in creation inseparable from Śiva, the Absolute.

upādhi: that which is put in place of another thing, a substitute; anything which may be taken for or has the mere name or appearance of another thing (applied to certain forms or properties considered as disguises of the Spirit); title; discriminative appellation.

Upanishad: (according to certain scholars) sitting down at the feet of a teacher and listening to his words (hence secret wisdom); (in Vedānta) the Knowledge of Brahman, which, when received from (*upa*) a teacher, loosens (*sad*) totally (*ni*) the pupil's bondage to the world, or surely (*ni*) enables him to attain (*sad*) the Self, or Supreme Reality; a class of philosophical treatises (supposed to be one hundred and eight in number) attached to the Brāhmana portion of the Vedas (with the exception of the *Iśa Upanishad*, which forms the fortieth chapter of the *Vājasaneyi Samhitā* of the Sukla Yajur-Veda). The purpose of the Upanishad is the exposition of the Vedic philosophy; it is regarded as the source of the orthodox systems of Hindu philosophy.

upāsanā: worship, especially worship associated with meditation on the deity.

vairāgyam: dispassion; distaste for worldly desires; indifference to worldly objects and life; a cardinal discipline practised by seekers of Liberation.

Vaiśvānara: relating to or belonging to all men; a name of Agni or the god of fire; the fire in the stomach which digests food; the name of the Supreme Spirit as identified with or controlling the aggregate of gross bodies (the same as Virāj); the Universal Self who exists in the form of the whole of humanity; the controller of all phenomenal changes; the Spirit functioning through the gross body in the waking state (*see also* Prājna).

vaiśya: 'a man who settles on the soil'; peasant; trader; farmer; member of the third caste in Hindu society (whose occupation is trade, cattle-rearing, and agriculture).

Vājapeya sacrifice: name of one of the seven forms of the Soma-sacrifice (performed by kings or brāhmins aspiring to the highest position in the world); it generally precedes the Rājasuya sacrifice.

vānaprastha: the third stage of life, succeeding the student and householder stages, when a member of the three upper castes, especially a brāhmin, abandons his home for an ascetic life in the forest. *See also* āśrama.

Varuna: name of an Āditya (in the Vedas commonly associated with Mitra, and presiding over the night, as Mitra over the day); one of the oldest of the Vedic gods; often regarded as the Supreme Deity, being then styled 'king of the gods', 'king of both gods and men', 'king of the universe'; described as fashioning and upholding heaven and earth, as possessing an extraordinary power and wisdom called māyā, as sending his messengers throughout the worlds, as hating falsehood, as seizing transgressors by means of a noose, as inflicting disease (especially dropsy), as pardoning sin, as the guardian of immortality; (in later mythology) the god of ocean, the god of rain, and the god of aquatic animals; *the deity identified with apāna (the downward breath) and the night.*

Vasus: a particular class of gods, whose number is usually given as eight, and whose chief is Indra, and later Agni or Vishnu. (The Vasus were originally personifications of natural phenomena. The eight Vasus, the eleven Rudras, the twelve Ādityas, together with Dyaus, or heaven, and Prithivi, or earth, constituted the thirty-three gods of the Hindus. For Dyaus and Prithivi some substitute Indra and Prajāpati, and others the two Aśvins.)

vāyu: wind, air; the prāna or vital breath; (with capital *v*) the god of wind; the same as Hiranyagarbha, Prāna, Sutrātmā, and Sutra (the first manifestation of Brahman in the relative universe), whose body is the aggregate of all subtle bodies, and whose mind, the aggregate of all minds.

Vedānta: the concluding part or essence of the Vedas; the name of the second and most important part of the Mimāmsā ('Inquiry') philosophy, called Uttara Mimāmsā, the first being designated as Purva Mimāmsā; (according to Śadānanda) the teachings embodied in the Upanishads, the Bhagavad Gitā, and the *Brahma Sutras*, together with their commentaries. (The chief doctrine of Vedānta, as explained by Śankarāchārya, is that of Advaita or non-dualism, according to which nothing really exists but the one Self or Supreme Soul of the universe, called Brahman, and the individual soul or jivātmā and all the phenomena of nature are non-different from Brahman. The system of Vedānta is also called Brahma Mimāmsā, the 'Inquiry into the nature of Brahman', or Śariraka Mimāmsā, the 'Inquiry into the nature of the embodied creature'. The founder of the Vedānta philosophy is said to have been Vyāsa, also called Bādarāyana.)

Vedas: knowledge; true or sacred knowledge; the name of the four celebrated works which constitute the basic scriptures of the Hindus and the ultimate authority of their religion and philosophy. (The four Vedas include the Rig-Veda, the Yajur-Veda, the Sāma-Veda, and the Atharva-Veda. The first three, called collectively the Trayi, or Triad, are sometimes said to constitute the Vedas. Certain scholars assign the oldest of the Vedic hymns, on astronomical calculations, to a period somewhere between 4000 and 2500 BC, but others who adopt a different reckoning assign them to the period between 1400 and 1000 BC. Each of the Vedas has two distinct parts, namely Mantra and Brāhmana. The Mantra contains chants and prayers addressed to deities for wisdom, health, wealth, long life, cattle, offspring, victory in battle, and sometimes forgiveness of sins. The Brāhmana gives directions for the details of the ceremonies at which mantras are to be used, and explains the legends etc. connected with the mantras. Both the Mantra and the Brāhmana are termed Śruti or revelation. The mantras of the Rig-Veda, called Riks, are verses of praise in metre, and are intended for loud recitation; those of the Yajur-Veda, called Yajus, are in prose and intended for recitation in a lower tone at sacrifices; and those of the Sāma-Veda, called Sāmans, are in metre and intended for chanting at the Soma-sacrifice. The mantras of the Atharva-Veda have no special name. Tradition makes Vyāsa the compiler of the Vedas in their present form. Out of the Brāhmana portion of the Vedas grew two other departments of Vedic literature, called the Āranyaka and the Upanishad. In the later Vedic literature the name of 'fifth' Veda is accorded to the Itihāsas, or legendary epic poems, and the Purānas. Certain secondary Vedas or Upavedas dealing with medicine, music, etc., are also enumerated.)

Vedānta Sutras: see *Brahma Sutras*.

vidyā: knowledge, science; also knowledge personified as and identified with Durgā, the Divine Mother. (According to some there are different forms of vidyā: the Trayi or the first three Vedas, Ānvikshiki or logic and metaphysics, Danda-niti or the science of government, and Vārttā or practical arts such as agriculture, commerce, medicine, etc. Manu adds a fifth, viz. Ātma-vidyā or knowledge of the Soul or Reality.)

vinā: a musical instrument of the guitar kind, supposedly invented by Nārada, usually having seven strings stretched above nineteen frets fixed on a long rounded board, toward the ends of which there are two large gourds. (Its compass is said to be two octaves, but it has many varieties according to the number of strings etc.)

Virāj: 'ruling far and wide'; the first manifestation of Saguna Brahman; a sort of secondary Creator, sometimes identified with Prajāpati, Brahmā, Agni, etc.; (in Vedānta) an epithet of the Supreme Spirit conditioned by the upādhi of the aggregate of gross bodies.

Virāt: the same as Virāj.

Vishnu: the all-pervader; *the deity who pervades the universe and is identified with the power that controls the feet*; one of the principal Vedic deities; (in the later mythology) regarded as the Preserver, and with Brahmā the Creator, and Śiva the Destroyer, constituting the well-known Trimurti or Triad of Hinduism. (Although Vishnu comes second in the Triad, He is identified with the Supreme Deity by His followers. As distinguished from other Vedic deities, Vishnu is a personification of light and the sun, especially in His stride over the heavens. In the Brāhmanas He is identified with the sacrifice, and in one of them is described as a dwarf. In the *Rāmā-yana* and the *Mahābhārata* He rises to the supremacy which He enjoys even now as the most popular deity of certain classes of dualistic worshippers. The distinguishing feature in the character of the post-Vedic Vishnu is His birth, in a portion of His essence, as the ten divine Incarnations. Vishnu's followers regard Him as the Supreme Being and often identify Him with Nārāyana.

Viśishtādvaita: *see* Qualified Non-dualism.

Viśva: *see* Prājna.

Viśve-devas: name of a particular class of gods; all the gods collectively; (according to the Purānas) sons of Viśvā, daughter of Daksha. (They are particularly propitiated at the after-death and Vaiśva-deva ceremonies.)

vrātya: a man of mendicant class; a low person; either a man who has lost caste through non-observance of the ten principal sacraments, or a man of a particular low caste descended from a śudra or a kshatriya; (according to some) an illegitimate son of a kshatriya who knows the habits and intentions of soldiers.

vyāna: one of the five modifications of the vital breath, that which circulates or is diffused through the body. *See also* prāna.

Vyāsa: a celebrated sage (often called Veda-Vyāsa), regarded as the original compiler and arranger of the Vedas, and author of the *Brahma Sutras* etc. (The son of Parāśara and Satyavati, and half-brother of Bhishma, he was also called Bādarāyana Krishna from his dark complexion, and Dvaipāyana on account of his having been brought forth by Satyavati on a dvipa, or island, in the Jamunā river. As he grew up he retired into the forest to lead a hermit's life, but at his mother's request returned home and married. Vyāsa was the father of Vidura by a slave girl, and of Śuka, the author of the *Bhāgavata Purāna*. He is also reputed to be the author of the *Mahābhārata*, many of the *Purānas*, and other sacred books of Hinduism. It appears that in olden times a writer would sometimes attribute his work to a celebrated person to enhance its prestige.)

vyāhritis: mystical words signifying the names of the seven worlds. *See also* Bhuh.

worlds: either the universe or any division of it. (A full classification gives seven worlds, namely Bhur-loka, or the earth; Bhuvar-loka, or the mid-region between the earth and the sun, inhabited by the munis or contemplatives and the siddhas or perfected souls; Svar-loka, or Indra's heaven above the sun and between it and the pole-star; Mahar-loka, a region above the pole-star inhabited by Bhrigu and other saints, who survive the destruction of the above-mentioned three worlds; Janar-loka, inhabited by such exalted souls as

Brahmā's son Sanatkumāra; Tapar-loka, inhabited by the deified renouncers of the world; Satya-loka, the abode of Brahmā, translation to which exempts one from rebirth. To these are sometimes added seven lower worlds, called, in the order of their descent below the earth: Atala, Vitala, Sutala, Rasātala, Talātala, Mahātala, and Pātāla.

yajna: worship; a sacrifice or religious rite in which oblations are offered in the fire to propitiate the deities (this is the prevailing meaning of the word as used in the Vedas); (with capital *y*) a name of Vishnu.

Yājnavalkya: name of an ancient sage (frequently quoted as an authority in the *Satapatha Brāhmana*); the first reputed teacher of the *Vājasaneyi Samhitā* or White Yajur-Veda, which was revealed to him by the Sun. (He is also the supposed author of a celebrated code of laws governing the social and individual life, which is second only to the laws of Manu.)

Yajur-Veda: one of the four Vedas. (The mantras of the Yajur-Veda, called Yajus, are composed in prose and are frequently identical with the mantras of the Rig-Veda. The Yajur-Veda is a sort of sacrificial prayer-book of the adhvaryu priests, formed out of the Rig-Veda, which had to be modified and arranged with additional verses for sacrificial purposes. The most characteristic feature of the Yajur-Veda is its division into two distinct collections of verses: the *Taittiriya Samhitā*, also called the Krishna or Black Yajur-Veda, and the *Vājasaneyi Samhitā*, also called the Śukla or White Yajur-Veda. The order of sacrifices, however, of both recensions is similar, the principal sacrifices being the Darśa-Paurnamāsa, which is to be performed on the days of the new and the full moon, and the Aśvamedha or Horse-sacrifice.

Yajus: Vedic mantras written in prose, as distinguished from Riks and Sāmans; name of the Yajur-Veda.

Yaksha: a supernatural being; ghost; name of a class of semi-divine beings, usually attendants of Kuvera the god of wealth. (Though generally regarded as creatures of a benevolent disposition like the Yakshas in Kālidāsa's *Meghaduta*, they are occasionally classed with malignant spirits).

yama: (in the Yoga philosophy) control of the mind; one of the eight disciplines for attaining samādhi; (with capital *y*) the deity who presides over the deceased ancestors and rules the spirits of the dead; (in the Vedas) a 'king' (gatherer of men), and the ruler over the Manes in heaven (the road to which is guarded by two broad-nosed, four-eyed, spotted dogs); (in post-Vedic mythology) the judge, restrainer, or punisher of the dead. (In this capacity Yama is called Dharma-rāja, the king of dharma or righteousness, who weighs in his balance the merits and demerits of the dead and rewards or punishes. His abode, in some part of the nether regions, is called Yama-pura, where the soul is said to go after leaving the body. A recorder reads an account of the soul's actions and Yama gives it a just sentence. In the *Mahābhārata*, Yama is described as possessing a glittering form and dressed in blood-red garments, with a crown on his head. He has glowering eyes and holds a noose with which he binds the soul, in size about the measure of a man's thumb, after drawing it from the body. In later mythology he is represented as a terrible deity inflicting tortures on wicked souls after death.)

yoga: the art of joining; a yoke; union with God or the Supreme Reality and the disciplines for such union; (with capital *y*) concentration practised as a discipline, as taught by Patanjali in the *Yoga Sutras*. (The philosophy of Patanjali's Yoga system is based upon that of Sāmkhya, one of the chief differences being that Yoga postulates a God, whereas Sāmkhya denies His existence. The chief aim of Yoga is to help a man suppress the states of his mind, achieve inner calmness, and realize the true nature of the soul by isolating it from matter and mind. Patanjali describes eight steps of yoga leading finally to samādhi, or complete absorption. Hatha-yoga, a branch of Yoga, recommends the withdrawal of the mind from external objects and prescribes various physical exercises, mainly to improve the health, increase longevity, and bring the body under control. Through the practice of Hatha-yoga a man can acquire various supernatural powers.)

yogin: one who practises the disciplines of yoga. *See also* yoga.

INDEX

hARPER ✦ ϹORϹhBOOKS

HUMANITIES AND SOCIAL SCIENCES

American Studies: General

HENRY STEELE COMMAGER, Ed.: The Struggle for Racial Equality TB/1300

EDWARD S. CORWIN: American Constitutional History. △ *Essays edited by Alpheus T. Mason and Gerald Garvey* TB/1136

CARL N. DEGLER, Ed.: Pivotal Interpretations of American History TB/1240, TB/1241

A. S. EISENSTADT, Ed.: The Craft of American History: *Recent Essays in American Historical Writing* Vol. I TB/1255; Vol. II TB/1256

CHARLOTTE P. GILMAN: Women and Economics ‡ TB/3073

OSCAR HANDLIN, Ed.: This Was America: *As Recorded by European Travelers in the Eighteenth, Nineteenth and Twentieth Centuries. Illus.* TB/1119

MARCUS LEE HANSEN: The Atlantic Migration: 1607-1860. *Edited by Arthur M. Schlesinger* TB/1052

MARCUS LEE HANSEN: The Immigrant in American History TB/1120

JOHN HIGHAM, Ed.: The Reconstruction of American History △ TB/1068

ROBERT H. JACKSON: The Supreme Court in the American System of Government TB/1106

JOHN F. KENNEDY: A Nation of Immigrants. △ *Illus.* TB/1118

LEONARD W. LEVY, Ed.: American Constitutional Law TB/1285

LEONARD W. LEVY, Ed.: Judicial Review and the Supreme Court TB/1296

LEONARD W. LEVY: The Law of the Commonwealth and Chief Justice Shaw TB/1309

RALPH BARTON PERRY: Puritanism and Democracy TB/1138

ARNOLD ROSE: The Negro in America: *The Condensed Version of Gunnar Myrdal's An American Dilemma* TB/3048

MAURICE R. STEIN: The Eclipse of Community: *An Interpretation of American Studies* TB/1128

W. LLOYD WARNER: Social Class in America: *The Evaluation of Status* TB/1013

American Studies: Colonial

BERNARD BAILYN, Ed.: The Apologia of Robert Keayne: *Self-Portrait of a Puritan Merchant* TB/1201

BERNARD BAILYN: The New England Merchants in the Seventeenth Century TB/1149

CHARLES GIBSON: Spain in America † TB/3077

LAWRENCE HENRY GIPSON: The Coming of the Revolution: 1763-1775. † *Illus.* TB/3007

PERRY MILLER: Errand Into the Wilderness TB/1139

PERRY MILLER & T. H. JOHNSON, Eds.: The Puritans: *A Sourcebook* Vol. I TB/1093; Vol. II TB/1094

EDMUND S. MORGAN, Ed.: The Diary of Michael Wigglesworth, 1653-1657: *The Conscience of a Puritan* TB/1228

EDMUND S. MORGAN: The Puritan Family: *Religion and Domestic Relations in Seventeenth-Century New England* TB/1227

RICHARD B. MORRIS: Government and Labor in Early America TB/1244

KENNETH B. MURDOCK: Literature and Theology in Colonial New England TB/99

JOHN P. ROCHE: Origins of American Political Thought: *Selected Readings* TB/1301

JOHN SMITH: Captain John Smith's America: *Selections from His Writings. Ed. with Intro. by John Lankford* TB/3078

LOUIS B. WRIGHT: The Cultural Life of the American Colonies: 1607-1763. † *Illus.* TB/3005

American Studies: From the Revolution to 1860

JOHN R. ALDEN: The American Revolution: 1775-1783. † *Illus.* TB/3011

RAY A. BILLINGTON: The Far Western Frontier: 1830-1860. † *Illus.* TB/3012

EDMUND BURKE: On the American Revolution. ‡ *Edited by Elliott Robert Barkan* TB/3068

WHITNEY R. CROSS: The Burned-Over District: *The Social and Intellectual History of Enthusiastic Religion in Western New York, 1800-1850* TB/1242

GEORGE DANGERFIELD: The Awakening of American Nationalism: 1815-1828. † *Illus.* TB/3061

CLEMENT EATON: The Freedom-of-Thought Struggle in the Old South. *Revised and Enlarged. Illus.* TB/1150

CLEMENT EATON: The Growth of Southern Civilization: 1790-1860. † *Illus.* TB/3040

LOUIS FILLER: The Crusade Against Slavery: 1830-1860. † *Illus.* TB/3029

WILLIAM W. FREEHLING, Ed.: The Nullification Era: *A Documentary Record* ‡ TB/3079

FELIX GILBERT: The Beginnings of American Foreign Policy: *To the Farewell Address* TB/1200

FRANCIS GRIERSON: The Valley of Shadows: *The Coming of the Civil War in Lincoln's Midwest: A Contemporary Account* TB/1246

ALEXANDER HAMILTON: The Reports of Alexander Hamilton. ‡ *Edited by Jacob E. Cooke* TB/3060

JAMES MADISON: The Forging of American Federalism: *Selected Writings of James Madison. Edited by Saul K. Padover* TB/1126

BERNARD MAYO: Myths and Men: *Patrick Henry, George Washington, Thomas Jefferson* TB/1108

---

† The New American Nation Series, edited by Henry Steele Commager and Richard B. Morris.
‡ American Perspectives series, edited by Bernard Wishy and William E. Leuchtenburg.
* The Rise of Modern Europe series, edited by William L. Langer.
** History of Europe series, edited by J. H. Plumb.
¶ Researches in the Social, Cultural and Behavioral Sciences, edited by Benjamin Nelson.
§ The Library of Religion and Culture, edited by Benjamin Nelson.
Σ Harper Modern Science Series, edited by James R. Newman.
o Not for sale in Canada.
△ Not for sale in the U. K.

2

WILLIAM MILLER, Ed.: Men in Business: *Essays on the Historical Role of the Entrepreneur* TB/1081
RICHARD B. MORRIS: Government and Labor in Early America TB/1244
HERBERT SIMON: The Shape of Automation: *For Men and Management* TB/1245
PERRIN STRYKER: The Character of the Executive: *Eleven Studies in Managerial Qualities* TB/1041
PIERRE URI: Partnership for Progress: *A Program for Transatlantic Action* TB/3036

Education

JACQUES BARZUN: The House of Intellect △ TB/1051
RICHARD M. JONES, Ed.: Contemporary Educational Psychology: *Selected Readings* TB/1292
CLARK KERR: The Uses of the University TB/1264
JOHN U. NEF: Cultural Foundations of Industrial Civilization △ TB/1024
NATHAN M. PUSEY: The Age of the Scholar: *Observations on Education in a Troubled Decade* TB/1157
PAUL VALÉRY: The Outlook for Intelligence △ TB/2016

Historiography & Philosophy of History

JACOB BURCKHARDT: On History and Historians. △ *Introduction by H. R. Trevor-Roper* TB/1216
WILHELM DILTHEY: Pattern and Meaning in History: *Thoughts on History and Society.* ○ △ *Edited with an Introduction by H. P. Rickman* TB/1075
J. H. HEXTER: Reappraisals in History: *New Views on History & Society in Early Modern Europe* △ TB/1100
H. STUART HUGHES: History as Art and as Science: *Twin Vistas on the Past* TB/1207
RAYMOND KLIBANSKY & H. J. PATON, Eds.: Philosophy and History: *The Ernst Cassirer Festschrift. Illus.* TB/1115
ARNALDO MOMIGLIANO: Studies in Historiography TB/1288
GEORGE H. NADEL, Ed.: Studies in the Philosophy of History: *Essays from History and Theory* TB/1208
JOSE ORTEGA Y GASSET: The Modern Theme. *Introduction by Jose Ferrater Mora* TB/1038
KARL R. POPPER: The Open Society and Its Enemies △
Vol. I: *The Spell of Plato* TB/1101
Vol. II: *The High Tide of Prophecy: Hegel, Marx and the Aftermath* TB/1102
KARL R. POPPER: The Poverty of Historicism ○ △ TB/1126
G. J. RENIER: History: Its Purpose and Method △ TB/1209
W. H. WALSH: Philosophy of History △ TB/1020

History: General

L. CARRINGTON GOODRICH: A Short History of the Chinese People. △ *Illus.* TB/3015
DAN N. JACOBS & HANS H. BAERWALD: Chinese Communism: *Selected Documents* TB/3031
BERNARD LEWIS: The Arabs in History △ TB/1029
BERNARD LEWIS: The Middle East and the West TB/1274

History: Ancient

A. ANDREWES: The Greek Tyrants △ TB/1103
ADOLF ERMAN, Ed.: The Ancient Egyptians TB/1233
MICHAEL GRANT: Ancient History ○ △ TB/1190
SAMUEL NOAH KRAMER: Sumerian Mythology TB/1055
NAPHTALI LEWIS & MEYER REINHOLD, Eds.: Roman Civilization. *Sourcebook I: The Republic* TB/1231
NAPHTALI LEWIS & MEYER REINHOLD, Eds.: Roman Civilization. *Sourcebook II: The Empire* TB/1232

History: Medieval

P. BOISSONNADE: Life and Work in Medieval Europe ○ △ TB/1141
HELEN CAM: England before Elizabeth △ TB/1026

NORMAN COHN: The Pursuit of the Millennium △ TB/1037
G. G. COULTON: Medieval Village, Manor, and Monastery △ TB/1022
CHRISTOPHR DAWSON, Ed.: Mission to Asia: *Narratives and Letters of the Franciscan Missionaries in Mongolia and China in the 13th and 14th Centuries* △ TB/315
HEINRICH FICHTENAU: The Carolingian Empire: *The Age of Charlemagne* △ TB/1142
GALBERT OF BRUGES: The Murder of Charles the Good. *Trans with Intro. by James Bruce Ross* TB/1311
F. L. GANSHOF: Feudalism △ TB/1058
DENO GEANAKOPLOS: Byzantine East and Latin West: *Two Worlds of Christendom in Middle Ages and Renaissance* △ TB/1265
DENYS HAY: Europe △ TB/1275
DENYS HAY: The Medieval Centuries ○ △ TB/1192
J. M. HUSSEY: The Byzantine World △ TB/1057
ROBERT LATOUCHE: The Birth of Western Economy ○ △ TB/1290
FERDINAND LOT: The End of the Ancient World and the Beginnings of the Middle Ages TB/1044
MARSILIUS OF PADUA: The Defender of the Peace. *Trans. with Intro. by Alan Gewirth* TB/1310
G. MOLLAT: The Popes at Avignon: 1305-1378 △ TB/308
CHARLES PETIT-DUTAILLIS: The Feudal Monarchy in France and England ○ △ TB/1165
HENRI PIRENNE: Early Democracies in the Low Countries TB/1110
STEVEN RUNCIMAN: A History of the Crusades. △
Vol. I TB/1143; Vol. II TB/1243; Vol. III TB/1298
FERDINAND SCHEVILL: Siena: *The History of a Medieval Commune. Intro. by William M. Bowsky* TB/1164
HENRY OSBORN TAYLOR: The Classical Heritage of the Middle Ages TB/1117
F. VAN DER MEER: Augustine the Bishop: *Church and Society at the Dawn of the Middle Ages* △ TB/304
J. M. WALLACE-HADRILL: The Barbarian West: *The Early Middle Ages, A.D. 400-1000* △ TB/1061

History: Renaissance & Reformation

JACOB BURCKHARDT: The Civilization of the Renaissance in Italy. △ *Illus.* Vol. I TB/40; Vol. II TB/41
JOHN CALVIN & JACOPO SADOLETO: A Reformation Debate. *Edited by John C. Olin* TB/1239
ERNST CASSIRER: The Individual and the Cosmos in Renaissance Philosophy. △ *Translated with an Introduction by Mario Domandi* TB/1097
FEDERICO CHABOD: Machiavelli & Renaissance △ TB/1193
EDWARD P. CHEYNEY: The Dawn of a New Era, 1250-1453. * *Illus.* TB/3002
G. CONSTANT: The Reformation in England: *The English Schism, Henry VIII, 1509-1547* △ TB/314
R. TREVOR DAVIES: The Golden Century of Spain, 1501-1621 ○ △ TB/1194
G. R. ELTON: Reformation Europe, 1517-1559 ** ○ △ TB/1270
DESIDERIUS ERASMUS: Christian Humanism and the Reformation: *Selected Writings. Edited and translated by John C. Olin* TB/1166
WALLACE K. FERGUSON et al.: Facets of the Renaissance TB/1098
WALLACE K. FERGUSON et al.: The Renaissance: *Six Essays. Illus.* TB/1084
JOHN NEVILLE FIGGIS: The Divine Right of Kings. *Introduction by G. R. Elton* TB/1191
JOHN NEVILLE FIGGIS: Political Thought from Gerson to Grotius: 1414-1625 △ TB/1032
MYRON P. GILMORE: The World of Humanism, 1453-1517. * *Illus.* TB/3003
FRANCESCO GUICCIARDINI: Maxims and Reflections of a Renaissance Statesman *(Ricordi)* TB/1160
J. H. HEXTER: More's Utopia: *The Biography of an Idea. New Epilogue by the Author* TB/1195

HAJO HOLBORN: Ulrich von Hutten and the German Reformation TB/1238
JOHAN HUIZINGA: Erasmus and the Age of Reformation.△ Illus. TB/19
JOEL HURSTFIELD, Ed.: The Reformation Crisis △ TB/1267
ULRICH VON HUTTEN et al.: On the Eve of the Reformation: "Letters of Obscure Men" TB/1124
PAUL O. KRISTELLER: Renaissance Thought: The Classic, Scholastic, and Humanist Strains TB/1048
PAUL O. KRISTELLER: Renaissance Thought II: Papers on Humanism and the Arts TB/1163
NICCOLÒ MACHIAVELLI: History of Florence and of the Affairs of Italy TB/1027
ALFRED VON MARTIN: Sociology of the Renaissance. Introduction by Wallace K. Ferguson △ TB/1099
GARRETT MATTINGLY et al.: Renaissance Profiles. △ Edited by J. H. Plumb TB/1162
MILLARD MEISS: Painting in Florence and Siena after the Black Death: The Arts, Religion and Society in the Mid-Fourteenth Century. △ 169 illus. TB/1148
J. E. NEALE: The Age of Catherine de Medici ° △ TB/1085
ERWIN PANOFSKY: Studies in Iconology: Humanistic Themes in the Art of the Renaissance △ TB/1077
J. H. PARRY: The Establishment of the European Hegemony: 1415-1715 △ TB/1045
J. H. PLUMB: The Italian Renaissance: A Concise Survey of Its History and Culture △ TB/1161
A. F. POLLARD: Henry VIII. ° △ Introduction by A. G. Dickens TB/1249
A. F. POLLARD: Wolsey. ° △ Introduction by A. G. Dickens TB/1248
CECIL ROTH: The Jews in the Renaissance. Illus. TB/834
A. L. ROWSE: The Expansion of Elizabethan England. ° △ Illus. TB/1220
GORDON RUPP: Luther's Progress to the Diet of Worms ° △ TB/120
G. M. TREVELYAN: England in the Age of Wycliffe, 1368-1520 ° △ TB/1112
VESPASIANO: Renaissance Princes, Popes, and Prelates: The Vespasiano Memoirs: Lives of Illustrious Men of the XVth Century TB/1111

History: Modern European

FREDERICK B. ARTZ: Reaction and Revolution, 1815-1852. * Illus. TB/3034
MAX BELOFF: The Age of Absolutism, 1660-1815 △ TB/1062
ROBERT C. BINKLEY: Realism and Nationalism, 1852-1871. * Illus. TB/3038
ASA BRIGGS: The Making of Modern England, 1784-1867: The Age of Improvement ° △ TB/1203
CRANE BRINTON: A Decade of Revolution, 1789-1799. * Illus. TB/3018
D. W. BROGAN: The Development of Modern France. ° △ Volume I: From the Fall of the Empire to the Dreyfus Affair TB/1184
Volume II: The Shadow of War, World War I, Between the Two Wars. New Introduction by the Author TB/1185
J. BRONOWSKI & BRUCE MAZLISH: The Western Intellectual Tradition: From Leonardo to Hegel △ TB/3001
GEOFFREY BRUUN: Europe and the French Imperium, 1799-1814. * Illus. TB/3033
ALAN BULLOCK: Hitler, A Study in Tyranny ° △ TB/1123
E. H. CARR: German-Soviet Relations between the Two World Wars, 1919-1939 TB/1278
E. H. CARR: International Relations between the Two World Wars, 1919-1939 ° △ TB/1279
E. H. CARR: The Twenty Years' Crisis, 1919-1939 ° △ TB/1122
GORDON A. CRAIG: From Bismarck to Adenauer: Aspects of German Statecraft. Revised Edition TB/1171
DENIS DIDEROT: The Encyclopedia: Selections. Ed and trans. by Stephen Gendzier TB/1299

WALTER L. DORN: Competition for Empire, 1740-1763. * Illus. TB/3032
FRANKLIN L. FORD: Robe and Sword: The Regrouping of the French Aristocracy after Louis XIV TB/1217
CARL J. FRIEDRICH: The Age of the Baroque, 1610-1660. * Illus. TB/3004
RENÉ FUELOEP-MILLER: The Mind and Face of Bolshevism TB/1188
M. DOROTHY GEORGE: London Life in the Eighteenth Century △ TB/1182
LEO GERSHOY: From Despotism to Revolution, 1763-1789. * Illus. TB/3017
C. C. GILLISPIE: Genesis and Geology: The Decades before Darwin § TB/51
ALBERT GOODWIN: The French Revolution △ TB/1064
ALBERT GUÉRARD: France in the Classical Age: The Life and Death of an Ideal △ TB/1183
CARLTON J. H. HAYES: A Generation of Materialism, 1871-1900. * Illus. TB/3039
STANLEY HOFFMANN et al.: In Search of France TB/1219
A. R. HUMPHREYS: The Augustan World: Society, Thought, and Letters in 18th Century England ° △ TB/1105
DAN N. JACOBS, Ed.: The New Communist Manifesto & Related Documents. Third edition, Revised TB/1078
LIONEL KOCHAN: The Struggle for Germany: 1914-45 TB/1304
HANS KOHN: The Mind of Germany ° TB/1204
HANS KOHN, Ed.: The Mind of Modern Russia: Historical and Political Thought of Russia's Great Age TB/1065
WALTER LAQUEUR & GEORGE L. MOSSE, Eds.: International Fascism, 1920-1945 ° △ TB/1276
WALTER LAQUEUR & GEORGE L. MOSSE: The Left-Wing Intellectuals between the Wars, 1919-1939 ° △ TB/1286
WALTER LAQUEUR & GEORGE L. MOSSE, Eds.: 1914: The Coming of the First World War ° △ TB/1306
FRANK E. MANUEL: The Prophets of Paris: Turgot, Condorcet, Saint-Simon, Fourier, and Comte TB/1218
KINGSLEY MARTIN: French Liberal Thought in the Eighteenth Century TB/1114
L. B. NAMIER: Facing East △ TB/1280
L. B. NAMIER: Personalities and Powers: Selected Essays △ TB/1186
L. B. NAMIER: Vanished Supremacies: Essays on European History, 1812-1918 ° △ TB/1088
JOHN U. NEF: Western Civilization Since the Renaissance: Peace, War, Industry, and the Arts TB/1113
FRANZ NEUMANN: Behemoth: The Structure and Practice of National Socialism, 1933-1944 TB/1289
FREDERICK L. NUSSBAUM: The Triumph of Science and Reason, 1660-1685. * Illus. TB/3009
DAVID OGG: Europe of the Ancien Régime, 1715-1783 ** ° △ TB/1271
JOHN PLAMENATZ: German Marxism and Russian Communism. ° △ New Preface by the Author TB/1189
RAYMOND W. POSTGATE, Ed.: Revolution from 1789 to 1906: Selected Documents TB/1063
PENFIELD ROBERTS: The Quest for Security, 1715-1740. * Illus. TB/3016
PRISCILLA ROBERTSON: Revolutions of 1848: A Social History TB/1025
GEORGE RUDÉ: Revolutionary Europe, 1783-1815 ° △ TB/1272
LOUIS, DUC DE SAINT-SIMON: Versailles, The Court, and Louis XIV. △ Introductory Note by Peter Gay TB/1250
ALBERT SOREL: Europe Under the Old Regime. Translated by Francis H. Herrick TB/1121
N. N. SUKHANOV: The Russian Revolution, 1917: Eyewitness Account. △ Edited by Joel Carmichael Vol. I TB/1066; Vol. II TB/1067
A. J. P. TAYLOR: From Napoleon to Lenin: Historical Essays ° △ TB/1268
A. J. P. TAYLOR: The Habsburg Monarchy, 1809-1918 ° △ TB/1187

4

G. M. TREVELYAN: British History in the Nineteenth Century and After: 1782-1919. △ *Second Edition* TB/1251

H. R. TREVOR-ROPER: Historical Essays ○ △ TB/1269

ELIZABETH WISKEMANN: Europe of the Dictators, 1919-1945 ** ○ △ TB/1275

JOHN B. WOLF: The Emergence of the Great Powers, 1685-1715. * *Illus.* TB/3010

JOHN B. WOLF: France: 1814-1919: *The Rise of a Liberal-Democratic Society* TB/3019

Intellectual History & History of Ideas

HERSCHEL BAKER: The Image of Man TB/1047

R. R. BOLGAR: The Classical Heritage and Its Beneficiaries △ TB/1125

RANDOLPH S. BOURNE: War and the Intellectuals: *Collected Essays, 1915-1919.* ‡ △ *Edited by Carl Resek* TB/3043

J. BRONOWSKI & BRUCE MAZLISH: The Western Intellectual Tradition: *From Leonardo to Hegel* △ TB/3001

ERNST CASSIRER: The Individual and the Cosmos in Renaissance Philosophy. △ *Translated with an Introduction by Mario Domandi* TB/1097

NORMAN COHN: Pursuit of the Millennium △ TB/1037

C. C. GILLISPIE: Genesis and Geology: *The Decades before Darwin* § TB/51

G. RACHEL LEVY: Religious Conceptions of the Stone Age and Their Influence upon European Thought. △ *Illus. Introduction by Henri Frankfort* TB/106

ARTHUR O. LOVEJOY: The Great Chain of Being: *A Study of the History of an Idea* TB/1009

FRANK E. MANUEL: The Prophets of Paris: *Turgot, Condorcet, Saint-Simon, Fourier, and Comte* TB/1218

PERRY MILLER & T. H. JOHNSON, Editors: The Puritans: *A Sourcebook of Their Writings*
Vol. I TB/1093; Vol. II TB/1094

MILTON C. NAHM: Genius and Creativity: *An Essay in the History of Ideas* TB/1196

ROBERT PAYNE: Hubris: *A Study of Pride. Foreword by Sir Herbert Read* TB/1031

RALPH BARTON PERRY: The Thought and Character of William James: *Briefer Version* TB/1156

GEORG SIMMEL et al.: Essays on Sociology, Philosophy, and Aesthetics. ¶ *Edited by Kurt H. Wolff* TB/1234

BRUNO SNELL: The Discovery of the Mind: *The Greek Origins of European Thought* △ TB/1018

PAGET TOYNBEE: Dante Alighieri: *His Life and Works. Edited with Intro. by Charles S. Singleton* TB/1206

ERNEST LEE TUVESON: Millennium and Utopia: *A Study in the Background of the Idea of Progress.* ¶ *New Preface by the Author* TB/1134

PAUL VALÉRY: The Outlook for Intelligence △ TB/2016

W. WARREN WAGAR, Ed.: European Intellectual History since Darwin and Marx TB/1297

PHILIP P. WIENER: Evolution and the Founders of Pragmatism. △ *Foreword by John Dewey* TB/1212

BASIL WILLEY: Nineteenth Century Studies: *Coleridge to Matthew Arnold* ○ △ TB/1261

BASIL WILLEY: More Nineteenth Century Studies: *A Group of Honest Doubters* △ TB/1262

Literature, Poetry, The Novel & Criticism

JACQUES BARZUN: The House of Intellect △ TB/1051

W. J. BATE: From Classic to Romantic: *Premises of Taste in Eighteenth Century England* TB/1036

RACHEL BESPALOFF: On the Iliad TB/2006

R. P. BLACKMUR et al.: Lectures in Criticism. *Introduction by Huntington Cairns* TB/2003

JAMES BOSWELL: The Life of Dr. Johnson & The Journal of a Tour to the Hebrides with Samuel Johnson LL.D: *Selections.* ○ △ *Edited by F. V. Morley. Illus. by Ernest Shepard* TB/1254

ABRAHAM CAHAN: The Rise of David Levinsky: *a documentary novel of social mobility in early twentieth century America. Intro. by John Higham* TB/1028

ERNST R. CURTIUS: European Literature and the Latin Middle Ages △ TB/2015

ÉTIENNE GILSON: Dante and Philosophy TB/1089

ALFRED HARBAGE: As They Liked It: *A Study of Shakespeare's Moral Artistry* TB/1035

STANLEY R. HOPPER, Ed.: Spiritual Problems in Contemporary Literature § TB/21

A. R. HUMPHREYS: The Augustan World: *Society in 18th Century England* ○ △ TB/1105

ALDOUS HUXLEY: Antic Hay & The Gioconda Smile. ○ △ *Introduction by Martin Green* TB/3503

ARNOLD KETTLE: An Introduction to the English Novel △
Volume I: *Defoe to George Eliot* TB/1011
Volume II: *Henry James to the Present* TB/1012

RICHMOND LATTIMORE: The Poetry of Greek Tragedy △ TB/1257

J. B. LEISHMAN: The Monarch of Wit: *An Analytical and Comparative Study of the Poetry of John Donne* ○ △ TB/1258

J. B. LEISHMAN: Themes and Variations in Shakespeare's Sonnets ○ △ TB/1259

ROGER SHERMAN LOOMIS: The Development of Arthurian Romance △ TB/1167

JOHN STUART MILL: On Bentham and Coleridge. △ *Introduction by F. R. Leavis* TB/1070

KENNETH B. MURDOCK: Literature and Theology in Colonial New England TB/99

SAMUEL PEPYS: The Diary of Samuel Pepys. ○ *Edited by O. F. Morshead. Illus. by Ernest Shepard* TB/1007

ST.-JOHN PERSE: Seamarks TB/2002

V. DE S. PINTO: Crisis in English Poetry, 1880-1940 ○ △ TB/1260

ROBERT PREYER, Ed.: Victorian Literature TB/1302

GEORGE SANTAYANA: Interpretations of Poetry and Religion § TB/9

C. K. STEAD: The New Poetic: *Yeats to Eliot* ○ △ TB/1263

HEINRICH STRAUMANN: American Literature in the Twentieth Century. △ *Third Edition, Revised* TB/1168

PAGET TOYNBEE: Dante Alighieri: *His Life and Works. Edited with Intro. by Charles S. Singleton* TB/1206

DOROTHY VAN GHENT: The English Novel TB/1050

E. B. WHITE: One Man's Meat TB/3505

BASIL WILLEY: Nineteenth Century Studies: *Coleridge to Matthew Arnold* ○ △ TB/1261

BASIL WILLEY: More Nineteenth Century Studies: *A Group of Honest Doubters* ○ △ TB/1262

RAYMOND WILLIAMS: Culture and Society, 1780-1950 △ TB/1252

RAYMOND WILLIAMS: The Long Revolution. △ *Revised Edition* TB/1253

MORTON DAUWEN ZABEL, Editor: *Literary Opinion in America*
Vol. I TB/3013; Vol. II TB/3014

Myth, Symbol & Folklore

JOSEPH CAMPBELL, Editor: Pagan and Christian Mysteries. *Illus.* TB/2013

MIRCEA ELIADE: Cosmos and History: *The Myth of the Eternal Return* § △ TB/2050

MIRCEA ELIADE: Rites and Symbols of Initiation: *The Mysteries of Birth and Rebirth* § △ TB/1236

THEODOR H. GASTER: Thespis △ TB/1281

DORA & ERWIN PANOFSKY: Pandora's Box: *The Changing Aspects of a Mythical Symbol.* △ *Revised Edition. Illus.* TB/2021

HELLMUT WILHELM: Change: *Eight Lectures on the I Ching* △ TB/2019

HEINRICH ZIMMER: Myths and Symbols in Indian Art and Civilization. △ *70 illustrations* TB/2005

Philosophy

G. E. M. ANSCOMBE: An Introduction to Wittgenstein's Tractatus. ○ △ *Second Edition, Revised* TB/1210

HENRI BERGSON: Time and Free Will ° △   TB/1021
H. J. BLACKHAM: Six Existentialist Thinkers ° △   TB/1002
CRANE BRINTON: Nietzsche   TB/1197
ERNST CASSIRER: The Individual and the Cosmos in Renaissance Philosophy △   TB/1097
FREDERICK COPLESTON: Medieval Philosophy ° △   TB/376
F. M. CORNFORD: Principium Sapientiae: A Study of the Origins of Greek Philosophical Thought   TB/1213
F. M. CORNFORD: From Religion to Philosophy: A Study in the Origins of Western Speculation §   TB/20
WILFRID DESAN: The Tragic Finale: An Essay on the Philosophy of Jean-Paul Sartre   TB/1030
A. P. D'ENTRÈVES: Natural Law △   TB/1223
MARVIN FARBER: The Aims of Phenomenology   TB/1291
MARVIN FARBER: Phenomenology and Existence: Towards a Philosophy Within Nature   TB/1295
HERBERET FINGARETTE: The Self in Transformation: Psychoanalysis, Philosophy and the Life of the Spirit ¶   TB/1177
PAUL FRIEDLÄNDER: Plato: An Introduction △   TB/2017
ÉTIENNE GILSON: Dante and Philosophy   TB/1089
J. GLENN GRAY: The Warriors: Reflections on Men in Battle. Intro. by Hannah Arendt   TB/1294
WILLIAM CHASE GREENE: Moira: Fate, Good, and Evil in Greek Thought   TB/1104
W. K. C. GUTHRIE: The Greek Philosophers: From Thales to Aristotle ° △   TB/1008
G. W. F. HEGEL: The Phenomenology of Mind ° △ TB/1303
F. H. HEINEMANN: Existentialism and the Modern Predicament △   TB/28
ISAAC HUSIK: A History of Medieval Jewish Philosophy   JP/3
EDMUND HUSSERL: Phenomenology and the Crisis of Philosophy   TB/1170
IMMANUEL KANT: The Doctrine of Virtue, being Part II of the Metaphysic of Morals   TB/110
IMMANUEL KANT: Groundwork of the Metaphysic of Morals. Trans. & analyzed by H. J. Paton   TB/1159
IMMANUEL KANT: Lectures on Ethics §   TB/105
IMMANUEL KANT: Religion Within the Limits of Reason Alone. § Intro. by T. M. Greene & J. Silber   TB/67
QUENTIN LAUER: Phenomenology   TB/1169
GABRIEL MARCEL: Being and Having △   TB/310
GEORGE A. MORGAN: What Nietzsche Means   TB/1198
PHILO, SAADYA GAON, & JEHUDA HALEVI: Three Jewish Philosophers. Ed. by Hans Lewy, Alexander Altmann, & Isaak Heinemann   TB/813
MICHAEL POLANYI: Personal Knowledge △   TB/1158
WILLARD VAN ORMAN QUINE: Elementary Logic: Revised Edition   TB/577
WILLARD VAN ORMAN QUINE: From a Logical Point of View: Logico-Philosophical Essays   TB/566
BERTRAND RUSSELL et al.: The Philosophy of Bertrand Russell   Vol. I TB/1095; Vol. II TB/1096
L. S. STEBBING: A Modern Introduction to Logic △ TB/538
ALFRED NORTH WHITEHEAD: Process and Reality: An Essay in Cosmology △   TB/1033
PHILIP P. WIENER: Evolution and the Founders of Pragmatism. Foreword by John Dewey   TB/1212
WILHELM WINDELBAND: A History of Philosophy
Vol. I: Greek, Roman, Medieval   TB/38
Vol. II: Renaissance, Enlightenment, Modern   TB/39
LUDWIG WITTGENSTEIN: Blue and Brown Books ° TB/1211

Political Science & Government

JEREMY BENTHAM: The Handbook of Political Fallacies. Introduction by Crane Brinton   TB/1069
KENNETH E. BOULDING: Conflict and Defense   TB/3024
CRANE BRINTON: English Political Thought in the Nineteenth Century   TB/1071
ROBERT CONQUEST: Power and Policy in the USSR: The Study of Soviet Dynastics △   TB/1307
EDWARD S. CORWIN: American Constitutional History: Essays edited by Alpheus T. Mason and Gerald Garvey   TB/1136

ROBERT DAHL & CHARLES E. LINDBLOM: Politics, Economics, and Welfare   TB/3037
F. L. GANSHOF: Feudalism △   TB/1058
G. P. GOOCH: English Democratic Ideas in Seventeenth Century   TB/1006
J. H. HEXTER: More's Utopia: The Biography of an Idea. New Epilogue by the Author   TB/1195
SIDNEY HOOK: Reason, Social Myths and Democracy △   TB/1237
ROBERT H. JACKSON: The Supreme Court in the American System of Government △   TB/1106
DAN N. JACOBS, Ed.: The New Communist Manifesto and Related Documents. Third edition, Revised   TB/1078
DAN N. JACOBS & HANS BAERWALD Eds.: Chinese Communism: Selected Documents   TB/3031
HANS KOHN: Political Ideologies of the Twentieth Century   TB/1277
ROBERT GREEN MC CLOSKEY: American Conservatism in the Age of Enterprise, 1865-1910   TB/1137
KINGSLEY MARTIN: French Liberal Thought in the Eighteenth Century △   TB/1114
ROBERTO MICHELS: First Lectures in Political Sociology. Edited by Alfred de Grazia ¶ °   TB/1224
JOHN STUART MILL: On Bentham and Coleridge. △ Introduction by F. R. Leavis   TB/1070
BARRINGTON MOORE, JR.: Political Power and Social Theory: Seven Studies ¶   TB/1221
BARRINGTON MOORE, JR.: Soviet Politics—The Dilemma of Power ¶   TB/1222
BARRINGTON MOORE, JR.: Terror and Progress—USSR: Some Sources of Change and Stability in the Soviet Dictatorship ¶   TB/1266
JOHN B. MORRALL: Political Thought in Medieval Times △   TB/1076
JOHN PLAMENATZ: German Marxism and Russian Communism. ° △ New Preface by the Author   TB/1189
KARL R. POPPER: The Open Society and Its Enemies △
Vol. I: The Spell of Plato   TB/1101
Vol. II: The High Tide of Prophecy: Hegel, Marx, and the Aftermath   TB/1102
HENRI DE SAINT-SIMON: Social Organization, The Science of Man, and Other Writings. Edited and Translated by Felix Markham   TB/1152
JOSEPH A. SCHUMPETER: Capitalism, Socialism and Democracy △   TB/3008
CHARLES H. SHINN: Mining Camps: A Study in American Frontier Government. ‡ Edited by Rodman W. Paul   TB/3062
BENJAMIN I. SCHWARTZ: Chinese Communism and the Rise of Mao   TB/1308
PETER WOLL, Ed.: Public Administration and Policy   TB/1284

Psychology

ALFRED ADLER: Individual Psychology of Alfred Adler △   TB/1154
ALFRED ADLER: Problems of Neurosis. Introduction by Heinz L. Ansbacher   TB/1145
ANTON T. BOISEN: The Exploration of the Inner World: A Study of Mental Disorder and Religious Experience   TB/87
ARTHUR BURTON & ROBERT E. HARRIS, Eds.: Clinical Studies of Personality   Vol. I TB/3075; Vol. II TB/3076
HADLEY CANTRIL: The Invasion from Mars: A Study in the Psychology of Panic ¶   TB/1282
HERBERT FINGARETTE: The Self in Transformation ¶   TB/1177
SIGMUND FREUD: On Creativity and the Unconscious § △ Intro. by Benjamin Nelson   TB/45
C. JUDSON HERRICK: The Evolution of Human Nature   TB/545
WILLIAM JAMES: Psychology: Briefer Course   TB/1034
C. G. JUNG: Psychological Reflections △   TB/2001
C. G. JUNG: Symbols of Transformation △
Vol. I TB/2009; Vol. II   TB/2010

6